Haydn, Mozart

and

Metastasio

Henri Beyle (Stendhal) and Giuseppe Carpani

Haydn, Mozart

and

Metastasio

by
STENDHAL
(1814)

Translated, Introduced & Edited
by
RICHARD N. COE

GROSSMAN PUBLISHERS
NEW YORK   1972

Published in 1972 by Grossman Publishers
625 Madison Avenue, New York, N.Y. 10022

This translation, introduction, notes, bibliography
Copyright © 1972 by Calder and Boyars, Ltd.

SBN 670-36417-7

Library of Congress Catalogue Card Number: 77-188310

Printed in Great Britain

CONTENTS

LIST OF PLATES

ACKNOWLEDGMENTS

Les Ateliers D'Art Graphique Meddens S.A., Brussels for *The Travels of Mozart* (p. 192).

The British Museum for *The Hour of Music* (p. 192); portrait of Metastasio (p. 224).

Eri. Edizioni Rai, Radiotelevisione Italiana for engraving by Guiliono Zuliani; sketch by Alessandro Bibiena (p. 256).

Mary Evans Picture Library for engraving of Joseph Haydn (p. xxxii); portrait of Wolfgang Amadeus Mozart (p. 160).

Musée Rodin, Paris for *Bust of Mozart*, — S.P.A.D.E.M., Paris (p. 192).

Museo Teatrale all Scala, Milan for stage set by Alessandro Sanquirico (p. 224).

Niederrosterreichischen Landesmuseum, Vienna for drawing by O. Zeiller and Haydn's birthplace at Rohrau (p. 32); the Haydn family making music (p. 160).

Osterreichischen Nationalbibliothek, Vienna for portrait of Carpani (frontispiece).

Theatermuseum, Munich, Abt. des Bayerischen Nationalmuseum for gouache of *L'Incontro improviso* (p. 160).

TRANSLATOR'S FOREWORD

"In music, as in all other matters, we have scarcely a notion of what the world was like a century ago." These words were written by Stendhal in 1814; and if they were true for the Napoleonic ex-administrator looking back to the closing years of the reign of Louis XIV, they may seem truer still for us, as we try and compel our imagination to adapt itself to the days when Napoleon himself was imprisoned in Elba and the Russians occupied Paris, when Talleyrand was preparing to pit his wits against Metternich at the Congress of Vienna, and when Schubert was an unknown young man who was rumoured to have written "one or two agreeable songs".

Even if there were no other justification for issuing a new translation of these *Lives of Haydn, Mozart and Metastasio*—even if their author had not, in later life, gone on to write *The Red and the Black* and *The Charterhouse of Parma*—this alone would suffice. What *was* the world of music like a hundred and fifty years ago? Or, to be more precise, how did it appear, not to the professional *maestro*, the concert-promoter or the concert-pianist, the impresario or the scholar, but to the typical *dilettante* of the period? Of course, the very word *dilettante* had a different meaning from that which our modern philistinism has chosen to attach to it. A *dilettante* (Stendhal was proud to be known as one of this privileged species) was a man of culture and refinement whose overmastering passion in life was music; more particularly, operatic music; more particularly still, *Italian* operatic music. For, compared with the reputation enjoyed by the masters of the Neapolitan school, few other composers could hope for more than the persevering reverence of pedants.

In this year 1814, Haydn was but five years dead, and Mozart but

1*

twenty. To the *dilettante*, Beethoven and Weber were little more than disquieting and cacophonous rumours in the distance; Handel was a purveyor of cantatas and oratorios, whose harsh chords and somewhat graceless solemnity were well suited to the tastes of those unmusical barbarians across the Channel (who invariably paid for quantity rather than quality, in music as in other commodities); while the name "Bach" meant Carl Philipp Emanuel, or occasionally Johann Christian; not one music-lover in a thousand had so much as heard of the (to us) immortal Johann Sebastian. Those "mountainous fugues"? Fit only to titillate the dull, lethargic sensibilities of beer-swilling, bread-crammed, half-frozen Prussians! True music began and ended within a hundred-mile radius of Mount Vesuvius.

This is the unfamiliar world which we are now to explore—a world whose deities are Cimarosa, Sacchini, Vinci, Leo, Guglielmi, Anfossi; in which Mozart is remembered almost exclusively as the composer of *Don Giovanni* and *Le Nozze di Figaro*; and where the title *Il Barbiere di Siviglia* conjures up the name, not of Rossini, but of Paisiello. Yet, even in 1814, there were hints of change in the air, and Stendhal was all too well aware of them. At heart, he disliked Haydn and all he stood for—he would rather that certain sections of the *Creation* had been re-written (more "harmoniously") by Sacchini—and this despite the fact that Haydn forms the main subject of these three *Lives*. He was aware of himself as a thorough-going reactionary, profoundly out of sympathy with the new trends and tendencies; ideally he would have liked to live in the age of Dr Burney and the Président de Brosses, in the heyday of the great castrati, when melody reigned supreme, and when the orchestra was never more than the humblest servant of the singer. Romanticism (in its more fulsome sense, musical or literary) held no appeal for him; he disliked Chateaubriand, he detested Madame de Staël, he was to have no high opinion either of Lamartine or of Victor Hugo. In spite of his enthusiasm for Shakespeare and Byron, his admiration for Jean-Jacques Rousseau and—at times—for Walter Scott, he remained at bottom immutably "classical" in outlook, and nowhere more so than in the field of music. Even in 1814, Stendhal was the better part of a generation behind his time. It needed all the perversity of genius to place Metastasio—that most ingenious of rococo librettists—on the same level as Virgil and Shakespeare. Nothing points more clearly than this ill-assorted trio to the most puzzling enigma concerning Stendhal's role in literary history: how did this belated classic emerge, almost in spite of himself, as one of the founders of the whole romantic movement? Nor have many books been written which are quite so illustriously and illuminatingly wrong-headed as these *Lives of Haydn, Mozart and Metastasio*.

Stendhal (whose real name was Henri Beyle) was born in Grenoble in 1783 and was expected to become a military engineer. However, seduced by the artistic life of Paris, he abandoned his studies at the École Polytechnique and decided to become a playwright—another Molière. In spite of a distressing amount of evidence that his talents did not lie in this direction, he persevered with drama for the better part of twenty years; and meanwhile, after a number of mishaps and adventures, including participation in the Retreat from Moscow, achieved some distinction as an administrator in the Napoleonic service. As early as the year 1800, as a 2nd Lieutenant in the 6th Dragoons, he had made a first discovery of Italy; in 1811 and again in 1813 he had continued his exploration of that "homeland of all the arts"; and so it was only natural that, with the fall of Napoleon, he should think of gravitating southwards from Paris towards that city which he loved most of all: Milan. It was on 31 March 1814 that the allied armies made their triumphal entry into Paris; the great *débâcle* of the Napoleonic Empire left Auditor Beyle unemployed, discouraged, and encumbered with 37,000 francs' worth of debts; yet before giving up hope altogether, he determined to pull such strings as lay within his grasp, in case the Restoration Government of Louis XVIII might overlook the past of this fairly obscure and only partially-committed Civil Servant so far as to grant him some minor post in his beloved Italy. Some years earlier, he had met and corresponded with a certain Countess Beugnot. This lady's husband was not without influence over the all-powerful Talleyrand; and Henri Beyle decided that, by assiduously paying court to the Count, and by an equally assiduous attendance in the Countess' *salon*—the formality leavened with a little judicious flirtation—he might perhaps descend on Milan or Florence, not as a friendless and penniless refugee, but adorned with the prestige and equipped with the income of some official function.

In those days, however, soliciting office was no rapid matter. The would-be Attaché or Fourth Secretary found time hanging heavily on his hands; and so, to while away the hours, he hired a copyist and began, in his own words, "to dictate an improved translation of the *Life of Haydn*, based on a work originally written in Italian"—namely, on Giuseppe Carpani's *Le Haydine*. When it was finished, the resulting volume (from which many of the more detailed analyses in the original had been excised, being judged by Stendhal "too pedantic") appeared uncomfortably slim. To pad it out, therefore, the author-translator decided to add a *Life of Mozart*, which he unashamedly copied out sentence by sentence from an earlier-published *Notice Biographique* by one C. Winckler; and then, finally, a *Life of Metastasio*, based mainly on an article by the Italian critic Giuseppe Baretti, and on ideas borrowed from the Swiss historian of politics and letters, J.-C.-L. Sismondi. To give this heterogeneous collection of borrowed material some semblance of unity, Beyle decided to address his "Letters" to one of his closest friends and colleagues in the Service, Louis Pépin de Bellisle (the "dear Louis" of our text), with whom, in 1811, he had shared a flat in the rue Neuve-du-Luxembourg—and who, by a curious irony, was also cultivating the Beugnot family in the hopes of a job under the new régime. As matters turned out, Louis de Bellisle was successful, whereas Beyle was not; none the less, the latter bore his rival no rancour, no more than he did towards the Countess Beugnot, who appears to have rejected his flirtations as courteously and as firmly as her husband deferred his requests for employment. Always ready to turn the most fleeting contact with a pretty woman into a Great Romantic Adventure, Beyle finally dedicated his *Lives* to the Countess, addressing her by the pseudonym of "Madame d'Oligny"; and if ever he felt the need for revenge (which is highly unlikely), the opportunity was almost miraculously presented some ten years later, when he became the lover of "Madame d'Oligny's" daughter—the beautiful, intelligent and passionate Countess Curial.

So far, so good. There is nothing reprehensible in the fact of a temporarily unemployed Civil Servant spending a few hours between jobs translating a *Life of Haydn* from the Italian, even if his knowledge of that language is perhaps not everything that it should be. Nor, if we look at the problem from another angle, is there anything fundamentally outrageous in Stendhal's method. Any conscientious modern journalist, commissioned by a publisher to write a *Life of Haydn*, would begin where Beyle began—namely, by looking up the latest work of scholarship on the subject, by taking his facts from there and by modifying them in the light of his own knowledge and experience. The trouble came in January 1815, when the new volume was actually published by the firm of Didot & Cie., in Paris:

Lettres écrites de Vienne en Autriche, sur le célèbre compositeur Haydn, suivies d'une vie de Mozart, et de considérations sur Métastase et l'état présent de la musique en France et en Italie, par Louis-Alexandre-César Bombet....

No mention of Carpani. No suggestion of a translation. Fulsome references to a certain Herr Schlichtegroll, whose *Obituary Notice* on Mozart Stendhal had certainly never read; but not a hint of Winckler's *Notice Biographique*,[1] most of which Stendhal had transcribed literally word for word, nor to Cramer's *Anecdotes sur Mozart*,[2] nor to Baretti's *Frusta Letteraria*,[3] nor to Sismondi's *De la Littérature du Midi de l'Europe*.[4] Behind the somewhat ludicrous pseudonym of "Bombet", Beyle preferred to pass the compilation off entirely as his own original work.

In view of this brazen attempt at plagiarism—an attempt which, even in our time, Stendhal has not quite lived down, so that even Henri Martineau declares himself "highly embarrassed"—it is not without a certain sense of relief that we read that the book was a total and lamentable failure, at least in its country of origin. Of the beggarly 1,000 copies printed in 1815, almost the totality remained unsold two years later. Convinced that this set-back must be due to the poor binding and the countless misprints of the original edition (Stendhal had finally left France for Italy in the latter part of July 1814, consequently had never had a chance to check the proofs), the "author" now had the text corrected and rebound, and some three hundred copies were issued, this time anonymously, in the so-called "second edition" of 1817, under a new and simplified title: *Vies de Haydn, de Mozart et de Métastase*. The result was not a jot more encouraging. By 1824, in spite of all his own efforts and those of his friend and agent, the Baron de Mareste, to

---

[1] *Notice Biographique sur Jean-Chrysostome-Wolfgang-Théophile Mozart*: extrait du *Magazin Encyclopédique*, Année VII, t. III, p. 29. Paris (J. J. Fuchs) An X (1801). 48 pp. Winckler acknowledges his own indebtedness to Schlichtegroll on p. 6, note.

[2] *Trente-Deux Anecdotes sur Mozart*. Traduites de l'Allemand [de Friedrich Rochlitz] par Ch. Fr. Cramer. Paris (chez l'Editeur), An IX 68 pp.

[3] Venice, 1763–5. Republished in his *Opere... scritte in lingua italiana*. Milan (L. Mussi), 5 vols., 1813–14.

[4] Paris (Treuttel et Würtz), 4 vols., 1813.

"puff" the book as hard as possible, affairs had come to a standstill. Here, Didot's royalty-statement is categoric: of the 1,000 copies originally printed, precisely 127 had been sold. Stendhal had written for the "Happy Few" with a vengeance!

In England, however, the public seems to have been more easily satisfied. As early as 1817 a first translation had been published in London, whether with or without Beyle's consent is uncertain. In the errata slip which appeared in the 1817 French edition he claimed, probably with more picturesque fantasy than truth, that "one day, when he chanced to be strolling down Albemarle Street, the Author observed in Murray's window the translation of his book. He desires to record his debt of gratitude to the Translator, whose name, however, he has yet to learn. . . ." This agreeable embellishment almost certainly conceals a more plain and prosaic reality: a common-or-garden business contract between himself and John Murray the publisher, followed by a brief (and otherwise unexplained) visit to London in August 1817, to see how matters were progressing. In any case, the English venture was an interesting one. Not only did Murray publish a far more accurate version of "Bombet" than "Bombet" had done of Carpani,[1] but he commissioned William Gardiner, "Author of the *Sacred Melodies*", to supply a quantity of learned (and at times very necessary) footnotes. Beyle was impressed, and recorded the fact that he felt almost inclined to translate them into French, had he not feared "to lend too *erudite* an air to his own production". In compensation, however, he borrowed a quotation from the English publisher's blurb for his own title-page; and, admonished by Gardiner, he admitted that he had perhaps underestimated Beethoven when writing the *Lives*. On the other hand, he reproached the London musical public with failing to appreciate Rossini.

This first English edition was promptly followed by a second, in which the cumbrous title of the original was once again happily simplified; and such was the success of this venture that within a couple of years the volume had been pirated across the Atlantic. In France, however, there was still no improvement. The original printing obstinately refused to sell. In 1817, Henri Beyle had adopted the pseudonym of "Stendhal" to replace that of the unhappy "Bombet"; and it was under

---

[1] For details of this edition, and of all others subsequently referred to, see *Bibliography*, under heading *Haydn*.

this name that, in the year 1831, he published the first of those master-pieces which mark him out as one of the greatest novelists the world has known: *The Red and the Black*. Yet in this same year, sufficient copies of the sixteen-year-old *Lives* were still unsold for it to become impera-tive once again to rebind and reissue the remaining stock. This time, the publisher was Levavasseur (who had just launched *The Red and the Black*); the refurbished copies were misleadingly inscribed "second edi-tion"; and for the first time the work was signed with the name Stendhal. From this point onwards, the fate of the remaining copies is obscure. We know that Stendhal's faithful cousin and factotum, Romain Colomb, was still trying to sell them off in 1834; and eight years later, Henri Beyle died. When next we hear of the *Lives of Haydn, Mozart and Metastasio*, in 1854, they are submerged in the first *Œuvres Complètes de Stendhal*; and from this point onward they will continue to take their place, albeit never entirely comfortably, in the general corpus of the novelist's writings.[1]

Meanwhile, what about the victims of this unscrupulous and inde-fensible piece of plagiarism? Winckler and Cramer are obscure figures of whom we know nothing; Baretti had died in 1789, Adolf Schlich-tegroll was obscurely buried away in his Ducal Library at Gotha, and it is highly unlikely that the illustrious Sismondi—to whom Stendhal was later to refer often enough, if only to criticise him—ever bothered to read this little-known publication, which had scarcely even the merit of being controversial and which, from the professional historian's point of view, was lamentably inaccurate. But Carpani was a different matter. Doubtless, the inevitable "kind friend" drew his attention to Bombet's compilation as soon as it appeared; and Carpani was justifi-ably incensed, although, let it be said in his honour, not so much of the fact of the theft of his work, as at the distortions, mistranslations and plain errors that "Bombet" had introduced into the original text in the course of his "improvements".

Nor is there any question but that "Bombet" had a pretty serious case to answer. The *Lives of Haydn, Mozart and Metastasio* are riddled with silly and irritating errors. Some of these, admittedly, are Carpani's own errors, which Stendhal had simply transcribed without checking

---

[1] The most important modern editions, from which this translation has been made, are those by Daniel Muller (Paris, Champion, 1914) and by Henri Martineau (Paris, Le Divan, 1928). Neither is wholly satisfactory, and both bristle with unsolved problems.

—for instance, the mis-spelling of names ("Manensdorf" for Mannersdorf, "Boselli" for Polzelli, etc.), the odd transplantation in time that makes Milton a contemporary of Handel, the statement that Haydn, while in London, was painted by Reynolds (in reality, by Hoppner) . . . and so on. But there are many others. Some of these are due to Stendhal's plain ignorance of the Italian language: he distorts the famous story about Haydn's expulsion from the choir-school at St. Stephen's Cathedral in Vienna, by translating *coda* as the "tail of a gown" instead of the "tail of a wig"; more ludicrously still, he translates Carpani's *le signore* Martinez as "Monsieur Martinez", thus citing, as a source for his information concerning the life of Haydn, old Niccolò, sometime Secretary to the Papal Nuncio in Vienna, who had been dead these thirty years or more, instead of his two famous and gifted daughters, Marianne and Antonia. On top of this, moreover, he makes a whole mass of senseless and inexplicable errors, most of which by no stretch of the imagination can be attributed either to Carpani or to "Bombet's" lack of Italian, but which appear to be due to plain carelessness. He situates the famous farewell performance of the *Creation* in the Palais Lobkowitz, whereas Carpani had stated, quite clearly and correctly, that it had taken place in the Aula Magna of Vienna University; he refers to Mislivicek's presence at an *evening* concert at the College of the Barnabite Fathers, whereas Carpani had noted, again correctly, that these concerts were invariably held in the morning. He had even, in adapting Carpani's epistolary form of narrative to his own purposes, simply transferred Carpani's "I" to himself—with the important consequence that he consistently makes himself out to be much older than he was in fact at this date, and with the ludicrous consequence that he assumes a number of Carpani's minor eccentricities and ailments, including, at one point, an attack of fever. For poor Carpani, this was the last straw. "He has stolen my fever! Let him at least give me back my fever!"

On the 18th, and again on 20 August 1815, Carpani, who was then in Padua, addressed a couple of open letters of protest to the leading Parisian daily paper, *Le Constitutionnel*.[1] At this stage of the controversy, the editor did not consider it worthwhile to publish them; but on 13 December the paper carried a humorous article making fun of the whole episode, admonishing both parties equally and finally

[1] For details of these, and of all other writings by Carpani, see *Bibliography*.

advising "Monsieur Louis-Alexandre-César Bombet", as a gesture of friendship, to restore to Signor Carpani the latter's property: "his book, his conversation and his fever!" Up to this point, the incident had remained something of a joke, even if manifestly a bad one. But now Stendhal embarked upon one of the very few completely discreditable adventures of his career. On 26 May 1816, *Le Constitutionnel* published a letter, either by Stendhal or directly inspired by him, in which he not only sneered ungenerously at the Italian scholar's complaints, but actually accused the old man of having plagiarised *him*—i.e., of having simply translated "Bombet's" *Vies* without permission or acknowledgment, and of having published the result as his own *Haydine*.

Carpani was understandably outraged and wrote off a violent reply, dated Vienna, 20 June 1816, which this time *Le Constitutionnel* saw fit to publish (20 August 1816). Stendhal of course retorted and, in a letter signed "H.-C.-G. Bombet" (a supposed younger brother of Louis-Alexandre-César)—a letter in which insolence, wit, bad taste and bad faith are combined in about equal proportions—he proceeded to pour scorn and ridicule on the Italian. After this, *Le Constitutionnel* deemed the matter closed; and thereafter, until his death in 1825, Carpani was left with no resources, other than those of the Italian press, through which to express his innocence. But the literary journals of Padua continue to bear witness to his grievances; and at one point he even threatens to unmask the true identity of *"questo figlio dell' Isera"*—the unspeakable Bombet-Stendhal-Beyle.[1] Nor is there a speck of evidence that Stendhal was ever ashamed of the episode.

This wretched question of plagiarism has bedevilled the whole problem of the *Lives of Haydn, Mozart and Metastasio*. Almost without exception, Stendhalian scholars have been so preoccupied by attempts to discover excuses for their hero, that they have missed the real points at issue. The "excuses" follow a well-worn and predictable track. Had it not been for Stendhal's "plagiarism", it is claimed, Carpani would have been long ago forgotten and consigned to dust—a poor consolation which has not even the advantage of being true: Carpani in his own right is still one of the basic sources used by musical historians and

[1] E.g.: "Lettera all' estensore del *Constitutionnel*", in *Biblioteca Italiana*, Jan.–Mar. 1817; etc.

biographers. Alternatively it is argued that Carpani's original was unreadable, whereas Stendhal, by virtue of his style, transformed it into a masterpiece—another claim which is untrue since, in 1814, Stendhal's own style is very far from flawless, while Carpani reads quite agreeably, even today. A third excuse is that the "plagiarism" of Carpani is merely the first instance of what will later prove to be Stendhal's essential literary method, even in his greatest works: he was incapable of inventing his *facts*—instead, he had to borrow them from some already-printed source, and then "embroider" them in such a way as to produce a new and original conception. And finally, it is alleged that only part of the book is borrowed, and that this part is exclusively technical, biographical or musicological—whereas the real value of the *Vies* lies in those chapters of paragraphs which owe nothing to Carpani, and in which Stendhal is already working out the ideas which later are to earn him immortality. "It is easy enough for anyone to spot those passages which belong to Stendhal," notes Daniel Muller[1]—and, of course, the temptation for the average reader is to attribute every good idea in the book to the author of *La Chartreuse de Parme*, and every poor or platitudinous one to Winckler, Cramer, Baretti, Sismondi . . . or Carpani. Poor Carpani!

Who *was* Carpani? Born on 28 January 1752 at Vill'Albese, near Como, he was educated by the Jesuits at their Collegio di Brera in Milan, and then sent to study law at the University of Pavia. Here he eventually acquired the degree of Doctor of Laws, for all that he is reported never to have opened a law-book in his life, whether as a student or later, as member of an eminent firm of Milanese lawyers. Two things only interested him in life: music and poetry. While still a student, he started writing both poems and plays in Milanese dialect; it was one of the former—a set of six sonnets on the death of Maria-Theresa in 1780—which won him the interest and protection of the highly-fashionable Parini, while it was a dialect comedy, *I Conti d'Agliate*, which earned him the favour of the ruling House of Austria. In the eighteenth century, Lombardy was an Austrian province, ruled by a son of Maria-Theresa, the Archduke Ferdinand, who kept his summer court at Monza; and here, in the presence of the Archduke and of his consort, Maria-Beatrice d'Este, *I Conti d'Agliate* was performed with such success that henceforward Carpani was never able to separate his fortunes from those of the House of Habsburg.

[1] *Vies*, ed. Champion, p. 414.

Carpani, then, was both a product of the Jesuits, and a protégé of the Austrian authorities in Italy—we need look no further than this to explain Stendhal's deep-rooted contempt for the man who, to make matters worse, was advocating the same type of musical and literary *avant-gardisme* as himself. By the time the French Revolution broke out, Carpani was irrevocably committed to the cause of Royalty; and from 1792–6 he was editor of the *Gazzetta di Milano*, one of the most implacably anti-revolutionary journals in Europe at the time. When Napoleon invaded Lombardy for the first time in 1796, Carpani fled, together with his Austrian patrons, to Vienna, which later became his second home; but the Treaty of Campo-Formio left him free to return, and in 1800 he was appointed Director and Censor of All the Theatres in Venice—a post which he held until 1805, in which year the French re-occupied the Venetian Republic, and the Director of All the Theatres retreated hurriedly once again to Vienna.

Back in the Austrian capital, he was nominated Court Poet and Official Librettist to the Emperor Franz I. It was at this point that he came into contact with Haydn, who had left Esterházy and retired to his little house in Gumpendorf, just off the highroad that led from Vienna to Schönbrunn. His admiration for the great composer was unbounded; and he was to devote much of his time henceforward to the self-imposed task of bringing Haydn's music to the ears of his compatriots in Italy. It was with this intention that he translated the texts of the *Creation*, the *Seasons* and even of the Imperial National Anthem, *Gott erhalte Franz den Kaiser*; and shortly after Haydn's death, he began to collect material for the first authoritative *Life*. But Haydn was by no means the only composer with whom he was on friendly terms: he knew Salieri, Weigl, Paër, Koželuck, Marianne Martinez and all the musical élite of the city; he was in contact with Beethoven and later with Rossini and on one famous occasion, in 1822, he actually managed to introduce these two uncompromising egoists to each other. His poem "*In questa tomba oscura*" was set to music over sixty times during the Romantic period; and his text, *The Passion of Our Lord*, with a score by Weigl, was to prove not without influence on the development of the modern Catholic oratorio. In 1825, when he died, he could be described by Michaud, who disliked his reactionary politics almost as much as did Stendhal, as a *poète et musicien célèbre*: a man, all in all, who deserves a better fate than Stendhalians have been in the habit of meting out to him.

As a librettist, he was among the most competent of his generation; and the "heroi-comic drama" which he adapted from Marsollier des Vivetières' *Camille* furnished the canvas for one of the most successful operas of the whole Napoleonic period: Paër's *Camilla, ossia Il Sotterraneo*, which held the stage in every country where Italian opera was performed (including Paris, where it was much appreciated by Stendhal) until the great Rossinian revolution of 1820–5. He was also a critic of considerable insight and importance. A controversy with the art-historian Andrea Majer over the significance of Tintoretto led him to compose an important treatise on the nature of Ideal Beauty; he wrote a study of the sculptor Canova and one of the earliest serious appreciations of the music of Rossini. By a supreme irony, this last work was eclipsed by Stendhal's *Vie de Rossini*, which was published in the same year, 1824, and this time was *not* a plagiarism—despite a last squeak of protest from Carpani who (understandably enough) assumed that somehow it must have been. But his unquestioned *chef-d'œuvre* is his study of Haydn, which was the fruit of many years' work and of a wide acquaintance with the music of the period. Its full title was as follows:

Le Haydine, ovvero Lettere su la Vita e le Opere del celebre Maestro Giuseppe Haydn; Milan (Buccinelli) 1812

and these seventeen letters (Stendhal makes twenty-two of them) enjoyed a lasting and deserved success. In 1823 they were reprinted in Padua with some additional material; and in 1837 a proper and accurate French translation came at last to replace Stendhal's brilliant but unscrupulous hotch-potch. In 1812, moreover, their originality was considerable. Haydn had died on 31 May 1809; and the immense literature which has since accumulated about the composer and his works was then in its extreme infancy. There was a scattering of *Memoirs* (notably Griesinger's), a few obituary discourses (e.g., Joachim Lebreton, *Notice sur Haydn*, read at the Institut de France on 6 October 1810) and the first faint beginnings of a critical assessment (e.g., N.-E. Framery, *Notice sur Joseph Haydn*. Paris (Barba) 1810). But there was as yet no general *Life and Works*—and this was the gap that Carpani came to fill.

If, instead of struggling with the intractable problem of plagiarism, we attempt to look at the Stendhal-Carpani relationship from a different point of view altogether, the enquiry may be more rewarding. *Why*, among all the many books on music that were available in 1814, did

Stendhal pick on the *Haydine*, whose principal subject was a composer for whom he felt remarkably little sympathy and whose death, in 1809, he had dismissed in a few words written in a letter to his sister Pauline, even though, thanks to his presence in Vienna as a member of the French army of occupation, he had actually attended the memorial service that was held in the Schottenkirche? The answer would seem to lie, not in Haydn at all, but in Carpani. It was the ideas, not the harmonies, that he found attractive. Again and again, notions which at first sight look typically "Stendhalian" turn out to be straightforward translations from the Italian. And when we find these same typical "Stendhalian" notions reappearing in volume after volume some five, ten or even twenty years later, the conclusion would seem to be inevitable: if Carpani was undeniably the victim of a piece of unforgivable plagiarism, this same Carpani was one of the major influences at work in the formation of the man who was eventually to emerge as "Stendhal".

To demonstrate this in detail obviously lies outside the scope of a simple Foreword, since not only would it involve analysing in depth all Beyle's earlier writings (letters, diaries, etc.) to show that certain ideas which we should perhaps label Carpano–Stendhalian were not present earlier, but it would also make necessary a careful study of the *Histoire de la peinture en Italie* which, it should not be forgotten, had been in preparation ever since 1811.

Indeed, the key idea of the *Histoire de la peinture en Italie* in its final version (1817)—an idea which was to have an incalculable influence on the whole aesthetic of Romanticism—is that there is no fixed and immutable standard of Absolute Beauty, as the Classics had believed. Now, the sources of this revolutionary concept can be traced back to a number of earlier philosophers, whose works Stendhal had studied with meticulous attention: to Montesquieu, to Helvétius, to Cabanis and in particular to the abbé Dubos, whose *Réflexions critiques sur la poésie et la peinture* (1719) expounded the first serious criticism of the classical aesthetic. Nevertheless, all these together do not quite make up the theory of "relative beauty" as it is developed in the *Histoire de la peinture*; and critics have often wondered what processes had intervened between Stendhal's concentrated reading of the philosophers (mainly 1800–10) and the first formulation of his own original conclusions in the *Lives of Haydn, Mozart and Metastasio*.

The answer would seem unquestionably to be Carpani. Three major themes are developed by Carpani and translated extensively and often word-for-word by Stendhal: namely, that the pleasure occasioned by music is physical, not intellectual;[1] that the ability to appreciate certain aspects of art will vary from country to country;[2] and finally, that since all music is, in its most primitive origins, *vocal* music, ideal forms of musical expression will necessarily vary from region to region under the influence of the language that happens to be spoken. Hence the "Ideal Beauty" of Italian music will, however remotely, reflect the tonal and inflectional structure of the Italian language, and thus will differ from any corresponding "Ideal Beauty" in Germany.[3]

The use to which Stendhal will put these arguments is, to anyone familiar with his later writings, quite evident. Under the influence of Cabanis and Montesquieu, he will tend to play down the linguistic emphasis of Carpani's last proposition, and to emphasise instead the theory of "national temperaments" suggested in the second. But otherwise all the essential ingredients of his relativist aesthetic are gathered together in these few pages of *Le Haydine*. So also are a number of other "typically Stendhalian" simplifications, of the variety that has so irritated serious musicologists ever since: the notion, for instance, that German music is based on harmony, while Italian is based on melody and that, beginning with Haydn and Mozart, the triumph of "Königsberg over Naples" will eventually spell the end of the Golden Age of music in Western Europe;[4] or the assertion that the most effective forms of music are invariably based on a kind of leitmotif, in which the monotony of repetition is avoided by an imaginative subtlety of variation.[5] While it is obviously not true that Stendhal learnt to *appreciate* music while working on Carpani (as he himself admits that he learnt to appreciate painting while working on the *Histoire de la peinture*), there is a very strong suspicion that it may have been through Carpani that he first learnt to formulate his *ideas* on music.

For obviously there was an immediate sympathy, a precise coincidence of likes and dislikes, that was present from the outset. Carpani

---

[1] *Le Haydine* (1812), pp. 127, 142, etc. This is a "typically Stendhalian" theme, if ever there was one, and one of the guiding notions in the *Vie de Rossini*.
[2] *Le Haydine*, p. 137.
[3] *Le Haydine*, pp. 191–200.
[4] *Le Haydine*, pp. 137, 161–2, etc.
[5] *Le Haydine*, p. 149, etc.

saves his highest admiration for Canova, Cimarosa, Napoleon (with reservations) and later Rossini—all of whom figure equally in the gallery of Stendhal's demi-gods. In Letter XVIII, Stendhal gives a list of what, for him, are the highest achievements of the human spirit in music before the death of Cimarosa—including Pergolesi's *Stabat Mater*, Paesiello's *Barbiere di Siviglia*, Mozart's *Nozze di Figaro* and *Don Giovanni*, the *Matrimonio segreto*, etc.—and most of these are destined to be repeated again and again until the day of his death. Yet this list is not his own, but basically Carpani's,[1] slightly abridged. This catalogue of fundamental similarities, not only between the *Haydine* and the *Lives*, which is to be expected, but between the *Haydine* and *Rome, Naples and Florence*, or the *Life of Rossini*, or *De l'Amour*, or the *Promenades dans Rome*, could be extended almost indefinitely. One further precise and most revealing instance, however, must be sufficient.

In the later nineteenth century, when Baudelaire and, after him, Rimbaud and the Symbolists, evolved the theory of "correspondences" and postulated a basic unity between all the arts, they naturally looked back to Stendhal as their great precursor. And indeed, it is one of Stendhal's claims to distinction that he first swept aside the rigid boundaries that hedged about the separate arts and so paved the way for a Mallarmé, a Debussy, ultimately a Diaghilev. "Those great ultramarine-coloured draperies which . . . Carlo Dolce tended to employ so lavishly in scenes where tenderness mingles with gravity," he writes in the *Life of Rossini*—describing, not a painting, but Rossini's scoring for the flute in his opera *Tancredi*. In the *Lives*, these "correspondences" are already worked out in detail. Haydn's use of sombre harmonies is equated with Rembrandt's use of chiaroscuro; Pergolesi and Cimarosa are "the Raphaels of music", while Sacchini is likened to Correggio and poor Simon Mayr identified with Carlo Maratta. "I am possessed with this mania for comparisons," admits Stendhal—and proceeds to give a list which, for all its idiosyncrasies, entitles his admirers to claim him as the founding father of the Symbolist aesthetic. Or rather, which *would* have entitled them to hail him as such, were it not for the fact that most of that list—and also the comparison between Haydn, Rembrandt and Caravaggio—is already in Carpani.[2] And Carpani, far from claiming

[1] *Le Haydine*, pp. 159–60.
[2] *Le Haydine*, pp. 99, 126, 174, 214–16, etc.

any glory for it, modestly ascribes the principle to old abbé Batteux, or even to Father Castel and his *"piano à couleurs"*.

Honour where honour is due. If the foregoing argument is correct, then the whole question of Stendhal's plagiarising of Carpani takes on a very different complexion. If Henri Beyle, in 1814, took the trouble to translate *Le Haydine*, it was not because he discovered there a conscientious but pedantic compendium of facts, mere raw material to be embroidered with his own ideas, but rather because he found there, in a significant and original formulation, certain basic ideas on the very nature of art and music which, henceforward, he was to make his own. In which case, Giuseppe Carpani is something very much more than the obscure victim of an unscrupulous predator; he is a figure whose ideas are destined to affect the whole development of sensibility in the nineteenth century.

Part of the fascination of the *Life of Haydn* lies precisely in this interplay of two minds, so closely attuned (in spite of their outward quarrels) that to attempt a clear division of ideas—*this* is Stendhal's, *this* is Carpani's—is virtually fruitless. It is almost as though we can watch Stendhal's mind being made up for him by Carpani as he goes along. The *Life of Mozart*, however, is a very different matter. Stendhal had already made up his mind about Mozart—or at least about his operas —long before he resorted to Winckler; he had seen them on the stage both in Paris and in Vienna, and what he had not seen had been sung for him in private by Angelina Bereyter, the little *seconda donna* from the Théâtre Italien in the rue de Louvois who was his mistress from 1810 until 1813. In this second section of the *Lives*, the conventional critical assessment is correct. Winckler was there to supply the facts and nothing but the facts (or better still, the anecdotes); the ideas would come from Stendhal himself; and most of them are in fact concentrated in the final *Letter concerning Mozart*, which is built around a most subtle and sensitive contrast between Mozart's and Beaumarchais' conception of the characters in *Le Nozze di Figaro*. Here, Stendhal is on his own ground; and no mere *dilettante* has even written more convincingly. If there is a problem, it concerns *Die Zauberflöte*. Almost alone among nineteenth-century critics, Stendhal appears to have thought highly of Schikaneder's controversial text. "The libretto, which seems to have much in common with the irrepressible fantasies of a tender imagination run riot, harmonises as though by some special dispensation of Providence with the genius of the composer." Yet had he actually ever *seen* the work in its original version on the stage? It appears more than doubtful. Outside Austria and Germany, *Die Zauberflöte* was anything but popular in the Napoleonic period; while the disastrous French adaptation which was given in Paris in 1801 under the title *Les Mystères d'Isis* was certainly not calculated to help its reputation. None the less, everything suggests that Stendhal had seen this grotesquely distorted version and no other. Schikaneder's text *is* delightful; but it is supremely ironical to discover that Stendhal's highly original appreciation of its qualities is based on little more than his own "tender imagination run riot".

And so to the third section of the *Lives*: the *Life of Metastasio*. Characteristically, Stendhal is happy to condense the poet's actual biography into less than a couple of pages (particularly since, in this instance, there are no anecdotes worth retailing); what interests him is Metastasio's art—the art of the libretto—and some of the pages in this final section are among the most interesting in the book.

Nowadays, except to students of Italian literature, Metastasio is largely a forgotten figure. Yet he was a considerable poet and certainly the greatest of librettists in a century when men of letters took the art of the libretto seriously. His glory waned with the passing of the Golden Age of "opera seria"; however, during the long interregnum between the death of Racine and the coming of the Romantic drama, the "opera seria" represented one of the highest forms of dramatic art —a form which deserves far closer attention than most historians of the theatre are prepared to pay it.

One thing is certain: that Metastasio understood the actual techniques of libretto-writing better than any other poet before him, and perhaps since. Above all, he understood the extremely delicate balance between action, words and music. His supreme quality, and his ultimate secret, was modesty; he taught his very poetry to be self-effacing. Powerful, original, self-assertive language has no place in a libretto, for either the music will kill it, or it will kill the music. The ideal libretto is unobtrusive, perhaps even a little platitudinous, a little dull. And yet it must still be poetry. The quality that Metastasio discovered, in which poetic beauty merges with unobtrusiveness, is *grace*—and this precisely is the quality which, for Stendhal, set him on a pedestal considerably higher than Racine.

In the last analysis, Stendhal's sensibility, and all his greatest writing, revolves about two opposing centres of awareness, ceaselessly in conflict and yet so exactly counterbalanced that neither will ever definitely predominate. On the one hand, an obsession with violence, with rash and even senseless acts of pure bravado, which, being aware of, he referred to as his *espagnolisme*, and attributed to the inheritance of a Spanish grandmother. On the other, a hypersensitive awareness of *la grâce*—that almost indefinable quality of controlled, delicate, unassertive, subtle and *sophisticated* beauty which he finds in Canova (but not in Michelangelo), in Cimarosa (but not in Haydn), in Raphael and in Correggio (but not in David or in Ingres). It is the *espagnolisme* which is uppermost in *The Red and the Black*, while it is the *grâce* which predominates in *The Charterhouse of Parma*. *Grâce*: the blue and misted curves of the hills that surround Lake Como, and which Stendhal loved above all other landscapes in the world; the delicate nuances of colour, shade and light, as the chestnut-trees of Windsor Forest faded into the golden mist; the elegant and sophisticated manners of an eighteenth-century *salon*; the arabesques of the Vatican Loggias, of the staircase of the Villa Melzi leading downwards to the Lake; the essentially similar arabesques of Mozart's *Dove sono* or of Cimarosa's *Cara, cara*. This quality of grace excludes high tragedy; but it also excludes boisterous comedy, while the harsh notes of realism will destroy it immediately. It can easily degenerate into simpering sweetness or, if it takes itself too seriously, into plain sentimentality, as it does in Greuze or in Boucher, as it does occasionally in Canova. But with Stendhal himself, never.

For Stendhal's ideal grace is not merely a delight of the senses, a caressing of the emotions; all great art (he maintains) is created first and foremost to satisfy the exigent intellect of the artist, and the intellect of the artist is self-aware, self-critical and more often than not self-mocking. So that the perfect grace is leavened with wit, with gentle satire, with delicate, non-corrosive humour; its urbanely rococo elegance, shot through with tenderness and a hint of melancholy, avoiding all the harsh angles and the disenchanting realities of power and servitude, is ironically self-conscious. Its sadness (the elegiac sadness of all things human) is discretely counterbalanced by absurdity; its farcicality is softened by the entrancing wonder of sustained and interwoven melodies. This, for Stendhal, is the miracle of the "opera buffa", the supreme example of the spirit of *la grâce* that man has yet invented; and, in a slightly more poetic context, it is also the miracle of Metastasio.

For Metastasio's dramas are graceful elegies with happy endings; not tragic, but of a touching melancholy; without asperities, without angularities, without reality; a dream-world of love, sadness and unmerited misfortune . . . Fabrice's dream-world in *The Charterhouse of Parma*. They are incomplete without music, and yet their very poetry suggests what the music must be. Their mood is not one of despair, still less of any harsh *catharsis*, but of "regretful sadness"—that mood which, for Stendhal, represented the profoundest of all emotional experiences, since it allowed the soul to explore the remotest depths of sensibility, yet at the same time offered it a promise of ultimate consolation—thus softening the austere curve of misfortune with an arabesque of hope. And if the "opera buffa" was the supreme instance of this perfection, the elegiac "opera seria" in the tradition of Metastasio ran it a close second.

What is emerging from these considerations is the answer to a question which has perplexed and exasperated critics—in particular, music-critics—for many years: namely, what (if any) were Stendhal's criteria in judging music? For by normal standards, of course, these criteria appear quite unbelievably narrow, idiosyncratic and biased. He loathed concertos and said quite frankly that practically every form of instrumental music, solo or orchestral, bored him stiff. His province was exclusively that of vocal music; but even here, there were whole categories which held no real meaning for him. To oratorios and cantatas in the eighteenth-century tradition, he listened only out of a sense of duty, if at all, unless they happened to be comic; he had a certain taste for popular songs, but no more than might be expected from any other soldier who had been through a few campaigns in a number of different countries; he paid lip-service to the concert-aria, but lip-service it remained, unless he knew and liked the context from which it was extracted; he had no more than the haziest knowledge of any music before 1720, and no interest in any after 1820—in a word, the total range of his musical interest spanned no more than that narrow field of Italian (or Italianate) opera that ran from Pergolesi to Rossini. And yet *within* this range, his sensibility is extraordinary; and he remains, even today, one of the supreme authorities on the subject. How is this possible?

His deep and enduring susceptibility to all manifestations of *la grâce*, which we have attempted to analyse, is part, but only part of the solution to the problem. There are "graceful" flute-concertos by Cimarosa, "graceful" andantes and allegrettos in Mozart's symphonies, "graceful" sonatas and sonatinas galore by Scarlatti, Galuppi, Tartini . . . none of which receives so much as a passing mention. Obviously, in music, grace by itself is not enough; some other condition remains to be fulfilled if it is to stir the very depths of Stendhal's soul; and to grasp the nature of this missing element, we must go back briefly into Stendhal's past, although all the clues are given, once again, in the *Life of Metastasio*.

Very early in life—certainly not later than 1804–5—Stendhal discovered that he was capable of occasional brief moments of "sublime exaltation", whose effect was so overwhelming that they bore no comparison with everyday experience; nor, more disturbingly, could they be expressed in any form of language that was normally associated with any of the commonplace acts of living. These *moments sublimes*, even though no more than half a dozen might be experienced in a lifetime, alone sufficed to justify a human existence on this earth; but Stendhal was more than an ordinary human being; he was an artist, and he considered it the fundamental purpose of his life to discover ways and means of *expressing* those perfect instants through the medium of art.

At first, however, the process was frustrating. He found that to attempt any direct description of the experience was not only to fail in the description, but actually to destroy the memory, and therefore the very reality, of the experience itself. "I have discovered beyond doubt that pure emotion leaves no memories whatsoever," he noted in his diary; there is, as it were, a series of events leading up to the great experience, and another series of events leading away from it; but in between the two, nothing but a tantalising and luminous blank, an indescribable *Néant*. In other words, the "supreme experience" has something in common with the method of locating a point in Euclidian geometry: the point itself has "neither length nor breadth nor thickness", but its position can be ascertained as the meeting-place of two straight lines.

Now, this Euclidian concept of a point (a situation) as the dimensionless meeting-place of lines (or forces) is clearly analogous to the basic dramatic concept of French classical tragedy—and it is to be recalled, once again, that Stendhal never wholly escaped from the influence of his classical heritage. In the ideal classical tragedy (or even comedy) we are not shown an *action*; we are shown a *situation* which is, as it were, the meeting-place of a number of lines of action in the past, but which, in itself, is static and dimensionless, outside space and time. It is a state of unbearable tension, resulting from the conflict of contradictory forces in a single human soul. "Tension", however, is something which is felt: it cannot (strictly speaking) be described, least of all in coherent and rational language. And this is precisely what we observe in the greatest of the classical tragedies: the language makes little or no attempt to describe (in any realistic or exact sense) the tension that is experienced by the characters in their inexpressible situation; the words are simply clues by which this *sense* of tension is conveyed to the spectator. The Racinian alexandrine is very rarely "poetic" in itself; it acquires its density, its significance and hence its poetry from the situation in which it is located.

French classical tragedy, then, consists in showing (usually in retrospect) the lines of force as they approach; and then in compelling the spectator to share the anguish of the situation that results when they meet. For Racine, as for Stendhal, no normal, everyday language can attempt to cope with this impossible task. The only words that can hope to convey the dimensionless *néant* of total tragedy are those which bear the least attachment to common wants and needs—a stylised, rigid, abstract, artificial chant or incantation which, in the last analysis, is closer to music than to ordinary speech.

For Stendhal, this magical incantation—the only form of language that could express the inexpressible—was melody: but, both from the evidence of his own emotional experience and from his life-long familiarity with the classical drama, it was clear that the supreme revelation of a *moment sublime* through music could only occur in the context of a precise situation. Music by itself was meaningless. To return to our original illustration: in order to define the dimensionless point, it is essential first to have the two straight lines. Without them, the point may be anywhere, or nowhere—and no music in the world can express a mere ubiquitous non-existence. For Stendhal, who had no conception whatsoever of the dramatic possibilities of musical form as such, a concerto appeared as formless, profitless and dull as a point whose whereabouts is not known, or as an alexandrine out of context. To the end of his life, and in spite of his dismal failure as a dramatist, Stendhal's imagination was to remain fundamentally dramatic. The supreme glory of music is to express a dramatic situation so tense, so moving and so sublime that it lies forever beyond the reach of ordinary language—but until there *is* a situation, there is nothing to express. Music exists exclusively in terms of theatre.

Yet the ultimate fascination of music is not only that it goes beyond language, but that it can also *use* language, even in the very act of going beyond it. In the very special dramatic context which, for Stendhal, constitutes the whole range of musical experience, words add a further dimension to the range of melody, not for their meaning, but for the *nuances* and variations of emotion which they enable the human voice to convey. Expressed by melody alone, a "sublime" situation might seem too abstract, too etherial; from these remote and lofty regions, the voice gently draws it back again to earth, to the level of humanity and of the human heart and understanding; for the human voice is never anything but individual.

Thus music, for Stendhal, is the sublimest of the arts when it expresses, in forms of beauty whose hallmark is melodious *grâce*, the extremest tension of a dramatic situation in which, as a result of "forces" acting upon them, mere mortals experience a degree of exaltation which no spoken language can convey unaided. But, once again, the lines of force must be there first; without them, the tension—consequently, the exaltation, the beauty and the music—will all evaporate.

It follows that Stendhal's exclusive preoccupation with the older Italian opera corresponds to some of the deepest impulses at work within his sensibility. For better even than Racinian tragedy or the comedies of Molière, a Metastasian opera embodies all the ideal requirements. In Racine's *Phèdre*, the borderline between "lines of force" and "situation" is to some degree ill-defined: both narrative exposition and scenes of high dramatic tension use the same language, are cast in similar dramatic mould. Not so in *L'Olimpiade*, in *Demofoonte*, nor even in *Il Matrimonio segreto*. Here, the "lines of force" are conveyed in recitative; and then, when the tension is built up, when the *moment sublime* explodes in all its inexpressible exaltation, the melody takes over, the words discard their commonplace significance, retaining nothing but their pure expressiveness, and that which *could* not be expressed now finds expression none the less, in all the subtle, generous and gracious beauty of a Mozartian or Cimarosan aria.

Possibly, moreover, it is because of Stendhal's love of opera that he failed so lamentably as a dramatist. He could construct his "lines of force" well enough; but when he reached the "situation", the language that he needed was denied him. It is as though a Mozart had been forced to construct his *Don Giovanni* entirely out of "recitativo secco". But this is neither here nor there. The fact remains that, of the three great artists whose lives are here described, Metastasio was the only one whose art Stendhal completely understood, or appreciated without reservation. Mozart at least is great enough in the field of Italian opera for what Stendhal has to say about him to be worth reading and remembering; but Haydn. . . ? There is a splendid irony, of the sort that Stendhal himself, in the Elysian Fields, might well appreciate, in the fact of a book on Haydn being written by a man who detested orchestral music in any form.

I have been, quite deliberately, an unfaithful—or better, an interfering —translator; for it appears to me that minor classics of this order, at once fascinating by their flashes of insight and exasperating by their lapses and their fallibility, require a sort of special compromise between exactness and readability. Neither Carpani nor even Stendhal at this stage was invariably lucid: and I have occasionally modified or clarified the text in order to avoid writing down sheer nonsense. I have standardised a number of Stendhal's more erratic spellings and corrected others (e.g., Wagenseil instead of "Wagensei"), and emended a quantity of misquotations, notably from Shakespeare. (The reader whose curiosity is sufficiently morbid to want to know what Stendhal can do with a line of the Bard is referred to the original edition.) I have also modernised as far as possible his extremely primitive method of identifying specific musical compositions—although here, in certain cases, I have had to admit defeat. Exactness, moreover, would have demanded the retention of a number of footnotes which today are totally irrelevant —for instance, the precise catalogue-numbers of certain paintings in the Musée de Paris in Napoleonic times. The scholar who needs such references will certainly look them up in the original French editions, while the ordinary reader will skip them anyway.

The thorniest of problems concerned the *List of Haydn's Works*, which concludes the first section of the book. Giuseppe Carpani, at the end of his *Haydine*, simply reproduced the famous MS list (now in the

Musik-Sammlung in Vienna) which Haydn himself had compiled from memory in his extreme old age; and Stendhal had copied it out, adding no more than the usual number of inaccuracies. The result is an unpalatable and unacceptable hybrid: it is neither an exact reproduction of Haydn's own recollection of his life's work, which is of considerable interest to musicologists; nor is it a valid reference-list for the general reader who wishes to identify a given piece. On the other hand, to replace this by a full modern list of Haydn's compositions—of vast length and bristling with problems of attribution—would have been completely out of keeping with the general tenor of Stendhal's book. After much deliberation, I have decided on a compromise which will probably satisfy no one: I have scrapped the Haydn–Carpani–Stendhal list altogether, and replaced it by an abbreviated modern list, of approximately the same scope as the original, but more easily accessible to the contemporary, non-specialist reader. Those who are dissatisfied are referred to A. Van Hoboken's *Thematisch-bibliographisches Werkverzeichnis*; to H. C. Robbins Landon's *Symphonies of Joseph Haydn*; or to Rosemary Hughes' *Haydn* in the Master Musicians Series.

On the other hand, the text of Stendhal's work is given complete and unabridged and I have used the Notes (to which references are indicated by an asterisk ★ in the text) at the end to expand, correct and elucidate wherever something more is required than a straightforward adjustment. The Biographical Index is likewise intended to help the reader identify those innumerable forgotten or half-forgotten personalities to whom references abound. In conclusion, I would like to record my gratitude to Mrs. Judy Rawson for her help with the numerous passages of Italian; to Dr. Hilde Burger for her advice in all matters relating to Vienna (and Vienna, after all, is the half-hidden theme which gives a deep and underlying unity to the book as a whole); and to Professor Basil Deane for his attempts to solve the conundrums of Stendhal's musical allusions.

Stendhal once described the "opera buffa" as an art created "solely for the purpose of ministering to the frivolous pleasures of sophisticated people". Even if this book serves no other purpose, its existence may perhaps be justified.

R.N.C.

JOSEPH HAYDN,

Joseph Haydn, a signed engraving

above: Pen and ink drawing of Haydn's house in Vienna by O. Zeiller

below: Haydn's birthplace at Rohrau

Haydn, Mozart and Metastasio

The present work is presumed to contain more musical information, in a popular form, than is to be met with in any other book of a size equally moderate.

(Preface to the original English edition)

PREFACE TO THE 1814 EDITION

In the year 1808, I was in Vienna★. At that time, I addressed to a friend a quantity of letters touching the celebrated composer, Joseph Haydn, whose acquaintance I had made, thanks to a fortunate accident, some years previously. Upon my return to Paris, I learned that my letters had enjoyed some small success, and that certain persons had thought it worth while to take copies of them. Now, I too am tempted to become an Author and to behold myself in print upon a page. In consequence of this desire, I have added a few explanations, eliminated a number of repetitions, and thus I introduce myself, in the form of a small octavo volume, to all good Friends of Music.

NOTE ADDED IN 1817

When the Author resolved, in the year 1814, to re-read his correspondence, and to make it into a volume, he was in search of an occupation to distract him from certain devouring sorrows,★ and so neglected the precaution of writing to Paris in order to ensure a due measure of acclaim. As a consequence, not a single periodical deigned to mention this little work; in England, however, it was accorded the honour of a translation,[1] and periodicals of the highest merit were readily inclined to comment upon the Author's notions. To which he here replies.

It was my plan to analyse the feelings that we in France commonly entertain towards music. In this task, an initial obstacle presented itself, in that the sensations which we owe to the magic of this Art are exceedingly difficult to recapture in words. I realised that, if I were to lend some grace to the philosophical analysis that I had undertaken, I should have to describe the lives of Haydn, Mozart and Metastasio★. Haydn provided me with examples of every type of instrumental music;

[1] Murray, 1817; 496 pages, with erudite annotations.

Mozart, compared at every point with his illustrious rival, Cimarosa, furnished instances of the two essential categories of dramatic music: that in which the voice is everything, and that in which the voice has scarcely any role, save to lend a name to those sentiments which the instruments evoke with such astonishing power. The life of Metastasio led by natural progression to an examination of those principles that govern the construction of libretti—dramatic poems designed to take Imagination by the hand and lead her, mad daughter of the household that she is, over the threshold of those Romantic countries that music renders accessible to those whose soul she sways.

The first law, so it appears to me, that our nineteenth century decrees for those who would meddle in the business of writing, is that of clarity. A further consideration transformed this general law, for me, into an imperative duty.

We in France are much given to talking about music; yet there is nothing in our education that prepares us to form any judgement of it. For it is a commonplace observation that the greater the *virtuosity* a man possesses in performing upon an instrument, the less he is capable of appreciating the effects of the spell that he weaves about his listeners. His soul is elsewhere, and he can admire nothing, save only that which is *difficult*. I was persuaded that young ladies about to come out into Society might find pleasure in discovering, between the covers of a single volume, all that it is useful to know upon this matter.

In the analysis of sensations fashioned of such delicate material, the essential is to avoid exaggeration. This suited me admirably; the gift of eloquence, which I possessed not at all, would have been wholly inapposite in such a study.

Isle of Wight*,
16 September 1817.

Haydn

LETTERS CONCERNING THE CELEBRATED COMPOSER
HAYDN

LETTER I

To Monsieur Louis de Lech   *Vienna, 5 April 1808.*

Dear Friend*,

Haydn, the composer of whom you are so fond—that rare being whose name sheds such a brilliant radiance in the Temple of Harmony —lives on; and yet the artist is no more.

At the furthest extremity of one of the suburbs of Vienna, extending towards the Imperial Park of Schönbrunn, there may be discovered, hard by the Mariahilfer Tollgate, a small unpaved street, frequented by so little traffic that it is overgrown with grass. About half-way down this thoroughfare there stands a small and humble house*, enveloped constantly in silence: this—and not the Esterházy Palace, as you would have it to be, and as indeed it might be, did he but so wish it—is the home of the founding father of orchestral music, one of the truest spirits of Genius in the eighteenth century, which was the Golden Age of that particular art.

It is but lately that Cimarosa, Haydn and Mozart have quitted the stage of this world. Their immortal compositions are still heard: yet soon they will be set aside. Other composers will capture the whim of fashion; and then we shall be fallen wholly into the dark abyss of mediocrity. Such are the musings which invariably possess my mind, when I draw near to the soundless house where Haydn lingers on. At your knock, an amiable little old woman, his former housekeeper, opens the door for you, all smiling: you climb a small wooden stair-case; and there, in the centre of the second room of a very plain apart-ment, you will behold a tranquil old man seated before a desk, lost in the melancholy thought that life is slipping through his fingers, and in all else, so void, so empty, that it needs the intrusion of visitors to re-mind him of what once he was. Whenever he catches sight of someone entering, a gentle smile comes to his lips, a tear moistens his eye, his voice grows clearer and, recognising his guest, he reminisces of his early years, which he recalls far more vividly than those which follow after; for an instant, you have the illusion that the artist is still there, still living; yet presently, before your eyes, he will relapse into his usual state of torpor and melancholy.

The Haydn of old, burning with ardour, teeming with inspiration, bursting with originality, who, seated at his piano, would invent sheer miracles of music and, in an instant, set every heart ablaze and transport every soul into a realm of delicious sensations—that being exists no more. The butterfly that Plato tells us of has spread its glittering wings towards Heaven, leaving behind it here on earth nothing but the rough, mis-shapen larva, in which disguise it was wont to appear before us.

Now and again I go to visit these cherished relics of a once-great man, and stir the ashes, still warm with the memory of Apollo's fire; and when I manage to dislodge some spark not yet totally extinguished, I take my leave, my soul filled with emotion and sadness. Behold all that now remains of one of the greatest geniuses that ever lived!

> *Cadono le città, cadono i regni,*
> *E l'uom d'esser mortale, par che si sdegni.*
> Tasso. *Canto ii*★.

That, my dear Louis, is all that I am able to tell you in truthfulness about that renowned being, news of whom you have, with such in-sistance, urged me to give you. Yet, since you are so fond of Haydn's music, and since you desire to become better acquainted with it, I can none the less furnish many other details of information, apart from such as concern Haydn the man. My residence here, and the society that I frequent, enable me to talk to you at length about Haydn the composer —that Haydn whose music is today performed from Mexico to Cal-cutta, from Naples to London, and from the suburb of Pera to the very salons of Paris.

Vienna is a delightful city. You must visualise a collection of palaces
and houses, of surpassing cleanliness and orderliness, inhabited by the
wealthiest landowners of one of the great Monarchies of Europe—by
the only *true aristocracy* that still has some just title to merit the appella-
tion. The inner city of Vienna, properly speaking, contains some
seventy-two thousand inhabitants, while her fortifications nowadays
serve no purpose other than to offer agreeable walks. Happily, however,
in order that the cannon (which no longer exist) might sweep the
ground before them with the maximum effect, a clear space★ some
twelve hundred paces broad was set aside, encircling the entire city,
whereon no building was permitted. This open space, as you may well
imagine, is covered with lawns and tree-lined avenues intersecting in
all directions. Beyond this circular crown of greenery lie the two-and-
thirty suburbs of Vienna, inhabited by a hundred and seventy thousand
persons, drawn from every class of society. On one side, the Danube,
that proud river, washes the walls of the Inner City, dividing it from
the suburb of Leopoldstadt, and, on one of its islands, is situated the
famous Prater, the noblest public promenade in all the world, beside
which the Gardens of the Tuileries, Hyde Park in London or the Prado
in Madrid are as those much-vaunted, yet common-or-garden views
in other lands when set against the panorama of the Bay of Naples, seen
from the Hermit's House on Mount Vesuvius. The Prater Island★, fertile as are all the islands formed by great rivers, is covered with noble
trees, which seem to grow taller there than elsewhere. This island,
which offers on every hand the prospect of nature in all her majesty,
combines the sight of straight-drawn avenues of chestnuts, laid out on
a truly noble scale, with the savage aspects of the most solitary forests.
A hundred winding paths criss-cross the island; and when one reaches
the edge of the mighty Danube, coming suddenly and unexpectedly
upon it, one's gaze is still held in fascination by the Leopoldsberg, the
Kahlenberg and many another picturesque hill-top, visible beyond the
further bank. This Garden of Vienna, upon which there intrudes no
trace of any of the unlovely labours of industry arduously seeking gain,
and whose expanse of forest is scarcely broken here and there by a few
meadows, is some six miles in length by some four and a half in width.
I do not know whether the notion is purely fanciful, but for me, the
noble Prater has always appeared visibly to incarnate the very genius of
Haydn.

2★

Within the Inner City of Vienna, winter residence of the Esterházys, the Pálffys*, the Trauttmansdorffs, and of so many other high-born aristocrats invested in a pomp and splendour scarcely less than regal, wit has not attained that glittering standard that it once reached in the *salons* of Paris in the days before our grim and gloomy Revolution. Nor, in Vienna, has Reason raised her altars, as in London. A certain reserve, which forms an intrinsic part of the ingenious policy of the House of Austria, has drawn the divers races that constitute the Empire towards pleasures of a more physical nature—pleasures less embarrassing for those who govern*.

The House of Austria has enjoyed frequent contact with Italy, a part of which belongs to it; several of its Princes were born there. The whole nobility of Lombardy converges on Vienna, soliciting the favour of employment; and the gentle art of music has grown to be the ruling passion of the Viennese. Metastasio lived for fifty years among them;[1] and it was for them that he composed those charming operas which our small-minded critics of the school of Laharpe mistake for misbegotten tragedies. The women of Vienna are decidedly attractive: their superb complexion is the jewel which sets off their elegant figure: that naïve and unsophisticated expression which among their sisters from the North of Germany*, tends now and then towards languor and even boredom, is here enlivened with a touch of coquetry, a hint of shrewdness—consequence of the presence of a numerous Court. In a word, in Vienna, as once of old in Venice, since politics, together with all the interminable arguments over possible improvements in the Commonweal, are forbidden to the human intellect, a gentle voluptuousness has gained possession of every heart. I would not take my oath that the *moral welfare* of the people—that moral welfare of which we hear so much, and at such tedious length—is entirely benefitted thereby: but there is one thing of which you and I may rest assured, and that is that no condition could be more propitious to the art of music. This bewitching art, here in Vienna, has conquered even in the face of haughty Germanic pride: the loftiest subjects of the Monarchy have secured the direction of all three of the lyric theatres; it is these same high-born Princes who control the Musical Society*; and more than one of them may well squander eight or ten thousand francs a year in the interest of the art. Italian sensibility, perhaps, may be profounder; yet it must

---

[1] Born in 1698, summoned to Vienna in 1730, he lived in that city until 1782.

be acknowledged that the Arts in Italy are very far from receiving such encouragement. Thus we may observe that Haydn was born some few leagues from Vienna, Mozart a little distance further away, towards the mountains of the Tyrol, while it was in Prague that Cimarosa composed his *Matrimonio segreto*.

LETTER II

Vienna, 15 April 1808.

It is my constant occupation, my dear Louis, to frequent those many *Musical Societies* which—Heaven be praised for it!—abound here in Vienna. All those delights, which I described to you in my last letter, are here united: and it is this which finally stayed my wandering courses in this city, and brought to haven

> *Me peregrino errante, e fra gli scogli*
> *E fra l' onde agitato, e quasi absorto.*
> Tasso, *Gerusalemme Liberata,*
> *Canto I*, st. iv, ll. 3–4.

I have good authority for all that I may tell you about Haydn; for I have had his story, first from his own lips, next from those persons who were closest to him at divers epochs of his life. I might name Baron van Swieten, the conductor-composers Frieberth and Pichl, Bertoja the 'cellist, Counsellor Griesinger, the composer Weigl, the two Martinez ladies*, Fraülein von Kurzböck, an unusually talented pupil who was also a friend of Haydn, and last but not least his faithful music copyist*. You will forgive me these details: my subject is one of those men of genius who, through the development of their powers, have dedicated the whole of their sojourn on this earth to increasing its pleasures, and to furnishing new distractions for its miseries—men whose genius is, in truth, sublime, but in whose place the common herd prefers others who make themselves a name by organising the mutual slaughter of some odd thousands of these same sad sheep in battle.

The Parnassus of Music already comprised a great number of illustrious composers at the time when, in an Austrian village, the creator of the symphony first made his appearance in the world. The experiments and the genius of Haydn's predecessors had been concentrated on the vocal element of their art—that element which, in the last analysis, forms the true basis of all the pleasure that we derive from music. They employed their instruments only in the role of a secondary embellishment, much as landscape is used in historical painting, or ornamentation in architecture.

The Realm of Music was a Monarchy: the human voice reigned as sovereign supreme, while the accompanying instruments were never more than subjects. That genre from which the voice is wholly excluded, that *Republic* of varied and yet concerted sounds, in which each and every instrument by turns may capture the attention, had, even by the end of the seventeenth century, scarcely begun to make its appearance. It was Lully, I believe, who first invented those symphonic pieces that we call *Overtures*; but even in such "Symphonies" as these, as soon as the fugal[1] passage was ended, the power of the Sovereign Monarch could be sensed. The melody was given wholly to the violin part, and the other instruments provided the accompaniment, just as they do in vocal music, accompanying the soprano, the tenor or the contralto, who

---

[1] The *fugue* is a form of music, in which a melody, known as the subject, is treated in accordance with certain rules which cause it to pass, through a series of successive alternations, from one part to another. Everybody is familiar with the canon:

> *Frère Jacques,*
> *Frère Jacques,*
> *Dormez-vous . . .?*

This is a kind of fugue. As a general rule, fugues serve to render music noisy rather than agreeable; this is the reason why they are better suited to choral compositions than to any other; and since their principal merit is to hold the attention constantly fixed upon the leading melody, or subject, to which end it is bandied about incessantly from part to part, the composer must of necessity take the greatest pains to ensure that this melody should be always perfectly distinct, and to guard against its being smothered by the other parts, or lost among them.

The pleasure afforded by this type of composition being invariably mediocre, it may be asserted that a fine fugue is the arid masterpiece of a conscientious harmonist.* [Cf. also Rousseau, *Dictionnaire de Musique*, Art. "Fugue".]

Everyone has heard Dussek performing on the piano his variations on the song *Marlbrough s'en va-t-en Guerre* or on the ditty *Charmante Gabrielle*. In this impoverished kind of music, the original tune, which is ruined by such a show of pretentiousness, is known as the *theme*, the *subject*, or else as the *motif*. This is the sense in which these terms will be employed here.

alone are deemed worthy to have the musical *idea*—that is, the melody
—entrusted to them.

Consequently, a "symphony" was nothing other than a theme played
on the violin, instead of being sung by a human performer. Scholars
will tell you that the Greeks, and later still the Romans, knew no other
form of instrumental music: be this as it may, however, one thing is
certain: namely, that before the coming of Lully and his symphonies, no
other species was known in Europe, save that which was needed for
dancing. Imperfect as it was, moreover, this kind of music, in which
one instrument alone provided the melody, was performed in Italy only
by exceedingly small groups. Paul Veronese, in his famous *Wedding-
Feast of Cana*, from the Convent of San Giorgio Maggiore, which is
at once the largest painting in the Musée de Paris* and one of the most
entrancing, has preserved the image of those instruments which were
practised in his time. In the foreground of the picture, in the empty
space that is left by the horse-shoe shape of the table, around which are
seated the wedding-guests of Cana, we see Titian playing on the
double bass, Paul Veronese and Tintoretto on the 'cello, an unknown
man wearing a pectoral cross performing on the violin, Bassano on the
flute, and a Turkish slave performing on the trumpet.

When the composer wanted more noise, he would simply add Bach
trumpets to the ensemble described. The organ, as a general rule, was
employed in solo compositions only. The majority of instruments used
by the troubadours of Provence remained unknown outside France, and
were extinct before the fifteenth century. At long last, Viadana,[1] having
invented the "basso continuo", and music making daily ever greater progress in Italy, the violins, originally known as *viols*, duly usurped the
place of all the other instruments; and towards the middle of the seventeenth century, orchestras began to be made up much as we see them today.

At this period, it goes without saying, no one, no matter how sensitive to music, could have conceived, even in his fondest dreams, an
ensemble such as that of the admirable Orchestre de l'Odéon, compris-
ing such a vast number of instruments, all emitting sounds so subtly
graduated for flattering the ear, and all playing together in such perfect
combination. The most beautiful overture that Lully wrote, heard now
as it was then by Louis XIV, surrounded by all his Court, would send

[1] Born at Lodi, in the neighbourhood of Milan: he was Kapellmeister at Mantua in
1644.

you running like a scalded cat to the furthest side of Paris. This reminds me of certain German and French composers who, in our own time, have thought fit to offer us a similarly pleasurable experience, by assailing us with kettle-drums: the fault here, however, lies no longer with the orchestra. The instrumentalists who make up the Orchestre de l'Odéon, taken separately, are one and all the most accomplished performers—their skill, in fact, is all too remarkable; for it is this very virtuosity* which gives these sadistic composers the occasion to torture our ears in such a fashion.

They tend to forget—composers such as these—that in all the Arts, nothing endures save that which continually gives pleasure*. They found no difficulty in seducing that numerous section of the public which gathers no immediate experience of pleasure from music, but which rather exploits it, as indeed it exploits all the other arts, as an excuse for exquisite conversation and manifestations of ecstatic sensibility. These elephant-hided purveyors of the well-turned phrase have led astray a small number of genuine *dilettanti*; yet this whole episode in the history of music is destined soon enough to lapse into the profound oblivion that it deserves, and, fifty years hence, the compositions of our current Great Masters will be keeping company with those of Rameau—that same Rameau whom we used to admire so fervently half-a-century ago. Even Rameau, however, had visited Italy, and appropriated there a fair number of delicious melodies, which he failed to smother entirely with his barbaric art.

In any case, that little sect of composers—those composers who exasperate you to such a degree in Paris, and against whom you rail so bitterly in your letter—has been in existence for many years: such a school is the natural product of much patience allied with a heart of ice, and with the disastrous notion that the Arts can be mastered by studious perseverance. It is the same breed of individual that does so much harm in painting: it is such as they who, after the death of Vasari, inundated Florence with artists who could draw with chilly perfection; and they are already the scourge of your own school of painting. Even in the days of Metastasio, German composers were striving to crush the singers with their instruments; and the latter, in their efforts to regain their lost sovereignty, began to retaliate with "Concertos for Voices", as this great poet used to say. Thus it came about, by a total topsy-turvydom of taste, that the human voice began to imitate those very instruments which seemed resolved to crush it out of existence: and so we heard Signora Agujari, for instance, or Marchesi,[1] or Signora Mara, or Signora Gabrielli,[2] or Signora Danzi, or Mrs Billington, together with countless other virtuosi, transforming their voices into flutes, issuing a challenge to every instrument in the orchestra, and triumphing over these rivals by the difficult and bizarre nature of the passages they performed. Before they could taste their true pleasure, the wretched *dilettanti* were obliged to wait in patience, until such time as these "Divine Virtuosi" lost the urge to show off. Pursued by the instruments of the orchestra, their singing, in the bravura passages, now afforded only one of the two qualities which together constitute Art; for if Art is to please, the imitation of impassioned nature must be united, in the spectator's mind, with the awareness of difficulties surmounted. When this latter quality alone is apparent, the audience's imagination remains cold and dead; and though for an instant the listener may be buoyed up by his vanity at being classed as a connoisseur of music, he belongs none the less to that genus of fond persons described by Montesquieu, who, though yawning fit to dislocate their jaws, still tugged each other by the sleeve and muttered in each others' ears: "Dear God! how vastly we are amused! how *splendid* it all is!"[3] A plethora of "beauties" of this sort is the reason why our present music is in such spanking fine fettle.

In France it is as true for music as for literature, that a writer is as pleased as Punch whenever he manages to startle the reader by some freakish turn of phrase. The honest public, having failed to notice that the author has said precisely nothing, finds something oddly original in his achievement, and applauds; however, after a due measure of applause has been accorded to two or three such odd originalities, our honest public starts to yawn; and on this sorry note, the majority of our concerts draw to a close.

Here you have the reason for the belief, so widespread in this land of bad music, that it is impossible to listen to *any* music for more than two hours on end without dying of sheer boredom. Yet in Naples or in Rome, at the houses of true music-lovers, where the programme is

---

[1] The "Divine Marchesi", born in Milan *c* 1755. Never again will any singer render, as he did, Sarti's rondeau: "*Mia Speranza*".

[2] Catterina Gabrielli, born in Rome in 1730, a pupil of Porpora and of Metastasio: singularly renowned for her caprices. When I was young, old men still spoke of the way in which she sang at Lucca, in 1745, together with Guadagni, who was then her lover.

[3] *Lettres Persanes*, Letter CXI.

carefully selected, a concert may easily afford a whole evening of effort-
less delight. It would suffice to mention those charming concerts that
used to be given by la Duchessa L★★★, for me to be persuaded that my
argument must carry conviction in the judgement of all those who
enjoyed the privilege of being admitted there.

To return, however, to the somewhat arid history of instrumental
music, I would remind you that Lully's original device, although most
fitting to its creator's purpose, which was to introduce, with proper
pomp and circumstance, a theatrical performance, none the less found
such a dearth of imitators that in Italy, for many years, the habit was to
perform Lully's "symphonies" as a prelude to operas by all the greatest
maestri, since these latter simply could not be bothered to write new
overtures of their own; nor were these *maestri* figures of lesser stature
than Vinci, Leo, and the divine Pergolesi. Alessandro Scarlatti was the
first to publish overtures of his own devising; they were immensely
popular, and his imitators included Corelli, Perez, Porpora, Carcano,
Bononcini, etc. All these "symphonies", modelled on those of Lully,
comprised a melodic line and a bass part and nothing else. The earliest
composers to introduce a third part were Sammartini, Palladini, C. P. E.
Bach, Gasparini, Tartini and Jommelli.

Only very occasionally did they attempt to vary the usual practice of
giving an identical rhythm to all three parts. Such were the feeble
gleams of light that heralded before the world the glorious sun of
instrumental music. Corelli had composed duets, and Gassmann quartets: yet it is enough to skip through the scores of these austere, erudite
and irremediably frigid compositions to know by intuition that Haydn
is the true inventor of the Symphony: and not only did he invent the
genre, but carried it to such sublime heights of perfection, that his successors must needs either draw upon his labours, or else slide backwards
into barbarism.

Experience is already bearing out the truth of this daring assertion.

Pleyel has reduced the number of his harmonies and cut down his
transition passages: his works, in consequence, have less dignity and
energy.

When Beethoven, when even Mozart himself, chose to make music
out of vast accumulations of ideas and notes; when they aimed at
quantity and sought after freakish effects by modulation, their symphonies, for all their erudition and technical ingenuity, produced no

effect whatsoever, whereas, whenever they followed in the footsteps of Haydn, they touched every heart.

LETTER III

Natura il fece, e poi roppe la stampa.   Vienna, 24 May 1808.
          Ariosto, *Orlando Furioso*, Canto X, st. LXXXIV.

Franz-Joseph Haydn was born on the last day of March 1732, at Rohrau*, a township situated some fifteen leagues from Vienna. His father was a wheelwright, and his mother, before her marriage, had been a cook at the *Schloss* of Graf Harrach, the overlord of the village.

To his trade as a wheelwright, Haydn's father added the office of sacristan* to the parish. He owned a fine tenor voice, loved his organ and adored all music, whatever its nature. In the course of one of those journeys that the skilled craftsmen of Germany frequently undertake, chancing to stay at Frankfurt-am-Main, he had learned to play a little upon the harp; and on Sundays and holidays, after Divine Service, he would take his harp and his wife would sing. The birth of Joseph brought no change into the habits of this peaceful household. Once a week, the little family concert would come round, and the child, standing in front of his parents, and holding in his hands two little pieces of wood, the one representing a bow, the other a make-believe violin, would constantly accompany his mother as she sang. I have myself witnessed Haydn, laden with years and with honours, recalling even today those simple melodies which she used to sing, so deep was the impression that these early tunes had made upon his imagination all steeped in music. A cousin of the wheelwright's, by name Franck, a schoolmaster at Hainburg*, came over one Sunday to Rohrau, and watched while this trio performed. He observed that the child, who was scarce six years of age, was beating time with a precision and a sureness that were truly astonishing. This Franck was a very competent musician; he proposed to the parents to take young Joseph into his household, and to give him lessons. Joseph's mother and father accepted the offer with delight, hoping as they did that they might the more readily succeed in enabling their son to enter Holy Orders, if he was acquainted with music.

And so it came about that he set out for Hainburg. Scarcely had he been there some few weeks, however, when he discovered in his cousin's house a pair of tympanis*, a sort of drum. By dint of trial and error combined with patience, he managed to coax out of this instrument, which possesses but two tones, a sort of melody which attracted the attention of every visitor who called at the schoolmaster's house.

It must be confessed, my dear friend, that in France, among a class of people as poor as was Haydn's family, music is scarcely to be thought of.

Nature had endowed Haydn with a fine-toned delicate voice. In Italy, at this period, a natural advantage of this kind might have proved fatal to the peasant lad: perhaps Marchesi might have had a disciple worthy of his talents, but Europe would still be awaiting its symphonist. Franck, by doling out to his young cousin—to use Haydn's own expression—"more kicks than ha'pence", soon brought the young tympanist to a stage where he could not only perform upon the violin and other instruments, but even was able to understand Latin, and could sing *solo* in the choir of the parish church in such a fashion as to earn himself a reputation throughout the province.

Now chance one day brought a visitor to Franck, one Reutter, choirmaster of St. Stephen's, the Cathedral of Vienna. He was on the lookout for voices to strengthen the complement of his choristers. The schoolmaster lost no time in suggesting his young relative*: Joseph appeared and Reutter gave him a canon to sing at sight. The precision, the tonal purity, the *brio*[1] with which the child performed the piece, struck him profoundly; his only criticism was that Haydn made no use of *trills*, and, laughingly, he enquired the reason. Quick as a flash, the other answered: "How do you expect me to have learned how to sing a trill, when my cousin himself doesn't know?"

---

[1] I apologise to the reader for resorting to this Italian, or rather Spanish, word, for which I can find no adequate translation: to sing *with ardour mingled with gaiety* would be no more than an imperfect rendering of what is understood in Italy by *cantar con brio*. On the further slope of the Alps, *portarsi con brio* implies praise: in France, it would be a monstrous absurdity. *Brio é quella vaghezza spiritosa che risulta dal galante portamento, o dall' allegra aria della persona.*

"Come here and I'll teach you," said Reutter. Whereupon he took him on his knee, and showed him how to juxtapose with rapidity the two notes, hold his breath and vibrate the uvula. The child produced a trill on the spot and did it excellently. Reutter, delighted at his pupil's success, took up a plate of luscious cherries that Franck had had brought in honour of his illustrious colleague, and poured the whole plateful into the child's pocket. The latter's joy may be imagined. Haydn has often recalled the incident for me, and he used to add, laughing, that every time he chanced to sing a trill, it still seemed to him that he could see those lustrous cherries.

You may well conceive that Reutter did not return to Vienna unaccompanied; he brought with him his new "vibratist". Haydn was then eight years old or thereabouts. In all the story of his modest fortunes, there is no single instance of advancement undeserved, nothing that may be put down to the influence of some wealthy patron. It was for no reason other than that the plain folk of Germany loved music that Haydn's father taught his son the rudiments of the art, that his cousin Franck took this teaching a stage or two further, until finally he was picked out by the Choir-Master of the greatest Church in the Empire. Each step represented a simple consequence of the basic mode of being in Germany, relative to this art which we love.

Haydn has told me that, from this time onwards, he cannot recall there having passed a single day when he failed to work for sixteen hours, and occasionally for eighteen. Yet—and this is note-worthy— he was always his own master and at St. Stephen's the compulsory attendance for the choristers amounted to no more than two hours a week*. Together, he and I, we sought the reasons for this astonishing industriousness. He would tell me that, from his very tenderest years, music had always afforded him an indescribable pleasure. To listen to someone performing on an instrument had always excited him more than racing about with his little school-fellows. He used to play with them on the great square next to St. Stephen's; but as soon as he heard the organ, he would run away from them and pass inside the Church.

By the time he was of an age to start composing, the habit of work was formed; in addition to which, the musical composer has the advantage over other artists: his productions are finished once they are complete in his imagination.

Haydn, whose mind was teeming with ideas of such beauty and in such quantity, was constantly possessed by the joy of creation, which is unquestionably one of the deepest experiences of delight that mortal man may know. The poet shares this advantage with the composer; yet the musician can work the faster. A fine ode, a beautiful symphony, need only to be imagined; immediately, they flood the soul of their creator with that secret admiration which constitutes the very life of artists.

By contrast, for the soldier, the architect, the sculptor, the painter, imagination alone cannot suffice to fill them with that perfect satisfaction with what they have achieved: further laborious tasks still remain to be performed. Projects which are the most admirable in conception may fail dismally in the execution; the most brilliantly conceived pictures may turn out to be badly painted—such considerations leave a hint of cloudiness in the artist's soul, a certain hesitancy regarding the final outcome which dims the perfect purity of the joy of creation. Haydn, on the other hand, had no sooner fashioned a Symphony in his mind, than he was perfectly happy; nothing was missing, save the physical pleasure of hearing it in performance, and the purely moral pleasure of seeing it applauded. I have often observed him, when he was conducting a performance of his own music, unable to stop himself smiling at the approach of certain passages that he approved of. I have observed also how, at those *Grand Concerts* which are given in Vienna at certain seasons of the year, divers so-called devotees of the Arts—persons gifted with every advantage save that of being able to appreciate the art to which they are devoted—exercise great skill in securing seats from which they can watch the countenance of Haydn, and thus, by following his smiles, are able to regulate to a nicety those outbursts of spontaneous applause which are destined to bear evidence to their neighbours of the breadth and the profundity of their transports. Absurd demonstrations! Such people are so remote from any appreciation of the beautiful in art, that they have never even learned to suspect that true emotion knows its own laws of modesty. This is one of the lesser truths of sensibility, which doubtless the female portion of our Romantic sect will be duly grateful to me for having enunciated. To which lesson I will now add an anecdote, which may prove valuable, both as a model in the domain of ecstatic appreciation, and also as a pretext, should some chilly spirit seek to make use of irony, or resort to disrespectful witticisms.

In one of the leading opera-houses in Rome, a company was giving Metastasio's *Artaserse*, with music by Bertoni; the inimitable Pacchiarotti,[1] if I am not mistaken, was singing the part of Arbace. At the third performance, when it came to the famous trial-scene, where the composer had inserted a few bars of orchestral music after the line:

Eppur sono innocente . . .

the beauty of the dramatic situation, the music, the expressive genius of the singer, had so overwhelmed the instrumentalists, that Pacchiarotti observed, after he had uttered these words, that the orchestra seemed to have forgotten its little interlude. He glanced down impatiently at the conductor. "Hey, there! What are you up to?" The latter, emerging as though from a trance, replied, still sobbing and in all simplicity: "We are weeping". Indeed, not a single member of the orchestra had given a thought to their passage and one and all had their eyes brimming with tears fixed upon the singer.

In Brescia once, in 1790, I saw the individual, who, in all the land of Italy, possessed the keenest sensibility to music. He spent his entire life listening to it; when it pleased him, he would remove his shoes, all unaware of what he was doing; and if the pathos grew unbearable, it was his habit to fling them over his shoulders, among the audience behind him.

Farewell. The length of this letter of mine fills me with dismay; my subject seems to grow and grow beneath my pen. I had thought to write you three or four epistles at the most, and I am tending towards infinity. I am taking advantage of the kind offer of Monsieur de C***, who will bear my letters to you free of postage as far as Paris, beginning with this present one. I am much relieved. If you were to be observed to receive through the post this series of enormous packages addressed to you from abroad, it might be suspected that we were engaged in matters of far graver import; and to be happy, if one possesses a heart, one's life must be kept secret.

Vale et me ama

---

[1] Pacchiarotti, born near Rome in 1750, was outstanding in pathetic roles. He is still alive, I believe, living in retirement at Padua.

LETTER IV

Baden*, *20 June 1808.*

Upon my soul, my well-beloved Louis, I begin to suspect that I am no longer fond of music. I have just emerged from a concert given to inaugurate the pretty new Baden Concert-Hall. You are aware that, in the matter of patience, I have long passed the stage of my novitiate; I have schooled myself to withstand the boredom of regular attendance at the sessions of a Parliamentary Assembly; amidst divers most attractive social gatherings, I have endured the friendship with which, for my sins, I was honoured by a gentleman of great consequence and little wit, who is numbered, I believe, in the circle of your acquaintance; yet for all that, I confess, in all the years that I have been listening to music, I have still failed to harden myself to the boredom of *concertos**. A concerto, for me, represents the direst of torments, much as I feel that there is no sillier example of simple-minded stupidity than to come and show off in public a set of five-finger exercises: exercises which must necessarily be mastered if one is ultimately to please the connoisseurs, and whose *results* are destined to be laid before them; but which it is sheer cruelty to oblige an audience to endure in the raw. It appears to me about as intelligent as it would be for your son, if, being away at school, instead of writing you a letter which told you something, he were to send you a collection of those capital Os and Fs that children are made to copy out in order to teach them to write.

Instrumentalists are like people who have learned to pronounce all the words of a language correctly, who can distinctly convey the difference between long and short vowels, but who, in the process of acquiring this mastery, have forgotten the meaning of the words they utter: were it not so, a flautist, instead of threading his way through an endless series of meaningless difficulties, and instead of dragging out his tonic closes for fifteen mortal minutes, would pick up some lively, tuneful melody, such as Cimarosa's

Sei morrelli e quattrobaj.*

spoiling it in the process, of course, and varying it with as many difficulties as his fancy dictated: and at least he would leave us only half-
bored. If ever he came back to his senses, he could bring tears to our
eyes by playing, without changing a single note, some noble aria instinct
with tenderness and melancholy; or else galvanise us with that lovely
thing, the "Queen of Prussia's Waltz".

Personally, I am feeling literally *stunned* by listening to three concertos, one after the other, during the same evening. I am in need of
some powerful distraction, and I have issued a ukase for myself that I
will not go to bed until I have finished telling you the tale of Haydn's
youth.

Less precocious than Mozart who, at the age of thirteen, wrote a
successful opera, Haydn, at this same age, composed a Mass*, which
our good Herr Reutter treated with well-merited derision. This verdict
surprised the lad; but he was already a sensible young fellow and he
appreciated the justice of it; he felt that he needed to learn counterpoint
and the rules of melodic composition—but who was there to teach him?
Reutter offered no instruction in counterpoint[1] to his choristers, and in
all his life gave Haydn only two lessons. Mozart enjoyed an excellent
teacher in his father, who was a violinist of repute; but the case was far
different with poor Joseph, a waif of a chorister alone and unbefriended
in Vienna, who could only get lessons by paying for them, and who
had not a penny. His father, despite his double trade, was so poor, that
when Joseph chanced to have his clothes stolen and announced this
misfortune to his family, it needed an effort for the old man to scrape
together half-a-dozen florins to refurnish his wardrobe.

None of the music-teachers of Vienna was prepared to give lessons
free and for nothing to an unknown chorister with no protecting influence behind him: and it is possibly to this misfortune that Haydn
owes his originality. All poets have imitated Homer, who himself
imitated no one: in this alone, his successors failed to follow his
example, and it is perhaps to this above all that he owes his stature as
the great poet who is universally admired. I personally, my dear friend,
would be glad to see all the *Elements of Literature* in the world at the
bottom of the ocean: all they achieve is to teach minds devoid of genius
to compose a syntax devoid of errors, while their innate mediocrity

1 Counterpoint is the basic art of composition.

ensures that their productions will equally be devoid of beauty. And
we, the readers, have then to suffer all these miserable abortions, and our
feeling for the Arts is thereby diminished; whereas surely no lack of
schooling would ever hold back a being whom Nature had destined
for true greatness. Look at Shakespeare, look at Cervantes; and such
also is the story of our Haydn. A music-master would have enabled
him to avoid some of the mistakes that he committed in later years,
when writing church and operatic music; on the other hand, he would
have been assuredly less original. The first definition of a genius is a
man who finds such delicious pleasure in practising his art, that he will
work at it in spite of every obstacle. Try but to dam these turbulent
mountain streams, the one which is destined to grow into a mighty
river will sweep aside the rubble in an instant.

Following the example of Jean-Jacques, he bought volumes of theory
from a second-hand shop—among others, Fux's *Gradus ad Parnassum*,
which he set himself to study with a degree of stubborn perseverance
that not even the fearsome obscurity of all these Rules could discourage.
Working in solitude, with no teacher to turn to, he made an infinite
number of minor discoveries which, later, he put to good use. Poor,
shivering with cold in his attic, with no fire in his hearth, studying into
the small hours of the night, dropping with weariness, beside a broken-
down harpsichord rapidly crumbling away to ruin at every corner, he
was happy. The days and the years flew by, and he often repeats that
never in all his life did he know such felicity. Haydn's passion was love
of music rather than love of fame; and even where love of fame did
play a part, there entered not the faintest shadow of ambition. In making music, his preoccupation was to afford pleasure to himself,
rather than to acquire the means to win a place among the ranks of
men.

Haydn did not learn recitative from Porpora as you have been informed—his own recitatives, which are so vastly inferior to those of the
inventor of the genre, would in any case suffice to prove the point.
From Porpora he learned the true style of Italian *bel canto*, and also the
art of piano-accompaniment, which is by no means as easy as is generally
believed. And here is the story of these lessons, and how he managed to
obtain them.

A Venetian nobleman, named Correr, was at that time in Vienna, as
the Ambassador of his Republic. He had a mistress who was obsessed

with music, and who provided a lodging for the aged Porpora[1] in the mansion which housed the Embassy. Haydn, employing no resources other than his passion for music, discovered the means to worm his way into this household. He made himself popular; and his Excellency took him, together with his mistress and Porpora, to the Spa of Mannersdorf*, which at that time was in the fashion.

Our young man, whose affections were wholly trained upon the aged Neapolitan, began to invent all manner of stratagems in order to enter into his good graces and to obtain his harmonic favours. Day after day he would rise early, brush the old man's suit, clean his shoes, dress to the best of his ability his antiquated wig. But Porpora was a crabbed old grumbler, cantankerous beyond description. At first, Haydn could obtain nothing from him save an occasional objurgation such as *Oaf*! when he entered his room in the morning. None the less, the old bear, finding himself valetted free, gratis and for nothing, and observing in spite of all certain highly unusual gifts in his self-appointed footman, from time to time would allow his good nature to get the better of him, and give him some sound advice. More especially Haydn received such good counsel when he was to accompany the beautiful Wilhelmine in some of Porpora's own arias, all of which were bristling with difficulties in the bass, which was hard to figure out correctly. It was in this household that Joseph learned to sing in the grand Italian style. On returning to Vienna, the Ambassador, astonished by the progress of this needy young man, made him a pension of six sequins a month (seventy-two francs) and admitted him to his secretaries' table. This generosity enabled Haydn to escape from the worst entanglements of poverty. He was able to buy himself a black suit. Thus dressed, he would leave the house at dawn, and go to the Church of the Barmherzigen Brüder, where he would take the first violin part; from there, he would proceed to the Chapel of Graf Haugwitz, where he would play the organ; later still, he would sing tenor at St. Stephen's. Finally, having spent the whole day running from place to place, he would spend a goodly portion of the night at the harpsichord. Thus, educating himself according to the precepts of each and every musician he could seize

---

[1] Born in Naples in 1685. Here are the life-spans of some of the notable artists whom I shall frequently have occasion to mention:
Pergolesi, born in 1704, died in 1733.
Cimarosa, born in 1754, died in 1801.
Mozart, born in 1756, died in 1792.*

hold of, grasping every opportunity to listen to music which was
reputed to be good, and having no steady teacher, he began to conceive
the notion of *Ideal Beauty* in music after his own fashion and, all unsus-
pecting, was making ready one day to create a wholly personal style.

LETTER V

Baden, 28 August 1808.

My dear Friend,

The ravages of Time soon came to overthrow Haydn's modest fortunes. His voice broke and, at the age of nineteen*, he quitted the
soprano-class at St. Stephen's; or rather, if we are to tell the precise
truth (and so avoid lapsing straight away into the panegyric style), he
was thrown out. Somewhat given to impertinence like all lively young
men, he saw fit, one day, to snip the tail off the gown of one of his
fellow-choristers: and the sin was deemed to be one for which there
was no forgiveness. For eleven years he had sung at St. Stephen's; on
the day when its doors were barred against him, his total fortune consisted but of his dawning talent, which is a poor enough resource when
it is known to no one. One admirer, none the less, he had. Being
obliged to seek a lodging, chance brought him the acquaintance of one
Keller, a wig-maker, who oft-times, in the Cathedral, had admired the
beauty of his voice, and who, in consequence, offered him shelter.
Keller took him in like a son, shared with him his meagre commons,
and charged his wife with the care of keeping him clothed*.

Haydn, thus freed of all temporal worries, and well-settled in the
wig-maker's obscure abode, was able to give himself up wholly and
without distraction to his studies: at which he made rapid progress.
This sojourn, however, exercised a fatal influence on his life: for the
Germans have a mania for marriage. Among a race which is fond,
gentle and timid, the joys of domesticity are esteemed desirable above
all others. Keller had two daughters: soon he and his wife began to

dream of marrying one of them off to the young musician. They spoke to him of the plan; he, being wholly absorbed in his meditations, and never giving a thought to love, showed no repugnance towards the proposal of such an engagement. In the event, he kept his betrothal-pledge with all that steadfast loyalty which formed the basis of his character; the union, however, was anything but happy.

A few short piano-sonatas constituted his earliest compositions; these he sold to the young ladies who came to him as pupils, for he had at length found some such. He was also writing Minuets, Allemandes and Waltzes for the *Redoutensaal**. For his own amusement, he wrote a Serenade for three instruments, which, on fine summer nights, he would go and perform in various parts of Vienna, accompanied by two of his friends. The Kärnthnertor-Theater[1] at that period had as director Johann-Joseph ("Bernardon") Kurz, a celebrated Harlequin, whose gift was to hold the public spell-bound with his puns. "Bernardon" used to attract the crowds to his theatre by the originality of his talent, and by producing first-class *opere buffe*. He had, on top of all this, a handsome wife; which was an added reason why our nocturnal adventurers chose to perform their Serenade beneath the windows of this *Arlecchino*. Kurz was so struck by the originality of the music, that he came down into the street himself to enquire who had composed it.

"I did," boldly replied Haydn.

"You? At your age? What do you mean?"

"One has to start sometime".

"'Fore Heaven! Remarkable! Come upstairs."

Haydn follows the Harlequin, finds himself being introduced to the handsome wife and comes down again furnished with the libretto of an opera entitled *Der krumme Teufel*. The music, written in the space of a few days, was acclaimed a great success, and was rewarded with a fee of twenty-four sequins. However, a certain nobleman who, it seems, was anything but handsome, soon found himself being ironically referred to by the nickname "the Crooked Devil", and consequently had the opera taken off the stage.

Haydn often mentions that he had more difficulty in discovering how to portray the movement of the waves in a storm-scene from this opera, than in writing double-fugues in later years. Kurz, who was a

---

[1] The most popular of the three theatres in Vienna.

man of both taste and intelligence, was not easily satisfied; but there was an added awkwardness, of a very different character. Neither of these two opera-makers had ever seen either the sea or a storm. If one is utterly ignorant of a thing, how is one to portray it? Were this gentle art to be invented, not a few of our Elder Statesmen might learn to speak more convincingly about Virtue. Kurz, in wild excitement, rushed madly round the room, revolving about the composer who was seated at the piano. "Imagine," he kept saying, "imagine a mountain towering up, and then a valley deeply delved, and then another mountain, and then another valley: mountains and valleys frantically chasing each others' tails, peaks and abysses coming one on top of the other, at every instant."

This splendid description failed to produce the desired effect. Harlequin added thunder and lightning—all in vain. "Come on, come on," he kept saying, "portray me all these horrors, but be sure you make the mountains and the valleys quite distinct."

Haydn ran his fingers rapidly over the keyboard, edged his way through the semitones, flung in handfuls of sevenths, leapt from lowest bass to highest treble. Kurz was still not satisfied. In the end, the young man lost patience, stretched out his hands to reach the most widely-separated notes on the harpsichord, drew them rapidly together, and cried: "Devil take your tempest!" "Got it! You've got it!" shouted *Arlecchino* flinging his arms round his neck and nearly choking him. Haydn would add that, many years later, when he found himself crossing the Channel from Calais in rough weather, he had laughed and laughed the whole time the journey lasted, remembering that storm-scene in *Der krumme Teufel*.

"But how on earth," I would say to him, "can you portray a tempest with sounds? And on top of that, *making everything quite distinct!*" To which, the great man being the very model of indulgence, I added that, by imitating the particular intonations of a man who is frightened or in despair, one might, given sufficient talent, convey to the audience sensations identical with those which a tempest would inspire. "But," I persisted, "music can no more *portray distinctly* a tempest than it can state: 'Herr Haydn lives hard by the Schönbrunn Tollgate'." "You may be right," he would reply. "None the less, you must remember that there are the words and above all there is the *décor*, to guide the audience's imagination."

Haydn was nineteen when he composed this storm. You will recall that Mozart, that prodigy of music, was only thirteen when he wrote his first opera, in Milan, in competition with Hasse who, having listened to it in rehearsal, went about saying to everybody: "This child will eclipse us all." No such similar fortune attended Haydn. His special talent was not made for the theatre; and although he has written operas that no *maestro* would disown, he has for all that never scaled the heights of *La Clemenza di Tito* or of *Don Giovanni*.

A year after *Der krumme Teufel*, Haydn embarked properly upon his real career: he entered the lists armed with six trios. The originality of the style and the attractiveness of this new manner immediately won for them the most widespread popularity; but the solemn musicians of Germany were furious in assailing the "dangerous innovations" with which the works were filled. This nation, which has always had a weakness for erudition, was still composing its chamber-music in all the rigorous severity of fugal counterpoint.[1]

The Academy of Music, which had been established in Vienna by His Most Contrapuntal Majesty—I mean, by the Emperor Charles VI —was still flourishing in all its vigour. This solemn ruler, who, it is said, had never laughed in all his life*, was one of the most knowledgeable music-lovers of his age; and all the composers with names in -*us* whom he kept about him were liable to burst with indignation at any piece that seemed to hold more promise of pleasure than of erudition. The delicious little themes of the young composer, the ardour of his style, the occasional licence that he took, roused up against him the anger of

---

[1] One must realise that there is nothing more absurd, nor more pedantic, than the 'rules" of this, the most fascinating of all the arts. Music is still awaiting its Lavoisier. I beg the Reader to excuse me from having to explain the baroque terms that I am occasionally obliged to make use of: there is always Rousseau's *Dictionnaire de Musique*. After taking infinite pains to understand, for instance, what is meant by *counterpoint*, one discovers that, if only music were treated with a minimum of order and method, some twenty lines would have sufficed perfectly to give a notion of this concept. The total range of material substances in nature, from the paving-stones of Paris to *Eau-de-Cologne*, assuredly comprises a far vaster number of different possibilities than are inherent in the diversity of circumstances attending some two or three sounds produced in sequence or in combination; yet the dullest-witted student of the *École Polytechnique*, after following a mere score of lessons by Fourcroy, would have all the categories of natural bodies neatly classified in his head. This is because, at the *École Polytechnique*, up to 1804, everything was preeminently rational; the clear air of Reason that was breathed there at that time repelled anything that was obscure or false.

all the sour-faced cenobites—the Pacomian Brethren!—of this musical
Monastic Order. They reproached him with contrapuntal ungodliness,
with heretical modulations, with rash and vainglorious rhythms.
Luckily, all this sound and fury caused not the slightest harm to the
emerging genius. One thing alone could do him harm: the silence of
contempt; and Haydn's beginnings were accompanied by circumstances of a totally different character.

You must realise, my dear Friend, that until Haydn's time, an
orchestra composed of eighteen different species of instrument was un-
dreamed of. It was he who invented the prestissimo, the very idea of
which sent a shudder down the spines of the antiquated old fogies of
Vienna. In music, as in all other matters, we have scarcely a notion of
what the world was like a century ago: the Allegro, for instance, was no
more than an andantino.

In instrumental music, Haydn has revolutionised details no less than
general conceptions; it was he who first compelled the wind-section to
play pianissimo.

He was twenty when he published his first Quartet in B flat major,
with two horns added*, that every music-lover in the country learned
by heart on the spot. I have never discovered why, towards this time,
Haydn abandoned the house of his friend Keller*; one thing is certain,
however, and that is that his reputation, now dawning under the most
brilliant auspices, had conspicuously failed to banish poverty. He now
went and lodged with a certain Signor Martinez, who undertook to
provide him with food and lodging, on condition that he should give
lessons in piano and singing to his two daughters. It was at this point
that one single house, standing near the Michaelerkirche*, contained,
in two rooms one above the other, on the third and fourth floors respectively, the greatest librettist of the century and the greatest symphonic writer in the world.

Metastasio was also a lodger of Signor Martinez; but as court-poet to
the Emperor Charles VI he was able to live in luxury, whereas in winter
poor Haydn was wont to spend his days in bed, for lack of firewood.
Nevertheless, he profited to no small extent from the company of the
Roman poet. A gentle, profound sensibility had endowed Metastasio
with impeccable good taste in all the arts: he was passionately fond of
music and understood it well; and this poetic spirit, wherein Harmony
reigned supreme, appreciated the talents of the young German. Dining

every day with Haydn, Metastasio instilled into him the general principles of the Arts and, incidentally, taught him something of Italian*.

This struggle against poverty, earliest companion of almost every artist who has made himself a name, lasted in Haydn's case for six long years. Had it only been given *then* for some great nobleman to "discover" him, and pack him off to Italy for two years' travelling, armed with a pension of a hundred golden *louis*—in that case, perhaps, no single aspect of his talent had remained unperfected. But, less fortunate than Metastasio, *his* Gravina was not forthcoming. However, at long last, he found a patron, and, in 1758, he left the Martinez household to enter the service of Graf Morzin.

This gentleman used to give musical *soirées*, and had an orchestra of his own. Now chance, one evening, brought old Prince Anton Esterházy, an impassioned devotee of music, to one of these concerts, which happened precisely to open with a Symphony by Haydn (Symphony in D major). The Prince was so enchanted by this piece, that then and there he begged Graf Morzin to let him have Haydn, whom he wished to appoint Deputy Director to his own orchestra. Morzin agreed. Unhappily, however, the composer, who was indisposed, chanced not to be present at the concert on that day; and since the whims of Princes, when they are not put into execution on the spot, are subject to many a delay thereafter, it was several months before Haydn, who was very eager to pass into the service of the most magnificent aristocrat in Europe, heard another word spoken of the matter*.

Frieberth*, Prince Anton's resident composer, who appreciated the new-found gifts of our young man, was on the look-out for a way to remind His Highness of his protégé. He had the inspiration of inviting Haydn to compose a Symphony to be performed at Eisenstadt, the Prince's residence, on the occasion of his birthday*. Haydn wrote it, and it is not unworthy of him. When the day of the ceremony arrived, the Prince, surrounded by his Court and seated on his Throne, graced by his presence the traditional concert. The orchestra embarked on Haydn's Symphony. But scarcely had they reached the middle bars of the opening Allegro, when the Prince interrupted his musicians and demanded to know who had written so exquisite a piece? "Haydn," replied Frieberth, meanwhile pushing the poor young man forward, all a-tremble. The Prince, perceiving him, exclaimed:

"What! Such music written by *this* blackamoor?" (It is to be confessed that Haydn's complexion was not wholly undeserving of the insult.) "Well then, Blackamoor, henceforward you shall be in my service. What is your name?"

"Joseph Haydn."

"But I know the name! You are already in my service. Why haven't I set eyes on you before?"

Haydn, tongue-tied by the majesty that surrounded the Prince, could answer nothing.

"Go, and fit yourself out with the livery of a *Kapellmeister*," added the Prince, "and let me never again see you looking like that. You are too small, you have mean features, go and get a new costume, a curled wig, red collar and red heels—but the heels are to be tall, mark you, so that your height may correspond to your ability. D'ye hear me? Then go away, and everything shall be given to you!"

Haydn kissed the Prince's hand and went and sat down again in a corner of the orchestra, slightly saddened, he would add, at being obliged to part with his own hair and all his young man's elegance. The following morning, he made his appearance at His Highness' *levée*, imprisoned inside the solemn uniform which the Prince had designated for him. He boasted the title of Assistant Master of the Music★: but his new colleagues called him simply the Blackamoor.

A year later, Prince Anton having died, his title passed to Prince Nikolaus, whose passion for the art of music was, if this is conceivable, even greater than his father's. Haydn was required to compose a large number of pieces for the baryton, a highly-complicated instrument which today has passed out of fashion, and whose timbre, somewhere between tenor and bass, is exceedingly agreeable to listen to. It was the favourite instrument of the Prince, who performed upon it every day, and every day desired to find, placed on his desk, a new piece of music. The larger part of all that Haydn composed for the baryton was subsequently lost in a fire★; the rest is unusable. He often used to say that the need to compose for this unusual instrument had taught him many things he might not otherwise had learned.

Before considering in detail Haydn's other works, I must say a few words about an event which, for many years, was grievously to trouble the even flow of his life. No sooner had he an assured income, than he recalled the promise he had made in earlier years to his friend Keller,

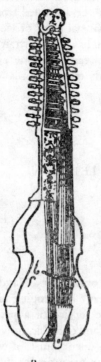

Baryton

the wig-maker: and he married Anna Keller, his daughter. It turned out, however, that the lady was an *honestà* who, besides being most inconveniently virtuous, was possessed of a mania for priests and monks. The lodgings of our poor composer were constantly swarming with such riff-raff. The cackle of noisy gossip stopped him working; and besides he was obliged, on pain of scenes with his wife, to keep supplied free, gratis and for nothing the monastery of each of these good Fathers with Masses and motets.

Ungrateful labour imposed by continual domestic nagging is the last thing needed by men who can work only by listening in silence to the promptings of their own soul. Poor Haydn sought consolation in the arms of Luigia Polzelli, an amiable mezzo-soprano attached to his

Prince's service. Peaceful relations between the couple were not improved by this. In the end, he separated from his wife whom he continued to treat, from a financial point of view, with perfect fairness.

So here, dear friend, you have the portrait of a period of calm youth, devoid of wild escapades, reason guiding every act—the portrait of a man advancing with steady tread towards his goal.

Adieu.

LETTER VI

Helenental*, 2 October 1808.

My dear Friend,

I am coming to the end of my story. Haydn, having once been taken into the House of Esterházy* and finding himself in charge of a large orchestra, attached to the service of a patron who was immensely wealthy and passionately fond of music, now benefitted from that combination of circumstances—a combination which is all too rare for our pleasures—which permits a great genius to spread its wings and take flight. From this moment onwards, his life flowed evenly and was fully occupied by his work. He would rise early in the morning, dress himself very neatly, sit down to a small table beside his piano; and rare were the days when the dinner-hour failed to find him still so seated. In the evening he would attend rehearsals, or else go to the Opera, which took place four times a week in the Prince's own Residence. Now and then—but only very occasionally—he would devote a whole morning to hunting. The few hours that remained to him on normal working-days he would divide between his friends and Signora Polzelli. Such was his life for more than thirty years. It is this feature which explains the extraordinary number of his works. They can be divided into three categories: Instrumental music, Sacred music and Operas.

In the Symphony he is the greatest of the great; in sacred music he opened up a new path, which may, in truth, be subject to criticism, but which, none the less, places his genius beside the highest. In the third of these categories, that of Operatic music, he rose little above the level of competence, and this for several reasons, of which one of the most persuasive is this: that in the Theatre, he was never more than an imitator.

Since you assure me that my interminable gossip does not displease you, I propose to talk in turn about these three genres.

Haydn's instrumental music comprises Chamber Symphonies for a greater or lesser number of instruments; and Symphonies for full orchestra, which, on account of the vast number of instruments required, can hardly be performed outside a concert-hall.

The first of these two categories includes duets, trios, quartets, sextets, octets and *divertimenti*, the piano sonatas, fantasias, variations and caprices. In the second category come the symphonies for full orchestra, concertos for various instruments, the serenades and marches.

Among all this mass of music, the most popular pieces have proved to be the quartets and the full orchestral symphonies. Haydn composed eighty-two quartets and 120 symphonies*. The nineteen earliest quartets are considered by connoisseurs as being mere *divertimenti*. In these, the originality and grandeur of Haydn's style are only fitfully displayed. By contrast, any single one of the quartets from No. 20 up to No. 82 would alone have sufficed to make the reputation of its composer.

It is a well-known fact that quartets are performed by four instruments: a first violin, a second violin, a viola and a 'cello. A lady of discernment used to remark that whenever she listened to Haydn's quartets, she could believe herself to be overhearing a conversation between four charming people. She found that the first violin resembled a man of the liveliest intelligence, who had reached some maturity of years, an inspired talker who kept the conversation moving by supplying it with topics. In the voice of the second violin, she recognised a friend of the first, who used every means in his power to make the other shine, rarely took thought for himself, and contributed to the conversation rather by approving what the others said than by advancing original ideas of his own. The 'cello was a solid, learned and sententious individual. He supported the eloquence of the first violin with a series of maxims, of laconic brevity yet of a devastating truth. As for the viola, she was a good soul, a bit of a feminine chatterbox, who never had really anything much to say, but who, none the less, always wanted to join in the conversation. Yet she contributed a certain gracefulness; and while she was talking, the other speakers had a chance to breathe. You might observe, however, that she had a secret hankering after the 'cello, whom she preferred to all the other instruments.

Haydn, in fifty years of labour, has given birth to 527 instrumental compositions; nor did he ever repeat himself, save when to do so was his deliberate intention. For instance, the aria given to Simon the Husbandman, in the Oratorio *The Seasons*, is an andante taken from one of his symphonies*, which has been transformed into a splendid bass aria—an aria which, it is true, weakens slightly towards the end.

You realise, of course, dear friend of mine, that the larger part of the comments that I would like to make at this point require a piano rather than a pen. At four hundred leagues' distance from you and from our delightful land of France, I can describe for you only the more poetic aspect of Haydn's style.

The allegros of his symphonies, being for the most part exceedingly lively and forceful, transport the listener far beyond the narrow bounds of self; they normally open with a theme that is short, easy and very distinctive; thereafter, by way of a complex process guided by the hand of genius, this theme, repeated by the various instruments, gradually begins to assume a character of heroism shot through with gaiety. These shades of seriousness correspond to the great shadows in Rembrandt* or in Guercino, which contribute so much to the effect of the brightly-lit portions of their paintings.

The composer seems to be leading you down among the valleys of shadow: yet a constant sensation of pleasure persuades you to follow him along the strange path that he had chosen. The characteristics that I have described appear to me to be shared also by the presto and rondo movements.

There is greater variety in the andante and adagio passages: here, the style is truly *grandiose*, shining forth in all its majestic splendour.

The phrases, or musical ideas, are given beautiful and massive development; each section is clear and distinct; the whole stands out in unforgettable boldness. The style is that of Buffon, in those passages where his ideas flow in abundance. To give a good performance of Haydn's Adagios, energy is required rather than gentleness. They are proportioned like Juno rather than like Venus. Steeped in grave solemnity rather than in simpering sweetness, they breathe that quiet dignity, full of strength with an occasional suspicion of heaviness, that is characteristic of the Germans.

In the Andantes, this dignity from time to time relaxes and yields to a moderate gaiety; yet it never ceases to be the dominant mood. Occasionally, in the Andantes and Adagios, the composer suddenly allows himself to be carried away completely by the power and the wealth of his own musical ideas. This madness, this superabundance of energy is like an explosion of joy, sweeping the entire composition along with it, yet not excluding either passion or the gentler emotions.

A certain number of Haydn's Andantes and Allegros appear at first to have no theme. The listener might be tempted to believe that the members of the orchestra have started playing from the middle of the score; yet little by little the true connoisseur comes to appreciate, by the gauge of his sensations, that the composer had both an intention and a plan.

His minuets are pure emanations of genius; so vast a wealth of harmony, of theme and inspiration, all crowded together in a tiny space, would have sufficed for any ordinary mortal to construct a full sonata. In similar vein, this is what Mozart meant, when he remarked of our comic-operas, that any normal man in good health should be able to toss off an opera like that every day before breakfast. The middle sections of Haydn's minuets, comic as a rule, are of enchanting originality.

In general, the characteristic of our composer's instrumental music is its wealth of romantic imagination. You would search in vain for controlled, Racinian self-discipline; the temper is that of Ariosto or of Shakespeare, and that is the reason why I still fail to understand the success that Haydn has had in France.

His genius flies abroad over every highway, with the swiftness of an eagle: superhuman miracles alternate with human fascination, and both are portrayed in the most glittering of colours. It is this variety of colouring, it is the absence of the style classico-tedious which perhaps accounts for the rapidity and the extent of his popularity. Certain of his symphonies were scarcely two years old when they were being performed in America and in India.

It is my impression that the magic of his style can be traced to two predominating characteristics: freedom and joyousness. Haydn's joyousness is an explosion of wholly natural exaltation—ingenuous, unsullied, unquenchable, unceasing. In the Allegros, it reigns supreme;

it can still be discerned in the solemn passages; and it permeates even the Andantes with an unmistakable presence.

In those pieces where it is quite evident, from the rhythm, the tone, the very genre, that the composer's intention was to generate melancholy, this obstinate joyousness, being unable to burst forth openly, is transmuted into energy and power. Mark well: this sombre gravity is not sadness, but rather joy constrained to don a mask. It suggests the concentrated, wild delight of a savage: but sadness, affliction, melancholy —never! Only two or three times in his whole career did Haydn succeed in expressing genuine sadness: in one versicle of his *Stabat Mater*, and in a pair of Adagios from the *Seven Words*.

And here you have the reason why he failed to excel in dramatic music. Without melancholy, there can be no *impassioned* music: which is why the French, lively, vain, feather-light, their emotions always ready-formulated on the tip of their tongue, occasionally bored but never melancholic, will never possess any music.

Since we have touched on this subject, and since I can see you already making a wry face, here is the tail-piece to round off my idea: I intend, quite purposely, to employ none but the most trivial of images—which, consequently are the clearest. And I invite all my literary colleagues, all concocters of paradoxes, to make use of the same method.

LETTER VII

Vienna, 3 October 1808.

Chance led me once into Italy by way of the Simplon Pass; I was travelling with a companion who was making this journey for the first time and, since we were passing within less than a mile of the Borromean Islands, it was a pleasure for me to be able to play the part of guide. We took a boat, we explored the gardens of this superb site, whose grandeur none the less touches the softer fibres of the heart. At long last we regained the little inn on the Isola Bella; here we observed that one of the tables was being laid for three; and, after the customary greetings, a young Milanese, whose aspect announced the easy circumstances of his life, took his seat beside us. I asked him a few questions, to which he replied unhesitatingly. While his attention was engaged in the carving of a partridge, my companion drew a letter from his pocket, and, pretending to read what was therein written, he said to me in English:

"Just look at that young man! Doubtless he has committed some crime, for which he is haunted by remorse. Observe the glances that he casts at us! He suspects that we are connected with the police; or else he may be some Werther, who has picked upon this celebrated spot to put an end to his days in high romantic fashion."

"Not a bit of it," I replied. "He is as affable a young fellow as any that we shall meet with and even an uncommonly cheerful one."

Every Frenchman who arrives in Italy for the first time falls into the same error. For the character of this people is of a sovereign melancholy. Falling on such a soil, the seeds of passion bring forth an hundred-fold; men such as this can scarce find amusement, save in the Arts. Thus it comes about, I believe, that Italy has engendered both her artists and also their admirers who, by revering them, and by paying them for their work, encourage their appearance. It is not that the Italian is incapable of enjoying himself—far from it. Set him down in the country, in the company of a few charming women, and he will surrender to a wild and extravagant gaiety, his imagination will reveal an astonishing vivacity.

Never once, when I have been in Italy, have I stranded myself in the sort of pleasure-party that is to be met with all too frequently in those lovely parks on the outskirts of Paris—parties which the least hint of disappointed vanity can turn into such funereal occasions. A mortal chill descends upon every amusement, and shrivels it; the head of the household glowers black as thunder because his chef has turned out a second-rate meal; as for myself, I am angry because, in the plain of Saint-Gratien, Monsieur le Vicomte de V***, inconsiderately showing off the paces of his English horse, cut me with the tails of his heavy riding-coat as he galloped past, and kicked up a cloud of dust to smother the ladies who were travelling in my fine new barouche—but I shall get my own back, mark my words, or else my coachman shall be turned

away! Sorry reflections such as these are a thousand leagues distant from
a young Italian preparing to receive a company of ladies at his villa.
Do you remember reading Shakespeare's *Merchant of Venice*? If you can
call to mind the speech where Gratiano says:

> *Let me play the fool,*
> *With mirth and laughter let old wrinkles come . . .*

—there you have the very spirit of Italian merriment. It is a merriment
that betrays the reveller's inner happiness; whereas with us, such a
humour would seem dangerously near to *bad taste*. It would involve
revealing that *I* am *profoundly happy*, thus, in a way, compelling others
to pay attention to myself. In France, gaiety consists in demonstrating
to all who are listening that one is gay exclusively for the sake of entertaining *them*; it is even necessary to wear a mask of extravagant joyful-
ness, so as to conceal the true joy that is the reward of the successful
entertainer.

French merriment demands much play of wit—it is the humour of
Lesage and his *Gil Blas*; Italian merriment is based upon sensibility, with
the result that, when there is nothing to make him merry, his merriment evaporates.

Our young acquaintance from the Borromean Islands could see
nothing positively side-splitting about the fact of having met, at the
common table of an inn, two well-bred French travellers. He was
polite; but *we* would have preferred him to be amusing.

It follows that, in Italy, since a man's actions depend more directly
than in France upon the quality of his profounder emotions, an individual whose soul is shallow will prove the dismallest companion in the
world. I was complaining of this one day to that amiable personage,
Baron W★★★. "What do you expect?" he answered. "We Italians, beside you Frenchmen, are like the melons of Italy compared with those
of France. In your country, you can buy melons anywhere in the
market-place, secure in the knowledge that they will all be more or less
palatable; here in Italy, the first twenty you buy will be nauseating, but
the twenty-first will be divine."

Among Italians, their way of life is almost invariably rooted in the
inner experiences of their soul. This fact clearly explains their love of
music, which, by conjuring up regrets, soothes the pains of melan-
choly★. By contrast, an active and sanguine temperament, such as that

possessed by three Frenchmen out of four, is incapable of any passionate fondness for music, since there is nothing there for music to soothe, nor can it normally give any ardent pleasure.

What say you now to my philosophy? It has the misfortune to bear a close affinity with the theory of those French philosophers whom nowadays you are wont to disparage: the theory which would attribute the origins of art to *boredom*.[1] I should prefer to replace the concept of boredom by that of *melancholy*, which assumes a degree of sensitivity in the soul.

The boredom of our average Frenchman, whose emotional experiences have never afforded him infinite happiness nor yet infinite despair, and whose deepest chagrins are the pricks and stings of vanity—such boredom evaporates in *conversation*, wherein vanity, which is his ruling passion, may constantly find means to make a glittering display, whether in the substance of what he says, or whether in the manner of saying it. In France, conversation is a game, an inexhaustible mine of eventualities. The art of conversation, as it is practised in France and as a foreigner may hear it every day in the Café de Foy*, and in other public places, is, in my estimation, the armed clash of two contending vanities.

The only difference between the Café de Foy and the salon of the Marquise du Deffand[2] is that, in the Café de Foy, which is frequented by members of the lower middle-classes struggling along on fixed and inadequate incomes, vanity relies on the *substance* of what is said. Each in turn retails anecdotes of flattering incidents that happened to him; his neighbour, who is supposed to be listening, awaits with ill-concealed impatience until *his* turn shall come, and then embarks upon a tale all of his own, not vouchsafing a single word of reply to his predecessor.

Good manners, which, in café or salon, stem from the same principle,[3] consist—in the context of the Café de Foy—in listening to one's neighbour with an appearance of concern, in smiling at the comical episodes in his tales and, when talking about oneself, in slightly veiling the anxious, wild-eyed aspect of self-interest. Would you observe this same self-interest in all its primitive uncouthness, delineated in frankest portraiture? Then just pay a fleeting visit to the Stock Exchange in some

---

[1] The *ennui* of a man of sensibility, ever mingled with regrets.
[2] In 1779.
[3] In any society of persons who are fundamentally indifferent to each other, good manners consist in a reciprocal effort to afford each other the maximum of pleasure.

3*

commercial city of the South, and watch a stockbroker proposing a deal to a business-man. This avid self-interest too patchily disguised occasionally lends to certain pairs of interlocutors in the Café de Foy the aspect of two mortal enemies dragged together by force to discuss their differences.

In wealthier and more sophisticated gatherings, it is not upon the substance of the tale, but upon the manner of the telling that the speaker must count, if he expects a goodly harvest of agreeable praise to flatter his vanity. The rule, therefore, is to chose a subject which is of the least possible interest to the speaker personally. Volney[1] notes that French settlers in the United States are dissatisfied with their isolated lives, and are never weary of repeating: "It is the end of the earth, you can't find anyone to talk to"—an attitude that contrasts sharply with that of other colonists, of German or of English origin, who are perfectly happy to spend days on end amid utter silence.

I am persuaded that this universal panacea, conversation, this sovereign remedy for boredom *à la française*, would prove incapable of exciting sufficient emotion to relieve Italian melancholy.

It is typical of the cast of mind resulting from this particular manner of seeking happiness, that Prince N★★★, whom I often used to hear mentioned in Rome as being one of the most charming men in Italy, and also one of the most dissolute, should make music for us at every conceivable opportunity, at the residence of the Countess S★★★, his mistress. He was rapidly dissipating a fortune of some two or three millions★: his rank, his wealth, his habits ought by all rights have turned him into a gilded coxcomb or quizzing-glass dandy; yet, although his dress-uniform was smothered in *Orders*, he remained immutably and exclusively an Artist.

In France, he who sets out for an assignation with his mistress, or he who steps forth to discover whether the Imperial Decree nominating him to some important Office of State has been signed, retains at least enough awareness over and above these preoccupations to allow him

---

1 "For Frenchmen, *visiting* and *chatting* are habitual needs, of such imperious urgency that, over all the length of the frontiers of Louisiana and Canada, it would be impossible to name a single colonist of that nation who has settled out of sight or earshot of another. In several places, having enquired how far away resided the most outlying of the settlers, I received the following reply: 'He is out in the desert, among the bears, a whole league distant from the nearest habitation, and *without a single soul to talk to*.'" Voleny,★ *Tableau des Etats-Unis*, p. 415.

to indulge in a flutter of jealousy at the sight of some fashionable gig. Nature has made the Frenchman vain and quick-witted, rather than merry. France produces grenadiers who are the finest in the world for carrying redoubts at the point of the bayonet; she also produces the most scintillating wits. Italy can boast no Collé, and has nothing even remotely resembling the delicious gaiety of his *Vérité dans le Vin*.

The inhabitants of the Peninsular are passionate, melancholy and of a tender sensibility: Italy has given us a Raphael, a Pergolesi—but also a Count Ugolino.[1]

LETTER VIII

Salzburg, 30 April 1809.

So, after all, my dear friend, you *have* received my letters: the war which here surrounds me on every side was causing me some anxiety about their fate. My walks through the woods are ever disturbed by the clash of arms; at this very instant, I can distinctly hear the rolling of the cannon in action on the Munich highroad, some four and a half miles distant; today, however, after having permitted myself a scattering of somewhat melancholy reflections upon that Fate which has robbed me of my Company of Grenadiers, and which, for twenty years, has held me in exile from my native land, I seated myself on the trunk of a mighty oak, now laid low upon the ground. Thus I find myself in the shade of a noble lime-tree; I can perceive around me nothing save the delightful green of trees sharp-etched against a dark blue sky; I have

---

[1] Count Ugolino, in Dante:

> La bocca solevò dal fiero pasto
> Quel peccator . . .
> *Inferno*, Canto xxxiii

Observe the large number of characters of this type in Sismondi's excellent *Histoire des Républiques d'Italie*.

taken out my little note-book and my pencil and once more, after this
long silence, I am going to talk to you about our friend Haydn.

Do you know, that I am almost tempted to charge you with heresy?
You seem to prefer him even to the divine singers of Ausonia! Ah no,
my friend. Pergolesi, Cimarosa and their peers are unrivalled in that
most deeply moving, yet at the same time most noble aspect of the
gentle art that is our consolation. You argue that one of the reasons for
your preference for Haydn, is that he can be heard in London and in
Paris as easily as in Vienna, whereas France, stricken by a dearth of
voices, will never enjoy the divine Pergolesi nor his *Olimpiade*. In this
respect, my opinion coincides with yours. The inflexible physiological
structure of the English, as of our good compatriots, may permit these
nations to bring forth some admirable instrumentalists; yet it debars
them for ever from the art of song. Here on the other hand, while
strolling through the suburb of Leopoldstadt, I have just heard a
wondrously sweet voice delightfully rendering the song:

Nach dem Todt bin ich dein.

As for your remarks addressed to myself, I discern all too clearly the
maliciousness of your criticism, emerging from its surrounding cloud
of compliments. You are still accusing me of that same flippancy*
which, praise be to Heaven, in days gone by used to form the gravamen
of your moralisings. You complain that I write to you of Haydn, forgetting only one thing, which is frankly to tackle the *manner* of the
Master and to explain, stooping from my high vantage-point as an
inhabitant of Germany to the abyss of your ignorance, just how and
why he is popular? Now to begin with, you are anything but ignorant.
You are passionately fond of music and, in the Arts, the fondness is all.
You argue that you can scarce pick out a simple tune: are you not
ashamed of this absurd objection? Do you take him for an artist, this
day-labourer, this rude mechanical, who for twenty years on end gives
piano-lessons, with as much inspiration as his peer in genius, the
tailor in the house next door, makes suits? Would you have considered
as an *art* that which is but a simple *trade*, in which, as in all other
trades, success will come with but a mickle of skill and a muckle of
patience?

You should do yourself more justice. If your love of music endures, a year's travel in Italy will furnish you with a more true scholarship than all your learned scholars in Paris.

There is one thing that I should never have believed: namely, that by studying the arts one might foster a true feeling for them. And yet . . . I used to have a friend who, in all the Musée de Paris, found nothing to admire save the expression on the face of Raphael's *St. Cecilia* and, to a lesser degree, the painting of the *Transfiguration*. All the rest left him utterly indifferent; and he preferred those pretty fan-paintings, which are on exhibition every other year, to all the smoke-darkened masterpieces of the Old Masters. In a word, for him, painting was a source of pleasure from which he was almost wholly excluded. Now it so happened that, merely to oblige an acquaintance, he had read through a *History of Painting** in order to correct the style; one day, by chance, he entered the Musée, and the sight of the paintings reminded him of what he had recently read about them. All unaware of what he was doing, he began confirming or revoking the verdicts that he had encountered in the manuscript; soon he learned to distinguish between the styles of the different schools. Gradually, and with no premeditated purpose, he found himself going three or four times a week to the Musée de Paris; and today there are few places in all the world from which he derives greater pleasure. He has discovered a thousand things to think about in this painting or in that which, previously, had meant nothing to him; and the beauties of Guido Reni, which in earlier days had struck him not at all, now hold him spellbound.

I am convinced that it is the same with music and that, if one were to make a start by getting by heart some five or six arias from *Il Matrimonio segreto*, one would end up by appreciating the beauty of all the others. However, there is one precaution to be taken, which is to deprive oneself of all music other than that of Cimarosa for a month or two. The friend whom I mentioned took great care each week, on his visit to the Musée de Paris, to look only at paintings by one given Master, or belonging to one given school.

Yet what a difficult task you are laying on me, my dear Friend, in asking about Haydn's symphonies. Not for lack of ideas, good or bad, for these I have in plenty; rather does the difficulty lie in transmitting them over a distance of some four hundred leagues, and transmuting them into words.

Since you insist upon it, my dear friend, take such precautions as you may against the contagion of boredom; for I, for my part, propose to set down for you verbatim those opinions which are current here in Austria concerning Haydn's style.

In the early days of our acquaintance, I would often ask him questions on this matter, for it is natural enough to enquire of a being who performs miracles: "How do you bring these things to pass?" Yet I observed my man always avoided anything like a direct answer. It occurred to me that a flank attack might succeed where a frontal assault had failed and so, with the effrontery of a journalist and with all the resources of inexhaustible lung-power, I embarked upon a series of obscure pontifications upon Handel, Mozart and other great Masters, whose pardon for this offence I humbly beg. Haydn, who is very indulgent and very kind, just allowed me to talk on, smiling the while; yet every now and then, after he had refreshed me with a glass of his Tokay wine, he would set me right with five or six sentences brimming with common-sense and ardour, delivered straight from his heart and revealing his theory: and no sooner had I stepped outside his house than I hastened to note down what I had heard. Thus it happened that, by plying a trade not unlike that of one of Monsieur de Sartine's *agents provocateurs*, I succeeded in learning the Master's true opinions.

Would you believe it? This great man, whom those poor uninspired devils, our *academic* composers, would gladly use as a shield to save themselves, was never weary of repeating:

"If you but start with a fine *tune*, then your piece, whatever it is, will be fine also, and will assuredly please the listener."

"Melody," he would continue, "is the soul of music, it is the very life, the spirit, the essence of a composition. Without it, a Tartini may discover harmonies of the rarest and most cunning variety, yet the listener will register nothing better than an ingeniously-contrived noise which, for all that it may not be displeasing to the ear, none the less leaves the mind vacant and the heart cold."

On one occasion, as I was contesting, with even more perversity than usual, these oracular pronouncements concerning the Art, Haydn, good fellow that he is, went and fetched for me a little, hastily-scribbled diary that he had kept during his stay in London. He made me read a passage that told how, having one day ventured into St. Paul's, he had heard a hymn there, sung by four thousand children. "That simple, natural melody," he added, "afforded me greater pleasure than I have ever received at any other time from a performance of music." Now, this melody which produced such an effect upon the man who, more than any other in the world, had listened to the most exquisite instrumental music, was nothing other than this:

Should I attempt, lest you accuse me of circumventing difficulties, to furnish you with a proper definition of melody? Listen to Signora Barilli, in *I Nemici generosi*, which I have just seen announced in the *Journal des Débats*, singing the aria:

> *Piaceri dell' anima*
> *Contenti soavi*. . . .

Listen to her in *Il Matrimonio segreto*, mockingly addressing her sister, who is as proud as a peacock to be marrying a Count:

> *Signora Contessina**. . . .

Listen to Crivelli, as Paolino, addressing this same Count, who has fallen in love with his mistress, in the aria:

> *Deh! Signor!*

—*that* is melody. Would you, by following so simple a method of instruction, now learn what melody is *not*? Then go to the Théâtre Feydeau, first making sure that the programme contains music neither by Grétry nor by Della-Maria, and avoiding the opera *La Mélomanie*. Listen now to the first arietta that chances to fall upon your ear, and you will perceive, better than by way of a thousand definitions, the meaning of music devoid of melody.

1 Haydn's memory has slightly embellished this tune.*

There is perchance more true love of music in any score or so of those
carefree beggars of Naples, known as *lazzaroni*, who, of an evening,
sing the length of the Riviera di Chiaja, than in the whole of those
elegant audiences that gather together of a Sunday at the *Conservatoire*
in the rue Bergère. Yet why should this fact upset us? Since when are
we grown so proud of qualities that are purely physical? The countryside of Normandy contains no orange-groves, and yet it is a fine and
goodly province: happy the man who owns his acres in Normandy—
and who is permitted to live on them! However, let us return to our
subject: melody.

How is one to define in a rational manner a thing that no rule in the
world can teach one how to produce? I have before my eyes some five
or six definitions that I have jotted down in my note-book: and on my
honour, if there were anything that might prove capable of destroying
the clear notion that I hold touching the nature of melody, it would
be the perusal of these definitions. They are just words: presentably
arranged, yet offering only the haziest outline of sense. For instance, what
is pain? We all of us, alas, possess enough experience to apprehend the
answer to this question; and yet, however we formulated our definition, we should merely have obscured the issue. I shall therefore, my
dear Sir, in absolving myself from furnishing you with a precise definition of melody, consider myself sufficiently secure from your reproaches.
Melody is that, for instance, which a sensitive yet untrained music-
lover retains in his mind after he has come home from the opera. Who
has ever listened to Mozart's *Figaro*, without singing to himself as he
leaves the building, in a voice as tuneless as any in the world:

> *Non più andrai, farfallone amoroso,*
> *Delle donne turbando il riposo* . . . etc.

The Masters will tell you: invent melodies which are clear and at the
same time easy, significant, elegant and which, without being far-
fetched, avoid lapsing into triviality. To avoid this latter pitfall, likewise the dullness of monotony, it is sufficient to introduce occasional
dissonances: these, at first, produce a slightly disagreeable impression;
the ear is eager to have them resolved and experiences an unmistakable
pleasure when at long last the composer brings about this resolution.

Mozart, that very genius of gentle melancholy, from whom ideas

flowed inexhaustibly, whose taste touched such heights of grandeur—
Mozart, who conceived the aria:

Non so più cosa son, cosa faccio . . .

was occasionally guilty of too lavish a use of modulation.

Here and there he would spoil those wonderful melodies whose
opening bars so perfectly express the sighs breathed by a soul to whom
tenderness is all. Towards the end, he torments them a little, thus frequently blurring them to the ear, for all that in the score they remain
perfectly distinct to the eye; occasionally, in his orchestral accompaniments, he introduces themes which are too much at variance with
those given to the singer on the stage; yet what would one not be prepared to forgive him, in consideration of the melody sustained by the
orchestra towards the middle of the aria:

Vedre mentr'io sospiro
Felice un servo mio!

from *Le Nozze di Figaro*—an aria that is truly divine, and which any
man in agony from the torments of love recalls whether he will or no.[1]

Dissonances in music correspond to *chiaroscuro*★ in painting: they
must be employed with moderation. Compare the *Transfiguration*,
with the *Communion of St. Jerome*, which hang opposite each other
in your Musée de Paris. The *Transfiguration* is slightly lacking in
chiaroscuro; by contrast, Domenichino makes a more skilful use of it,
and demonstrates the point at which it is essential to stop. Otherwise
you will tumble headlong among the sect of the *tenebrosi* who, in the
sixteenth century, occasioned the demise of painting in Italy. Professional musicians will tell you that Mozart is over-lavish with his use of
certain intervals: above all, the diminished and the augmented.

[1] I offer no excuses for taking my examples from music that I have heard in Paris since
my return to France and which belongs to a period later than the original date of these
letters.★ It is not given to everyone to imitate a certain great writer who, striving to give
his friend an exact idea of the deserted countryside that the traveller must cross in order
to reach Rome, writes to him:

"You have read, my dear friend, all that has been written about this landscape, yet I
know not whether actual travellers have afforded you any truly precise notion of it. . . .
You are to imagine something of the desolation of Tyre and of Babylon, of which it is
written in the Scriptures. . . ." (*Génie du Christianisme*, vol. III, p. 367).

Here in Paris, were I to quote you the larger number of the masterpieces of Pergolesi,
Galuppi, Sacchini, etc., it would be rather similar to talking about the "Plains of Babylon".

Some years after Haydn had taken up his residence at Eisenstadt*, and as soon as he had firmly established his own style, he resolved to re-stock his imagination by making a careful collection of those ancient and original folk-melodies that are handed down among the people of every nation.

The Ukraine, Hungary, Scotland, Germany, Sicily, Spain, Russia—he exploited the resources of all these countries.

You may gather an idea of the originality of these tunes from that Tyrolean folk-song, which was brought back to France by officers who had served in the Austrian campaign in 1809:

Wenn ich war in mein. . . .

In Naples, every year shortly before Christmas, bands of wandering musicians may be observed flocking in from Calabria. These performers, armed with a guitar and a violin, which they play, not by resting it against their shoulder, but by holding it rather as we do the double-bass, provide accompaniment for their barbaric folk-songs, which are as unlike any music that can be heard elsewhere in Europe as can con-ceivably be imagined. These melodies, despite their fantastic weirdness, are not devoid of charm, and are by no means displeasing to the ear.

It is possible, after a fashion, to form some idea of the genre by re-calling that *Romance* which is sung so enchantingly by Crivelli in Paisiello's *Nina*. Paisiello spent some time in collecting antique melo-dies which are believed to be Greek in origin and which are still sung even today by the semi-barbaric peasants from the extreme tip of Italy; and it was one of these melodies that he arranged, and from which he derived this *Romance*, at once so simple and so exquisite.

Is it possible to conceive any two melodies more vastly different from each other than the Spanish *Bolero* and Henry IV's tune, *Charmante Gabrielle*? Add to these a Scottish reel and a Persian romance, such as you will hear sung in Constantinople, and you will realise the extent to which variety is possible in music. Haydn fed his imagination on all this material, and knew by heart all these singular melodies.

Just as Leonardo da Vinci used to make sketches, in a little notebook that he carried always on his person, of any curious human features that he encountered, so also Haydn carefully used to note down all the passages and themes that passed through his head.

When he felt happy and cheerful, he would rush across to his little writing-table, and jot down themes for minuets and songs; on the other hand, on days when he felt a prey to gentle languor and inclined towards melancholy, he would scribble down ideas for Andantes and Adagios. Later on, when in the throes of composition he found that he had need for a passage of such and such a character, he would resort to his musical arsenal.

Normally however, Haydn would embark upon a Symphony only when he felt in a propitious mood. It has been said that noble thoughts spring direct from the heart; moreover, the remoter the art that one practises from the precision of the mathematical sciences, the truer this dictum appears. Tartini, before sitting down to compose, would read one of Petrarch's gentle sonnets. Alfieri, that bilious-tempered poet who, by dint of depicting tyrants, became at length infected with the embittered savagery that devours them, used to love to listen to music before settling down to work. Haydn—similar in this to Buffon— needed to have his wig dressed with the same care as though he were going forth into Society, and to dress with something resembling splendour. Frederick II had once sent him a ring set with diamonds; and Haydn confessed on more than one occasion that if, when he sat down at the piano, he forgot to wear this ring, not a single idea would come to him. The paper on which he wrote his scores had to be of the finest quality available and of perfect whiteness. Thereafter he would write with such scrupulous care and neatness, that not even the most skilled of copyists could have surpassed him in the clarity and evenness of his notation. It is true that his notes had such small heads and such fine tails that he used to refer to them, with some semblance of justice, as "a fly walking over the paper".

Having seen to all these purely mechanical precautions, Haydn would begin his work by noting down his principal idea, his *main theme*, and by selecting the keys through which he desired to make it pass. His sensibility had endowed him with the most profound knowledge of the greater or lesser effect produced by one key succeeding upon another.[1] As a next step, Haydn would invent a kind of simple

[1] A trivial example: go to the piano and pick out the chord of C major; now jump immediately to G major, and you will find that this transition is not unpleasing. If, however, instead of jumping to G major, you proceed directly from C major to E flat major, you will observe the extent to which this second transition appears more sonorous, more majestic and more agreeable than the first*. It would be easy to discover a thousand more complex instances: Mozart and Haydn are full of them.

story, to provide a canvas for the necessary emotions and musical colours.

On occasions, he would imagine that a friend of his, father of a large family and ill-provided for by fortune's favours, was about to set sail for America, hoping thereby to alleviate his destiny.

The chief incidents of the voyage would form the Symphony. It would open with the departure. There is a favourable wind gently stirring the waves, and the vessel sails bravely out of harbour, while, left behind on shore, the traveller's family is watching him with tear-filled eyes, and his friends are waving him goodbye. Amid the waves the vessel prospers; and in due course drops anchor off an unknown shore. Towards the middle of the Symphony, there are echoes of savage music, of dancing and barbaric cries. The fortunate navigator makes profitable exchanges with the natives of the country, loads his vessel to the gunwales with rich merchandise and at long last sets sail again for Europe wafted by a favourable breeze. At this point, the opening theme of the Symphony returns. But soon the sea begins to grow rough, the sky darkens and a fearful tempest advances with a clashing of key-signatures and a quickening of the tempo. Aboard the ship all is wild disorder. The cries of the sailors, the pounding of the waves, the howling of the gale whip up the melody from chromatic to pathetic. Chords augmented and diminished, modulations sliding through cataclysms of semitones, depict the terror of the crew.

And now, little by little, the seas subside, while propitious breezes come to fill the sails. The harbour-bar is passed. The happy father drops anchor amid the blessings of his friends and the joyful shouting of his children and their mother; and as at last he sets foot on land, he takes them in his arms. As the Symphony draws to its close, all is merriment and laughter*.

I am unable to recall precisely which one of Haydn's Symphonies has this simple narrative as its guiding thread. I know that he specified it, not only to me, but also to Pichl the composer, but it has completely slipped my memory.

In another of his Symphonies, our good Haydn imagined a kind of dialogue between Jesus and the hardened sinner; after which he followed with the parable of the Prodigal Son.

From these simple stories are derived the nicknames by which our composer occasionally was wont to designate his Symphonies. Without this clue to their origin, it is impossible to understand names such as the *Beautiful Circassian Maiden*, *La Roxolane*, the *Hermit*, the *Infatuated Schoolmaster*, the *Persian Maid*, the *Coward*, the *Queen of France*, the *Laudon*—all titles which betray the little tale which served to guide the composer's inward soul*. I could dearly wish that all Haydn's Symphonies had kept names, rather than numbers. A number says nothing; a title, such as the *Shipwreck*, the *Wedding*, etc., acts in a gentle way as a spur to the listener's imagination, which cannot be too early set in motion.

It is said that no man ever better understood the divers effects of colours, their relationship one with another and the contrast of which they are capable, than did Titian. Haydn similarly possessed an incredible knowledge of each of the instruments that made up his orchestra. No sooner had his imagination offered him a development, a chord, a simple phrase even, than he perceived in a flash the instrument by which it must needs be performed in order to produce the most agreeable, and at the same time the most musically effective, impression. And were he in any doubt while composing his symphony, his official position at Eisenstadt furnished him with an easy means of resolving it. He would ring a bell in the recognised manner for announcing a rehearsal; the musicians would come trooping into the *foyer*. He would have them play through, in two or three different ways, the passage that was running through his head, select one version and reject the others, dismiss the orchestra, and hurry back to his work.

Call to mind, my dear Louis, the Orestes scene in Gluck's *Iphigénie en Tauride*. The amazing effect of those agitato passages on the violas would have vanished altogether had these same passages been allotted to any other instrument.

Haydn's music frequently contains unexpected modulations; yet he sensed perfectly that the least hint of extravagance served only to diminish the impression of pure *Beauty* that haunted the soul of the listener; nor does he ever risk any key-change that is odd or unusual without first having imperceptibly prepared it by the preceding chords. Thus, when the moment for this key-change comes, it is felt to be neither crude nor arbitrary. He used to maintain that he had discovered the idea for several modulations of this type in the works of C. P. E. Bach. And you know that Bach himself brought them back from Italy.

In general, Haydn was all too willing to acknowledge his debt to

Carl Philipp Emanuel Bach who, before the birth of Mozart, used to be reputed the greatest pianist in the world; but at the same time he would protest that he owed nothing at all to Sammartini who, he added, was nothing but a muddle-headed old blunderer.

Despite this, however, I perfectly recall being in Milan some thirty years ago and attending a *soirée musicale* which was being offered to the celebrated Misliviček*. On that occasion, the orchestra chose to perform a number of half-forgotten symphonies by Sammartini; whereupon the Czech composer suddenly exclaimed: "I have discovered the ancestor of Haydn's style!"

This was undoubtedly an exaggeration; yet these two artists were both endowed by Nature with a temperament that was roughly similar and it is a proven fact that Haydn enjoyed every opportunity of studying the works of the Milanese. As for specific resemblances, observe, in Haydn's first Quartet in B, at the opening of the second section of the first movement, the rhythms of the second violin and viola: nothing could be purer Sammartini.

This Sammartini, a man of wildly ardent temper and considerable originality, was also, albeit *in absentia*, in the service of Prince Nikolaus Esterházy. A Milanese banker named Castelli was commissioned by the Prince to hand over to Sammartini the sum of eight sequins (96 francs) in cash for every piece of music that he should place in his hands: the composer was to furnish a minimum of two per month, but he was at liberty to pass on to the banker as many as he liked. Towards the end of his life, however, old age made him lazy; and I recall most distinctly having heard the banker complaining to him of the reproaches that he himself received from Vienna, on account of the infrequency with which he was transmitting new pieces. "I'll do them, I'll do them; but the harpsichord is stealing my life away!" replied Sammartini, grumbling darkly.

In spite of this laziness of his, the library of the Pálffy family mansion contains over a thousand pieces by Sammartini. Consequently, Haydn enjoyed every possible opportunity to know and study them, if ever he had the intention.

Haydn, by an intense study of sound, early discovered, to use his own terms, "what goes well, what goes better, what goes badly."

Now there, my dear Friend, you have an instance of that art of giving a simple answer which so many people find so embarrassingly difficult. If you asked Haydn the reason for a certain chord, or for a passage given to one instrument rather than another, he would scarcely vouchsafe any reply save: "I did it that way because it goes well."

This extraordinary man, having been refused admission in his youth to the Temples of Knowledge by the avarice of the music-masters, had found all his learning in his own heart; he had taught his soul to submit to the effect of music; he had observed what was taking place within himself, and had striven to reproduce what he had experienced. A mediocre artist, by contrast, is content simply to quote the rule or the model that he has followed: for *that* is the one thing that he can conceive quite clearly in his little mind.

Haydn had discovered for himself a unique rule, about which I can tell you nothing, save that he himself had always refused to divulge what it was. You are too familiar with the Arts for there to be any need for me to remind you in detail that the ancient Greek sculptors had certain invariable rules of Beauty, known as *canons*.[1] These rules are lost, and their existence is surrounded by impenetrable darkness. It would appear that Haydn had discovered something similar in music. The composer Weigl*, having begged him one day to reveal these rules to him, could get no reply from him other than this: "Try and see."

You will hear it maintained that Sarti, that charming composer, would occasionally work according to a numerical system: he even used to boast that he could teach this *science* in a small number of lessons; yet the real secret of his method consisted in extracting money from the pocket of wealthy music-lovers, who were naïve enough to have high hopes of being able to speak a language without knowing it. How can one expect blindly to make use of the general language of sounds, without first having studied the specific meaning of each one in particular?

As for Haydn, whose heart was the very Temple of Scrupulousness, all those who knew him are aware that he possessed a secret, and that he had never consented to reveal it. He never made known to the world anything, in this connection, save a sort of "philharmonic game", in which the players select numbers by the chance of a throw of dice; each of these numbers corresponds to a given passage of music; and

[1] See Winckelmann and Visconti; or rather, Visconti and then Winckelmann.

these passages, when put together by someone to whom counterpoint is a sealed book, form regular minuets.

Haydn had one other principle, of a singular strangeness. Unless his aim was to express a specific emotion, or to depict a specific image, *any* theme would serve his purpose. "The whole of art," he would maintain, "consists in the manner of *treating* a theme and of developing it." Frequently, one of his friends would drop in to visit him just as he was about to begin on a piece. "Give me a tune," he would say, laughing. Give a tune to Haydn! Who would have dared? "Come on! Out with it! Don't be scared! Give me a tune, *any* tune, never mind which." And his order had to be obeyed.

A number of his astonishing Quartets show evidence of this *tour de force*. They open with the most insignificant of themes; yet bar by bar this theme takes on a recognizable personality, grows, spreads forth; and the dwarf becomes a giant before our astonished eyes.

LETTER IX

Salzburg, 4 May 1809.

My dear Friend,

In the year 1741, Jommelli, a genius in the field of music, was summoned to Bologna to compose an opera. On the day following his arrival, he went to see the famous Father Martini and, without revealing his identity, begged him to accept him among his pupils. Father Martini gave him a subject for a fugue; but then, observing that he was developing it with extraordinary skill, he exclaimed:

"Who are you? Do you take me for a fool? *I* am the one who should learn, and I want to learn from you!"

"I am Jommelli, the *maestro* who has been commissioned to write the opera that is to be performed here this coming autumn, and I have come to beg you to teach me the great art of never being nonplussed in the handling of my own musical ideas."

We, having no business with music save to enjoy it, have no conception of the difficulty that there is in arranging noble melodies in such a way that they shall delight the listener, without thereby infringing certain rules, of which a good quarter at least—let it be admitted—are pure convention. It happens to writers every day: we have ideas that appear valid, yet which turn out to present extraordinary difficulties as soon as it comes to finding words in which to formulate them attractively, or to setting them down on paper. This prickly art, which Jommelli had begged Father Martini to teach him, Haydn had mastered all alone. In his younger days, he would often jot down on paper a number of notes taken at random, mark them with a beat, and force himself to construct something out of this arbitrary jumble, using it as basic thematic material. Sarti is reputed to have practised a similar exercise. In Naples the *abate* Speranza used to require his pupils to take a lyric by Metastasio, and then to compose straight off some thirty different tunes to fit the same words. It was by methods such as these that he trained the celebrated Zingarelli, whose glory still shines undimmed to this day in Rome, and who could contrive to write his best works within a week, and sometimes even less. I personally, unworthy witness that I am, can testify that in the space of forty hours, distributed over ten working days, he produced his inimitable *Giulietta e Romeo*. At Milan, he had written his opera *Alsinda*, the work that first established his reputation, in seven days. He possesses an absolute mastery over all the technical difficulties of his art.

One of Haydn's more remarkable qualities, and the most significant among those which were not the direct gift of Nature, was his ability to create a *style*. A musical composition is simply a discourse which is fashioned out of sounds instead of words. In his "discourses", Haydn possesses to a supreme degree, not only the art of enhancing the effectiveness of the principal theme by relating it to various subsidiary themes, but also that of formulating both principal and secondary material alike in the manner which is supremely well-suited to the complexion of the subject. This is by and large what is known in literature as stylistic appropriateness. Thus the sustained style of Buffon excludes those lively, original and slightly colloquial turns of phrase which are such a constant delight in Montesquieu.

The main theme of a symphony is the proposition which the composer intends to demonstrate, or rather, to be more precise, whose truth he proposes to establish by the irrefutable evidence of the senses. In the same way as the orator, having first stated his subject, then proceeds to develop it, introduces his proofs, repeats what he intends to demonstrate, adduces more proofs, and finally concludes, so also Haydn is ever striving to convince us of the *motif* of his symphony.

This theme must be restated, lest it be forgotten. The vulgar run of composers are content with servile repetitions, merely tossing their subject from one key to another; by contrast Haydn, at each restatement, decks it out in a garment of novelty, at times invigorating it with a sharp touch of asperity, at others embellishing it with delicate ornamentation, yet always permitting the listener, in his surprise, to recognize the original beneath the fascinating trappings. You tell me that you have been deeply stirred by Haydn's symphonies: consequently, if you have followed this emotional exegesis, I am convinced that, at this very moment, one or other of his admirable Andantes must actually be running through your mind.

Impelled ever onward by this rushing torrent of ideas, Haydn none the less possesses the ability to remain constantly within the bounds of nature; he is never freakishly fantastic; everything is allotted to its right and proper place.

Haydn's symphonies, like Cicero's speeches, constitute a gigantic arsenal, wherein there lie gathered together all the resources of art. Had I but a piano beside me, I could train you to distinguish more or less clearly some twelve or fifteen musical devices, as different one from the other as the equivalent devices in rhetoric, as antithesis is from metonymy;[1] here, however, I will confine myself to drawing your attention to the pauses.

I am referring to those unexpected hushes that grip the whole orchestra, as Haydn, rushing headlong down from the climax towards the recapitulation and, being at last just about to reach that final note which resolves and concludes the development section, stops suddenly dead, at that very instant when the instruments appear to be committed to the most violent animation, and imposes silence on them all.

As soon as they resume, the first sound that will be heard, you may assume, will be that long-heralded, expected final note, the note that was to conclude the development, and which, so to speak, you could

---

[1] "Resounding words, that Pradon takes for terms in chemistry" (Boileau).

already hear in your own mind as the beginning of the recapitulation. Far from it. At this point Haydn dodges away, escaping normally towards the dominant, by way of some deliciously graceful little passage which he has already hinted at earlier in the movement. After having distracted your attention for an instant by this feather-light interlude, he returns to the tonic and now at last gives you, complete, entire and for your utter fulfilment, that recapitulation which he had at first pretended to withhold from you, only to increase your eventual satisfaction.

He is most adept at exploiting one of the great advantages that instrumental music can claim over vocal music: namely, that instruments can depict the most rapid and energetic movements of the human soul, whereas the singing voice is incapable of delineating the passions whenever these require a comparatively swift utterance of words. The composer needs *time*, just as the painter needs *space* on his canvas. Such are the limitations of these particular arts.

If you recall the duet:

Sortite, sortite,

between Susanna and Cherubino, at the instant when he is about to leap through the window, you will agree that while the accompaniment is sheer delight, the words come tumbling out too quickly to give complete pleasure; in the duet:

Svenami . . .

from Act III of *gli Orazi e Curiazi*, is it not quite shockingly improbable that Camilla, possessed of all her fury, and arguing with the ferocious Horace, should speak so slowly? This duet, in my opinion, is musically a fine piece of work; but these slow, dragging words, at variance with so dynamic a situation, kill all the delight one might take in it. I would even undertake to compose a set of Italian words, in which Camilla and Horace would be a pair of lovers lamenting with each other over their dismay at being unable to see each other for a day or two; I would adapt this dialogue to the tune of the duet *Svenami*; and I maintain that the music would now just as happily depict the mitigated chagrin of my lovers, as it does the furious patriotism and the despair of Signora Grassini and Signor Crivelli. Yet, if Cimarosa failed to find a form of musical expression suited to these words, who else would be bold enough to claim that he could attempt it? For my part, I am persuaded that here we are up against one of the limits of the art of Music.

A regular devotee of the *Grand Opéra* in Paris once said to a friend of mine: "Ah, Gluck! Now *there's* a great man for you! His melodies, admittedly, are not particularly pleasant; but what *expression*! Listen to Orpheus singing

> *J'ai perdu mon Euridice,*
> *Rien n'égale mon malheur.*

My friend, who has an excellent voice, retorted by singing to exactly the same tune:

> *J'ai trouvé mon Euridice,*
> *Rien n'égale mon bonheur.*

I urge you to try this little experiment for yourself, keeping you eyes meanwhile on the score.

If you wish for sorrow, remember the aria:

> *. . . lascia, o cara,*
> *La rimembranza amara!*

from the opening of *Don Giovanni*. Observe that here the tempo is necessarily slow, and that perhaps even Mozart himself would not have succeeded in portraying an *impetuous* despair, such as that, for instance, of the churlish lover upon receipt of that fearful letter which consists of these three words "Indeed, sir—*No*!" This situation is admirably expressed in Cimarosa's aria:

> *Senti, indegna! io ti volea sposar,*
> *E ti trovo innamorata.*

Here again, the poor unhappy lover is on the point of shedding tears, his reason is wandering, but he is in the grip of no mad fury. Music can no more portray wild fury than a painter can show the same action at two different instants in time. The ideal tempo for vocal music is that of a nocturne. Think of the nocturne from *Ser Marcantonio*. This is a truism that was well understood by composers such as Hasse or Vinci and by singers such as la Faustina and la Mingoti; yet it is one which has been forgotten in our own time.

Still less is music able to depict divers objects in nature: the instruments of the orchestra, admittedly, can convey rapidity of movement; yet, being bereft of language, they can transmit no *precise* image. If you take any fifty people, all of some musical sensibility, listening with pleasure to the identical symphony, I would wager that no two among them will have been stirred by the same image.

It has often occurred to me that the effect of Haydn's and of Mozart's symphonies would be markedly increased, were they to be given in the orchestra-pit, and if, during the performance, a series of skilfully-contrived décors, reflecting the chief moods of the different passages, should be revealed one after the other on the stage. A well-painted backdrop, representing a calm sea and a boundless vista of pure sky, would, it seems to me, increase the effectiveness of many an Andante by Haydn which depicts a serene tranquility.

In Germany, there is a tradition of contriving *tableaux vivants* to represent the Old Masters. A whole society of people, for instance, will dress up in Dutch costume, divide into groups and thus, frozen into perfect immobility, and echoing the original with absolute exactness, constitute a living reproduction of some painting by Teniers or Van Ostade.

Some such *tableaux* on the stage would be an admirable commentary on the Symphonies of Haydn and would imprint them indelibly on the memory. I shall never be able to forget the "Symphony of Chaos" which preludes *The Creation* since I saw the ballet *Prometeo*, and in it, Vigano's delightful ballerinas depicting, along the lines suggested by Haydn's music, the astonishment of the Daughters of Earth, for the first time penetrated by the charms of Art. This is a truth not to be gainsaid: that music, the most etherial of all the arts, cannot unaided attempt description.

When music realises one of the conditions necessary for description, rapidity of tempo for example, it must needs abandon language and the deeply-stirring intonations of the human voice; when the voice is present, the prerequisite of rapidity vanishes.

How should music portray a meadow starred with flowers in patterns of sound that are in any way distinguishable from those suited to suggesting the joyous breeze that blows, propitiously filling the sails of the vessel on whose deck Paris bears away fair Helen?

Paisiello and Sarti share with Haydn his notable skill in the proper distribution of material over the various sections of a work. By a similar process of prudent interior economy, Paisiello manages to compose, not a single aria, but indeed a whole opera, out of two or three exquisite basic thematic statements. He will disguise them, recall them, combine them, deck them out in majesty; gradually with each new repetition, he drives them deeper into the imagination of his listeners, fostering in them a consciousness of the suavity even of those notes which are least striking and in the end creating that inexpressibly graceful style that is his, and which is so easy to understand. Think of *La Molinara*, of which you are so fond. Or think of the accompaniments to *Pirro*, compared for instance with those of Mayr's *Ginevra*; or, if you prefer a setting of solemn black to serve as foil to your woes, call to mind the accompaniment in Gluck's *Alceste*.

Our imagination needs a certain amount of time to grasp a passage of music, to *feel* it, to allow it to sink in. The loveliest theme in all the world will produce but an ephemeral impression, if the composer fails to dwell upon it. If he hurries on too quickly to another theme, all the graciousness of the music vanishes. Haydn's skill in this particular art, which is so essential to symphonic music, where there are no words to explain the structure, no recitatives, no instants of silence to interrupt the flow, is another of his admirable qualities. Think of the Adagio of Quartet No. 45; yet similar instances abound in all his works. As soon as his principal theme begins to show signs of exhaustion, he offers you some agreeable digression, and in divers varied and stimulating forms the listener's pleasure is rekindled. For he understands that, in a symphony as in an epic poem, the function of episodic material is to embellish the essential subject, not to obliterate it. In this respect, Haydn is unique.

Take, for instance, the Peasants' Dance in *The Seasons*: gradually it evolves into a vigorous fugue, and forms an entrancing digression.

The properly-handled distribution of thematic material over the various sections of a symphony produces on the listener's imagination a curiously satisfying impression, combined with a certain soothing sense of calm—an impression similar, if I am not mistaken, to that which the eye receives from the harmony of colours in a well-painted picture. Take, for instance, Correggio's *St. Jerome*; the spectator is all unconscious of his motives; yet his feet turn ever and again and of their own accord towards this *St. Jerome*, whereas it is only by virtue of a conscious resolution that he will turn a second time in the direction of Caravaggio's *Christ laid in the Tomb*.[1] In the realm of music, how many Caravaggios do we meet, against one Correggio! On the other hand, a painting may have remarkable qualities, and yet afford no sensible pleasure to the eye; into this category fall several works by the Brothers Carracci, which are sombre to the point of distastefulness. Whereas any music which does not *begin* by appealing to the ear, is simply not music. The science of sounds is so little understood, that one can be sure of nothing in this domain, save of the pleasure experienced in the present instant.

Haydn shares out his musical themes or melodies among the various instruments of the orchestra in accordance with the demands of profound and complex combinations. Each instrument has its part, and exactly the part best suited to it. I could dearly wish, my good Friend, that in the interval between this letter and the next you might pay a visit to the *Conservatoire*, there in your own city of Paris, where, you tell me, they perform in so admirable a fashion the symphonies of our composer. Consider, while you are listening to them, whether you acknowledge the truth of these my musings: in the contrary case, assail me mercilessly. For in the latter event, it signifies, either that I have expressed myself badly; or else that my ideas have as much foundation in fact as those of that dear old soul who, looking at the dark configurations of the moon, believed with all her heart that she could see happy lovers leaning one towards the other.

Certain operatic composers have tried to achieve the same result, sharing the statement of their theme between the orchestra and the singer's voice. They neglected to observe that the human voice has one peculiar characteristic, namely, that as soon as it is heard it attracts the *whole* of the listener's attention exclusively to itself. We all of us, unhappily, find as we grow older and as our learning increases at the expense of our sensibility, that we listen with ever-growing attentiveness to the instruments in the orchestra. However, for the majority of those who are endowed with sensibility and whose souls were truly fashioned for music, the clearer the melody entrusted to the voice and the more

[1] This distinction would be even more striking, if I were able to instance the *St. George*, which is in the Dresden Gallery. In the *St. Jerome*, which is in Paris, the beauty of the Virgin and the celestial expression on the countenance of Mary Magdalene are so striking that one has no leisure to reflect how skilfully this picture is painted.

distinctly it is rendered, the more penetrating the pleasure they receive. I can observe no exception to this rule unless it be in certain pieces by Mozart. But Mozart is the LaFontaine of music; and just as those who have tried to imitate the natural simplicity of the greatest poet in the French language have achieved nothing but a kind of silliness, so also those who strive to imitate Mozart plunge headlong into an abominable morass of elaborate absurdities. The sweetness of the melodies created by this great genius softens all his harmonies, makes everything acceptable. Whereas those German composers who form my daily fare have given up the ideal of graciousness (all too understandably!) as a bad job; and yet the genre imperiously demands it. They are determined at every bar to assail us with Terror. The overture to the most trivial of comic-operas sounds like a funeral, or like a battle. *They* retort, that the overture to *La Frascatana* is harmonically feeble.

It is as though a painter, all ignorant of the *nuances* of colour, knowing nothing of soft shades or tender harmonies, were to insist against all the odds on painting portraits of women. Thereafter, in oracular tones, he will harangue his pupils: "Whatever you do, take care not to copy that wretch Correggio, that insipid bore Paolo Veronese: be hard and harsh—like me."

> *Jadis en sa volière, un riche curieux*
> *Rassembla des oiseaux le peuple harmonieux;*
> *Le chantre de la nuit, le serin, la fauvette*
> *De leurs sons enchanteurs égayaient sa retraite;*
> *Il eut soin d'écarter les lézards et les rats.*
> *Ils n'osaient approcher: ce temps ne dura pas.*
> *Un nouveau maître vint; ses gens se négligèrent,*
> *Ils dirent aux lézards: "Illustres compagnons,*
> *Les oiseaux ne sont plus et c'est nous qui régnons."*
> Voltaire. *Les deux Siècles.*

LETTER X

Salzburg, 6 May 1809.

I have frequently heard it asked of Haydn, which of his own works he preferred. He used to reply: *Die Sieben Worte des Erlösers am Kreuze.* Here, first of all, is an explanation of the title. Some fifty years ago, I believe, Maundy Thursday used to be celebrated, both in Madrid and in Cadiz, with a prayer known as *el Entierro*—the Burial of the Saviour. The piety and the grave demeanour of the Spanish people used to envelop this ritual in unusual solemnity: a preacher would expound in turn each of the Seven Words spoken by Christ from the Cross; while music, of a dignity befitting this awe-inspiring subject, was required to fill the intervals accorded to the sacred meditation of the Faithful between the exegesis of each of the Seven Words. The organisers of this ritual drama caused a proclamation to be published throughout the whole of Europe, offering a considerable prize to the composer who should submit seven full-scale symphonic pieces, each expressing the emotions that one of the Seven Words was deemed to inspire in the breast of the believer. Haydn was the only competitor*. He submitted seven symphonic pieces, in which

> *Spiega con tal pietate il suo concetto,*
> *E il suon con tal dolcezza v'accompagna,*
> *Che al crudo inferno intenerisce il petto.*
>
> Dante

What is the sense in praising them? The only thing is to hear them, have Faith in Christ, weep, believe and shudder. At a later date, Michael Haydn, the brother of our composer, added words and wrote a voice-part for this sublime orchestra music*: without altering a note, he transformed it into an accompaniment—a Herculean labour, which

4

would have terrified a Monteverdi or a Palestrina. This superimposed vocal part is written for four voices.

A number of Haydn's symphonies were written for religious festivals.[1] Beneath the all-pervading sorrow that they express, I still seem to perceive Haydn's characteristic vivacity, with, here and there, a hint of anger, by which the composer perhaps contrives to suggest the Jews crucifying their Saviour.

Here follows, my dear Louis, a brief summary of what I have so often felt while listening to Haydn's finest symphonies, and while trying to decipher in my own soul the secrets of their attraction for me. I would start by trying to distinguish clearly what these symphonies have altogether in common, and by striving to lay my finger on the general style which informs them.

As a further step, I would attempt to trace resemblances that might exist between this style and that of the best known Masters. Occasionally, one can discover Haydn putting into practice precepts formulated by C. P. E. Bach; one can observe that, in the handling and in the development of the tonal qualities of the various instruments, the composer has borrowed something from Fux and something from Porpora; and, in the elaboration of his thematic material, he has developed some exquisite ideas that can be found in embryo in the works of the Milanese composer Sammartini, or in those of Jommelli.

Yet these faint suggestions of plagiarism are far from robbing him of the incontestable merit of having a style all of his own, one fitted to bring about, as in fact has happened, a total revolution in the art of orchestral music. In similar fashion, it is not beyond the bounds of possibility that my beloved Correggio may have borrowed a few notions of that sublime *chiaroscuro*, which explains the fascination of his *Leda*, his *St. Jerome*, his *Madonna alla Scodella*, from certain paintings by Fra Bartolomeo or by Leonardo da Vinci. He is none the less rightly reputed to be the discoverer of that art of *chiaroscuro* which has endowed modern generations with the knowledge of a second source of ideal beauty. Just as the *Apollo Belvedere* exemplifies all beauty of form and contour, so Correggio's *Night*, in the Dresden gallery, by its shadows and half-tones, affords to the soul lost in gentle reverie that sensation of pure happiness that exalts it and bears

[1] These include the Symphonies* in D minor, No. 26 ("*la Lamentatione*") and in F minor, No. 49 ("*la Passione*").

it away out of itself—that sensation which has been referred to as "the Sublime".

LETTER XI

Salzburg, 11 May 1809.

My dear Friend,

Despite a somewhat loutish cast of feature and, in his speech, a kind of laconic brevity, Haydn was gay, of cheerful temper and of a sociable character. This vivacity of his, admittedly, was easily constrained by the presence of strangers or of persons of a higher rank than himself. In Germany there is no bridging of distances, it is the land of bowing and scraping. In Paris, Gentlemen of the Bedchamber, Companions of the Order of St. George, would call on d'Alembert in his garret; in Austria, Haydn frequented no company save that of his fellow-musicians. Doubtless he was the poorer for it; but Society was the poorer also. His cheerfulness and his rich melodic inventiveness designated him as the ideal composer to introduce a strain of comedy into orchestral music—a field that was almost wholly unexplored, and in which he might have gone far, were it not for the fact that, in all things relating to comedy, it is imperative that the writer or composer should move in the very centre of the most elegant circles. Haydn saw nothing of fashionable society, save in his old age, in the course of his visits to London.

The natural bent of his genius inclined him to employ his instruments with deliberate comic intent. Frequently, at rehearsals, he would give his friends in the orchestra short pieces to play in this style—a style which, to date, has been very little developed. Because of this, I trust that you will forgive me some small display of my limited stock of comic erudition.

The earliest of all musical jokes that I know is that perpetrated by Merula,[1] one of the most learned contrapuntalists in a period when

[1] Floreat *c.* 1630.

melody still played a very secondary role in music. He devised a fugue which figured schoolboys reciting the Latin pronoun *qui, quae, quod* at the behest of their schoolmaster. But their lesson was ill-learned. The muddles, the desperate stumblings and stammerings, the howlers committed by the schoolboys, all mingled with the shouting of the pedagogue, who loses his temper and canes them each in turn, produced a most successful comic effect.

Benedetto Marcello, the Venetian, a composer so staid and of such sublime gravity in his sacred style, the very Pindar of music, is the composer of the well-known piece entitled *Il Capriccio*, in which he makes fun of the *castrati*, whom he cordially detested.

Two basses and two tenors begin by singing together the three following lines:

> *No, che lassù nei cori almi e beati,*
> *Non entrano castrati,*
> *Perchè scritto è in quel loco . . .*

At this point our male soprano soars off all alone, enquiring:

> *Dite: che è scritto mai?*

The tenors and basses reply somewhere right at the bottom of the register:

> *Arbor che non fa frutto*
> *Arda nel fuoco.*

—to which the castrato, far away at the other end of the scale, answers:

> *Ahi! Ahi!*

The effect created by this highly expressive little piece is incredibly funny. The extreme distance that the composer has placed between the high, squeaky notes of the unfortunate castrato and the sombre rumbling of the *bassi profundi*, combines to produce the most absurd melody in the world.

The everlasting nasal droning of the Capucins, who are expressly forbidden by their Order to sing or to depart from the tones of common speech, provides Jommelli with the subject for an agreeably satirical composition.

The elegant Galuppi, who is so famous for his *opere buffe* and for his church music, did not disdain to offer a musical version of the chanting in a synagogue, nor to depict a quarrel between a bevy of market-women—fruit-stall owners—in a crowded market-place in Venice.

In Vienna, the spirit of order and method that reigned in the land established one particular day of the year for drolleries of this description. The evening of St. Cecilia's day was traditionally devoted to making music in every household and, from the middle of the eighteenth century onward, it grew customary for the most staid and solemn of musicians to present, on that one occasion, some comic composition to their friends. A certain Augustinian Father*, attached to the fine Monastery of Sankt Florian in Austria, selected a most singular text as material for his musical joke: he actually composed a Holy Mass which for many years—and without a hint of scandal—enjoyed the unique privilege of keeping both singers and congregation in a constant fit of laughter.

You are familiar with the ale-house rounds written by Father Martini of Bologna: the "Drunkards' Round", the "Round of Bells", the "Decrepit Nun's Round".

Among the piano-works of the celebrated Clementi, he who sought to emulate Mozart, there is an interesting collection, published in London, that very homeland of caricature: a *Collection of Musical Caricatures*, in which he takes off all the best-known composers of piano-music that have ever lived; and anyone who has the slightest acquaintance with the styles of Mozart, Haydn, Koželuck, Sterkel, etc., has only to listen once to these miniature sonatas, each consisting of a prelude and a development, to guess immediately which of the Masters it is who is being treated so irreverently; his style is unmistakable and, above all, his trifling mannerisms and the minor inaccuracies to which he is prone are pounced on with merciless penetration.

In the days of the Emperor Charles VI, the famous Porpora used to live in Vienna, poor and unemployed: his music failed to please this royal connoisseur, since it was too full, so the latter complained, of shakes and mordents. Hasse composed an Oratorio for the Emperor, who promptly commissioned a second. Hasse pleaded with His Majesty to allow Porpora to carry out this royal command; at first, the Emperor refused, saying that he did not care for Porpora's bleating style: in the end however, being touched by Hasse's generosity, he relented and gave consent to the request. Warned by his colleague, Porpora refrained from scoring a single trill in the whole Oratorio. At the dress-rehearsal, the astonished Emperor could do nothing but exclaim, over and over again: "But it's a different man! No trills!" However, when it came to the fugue by which this piece of sacred music was to conclude, he observed that the principal subject opened with four notes, all armed with trills. Now, as you know, in a fugue the main subject is handed on without variation from part to part; and when the Emperor, whose royal prerogative it was never to smile, heard at the full final climax of the fugue this immense deluge of trills, seemingly the musical embodiment of a very Bedlam of paralytics, he could restrain himself no longer, and gave a great guffaw of laughter, perhaps for the first time in his life. In France, which is the land of ingenious jests, this particular one might perhaps have seemed in doubtful taste; but in Vienna it laid the foundation-stone of Porpora's fortunes.

Among all the comic pieces that Haydn wrote, only one has survived: that well-known symphony in the course of which all the instruments, one after the other, vanish into silence, until at the end the leader of the violins is left playing on all by himself*. This curious piece has given rise to three conflicting stories, each of which, in Vienna, is sworn to utterly by actual eye-witnesses—so I leave you to judge of my perplexity. According to one version, Haydn, observing that his innovations were unpopular with the members of the Prince's orchestra, resolved to play a joke on them.

He arranged for the symphony to be performed, without preliminary rehearsal, in the presence of His Highness, who had been let into the secret. The worried looks on the faces of the musicians who all thought that they had misread the score, and above all the utter embarrassment of the leader when, at the end, he heard himself performing in glorious isolation, provided amusement for the whole Court of Eisenstadt*.

The second version maintains that on one occasion, when the Prince had threatened to dismiss his entire orchestra, save only Haydn, the latter devised this ingenious means of illustrating the general exodus and the mournful silence that would ensue: one after the other, as their parts concluded, the players left the hall. You shall be spared the third and final version*.

On a different occasion, being resolved to amuse the society that was gathered about the Prince, Haydn paid a visit to a fair in some little Hungarian township not very distant from Eisenstadt, and purchased there a whole basketful of penny-whistles, toy violins, a thing that made a noise like a cuckoo, wooden trumpets and all sorts of instruments that children love to play with. He took the trouble to study the range and the timbre of each of them, and composed the most entertaining little symphony exclusively for these instruments, of which some are even given solo passages to play: the running bass of the piece is provided by the cuckoo*.

Many years later, when he was in England, Haydn observed that his English audiences, who were highly appreciative of his orchestral pieces so long as the tempo remained that of a lively Allegro, tended on most occasions to fall asleep during the Andante or Adagio, no matter how many musical treasures he sought to accumulate in these movements. As a result, he composed an Andante that was the merest sigh of softness, of soothing calm and of sweet, tranquil melody; little by little, all the instruments seemed to rock themselves to sleep: and then suddenly, in the middle of the most hushed pianissimo, they all leapt into action at once, reinforced by a great bang on the tympany, and awakened the sleeping audience with a start*.

LETTER XII

Salzburg, 17 May 1809.

My dear Friend,

We have spent long enough now tracing Haydn's career in a field where his mastery was unquestioned; let us now look at his achievement in the realm of vocal music. He has given us Masses, Operas and Oratorios; and each of these represents a separate genre.

We have little to go on save conjecture, if we would discover what Haydn achieved in the field of operatic music. The operas that he wrote for Prince Esterházy never emerged from the archives at Eisenstadt, which one day were burned to the ground, as was Haydn's own house. He lost on that occasion the larger part of all that he had composed for the stage. All that survived was an *Armida*, an *Orlando Paladino*, and two comic-operas, *La Vera Costanza* and *Lo Speziale*, which were perhaps the least satisfactory of all his operatic works.

Jommelli, being called to Padua on one occasion to write an opera for the season there, and discovering that the singers, male and female alike, were not only hopelessly incompetent, but in addition had not the slightest intention of putting themselves to any trouble, turned on them with these words:

"All right, you blackguards, I'm going to make the *orchestra* do all the singing! The opera will be praised to high heaven and *you*, consigned to the depths of hell!"

The company that was in the service of Prince Esterházy, without being precisely similar to the one in Padua, was distinctly second-rate. Moreover Haydn himself, whom a thousand ties kept at home in the region where he was born, and who was already an old man by the time he first ventured abroad, never wrote for the great opera-loving public.

These general considerations, my dear Louis, will have prepared you for the confession that I have to make in relation to our composer's operatic music.

Orchestral music, when he had discovered it, was in its infancy; by contrast, vocal music, when he appeared upon the scene, was at the very height of its glorious career. Pergolesi, Leo, Scarlatti, Guglielmi, Piccinni and a score of others had carried it to a peak of perfection— a peak which, since that time, has been reached and occasionally surpassed only by Cimarosa and by Mozart. Haydn never rivalled the melodic beauty of these illustrious men; indeed, it must be confessed that, in this particular field, he was outdistanced, not only by his contemporaries, Sacchini, Cimarosa, Zingarelli, Mozart, etc., but even by his successors, Tarchi, Nazolini, Fioravanti, Farinelli and so on.

You who love to delve deep into the inspiration of artists, in order to discover there the secrets of the qualities of their work, you will perhaps not care to dispute my conjectures about Haydn. It is beyond all manner of doubt impossible to deny him a vast and vigorous imagination; an imagination which was to the highest degree *creative*. Yet perchance in the matter of sensibility he may prove to have been less richly endowed; and without this unhappy gift, farewell to song, farewell to love, farewell to opera! This spontaneous hilarity of his, this characteristic cheerfulness of which I have already spoken, for ever barred the way against a certain species of tender melancholy, and forbade it access to his contented and tranquil soul. And yet, to create no less than to enjoy the music of the opera, it is essential to be able to say, as did fair Jessica:

> *I am never merry when I hear sweet music*
> *Merchant of Venice*, Act V, Scene i

A heart disposed to tenderness, together with a touch of melancholy, is needed if you are to find pleasure even in *le Cantatrici villane*,[1] or in *i Nemici generosi*;[2] the explanation is extremely simple: if you are in high good humour your imagination has no need to be *distracted* from the visions that obsess it.

But there is a further reason. In order to dominate the minds of his listeners, Haydn's imagination demands the privilege of undivided sovereignty; as soon as it is chained in slavery to *words*, it grows unrecognisable. It would appear that the text of most operatic dialogues forces his imagination in a direction whither it cannot proceed, namely, that of sensibility. Thus Haydn will always hold first place among the Great Masters in the art of landscape: he is destined to be the Claude Lorrain of music. Yet in the theatre, that is to say in a domain of music which is wholly and exclusively compounded of emotion, he will never merit the place of Raphael.

You will retort, of course, that he who holds that place was himself the cheerfullest of mortals. Cimarosa, it is not to be denied, was gay in company. If one frequents Society, is it not the best thing a man can be? Yet I should be distinctly vexed on behalf of my theory, if it should prove that the passions of love or vengeance had never driven him to some act of madness, nor placed him in some situation of unspeakable absurdity. Was it not but recently reported that one of the most likeable of his successors* spent a whole long night, in the depth of January, waiting with untiring patience for the most laughter-loving of *prime donne* to keep the promise she had made to him?

I would be prepared to wager that Cimarosa's gaiety was anything rather than a mere compound of quips and epigrams, like that of Gentil-Bernard.

---

[1] Fioravanti's masterpiece, which is very popular in Paris.
[2] An exceedingly comic opera by the admirable Cimarosa.
4*

You will observe, my good friend, that my adoring devotion to my Saint knows well how to stop this side idolatry. I would place symphonic composers in the same category as landscape-painters, and class operatic composers together with painters of historical scenes. On two or three occasions only* in all his life did Haydn rise to the heights of this noble genre; but then he was both Michelangelo and Leonardo da Vinci rolled into one.

Let us take consolation, however, for we shall see his genius emerge again when we consider his church music and his Oratorios; in these last especially, where the Pindaric rather than the dramatic genius finds opportunity to display itself, he once more scaled the sublime heights, and added to the glory that he had already won with his symphonic music.

I observe that, in my striving after impartiality, I am inclined to deal perhaps too harshly with our friend. Have you ever listened to his Ariadne, abandoned upon the Isle of Naxos? This Cantata gives the lie to all my calumnies.

It appears to me that music differs from painting and the other Arts in this, that in music the element of physical pleasure, experienced through the sense of hearing, is at once more predominant and at the same time more profoundly essential than satisfaction of the intellect. The root of music lies in physical pleasure; and I am persuaded that it is our ear, even more than our heart, that is bewitched as we listen to Signora Barilli singing

> *Voi che sapete*
> *Che cosa è amor*

rom Mozart's *Nozze di Figaro*. A well-conceived harmony enchants the ear; a discord rends it asunder; yet neither of these phenomena contains anything of substance to inform the mind, nor anything that we could write down on paper, were it required of us. We experience simple pain, or simple pleasure. Of all our organs, it would seem that the ear is that which is the most sensitive to agreeable or disagreeable vibrations. The sense of smell, like that of touch, is also highly susceptible to pain or pleasure; the eye is the most hardened of all and in consequence is capable of experiencing physical pleasure only to a very limited degree. Show a fine painting[1] to some dull-minded oaf: he will feel no particular pleasure, since the enjoyment that is to be derived

---

[1] Correggio's *Marriage of St. Catherine*.

from the sight of a noble painting comes almost wholly through the mind. Our oaf will most assuredly prefer any brightly-painted shop-sign to Lodovico Carracci's *Christ calling St. Matthew*. By contrast, take this same sorry oaf, and let him listen to some great aria exquisitely sung: who knows, he may even betray a hint or two of enjoyment, whereas the same thing badly sung might well cause him a suspicion of uneasiness. If you betake yourself of a Sunday to the Musée de Paris, you will observe, at a certain point along the gallery, the whole passage blocked by crowds gathered before a single painting: and every Sunday, it will be the same painting. You may be persuaded that it is some masterpiece. Far from it—it is some feeble daub of the German School, representing the "Last Judgment". The vulgar herd enjoys gloating over the tortured expressions of the damned. Now, any evening, if you follow this same vulgar herd into the free seats at the Grand Opéra, you may observe them applauding furiously at number after number sung by Madame Branchu; whereas in the morning, the paintings of Paolo Veronese had left them merely cold and indifferent.

I would conclude from all this that if a composer should sacrifice to any other aim the pure physical pleasure which it is the primary duty of music to afford us, then what we hear is no longer music; it is just plain noise, intruding upon and insulting our ears, under the pretext of speaking to our soul. It is for this reason, I am persuaded, that I cannot without discomfort sit through a complete opera by Gluck.

Adieu.

LETTER XIII

Salzburg, 18 May 1809.

Melody, in other words a pleasing succession of related notes that act soothingly upon the ear without ever distressing it; melody—for instance, the aria:

Signora contessina,

as sung by Signora Barilli in *Il Matrimonio segreto*[1]—is the primary means

[1] I make so many allusions to *Il Matrimonio segreto*, which is Cimarosa's masterpiece, and which, in my experience, is tolerably familiar to all who live in Paris, that I have been advised to set aside some small corner of this book, in order to furnish music-lovers who do not reside in the capital with a brief résumé of the plot.

Geronimo, an extremely wealthy albeit slightly deaf Venetian merchant has two daughters, Carolina and Elisetta. The charming Carolina has recently contracted a secret marriage with Paolino, chief clerk to her father (a); the latter, however, is a prodigious snob, and the lovers are sorely perplexed to find a way of revealing their marriage to him. Paolino, who is alert for every opportunity to get into his father-in-law's good graces, has arranged the marriage of Geronimo's elder daughter, Elisetta, with a certain Count Robinson: Geronimo is in the seventh heaven of bliss at the prospect of this alliance with a titled member of the aristocracy, and at the thought of seeing his own daughter become a Countess (b). The Count arrives and is introduced to the family (c); but the charms of Carolina alter the direction of his resolve (d); he declares to Paolino, the lover of Carolina, that it is she, rather than Elisetta, whose hand he proposes to demand in marriage and in order to win the elderly merchant's consent to this exchange—which, after all is simple enough in a marriage of convenience—he announces that he will be content with a dowry of a mere fifty thousand crowns instead of the hundred thousand that he had been promised (e). Elisetta, very much on her dignity on account of the Count's coldness towards her, surprises her supposed suitor kissing the hand of Carolina; whereupon she denounces him to Fidalma, the old man's sister (f), who, for her part, is convinced that her considerable fortune makes her an ideal match for Paolino. Geronimo, being deaf, has difficulty in grasping either the Count's proposal, or the lamentations of Elisetta (g), and indulges in a fit of bad temper which constitutes the finale of Act I (h).

Act II opens with a quarrel between the Count and Geronimo; this is the famous duet,

(a) The work opens with Two duets, both of inspired tenderness, which immediately win our hearts in favour of the lovers, and which at the same time expound the plot. The first of these duets begins with the words *Cara! cara!*; the second with the words *Io ti lascio, perche uniti* . . .

(b) At this point, Geronimo has a notable bass aria, *"le Orecchie spalancate"*, which contrives a most original combination of highly-naturalistic absurdity and touching kind-heartedness. We laugh at Geronimo, yet we are fond of him all the same; and the listener's imagination is freed from any sense of *odium* for the remainder of the opera.

(c) At his firs entry, he sings the aria: *"Senza tante cerimonie"*.

(d) *"Il core m' ha ingannato"*; followed by a splendid quartet portraying the profoundest of passions without the faintest admixture of melancholy. This is one of those passages which reveal most clearly the difference between the paths followed respectively by Cimarosa and by Mozart. Try and imagine the latter creating a musical setting appropriate to the theme of this particular quartet.

(e) A moving duet, opening with this fine phrase sung by Paolino: *"Signor, deh concedete"*.

(f) Aria: *"Io voglio sussurrare la casa e la città"*.

(g) Aria: *"Voi credete che gli sposi faccian come i cicisbei"*.

(h) Of passages of this description, veritable masterpieces of verve and merriment, there is no trace in Mozart; on the other hand, an aria such as *Dove sono i bei momenti*, were it given to Carolina at this juncture, would portray her situation in a far profounder fashion.

employed in producing this physical pleasure. Harmony is entirely secondary. It is *melody*, Haydn was never weary of repeating, that constitutes the charm of music. But it is also that part which presents the composer with the greatest difficulties. To invent agreeable harmonies requires no more than patience and application; but to create a beautiful melody is the prerogative of genius. It has often occurred to me that if we in France possessed, in the field of music, an institution that played a part corresponding to the *Académie Française* in the field of letters, the election of its Immortals might be determined by the simplest of tests: each competitor would be required to submit ten lines of original melody: nothing more.

Mozart would submit *"Voi che sapete"*, from *Le Nozze*; Cimarosa, *"Da che il caso è disperato"*, from *Il Matrimonio segreto*; Paisiello, *"Quelli là"*, from *La Molinara*—but what of Monsieur ***? Or Monsieur ***? Or even of Monsieur ***? Indeed, to give pleasure, a true melody requires neither ornamentation nor frills nor accessories. Would you like to learn a simple test, to decide whether or not a melody is genuinely beautiful?—then just strip it of all its accompaniments. Of a fine melody it is possible to say what Aristaenetus declared once of his mistress:

"Se fiato in corpo avete". Picture of Carolina in despair at the threat to send her off to a convent. Fidalma proposes marriage to Paolino (i). Now comes a magnificent aria, sung by Carolina distracted by jealousy, yet cut in the Parisian production: she forgives Paolino, who tells her of all the arrangements he has made to ensure their secret flight. This is the *pièce de résistance* of the whole opera, the virtuoso tenor aria: *"Pria che spunti in ciel l'aurora"*.

The Count and Elisetta meet by chance as they enter the drawing-room intent on gathering candles to light them to bed in their respective rooms. The Count declares to her face that he cannot marry her (j). It is close on midnight: Carolina, all a-tremble, enters in the company of her lover; but as they cross the drawing-room to embark upon their flight, they are disturbed by some noise still coming from within the house, and Paolino retreats together with his bride into the latter's bedroom. Elisetta, who has been kept awake by her jealousy, hears voices distinctly coming from this room and, believing that it is the Count, arouses her father (k), and her aunt, who had already retired to their several appartments. They knock on Carolina's door: the whole plot is uncovered; but finally, upon the insistence of the Count, who addresses Geronimo in a fine aria, *"Ascoltate un uom del mondo"* and who, in order to obtain forgiveness for Carolina, consents to marry Elisetta, the old man grants his pardon to the lovers.

Originally, this opera was a play by Garrick, the famous actor. In the English version, the character of the sister is atrocious, and the whole drama is sombre and foreboding; by contrast, the Italian libretto furnishes a pretty little comedy, into which the musical episodes fit admirably.

(i) Aria: *"Ma con un marito, via, meglio si sta"*.
(j) A pretty little aria, sung by Farinelli: *"Signorina, io non v'amo"*.
(k) Aria: *"Il conte sta chiuso con mia sorellina"* .

Induitur, formosa est; exuitur, ipsa forma est[1]

As for the music of Gluck, which you are always quoting at me, Caesar once said to a poet who was reciting verses to him: "You sing too much for a man who reads, and you read too much for a man who sings." Occasionally, however, Gluck discovered the secret of speaking directly to the listener's heart: either with delicate and wistful melodies, as when the Nymphs of Thessaly breathe their laments over the tomb of Admetus;* or else with violent and vibrating sound, as in the scene between Orpheus and the Furies.

Music is to the drama as love is to the heart: unless it be a despot, reigning in sovereignty unchallenged, unless all other things be sacrificed to it, then it is not love.

Now, if we accept this as a principle, what is the secret of inventing a noble melody? Precisely that same method which Corneille followed in order to light upon the famous interjection *Qu'il mourût!*★ Take a couple of hundred correct Academic Dramatists—witness Monsieur Laharpe—all busy turning out tragedies according to the Precepts of Reason: here you have the current equivalent of that similar number of impeccable Academic Composers deeply versed in the Principles of Harmony, who, at this very instant, swarm over the face of Germany. Their music is unimpeachable; it is erudite; and every note is where the text-book says it ought to be. It has but one demerit—it sets the listener yawning.

I am persuaded that the Fates, if they are to raise up a Corneille in the field of music, must needs bring together in one single being an excessively sensitive ear and an exceedingly passionate soul. It is essential that these two manners of sensation should be intimately linked one with the other, in such a way that, in his most desperate moment of sadness, as when he believes his mistress unfaithful to him, our young Sacchini may yet receive some consolation from those few scattered notes that he chances to hear sung half-aloud by some chance passer-by. Now, until this present day and age, souls such as this have scarce been brought into the world, save in the neighbourhood of Mount Vesuvius. The reason? I have no idea—yet do but run your eye over the list of great composers.

In Germany, music is too often impaired by an over-frequent use of

[1] Clothed, she is beautiful; naked, she is Beauty in person.

modulation and a surfeit of harmony. The German nation desires to set the seal of learning on everything it touches; and doubtless would boast a finer musical tradition, or rather a more Italianate tradition, if its young folk were less addicted to erudition and more attracted to pleasure. Just take a stroll through the city of Göttingen, and watch those fair-haired tall young men of faintly pedantic aspect, walking along the streets as though propelled by clockwork, scrupulously punctual at their lectures, dominated by their imaginations, yet rarely steeped in passion.

The antique music of the Flemish school was nothing but a cunning web of chords devoid of inspiration. This people made its music much as it did its painting: a great deal of labour, an infinitude of patience—and nothing more.

Throughout Europe, all music-lovers of all nations—with the solitary exception of France—are persuaded that the music of any neighbouring nation is well-nigh intolerable. It seems irregular and jerky; it appears at one and the same time pretty-pretty and barbaric; above all, it tends to be excessively boring. The tunes that appeal to the English are too monotonous—always assuming that there *are* any. It is the same thing with the Russians; the same again, astonishingly, with the Spaniards. Is it conceivable that this land so blessed with sunshine, that the country which gave birth to the Cid and to those warrior-troubadours who could still be counted among the hordes of Charles V, should yet have failed to produce illustrious composers? This brave nation, so excellently fashioned for great things, and whose romances exude such a wealth of sensibility, such a store of melancholy, possesses in all some two or three styles of melody—and nothing more. It might be suspected that the Spaniards, in their emotional life, have no love for any great variety of ideas: just one or two recurrent themes, yet deep and constant, indestructible.

The music of the East is lacking in distinctness, and has more likeness to a continuous wail than to any species of melody.

In Italy, an opera consists of singing on the one hand, and of continuo, or of orchestral accompaniment*, on the other. The orchestra is required to be the most humble and obedient servant of the singer, and its task is limited to augmenting the effectiveness of the voice; now and again however, the portrayal of some momentous upheaval in Nature may afford the orchestra a chance—a logically justifiable chance—of showing its paces. The various instruments, having a much wider compass than the human voice, together with a greater variety of sounds, are able to depict phenomena that the voice could never hope to portray: a storm at sea, for instance, or a forest at night, made fearful by the howling of wild beasts.

In opera, the orchestra can every now and then furnish just those characteristic touches, clear and energetic, which bring the whole composition suddenly to life. As an instance, take the Quartet from Act I of *Il Matrimonio segreto*, and observe that orchestral passage which follows the lines:

> *Così un poco castigato*
> *Il suo orgoglio resterà.*

Haydn, accustomed as he was to yield to the imperious violence of his own imagination, and to handle his orchestra much as Hercules wielded his club—Haydn, whenever he found himself forced to follow the inspiration of the librettist and to prune the luxuriance of his instrumentation, gives the impression of a giant in chains. The result is music that is correct and well-constructed; but the ardour has vanished, together with all the genius, and all the spontaneity. The glittering originality has evaporated into air and, strange to say, this same being who, from dawn to dusk, is never weary of hymning the praises of melody, for whom melody is the great First Principle to which he incessantly returns—this same man writes works which are insufficiently melodious. I am reminded of your authors in the current fashion who, in a style compounded of luxuriating arabesques and nonsense, everlastingly sing the praises of that fine, stark simplicity that characterised the classics in the Age of Louis XIV.

Haydn, after a fashion, admits his mediocrity in this field. He claims that, if only he had been able to spend a few odd years in Italy, listening to the inimitable voices and studying the *maestri* of the Neapolitan school, he would have succeeded as well in opera as in orchestral music. Of this, I have my doubts. Imagination is one thing, sensibility is another. A poet might well compose the fifth book of the Aeneid, describing the funeral games with glittering and majestic touch, leading Entellus into combat against Dares, and yet fail utterly in giving us the death of Dido in credible and moving fashion. The passions cannot be simply observed and copied, like a sunset. Some twenty times a month, in Naples, Nature offers splendid sunsets to any competent Claude Lorrain who is present to observe them: yet where did Raphael discover the expression that lights up his *Madonna alla Seggiola*? In his own heart.

LETTER XIV

Salzburg, 21 May 1809.

You express a desire, my dear Louis, that I should write to Naples and send for some pamphlet describing the music of that region; since I so frequently allude to it, you urge it as my duty to make you familiar with it. You have heard it claimed, that the further one ventures towards the toe of that kind of boot which is the configuration of Italy, the more original the music that one finds there; you have a great affection for that "gentle Parthenope" in which Virgil found his inspiration; you are envious of her destiny; while we, exhausted by storms of revolution, *we* do dearly wish that we might declare:

> . . . *Illo me tempore dulcis alebat*
> *Parthenope, studiis florentem ignobilis oti.*

Finally, you argue that the music which was composed during this blessed period of "idleness" was specifically created to please the Neapolitan fancy; and that, since it has so admirably answered its purpose, it should be judged by a native of that country.

Your wish is already granted; in fact, I have had precisely such a pamphlet in my possession for a long while. So here follows a sketch of the music that was created by the school of Naples—a sketch which was furnished for me, some years ago, by a great, lanky, parchment-skinned priest* with an obsessive mania for the 'cello; a man who, as a regular *habitué* of the San Carlo theatre, had not, to the best of my belief, missed one solitary performance there in forty years.

My own role is confined to that of translator, and I have altered none of his judgements, which are not necessarily my own. You will observe that he makes no reference to Cimarosa: the reason is that, in the year 1803, it was unwise to mention Cimarosa in Naples*.

Naples, 10 October 1803.

Amico stimatissimo,

In days gone by, Naples used to have four Academies of vocal and instrumental music; today, however, there remain but three, holding in all some two hundred and thirty students. Each Academy has a distinctive uniform: the students of Santa Maria di Loreto wear white; those of La Pietà, sky-blue or rather slate-blue (called in Italian, "Turkish blue", hence they are known as *i Turchini*); while those of Sant' Onofrio are dressed in puce and white. These are the Academies which turn out the finest musicians in the world—as is only natural, since of all countries in the world, ours is that where music is most passionately loved. The greatest composers that Naples has produced flourished toward the beginning of the eighteenth century.

It is evidently normal to distinguish between those founders of schools who inspired a revolution in every branch of music, and those who specialised in one type of composition only.

In the first category, we find, pre-eminent above all others, Alessandro Scarlatti, who must be considered as the founder of the whole modern art of music, since it is to him that we owe the science of counterpoint. He was from Messina and died towards 1725.

Porpora died in poverty, at ninety years of age, in 1770 or there-abouts. He enriched the stage with a large number of pieces which are considered as models of the genre. His cantatas are even more remark-able than his operas.

Leo was his disciple, and outshone his master. He died at the age of forty-two, in 1745. His style is inimitable; the aria:

Misero pargoletto,

from *Demofoonte*,[1] is a masterpiece of expressiveness.

---

[1] The dramatic situation which gives rise to this aria is one of the most moving that Metastasio ever conceived, and Leo has expressed it with divine perfection. Timante, a young Prince who believes himself to be the son of that grim tyrant, Demophon, King

Francesco Durante was born at Grumo, a village in the neighbourhood of Naples. For him was reserved the glory of making counterpoint appear easy. In my opinion, his finest works were duets, arranged from a group of Scarlatti cantatas.

In the second category, we would give pride of place to Vinci, the great precursor of all those who have composed for the theatre. His highest quality resides in a most lively expressiveness combined with a profound understanding of counterpoint. His masterpiece is a setting of Metastasio's *Artaserse*. He died in 1732, in the prime of his maturity, and some say poisoned by a relative of a certain lady of Rome, whom he had loved.

Giambattista Jesi was born in Pergola, in the Marches, whence derives his familiar name of Pergolesi. He was trained in one of the

of Epirus, has for two years been secretly married to Dirce; and by her he has a son. Demophon surprises the secret of this marriage and, among the laws of his kingdom, discovers one which will send both the lovers to their death. They are led out to execution; but the despot's cruel soul is softened by the prayers of the people, and he pardons them. But at the very instant when Timante is flying into the arms of his Dirce, a faithful friend brings him irrefutable evidence that Dirce is the daughter of Demophon himself.

Stricken with horror for the involuntary crime that he has committed in marrying his own sister, and filled with despair at having to abandon his beloved Dirce, Timante sees himself as some new Oedipus; motionless he stands, plunged into the deep shades of horror.

Dirce, who cannot understand this strange coldness, begs him, in the name of their love, to speak; but his horror is only intensified. She shows him his son, beseeching him at least to cast a glance upon this child who clasps him so fondly. At this point, the unhappy Timante can no longer contain his anguish; he embraces his son, and the aria begins:

> Misero pargoletto,
> Il tuo destin non sai;
> Ah! non gli dite mai
> Qual era il genitor.
>
> Come in un punto, oh Dio!
> Tutto cambiò d'aspetto!
> Voi foste il mio diletto
> Voi siete il mio terror.

which, being translated, reads:

> Ill-fated child,
> All ignorant of thy destiny;
> Ah! Let none reveal to him ever
> The name of his father!
>
> Ye Gods! In the space of an instant
> How the face of all things is changed!
> Thou who wert once my delight
> Art now the torment of my days!

At each repeat of these words, which Timante addresses, now to his son, now to Dirce, Leo's genius managed to portray yet a further nuance of his unfathomed despair.

Academies of Naples, where his teacher was Durante, and he died in 1733, at the age of twenty-five. Pergolesi was an unquestioned genius. His masterpieces are his *Stabat Mater*, the aria *"Se cerca, se dice"* from *L'Olimpiade* and, in the comic vein, the intermezzo *"La Serva Padrona"*. Father Martini has said that Pergolesi was such an absolute master of this latter genre, while his temperament was by nature so irresistibly impelled towards comedy, that there are *buffo* themes even in the *Stabat Mater*. Yet in general his style is melancholy and expressive.

Hasse, known as *il Sassone* ("the Saxon") was a pupil of Alessandro Scarlatti, and the most spontaneous of all composers at that time.

Jommelli was born in Aversa and died in 1775. His talent extended over a wide field. His *Miserere* and *Benedictus* represent his finest achievements in the noble and simple manner; his *Armida* and *Iphigenia* are his most successful operas. He tended to score too heavily for the orchestra.

David Perez, who was born in Naples and who died round about 1790, wrote a *Credo* which, on certain high feast days, is still sung in the church of the Oratorian Fathers, where music-lovers go to hear it in its traditional setting. He is one of those who adhered longer than others to the rigorous traditions of the contrapuntal style. He worked with some success both for the Church and for the stage.

Traetta, first the teacher, later the colleague of Sacchini at the Conservatorium of Santa Maria di Loreto, followed an identical career. He possessed greater technical ability than Sacchini who, for his part, is reputed to have had more native genius. The characteristic feature of Sacchini's style is facility shot through with light-heartedness. Outstanding among his compositions in the genre of the *opera seria* is the recitative *"Berenice che fai?"* with the aria that follows it.

Johann Christian Bach, though born in Germany, was trained in Naples. He is appreciated on account of the tender lyricism that inspires his compositions. The music he wrote for the duet:

Se mai più saro geloso . . .

is by no means the least considerable item in that published collection of the settings that the most renowned of *maestri* have composed for these words. It might be claimed that Bach was unique in his peculiar talent for expressing irony.

All these composers died in 1780 or thereabouts.

Piccinni was the rival of Jommelli in the *style noble*. His duet:

Fra queste ombre meste, o cara!

is beyond compare or criticism. Perhaps he should also be regarded as the founder of the current *opera buffa* tradition.

Paisiello, P. A. Guglielmi, and Anfossi are among those of his disciples who have earned themselves some reputation. However, in spite of their contributions, the decadence of music in Naples has been unmistakable and all too swift.[1]

---

[1] Here follow the dates of a number of composers:

Durante	born in 1693	died in 1755
Leo	1694	1745
Vinci	1705	1732
Hasse	1705	1783
Handel	1684	1759
Galuppi	1703	1785
Jommelli	1714	1774
Porpora	1685	1767
Benda	1714	
Piccinni	1728	1800
Sacchini	1735	1786
Paisiello	1741	
Guglielmi	1727	1804
Anfossi	1736	1775
Sarti	1730	1802
Zingarelli	1752	
Traetta	1738	1779 (a)
J. C. Bach	1735	1782
Mayr, born circa	1760	
Mosca, born circa	1775	

(a) Traetta, a profound and melancholy artist, possessed an outstanding talent for sombre and picturesque harmonic effects. In his *Sofonisbe*, the Queen throws herself between her husband and her lover, who are on the point of drawing their swords. "Ah! cruel ones!" she hurls at them. "What possesses you? If it is blood that you require, then strike it from my bosom!" And when her pleading proves vain, and they turn from her to embark upon their duel, she cries out: "Whither go ye? Ah! No!" On the word *Ah!*, the actual melody is interrupted; the composer, realising that normal rules of scoring for the voice could no longer apply at this point, yet not quite knowing how to indicate the sort of scream that the actress was supposed to emit, added in brackets, over the G-natural, the expression-mark: (*Un urlo francese*).

LETTER XV

Salzburg, 25 May 1809.

My dear Friend,

On the occasion of my most recent journey to Italy, I visited once again that little villa at Arquà and contemplated the antique chair in which Petrarch had sat while composing his *Trionfi*. Nor do I ever pass through Venice without requesting the sacristan to open up the little treasure-house of relics that has been established in the church where our divine Cimarosa was buried in 1801.

You may therefore find something of interest in the details—none remarkable in themselves—that I have gathered together touching the life of our composer.

In setting out the programme of a single day in Haydn's career, from the moment that he entered the service of Prince Esterházy, we have described his life as it was lived for thirty years. He laboured incessantly: yet all his work was a hard uphill struggle. This was certainly not due to any lack of inspiration, but rather to the delicate refinement of his taste, which was rarely satisfied with anything less than perfection. A symphony would cost him a whole month's work, a Mass more than twice that amount of time. His rough sketches are full of variant passages. For a single symphony, his notebooks contain themes enough for three or four. In much the same vein, I once beheld in Ferrara the original sheet of paper on which Ariosto had composed sixteen different versions of his beautiful octave describing the Tempest, and it was only at the very bottom of the sheet that one might discover the version to which he finally gave preference:

Stendon le nubi un tenebroso velo . . . * etc.

However, as Haydn used to say himself, work was always the greatest happiness he knew.

It is this circumstance that renders it conceivable that he should have given birth to so truly immense a quantity of works. Society, which robs those artists who reside in Paris of three-quarters of their time, stole from him only those instants during which work is in any case impossible.

Gluck, in order to fire his imagination, to spread his soul's wings and fly away to Aulis or to Sparta, had need to establish himself in the middle of a flowery meadow; there, with his piano before him and a couple of bottles of champagne at his side, he would compose, beneath the open sky, his two *Iphigénies*, his *Orfeo* and all his other works.

Sarti, by contrast, required a dark and cavernous chamber, fitfully illuminated by the gleam of a funerary lamp suspended from the ceiling; and it was only in the stillest silence of the night that musical inspiration would come to him. It was in these circumstances that he composed his opera *Medonte*, the rondo

Mia speranza,

and one of the finest arias that has ever been written, namely:

la dolce Compagna.

Cimarosa was fond of noise: he preferred to have his friends about him while he composed. In their company, he would give himself up to frenzied amusements, in the course of which there descended upon him the inspiration for both *Gli Orazi e Curiazi*, and *Il Matrimonio segreto*—that is to say, for the finest, richest and most original of all *opere serie*, and the most masterly *opera buffa* in the whole of the Italian repertoire. Frequently, in the course of a single night, he would jot down the themes for eight or ten of these delightful arias, elaborating them immediately after, surrounded by all his friends. It was after spending a whole fortnight in total idleness, strolling aimlessly around the outskirts of Prague, that the aria *"Pria che spunti in ciel l'aurora"* came to him all of a sudden, at an instant when his thoughts were a hundred miles away from composition.

Sacchini's powers of melodic invention dried up and withered unless his mistress were beside him, and unless his kittens, whose graceful movements inspired him with boundless admiration, were playing about his feet.

Paisiello composes in bed. *Il Barbiere di Siviglia, La Molinara,* and so many other masterpieces of easy lyric gracefulness all came to him as he lay between the sheets.

Zingarelli requires to peruse a chapter from one of the Holy Fathers, or else a passage from the Classics: whereupon, in less than four hours, he will improvise a whole act of *Pirro* or of *Giulietta e Romeo.* I recall also a brother of Anfossi's, who was full of promise but who, alas, had scarce attained to manhood when he died. This young man was unable to compose a note unless he was completely surrounded by roasted chickens and steaming sausages.

But Haydn was as solitary and as sober as Newton; and provided only that he had upon his finger the ring that Frederick the Great had sent him and which, he maintained, was essential to his imagination, he would sit down at his piano, and in a few instants his fancy would be soaring in the company of angels. At Eisenstadt, nothing came to disturb him: his life was wholly devoted to his art, and he dwelt remote from worldly cares.

This even, gently-flowing existence, filled with a work which he loved, continued unbroken until the death of Prince Nikolaus, his patron, in 1789.

One curious effect of his retiring disposition was that our composer, who never so much as set foot outside his own little township—a fief of the Esterházy's—was perhaps the only man in the whole of Europe, among those who cared a fig about music, who for years on end had no inkling of the fame of Joseph Haydn. The first tribute that was paid to his genius was bizarre. As though it was one of Nature's inexorable laws, that all ultimate absurdities in the field of music first see the light of day in Paris, Haydn suddenly received from a celebrated music-lover of that city a commission to write a piece of vocal music. Accompanying the letter, in order to provide the composer with a model, there were attached a number of "selected pieces" by Lully and Rameau. You may imagine the effect that this antiquated nonsense, in the year 1780, was destined to produce on Haydn, brought up on all the masterpieces of the Italian school, which for half a century had been at the very summit of its glory. He returned the precious relics to the sender, replying with a simplicity not devoid of malice, "that he was Haydn, not Lully, nor yet Rameau; that if the gentleman required music by those great composers, he should address his request to them, or to their pupils; for his part, much to his regret, he could compose no music, save only music by Haydn."

His name had been a household word for many years when suddenly and almost simultaneously he was invited by the most celebrated *impresari* of the opera-houses of Naples, Lisbon, Venice, London, Milan, etc., to compose operas for them. However, a fondness for tranquillity, a quite understandable attachment to the Prince his patron and to his own habitual way of life, kept him at home in Hungary★ and triumphed over his constant urge to cross the Alps. Indeed, he had very likely never set foot outside Eisenstadt, had it not been for the death of Signora Polzelli. As a result of this loss★, Haydn began to feel that time hung heavy and empty on his hands. He had recently declined an invitation from the managers of the *Concerts Spirituels* in Paris. However, after the death of his mistress, he accepted the proposals of a London violinist, named Salomon, who was the manager of a Concert Society in that city. Salomon calculated that such a man of genius, prised loose expressly for the pleasure of London's music-lovers, would suffice to set his concerts in the fashion. He normally offered twenty concerts in a year; and he promised Haydn a hundred sequins (1,200 francs) per concert★. Haydn accepted these conditions, and so, in the year 1790, set out for London, in the fifty-ninth year of his age. He spent there more than a year. The original music that he wrote for these concerts was enormously appreciated. His cheerful, unpretentious manner, coupled with the undoubted presence of genius, was certain to be well-received amid a people that is at once generous and serious-minded. Frequently an Englishman would come up to him in the street, stare him up and down from head to foot, then move away, saying, "So *that* is what a great man looks like."

Haydn, in the days when he could still tell stories, used to enjoy himself hugely relating numerous anecdotes concerning his stay in London. A certain noble Lord, who (according to himself) was verily devoured by his passion for music, called upon him one morning and requested lessons in counterpoint for the fee of one guinea a lesson. Haydn, observing that his Lordship was not entirely barren of musical knowledge, accepted.

"When would it suit your Lordship to begin?"

"Now, if you like," replied this gentleman, drawing from his pocket the score of a Haydn quartet. "For the first lesson," he continued, "pray let us consider this quartet, and be so good as to explain to me the reason for certain modulations and the principles that determine the general structure of the piece, which I confess I cannot but disapprove of, in part, since these modulations infringe the true principles of music."

Haydn, not a little surprised, averred that he was ready to begin. His Lordship plunged into the score and, from the very first bars, proceeded to find fault with every note. Haydn, who was wont to rely on his own untutored inventiveness, and who was anything rather than a stickler for the rules, found himself completely at a loss and again and again could only answer: "I did *that*, because I liked the effect; I placed that passage *there*, because it sounded right." The Englishman, in whose opinion these replies proved nothing, recommenced his argument from first principles, and demonstrated by sound logic that Haydn's quartet was not worth a bean.

"Well then, my Lord, why not arrange this quartet according to your fancy; have it performed, and then you will be able to judge yourself, which of the two versions is the better."

"But how is it possible that yours, which is contrary to the Rules, should be the better of the two?"

"Because it gives the listener more pleasure."

His Lordship had a retort ready for this, while Haydn continued to argue as best he could; yet in the end he lost patience.

"I perceive that it is his Lordship who, out of the goodness of his heart, is pleased to give me lessons; I am forced to confess, however, that I do not deserve the honour of having such a master."

The Defender of First Principles at this point left the house; nor, to this very day, has his puzzlement diminished, that a man may faithfully observe the very letter of the law, and *still* not infallibly create another *Matrimonio segreto*.

One morning, a sea-captain knocked at Haydn's door:

"Are you Mr. Haydn?"

"I am he, Sir."

"Are you willing to write me a March, to cheer the spirits of the troops that I am carrying aboard my vessel? I will give you thirty guineas; but I must have it today, for tomorrow we hoist sail for Calcutta."

Haydn accepted the commission. The sea-captain rose; whereupon the composer sat down at his piano and in quarter of an hour had completed the March.

However, being somewhat uneasy in his conscience at having earned so rapidly a sum which, to him, appeared more than considerable, he returned home early that same evening, and composed two further Marches, intending to offer the brave captain a choice, and then, requiting his generosity, to make him a present of all three. At dawn next day, the captain made his appearance.

"Well now, that March of mine?"

"Here it is, all ready."

"Would you play it through for me on the piano?"

Haydn obliged. Without a word, the captain counted down his thirty guineas on the lid of the piano, snatched up the March, and stalked out. Haydn ran after him and stopped him.

"I have written two others," he said, "which are better. Come back and hear them and then make your choice."

"The first one suits me well enough."

"But listen. . . ."

The captain plunged ahead down the staircase, refusing to listen to a word. Haydn ran after him, shouting:

"I'll give you them for nothing!"

"I don't want 'em, I tell you," replied the captain, running ever faster down the stairs.

"But come and listen to them, at least!"

"The Devil himself wouldn't make me listen to 'em!"

Haydn, greatly incensed, ran straight out of the house, rushed to the Exchange, ascertained the name of the vessel that was due to sail that very day for India, discovered the name of the officer in command; he then rolled the two Marches up into a cylinder, added a polite note, and sent the packet round to the captain on board his ship.

This pig-headed old sea-dog, however, suspecting that it was the composer who was thus persecuting him, refused so much as to open Haydn's note, and sent the whole lot back again. Haydn tore the Marches into shreds, and till his dying day never forgot the features of the English sea-captain.

He used to derive great delight from telling us of his quarrel with a London music-seller. One morning, Haydn, who had been amusing himself wandering round the shops, as is the English habit, walked into the establishment of a music-seller, and enquired whether he had any choice pieces of high quality.

"I've just the very thing for you, Sir," replied the shop-keeper. "*Sublime* music, Sir, by Mr. Haydn, straight off my own press!"

"Oh, *that* stuff," countered Haydn, "I have no time for that sort of thing."

"What, Sir! No time for the music of Mr. Haydn, Sir? And what, pray, do you find wrong with it?"

"Oh, there are lots of things wrong with it; but there is no sense in arguing about it, since I tell you it doesn't appeal to me. Show me something else."

"No, indeed, Sir, I shall *not*!" replied the print-seller, who was an impassioned *Haydinist*. "I will not deny that I have other music in my shop, Sir, but it is not for you, Sir," upon which he turned his back on his customer. Just as Haydn, laughing heartily, was leaving the shop, there chanced to enter an acquaintance of his, another music-lover. The latter greeted Haydn, calling him by name. The shop-keeper, hearing the name spoken, swung round, still boiling over with anger, and addressed the newcomer.

"Ah yes, Haydn! Haydn! Now here's a gentleman who actually says he doesn't *like* the great man's music!"

Haydn's English acquaintance laughed; the enigma was explained, and the music-seller was introduced to this strange individual who found matter to complain of in the compositions of Mr. Haydn.

During his residence in London, our composer had two outstanding pleasures; the first consisted in listening to the music of Handel★; the second, in hearing concerts presented by the "Society for Ancient Music"★. This Society had been established with the aim of preserving for posterity music which people of fashion were wont to call "antique"; and it organised concerts at which the audience might hear the masterpieces of Pergolesi, Leo, Durante, Marcello, Scarlatti, and others—in a word, the music of that group of men of such rare talent who, almost without exception, flourished simultaneously towards the seventeen-thirties.

Haydn used to tell me with astonishment that many of these pieces, which had transported him to the very gates of Heaven when he used to study them in his youth, now seemed to him, some forty years later, singularly diminished in beauty. "It was a melancholy experience," he

used to add, "almost like that of renewing acquaintance with some
mistress from the distant past." Was the reason for this merely the
normal consequence of advancing years, or was it that these wondrous
pieces at this stage appealed less strongly to our composer, because the
charm of *novelty* was gone out of them?

In 1794, Haydn made a second journey to London. Gallini, the
impresario of the Haymarket Theatre, had commissioned him to compose an opera which he intended to present with an unprecedented
extravagance of luxury. The libretto dealt with the theme of Orpheus
descending into the Underworld. Haydn set to work; but Gallini ran
into difficulties* in securing a licence to open his theatre to the public.
The composer, who was hankering after the comforts of his home, lost
patience and declined to wait until the licence had been granted; thus
he left London with eleven completed numbers of his *Orfeo* among his
baggage—eleven numbers which, I have been credibly assured, represent his finest achievement in operatic music—and so returned to
Austria, which he was destined never again to leave.

While in London, he much frequented the society of the celebrated
Mrs. Billington, of whose talents he was an ardent admirer. He discovered her one day in the company of Reynolds, the only English
painter who understood the art of portraiture; he had at that time
recently completed a portrait of Mrs. Billington as St. Cecilia, listening
(in the inevitable traditional manner) to the strains of Heavenly Music.
Mrs. Billington showed Haydn the portrait: "A good likeness," approved the latter, "and yet there is one most singular error."

"Which?" broke in Reynolds sharply.

"You have portrayed her listening to the angels; you should rather
have shown the angels listening to the divine voice of Mrs. Billington."
La Billington threw her arms about the great composer's neck. It was
for her that he wrote his *Arianna a Naxos*, which bears comparison with
that of Benda.

A scion of the English royal family commissioned Reynolds* to
paint Haydn's portrait. Haydn, flattered by this honour, went round to
the painter's studio and posed. Before long, however, boredom began
to creep over him; Reynolds on the other hand, by no means indifferent
to his own reputation, was reluctant to portray a man universally reputed as the possessor of genius, with the features of a congenital
idiot, and postponed the session until another day. At the second

appointment, renewed boredom, renewed lapse of features into idiocy. Reynolds hurried off to find his royal patron, and told him of the distressing occurrence. Whereupon His Royal Highness devised a stratagem: he discovered in the suite of his mother the Queen a beautiful Teutonic damsel, and sent her off post-haste to the painter's studio. For a third time Haydn came to pose; but, just as the conversation was faltering into silence, a veil fell to the floor and our ravishing *Mädchen*, all elegantly draped in fine white gauze, and bearing a crown of roses on her head, spoke yearningly to Haydn, addressing him in his mother-tongue: "Oh illustrious genius! How happy am I to behold thee! How happy to be near thee!" Haydn, delighted, was soon eagerly plying the fair enchantress with questions; his features lit up and Reynolds was able to catch them hurriedly on his canvas.

King George III, who never took true pleasure in any music save Handel's, nevertheless was not wholly insensitive to that of Haydn; the Sovereign and his Queen gave a distinguished welcome to the German virtuoso; as a final gesture, the University of Oxford sent him the Degree of *D.Mus.*⋆, an honour which, since its inception in the 1400, had only been conferred *honoris causa* upon four persons, and which even Handel himself had failed to obtain.

The tradition now required that Haydn should present the University with a piece of learned music; he therefore contrived, for the benefit of this ancient foundation, a page of manuscript so complex, that whether it were read from the top or the bottom of the page, whether it were begun in the middle or back to front, in a word, whichever way you might conceivably choose to read it, it still formed a melody together with its correct accompaniment⋆.

He left London enchanted with Handel's music and with several hundred guineas in his pocket, a sum which, to him, seemed like a royal treasure. Returning by way of Germany, he gave a number of concerts; and, for the first time in his life, his exiguous personal fortune received an increase. The pension that he received from the House of Esterházy was niggardly; yet the kindness with which he was treated by the members of this illustrious family was worth more to the man who works with his emotions than any conceivable salary. His place was always laid for him at the Prince's own table; and whenever His Highness distributed new uniforms to his orchestra, Haydn received the ceremonial costume that persons of rank, coming to Eisenstadt to pay their court to the Prince, were accustomed to wear. It is by a long series of favours of this nature that the great nobles of the Austrian Empire win the true loyalty and affection of all those who surround them; it is by such moderation that they persuade the people, not only to bear with, but even to cherish, privileges and manners which place them almost on a level of equality with the crowned heads of Europe. The traditional stiff-necked Teutonic pride appears absurd only in printed accounts of public ceremonies; observed in its natural surroundings, the prevalent air of kindness excuses all the rest. Haydn returned from London with a fortune of fifteen thousand florins; a few years later, the sale of the scores of the *Creation* and *The Seasons* brought him the sum of two thousand sequins (24,000 francs), with which he purchased the little house and garden where he now lives, in the suburb of Gumpendorf, hard by the highroad to Schönbrunn. Such is his whole fortune*.

I was with him in this new house of his, on the occasion when he received the flattering letter addressed to him by the *Institut de France*, announcing that he had been nominated a Foreign Associate Member. As Haydn read it, he suddenly burst into tears; nor ever afterwards could he remain unmoved, whenever he brought out this letter, which is truly inspired with that noble, yet gracious tone which we in France can more readily command than any other nation.

LETTER XVI

Salzburg, 28 May 1809.

Come, my Friend: for Haydn, who touched the celestial heights in his orchestral music, who was of an honest competence, no more, in his operatic works, now invites you to follow him into that sanctuary, where

> *La gloria di Colui che tutto muove*
> Dante, *Paradiso*, Canto I, St. 1.

inspired him to compose sacred pieces which, at times, are almost worthy of their Eternal Subject.

Nothing has been more properly admired, nor at the same time more heatedly criticised, than his Masses; however, in order to appreciate the beauties of this music, its faults and the reasons which compelled him to commit them, the best expedient is to consider the original state of Church Music towards the year 1760.

No one is ignorant of the fact that both the Jews and the Gentiles were wont to associate music with their religious ceremonies; it is to this admixture that we owe those melodies, devoid of rhythm yet instinct with a grandiose beauty, which have been preserved for us by the Gregorian and Ambrosian chants. Scholars have established with a wealth of sound argument that these chants, whose vestiges are known to us, were the same as those which were used in Ancient Greece, in the worship of Jupiter and of Apollo.

Soon after the days of Guido d'Arezzo, who is reputed, in the year 1302, to have discovered the earliest notions of counterpoint, this art was introduced into church music; however, until the age of Palestrina, that is to say towards the year 1570 or thereabouts, such music was never more than a pattern of harmonies, almost entirely devoid of any-thing recognisable as melody. During the fifteenth century, and also during the first half of the century following, composers, in order to lend pleasurable colouring to their Masses, would tend to base them on some popular air; thus we find more than a hundred Masses written during this period, based on the well-known tune of the *Song of the Man-at-Arms*.

The eccentric scholasticism of the Middle Ages induced other com-posers to construct their sacred music by a throw of dice: every number that turned up had specific passages of music to correspond with it. At long last, the world saw Palestrina.[1] This immortal genius, to whom we owe our modern concept of melody, shook himself free of the dragging chains of barbarism: he introduced into his works a distinctive melody, solemn admittedly, yet continuous and unmistakable; and still today his music may be heard at St. Peter's in Rome.

By the middle of the sixteenth century, composers had developed such a taste for fugues and canons, and in their sacred music combined these figures in so grotesque a fashion, that for the most part their pious

[1] Born in 1529 (nine years after the death of Raphael), died in 1594.

compositions contrived to sound excessively comic. For many years, this particular abuse had provoked the complaints of pious folk; indeed, on more than one occasion, it had been proposed that music should be banned altogether from the churches. Finally, Pope Marcellus II, who occupied the Holy See in 1555, was on the very point of signing the edict decreeing its suppression, when Palestrina requested the Pope's permission to perform for him a Mass of his own composition. The Pope consented; whereupon the young composer had sung in his august presence a Mass for six voices, which seemed so beautiful and so full of noble solemnity that the Sovereign Pontiff, far from putting his edict into effect, commissioned Palestrina to compose further works in similar style for his own chapel. The Mass in question has been preserved to this very day; it is known by the name of Pope Marcellus' Mass.

There is a distinction between composers who are great by virtue of what they promise, and those who are great in what they actually perform. Palestrina and Scarlatti wrought an astonishing transformation in their art; they possessed perhaps quite as much genius as Cimarosa; yet Cimarosa's actual works afford much more pleasure than theirs. What might not Mantegna have achieved—this same Mantegna whose paintings simply provoke laughter from three people out of four who see them in the Musée de Paris—if, instead of contributing to the education of Correggio, he had been born in Parma some ten years later than this great genius? Above all, what might not the world have received from the great Leonardo, he who of all men that ever lived was perhaps the most richly endowed with natural gifts, he whose very soul was especially created to adore Beauty, had it been granted to him to behold the paintings of Guido Reni*?

A simple mechanic in painting or in music in our own day can easily outstrip Giotto or Palestrina; but to what heights had these truly inspired artists not attained, had they enjoyed the same formative background as the mere mechanic, our contemporary? Monsieur de Laharpe's *Coriolan*, had it been published in the days of Malherbe, would have earned its author a reputation almost equal to that of Racine. Any man born with a modicum of talent is inevitably swept along by the tide of his century to that point of perfection which the century as a whole has reached; the education he receives, the general level of culture prevalent among the spectators who applaud him,

5

everything conspires to take him to that particular high-water mark;
but the moment he goes *beyond* that point, then he has risen above his
century, he has genius—in which case, his works will be destined for
posterity; yet at the same time are liable to be less appreciated by his
contemporaries.

It will be evident that, towards the close of the sixteenth century,
church music was drawing closer to dramatic music. It was not long
before composers started enriching their sacred canticles with orchestral
accompaniments.

At long last, in 1740 (certainly not earlier), Durante[1] had the idea of
using music to point the meaning of words and began to hunt for
melodious phrases specifically designed to emphasise and magnify the
sentiments embodied in the text. South of the Alps, the transformation
brought about by this notion—which, after all, appears so natural—
was universally acclaimed; in Germany, however, composers remained
faithful to the old traditions, and their sacred works continued to preserve something of the primitive rudeness and monotony of the Middle
Ages. In Italy, the contrary development occurred: sentiment eclipsed
all sober decency, and before long church music and operatic music
were indistinguishable. A *Gloria in Excelsis* grew to be nothing other
than a merry little air, to the tune of which some lover might just as
appositely have expressed his delight in his mistress' favours; a *Miserere*
was hardly to be told apart from some lover's lament, brim-full of
tenderness and languor.

Arias, duets, recitatives, even merry and skipping little rondos—all
these found their way into the prayers. Benedict XIV made an attempt
to put an end to the scandal by forbidding wind-instruments in church;
but the root of the trouble lay, not in the instruments used, but in the
very genre which had developed.

Haydn who, from an early age, was acquainted not only with the
aridity of the medieval sacred tradition, but also with the profane
luxuriance which the contemporary Italian style had imported into the
holy places, and further with the monotonous and expressionless
dreariness that characterised church music in Germany, realised that he
had only to develop what he himself felt to be decent and proper, to
create a style which would be completely original. In consequence, he

---

1 Durante, born in Naples in 1693, a pupil of Scarlatti; died in 1755, in the same year
as Montesquieu.

borrowed little or nothing from operatic tradition; he preserved, in the solid texture of his harmonies, something of the grandiose and sombre austerity of the medieval school; and he used the full rich resources of his orchestration to sustain melodies which were solemn, tender, dignified—yet still resplendent since, from time to time, grace-notes and *fioriture* were permitted to soften the austere grandeur of these canticles praising the glory of God and thanking Him for all His mercies.

In the elaboration of this style, his only precursor had been Sammartini, the Milanese composer of whom I have already spoken.

If you should ever hear, in one of those immense Gothic cathedrals which are frequently to be met with in Germany, and where feeble gleams of daylight penetrate fitfully through the stained-glass windows, one of Haydn's Masses, the first impression is of a profound disturbance, the second, one of exaltation, as you are gradually swept away by the combination of grave solemnity, noble melody, antique austerity, imaginative splendour and deep piety which characterises them.

In the year 1799, I was in Vienna*, lying sick of a fever, when I heard the bell ringing for High Mass in a church hard by the little room which I occupied. Boredom got the better of caution: I got up and went out, so as to enjoy the consolation of a little music. At the church-door, I made enquiries: it was St. Anne's Day, and the Mass to be performed was one of Haydn's—the Mass in B flat major*—which I had previously never heard. Scarcely had the first notes sounded, when I was possessed of a strange emotion; I found that I was sweating profusely, my headache had vanished; and some two hours later I emerged from that church lighter of heart than I had been for many years. Nor did the fever ever return.

I suspect that not a few of the ailments that afflict the feminine nervous system might well be cured by this remedy of mine; not, however, by the sort of empty, tinkling music which the gentler sex commonly expects for entertainment at a concert, having first put on the prettiest of its bonnets. Women all their life long, and men similarly when they are young, are incapable of devoting full attention to music, unless the hall is darkened. In darkness, we are freed from the pretence of social graces; no longer are we obliged to keep up appearances; and so at long last we may surrender to the music. Concert-going in France, however, is a very different matter—indeed, the frame of mind induced is

diametrically opposite. There are few social occasions when I feel myself under a stronger obligation to shine in the eyes of my fellow-
mortals, than at a concert. By contrast, should you chance to be taking
the morning air in the Parc Monceau, being seated alone with a book
in some green arbour and knowing yourself secure from curious eyes;
and should you then suddenly have your attention caught by the sound
of instruments—a few scattered chords—and singing, welling up from
one of the houses in the neighbourhood and finally resolving itself into
a graceful melody; should you now desire to return to your reading, it
would be in vain. For your heart will be held captive by the music, you
will find yourself lulled by lapping waves of reverie; and some two
hours later, as you climb back into your carriage, you will find yourself relieved of that secret sorrow that ever and again weighed heavily
upon your heart, often without your even being aware yourself in
what it consisted, or by what it was engendered; you will feel gently
wistful, ready to weep tears over your own destiny; you will have
discovered the sensation of *Regret*, and regret is the consolation which is
lacking to those who are truly unhappy, for they can no longer believe
that happiness is possible. He who knows the experience of Regret,
feels the existence of that happiness that once he knew and, gradually, he
will come to believe once more in the possibility of regaining this lost
paradise. Good music makes no error: it plunges straight into the
uttermost depths of the soul, to seek out thence the sorrow that devours
us.

In all cases of treatment and cure by music, I am persuaded—speaking
now in serious medical terms—that it is the brain that exercises a
powerful pressure over the rest of the nervous system.[1] The principle
involved is that the music must begin by lifting the patient out of his
normal frame of mind, and by convincing him of the possibility of
things which hitherto he had not dared hope for. One of the most
singular instances of this temporary mental derangement, this total
forgetfulness of the Self, its vanity and the part that it is required to
play, is the case of Senesino who, on one of the London stages, was
engaged to sing the part of the Tyrant in some opera or other—I cannot
recall which—while the celebrated Farinelli was to sing the part of the
youthful Prince, his piteous victim. Farinelli, who was involved in a

---

[1] One of the first effects is a rigid sensation in the stomach; this is caused by the irritation
of the nerves of the diaphragm.

THE CELEBRATED COMPOSER HAYDN

concert-tour in the provinces, reached the theatre only a few hours before the actual performance, so that in fact ill-fated Hero and cruel Tyrant met for the first time actually on the stage. When he came to his first aria—that in which he besought the Tyrant's compassion—he sang it with such sweetness, such heartbreaking expression, that the wretched Tyrant, the tears streaming down his face, was forced to fling his arms about his neck and to embrace him three or four times, being utterly beside himself with emotion.

Here is another anecdote. One day in the high heat of summer, when I was still very young, I sallied forth with a company of other carefree young men to seek the cool altitude and the pure air on one of those high mountains that encircle Lake Maggiore, in Lombardy*. By day-break, we had half-completed the climb; and while we were halted to admire the view of the Borromean Islands which lay at our feet, sharp-outlined by the waters of the lake, we suddenly found ourselves surrounded by a great flock of sheep, which had just emerged from the fold on their way to the high pastures. One of our company, who could play better than many another upon the flute, and who never stirred abroad without this instrument, promptly drew it from his pocket. "I shall now," he declared, "pretend that I am Corydon or Menalcas. Let us see if Virgil's ewes still recognise their shepherd"; whereupon he struck up a tune. The sheep and the goats, which up to that instant had been proceeding in solemn Indian file up the mountain, noses to the ground, now, at the first sound of the flute, all raised their heads; then, as of one common and immediate accord, turned to face the direction whence proceeded these agreeable sounds. Gradually the whole flock gathered about the musician, and there stood motionless, listening. The shepherd's stick began, in peremptory fashion, to urge those nearest about him to move on; those whom be belaboured obeyed; but no sooner did the piper begin his tune anew, than his audience of innocents came flocking back around him. The shepherd grew impatient and with his crook started to bespatter the backs of his flock with lumps of turf: not a beast moved. The flute went more and more merrily; the shepherd, losing his temper, whistled and swore; lavished blows and hurled stones at those piteous music-lovers. The ones whom the stones actually hit began to drift away; but the rest remained exactly where they were. Finally, the shepherd was obliged to beg our Orpheus to desist from the magic of his music; whereupon the flock once more resumed its course. Yet even when they were far ahead, the sheep would still stop dead the moment that our friend uttered a note on the instrument that so delighted them. The tune he had played was nothing more elusive than the latest fashionable ditty from the opera currently running in Milan.

As we were never weary of music and all things musical, we were enchanted by our little adventure, and we concluded that physical pleasure is the primary element in all forms of musical experience.

But . . . what about Haydn and his Masses? You are right, of course, but then, what would you? If I write, it is but for my own amusement, and we have long ago agreed, you and I, never to be other than *natural* with each other.

Haydn's Masses, then, are informed by the yearnings of a tranquil sensibility; the underlying inspiration is brilliant, and in general solemn and majestic; the style is ardent, noble, and gives rise to exquisite developments; the Amens and the Alleluias express a deep-felt joyousness and are of unparalleled vivacity. At times, when the tone of a passage threatens to appear too light-hearted and profane, Haydn will darken it with deep and resonant chords which sober its worldly gaiety. His *Agnus Dei* passages are wistful and tender: in particular, that of No. 4, the *Saint Nicholas Mass* in G major—of such stuff is the music of Heaven. His fugues are torrents of spontaneous movement: they are compounded of fire, dignity and the exaltation of a soul enthralled.

Here and there he employs the following device, which is characteristic of Paisiello.

From the very first bars of his work, he will pick out some particularly attractive passage, and then repeatedly allude to it during the remainder of the composition; not infrequently, instead of a whole passage, he will be content with some brief and fragmentary motif. It is incredible how effectively so simple a device, the mere repetition of the same passage, establishes the unity of the whole, and creates an atmosphere of profound and moving piety. You can appreciate that such a procedure may easily verge upon monotony; yet the truly great composers always manage to avoid it. Take, for instance, *La Molinara*; or rather take Cherubini's *Les Deux Journées*. In the Overture to this fine work there is a certain phrase that seems to stand out from all the rest, a phrase which the ear distinguishes from its surroundings because there is something half-choked, something odd about it. In the Trio of Act I, it reappears; again in an aria, and yet again in the Finale; and at each successive appearance, it gains in fascination. In Paisiello's *La Frascatana*, this dominant motif is so pervasive, that it alone gives rise to the whole of the Finale. In Haydn's Masses, themes such as this, at first encounter, are hardly remarkable for their charm; yet as the work develops, at each new appearance they acquire more forcefulness and ever greater beauty.

At this stage, however, let us give heed to Counsel for the Prosecution; and I assure you that, whatever else may be lacking in Haydn's detractors, it is not energy. They accuse him first of all of having destroyed the established traditions of Sacred Music, which had been adopted by all the Schools. Yet in practice, this species was already extinct in Italy, while in Germany the trend was ever backward, towards that monotonous and (worse still) utterly expressionless intoning of the Middle Ages. If the hallmark of gravity is held to be *monotony*, then most assuredly no style was ever graver.

Either ban music from the churches altogether; or else allow *true* music to have its place there. Did you forbid Raphael to introduce human faces of celestial beauty into his religious paintings? Guido Reni's all-too-handsome Archangel Michael, a figure apt to set the thoughts of many a pious feminine head a-wandering—is this Archangel Michael not still to be seen in Rome, in very St. Peter's? Why then should music not be allowed to offer its attractions? If you should seek an argument in theology, the example of the Psalms of David lies before us. "If the Psalmist laments," writes St. Augustine, "lament ye with him; if he utters forth the praises of God, praise ye also the wondrous works of the Creator."

It is nonsense, therefore, to sing an Alleluia to the measure of a *Miserere*. On this issue, our good Teutonic academics are now prepared to give a little ground: they will agree that the melody may encompass some small element of variety, yet still insist that the accompaniment should none the less remain austere, heavy-footed and noisy. Are they wrong? I recall that a famous doctor from Hanover, worthy compatriot of Frederic the Second and Catherine the Great, of Mengs and Mozart and others of their stamp, once confided to me, laughing: "The ordinary run-of-the-mill German requires more physical effort, more movement and more noise before he will be stirred, than any other race on earth; we drink too much beer, we need to be skinned alive before we feel it tickling."

If the aim of music, in church as elsewhere, is to lend added emotional impact to the sentiments expressed by the words as they penetrate the listener's breast, then Haydn has attained perfection in his art. I defy any Christian who listens, on Easter Day, to one of Haydn's *Glorias*, to leave the church without a heart brim-full of holy joy—an effect, apparently, that Father Martini and the German harmonists consider undesirable; however, if their aim is to avoid at all costs such experience, it must be confessed that they have singularly well succeeded.

If these gentlemen are wrong, then, in their principal accusation against Haydn, they are none the less correct in certain details. Correggio likewise, in his search for *graceful* beauty, fell now and then into the pit of simpering affectation. Consider, for instance, that divine *Madonna alla Scodella*, which hangs in the Musée de Paris. At times, when you are out of mood and temper, you may find the movement of the angel engaged in tying up Joseph's ass to be affected; yet on more propitious days, this same angel will seem charming. Occasionally Haydn's failings are of a more positive character: in the *Dona nobis pacem* of one of his Masses⋆, the principal theme, frequently repeated, is this poor tinkling little ditty, marked "tempo presto":

In one setting of a *Benedictus*⋆, after much orchestral heralding, we meet this Great Thought, in many multiple repeats and invariably in "tempo allegretto":

The identical theme may be found in an *aria buffa* by Anfossi, where it is in fact most excellently effective—being in this case truly apposite. Haydn has written certain fugues in "tempo di sestupla", which, as

soon as the movement livens up, are as ridiculous and as absurd as anything in the *opera buffa*. When the repentant sinner weeps for his sins at
the foot of the altar, too often Haydn portrays the delights of an all-too-
tempting transgression, instead of dwelling on the true Christian's
repentance. Here and there, his tempo lapses into 3/4 or 3/8, thereby
irresistibly putting the listener in mind of waltzes and quadrilles.

Such errors as these are an infringement of the physical laws on which
all music is based. Cabanis will tell you that joy accelerates the circulation of the blood, and requires a corresponding presto; sorrow diminishes and slows down the movement of the humours, and thus seeks its
expression in a "tempo largo"; the mood of satisfaction demands a
major key, while melancholy finds its echo in the minor—this latter
observation being the one upon which the styles, both of Cimarosa and
of Mozart, are founded.

Haydn was wont to make excuses for these defects, which his reason
could not but recognise as such, by saying that whenever he contemplated the nature of God, he was unable to conceive of Him, save as a
Being of infinite greatness and goodness. He would add that these latter
attributes of the Divinity so filled his heart with trust and joy, that he
could gladly have marked everything Allegro, even the *Miserere*.

Personally, I find his Masses to be slightly too *Germanic* in style: by
this I mean that the accompaniments are often over-elaborate, thus to
some extent obscuring the effect of the melody.

There are fourteen Masses in all, of which a number were composed
during the period of the Seven Years' War, on occasions when the
fortunes of the House of Austria were at their lowest ebb. These are
shot through with a truly martial ardour★: in this sense, they bear some
resemblance to those sublime songs which have newly been improvised, in this very year of grace 1809, upon the approach of the French
armies, by the famous Viennese tragic dramatist, Heinrich Josef von
Collin★.

LETTER XVII

My dear Louis,

The one work of Haydn's that there remained for me to discuss was the *Creation*. It represents our composer's finest achievement; it is the true *epic poetry* of music. Now, as you are aware, I have entrusted the secret of these letters of mine to a charming Viennese lady of my acquaintance—a lady who, like many others from among the leading families of this unhappy city, has taken refuge here among these mountains*. This acquaintance of mine has a secretary and he it is who transcribes these letters for me, thus sparing me what is in my view the most desperately tedious of occupations, namely that of going back a second time over the same sequence of ideas. I told my charming friend that I should be obliged to pass over the *Creation* with scarcely a mention, since I had listened to it but once or twice in all my life. "Indeed!" she replied. "Then it is *I* who shall compose this letter to your friend in Paris." I ventured upon a few slight objections, such as politeness demands. "Would you have it, then," she protested, "that I am incapable of writing to a cultivated Parisian, who is as fond of you as he is of music? Come, Sir! At most you will discover in my letter some occasional faults in the French language that deserve correction; but when you correct them, pray strive not to disfigure my ideas too grossly in the process—that is all I ask of you."

As you will observe, this preamble is in the nature of a betrayal. I beg you, do not fail to write me an answer when you receive this letter on the *Creation*; and above all, criticise it mercilessly. Tell me that my style is effeminate, that all the broader concepts are lost amid an infinitude of pettifogging details, that I observe things that never existed, save in my own head. And more especially, I beg you to reply promptly, so that there may be no suspicion of conspiracy between us. Your criticisms, here in Salzburg, are destined to provoke a most lively reaction, which promises delightful entertainment.

LETTER XVIII

Salzburg, 31 May 1809.

We are forever complaining, my dear Friend, that we are come into the world too late, that nothing remains for us to do save to admire the achievements of past ages, and that we are contemporary with naught that is of true greatness in the Arts. Yet great men are like the summits of the Alps: when you are close at hand, in the valley of Chamonix, for instance, the Mont Blanc itself, dwindling amidst a host of neighbouring peaks snow-mantled like itself, seems to be nothing save just one more high mountain among others; but when, having returned again to Lausanne, you behold it dominating everything that surrounds it; and when, separated from it by a greater distance still, you stand in the centre of the plains of France, whence the panorama of the mountains has entirely vanished, and yet you still continue to perceive, upon the far horizon, this white, enormous mass, it is indeed then that you must recognise it for what it is: the Colossus of the Old World. By what process of discovery have you in France, O vulgar species of mankind that you are, come to perceive to its full extent the genius of Molière? By that unique process, which is experience; and by observing that, at a distance of a hundred and fifty years, he still towers in majestic solitude upon the horizon. In music we stand now where, at the close of the century of Louis XIV, the people of Paris stood in relation to literature. The constellation of genius has but lately sunk below the horizon.

And of this constellation, no single member ever produced, in the academic genre, a work more celebrated than the *Creation*, which, perchance, may survive even for posterity.

It is my belief that Pergolesi's *Stabat Mater*, together with one short opera, *La Serva Padrona*, Piccinni's *Didone* and *La buona Figliuola*, Paisiello's *Barbiere di Siviglia* and *La Frascatana*, Cimarosa's *Matrimonio segreto* and *Gli Orazi e Curiazi*, Mozart's *Don Giovanni* and *Le Nozze di Figaro*, Jommelli's *Miserere*, together with the merest handful of other pieces, will keep it faithful company*.

Now you shall learn, dear Friend of mine, what we here in Vienna find to admire in this work. Yet remember always that the more lucid my ideas might appear were we but seated together, you and I, conversing beside a piano, the more I fear that they may prove obscure when sent by post from Vienna to Paris—to Paris, that disdainful city, which believes that anything that it fails to grasp effortlessly and without delay is not worth grasping. The mechanism of this contempt is plain: for, being forced to acknowledge, either that the writer of the letter is a fool, or else that there are realms to which your own intellect, with all its penetration, has no access, how should you hesitate?

Many years before he scaled the heights of the *Creation*, to be precise, in 1774, Haydn had composed his first Oratorio, entitled *Il Ritorno di Tobia*, a mediocre piece of work, wherein no more than two or three sections bear the imprint of the future Master. You will recall that, during his visits to London, Haydn was much struck by the music of Handel; and it was by studying the works of England's adopted musician that he learnt the secrets of a majestic style. On one occasion, chancing to be seated next to Haydn during a performance of Handel's *Messiah*, given in the Palace of Prince Schwarzenberg, I ventured to praise one of the noble choruses in this work. Haydn, deep in thought, replied: "*He* was the father of us all."*

I am persuaded that, had he not studied Handel, Haydn could never have written the *Creation*; his own genius was set ablaze by the sparks thrown off by Handel's. Everyone has acknowledged the fact that, following his return from London, his themes became more grandiose; in a word, that he drew near, in so far as human genius *can* draw near, to the unapproachable Subject of his anthems.[1] Handel's music is

---

[1] In 1791, Haydn had listened to a performance of Handel's *Messiah*, given in Westminster Abbey*. For the first time in his life, he heard an orchestra of 1,067 players, made up as follows:

Violins	250	Oboes	40
Violas	50	Bassoons	40
'Cellos	50	Horns	12
Double-Basses	27	Trumpets	14

simple: his accompaniments are scored for three parts only; yet, to use a Neapolitan expression adopted by Gluck, there is not a single note *che non tiri sangue*. Handel is particularly keen to avoid any continuous scoring for the wind-section, since the suavity and timbre of these instruments will eclipse even the human voice. Cimarosa used no flutes except in the opening numbers of *Il Matrimonio segreto*; Mozart, by contrast, employs them all the time.

The Oratorio is a form invented in the year 1530 by St. Philip Neri, who believed it to be a means of awakening religious fervour in the somewhat profane city of Rome, by captivating the senses, partly through the dramatic intensity of the narrative, and partly through a degree of innocent voluptuousness. Up to the time of Haydn, men were convinced that the form had attained to its perfect state in the hands of Marcello, Hasse and Handel, who had composed such a quantity of pieces in this manner, and of such unrivalled quality. Zingarelli's *Distruzione di Gerusalemme*, which is sometimes given in Paris*, and which still attracts its audiences, despite the gross and unworthy mutilation it has suffered at the hands of its "arrangers", is already something other than a genuine Oratorio. A true and perfect specimen of the genre, such as those favoured by the Masters to whom I have just alluded, must reveal aspects of the grave and frugal style of church music, in combination with the clear-textured and expressive style of the opera. The Oratorios of Handel and Marcello include fugues in almost every section; Weigl employed them similarly in his superb Oratorio, *Das Leiden Jesu Christi*; whereas contemporary Italian composers have tended to make Oratorio almost indistinguishable from opera. Haydn desired to imitate the former school; but the burning genius of the man could ill be satisfied with imitation: his enthusiasm caught fire only when he was himself *creating*.

Haydn was a friend of Baron Gottfried van Swieten, Curator of the Imperial Library, a man of great erudition even in the field of music and, in addition, himself no inconsiderable composer. It was a theory of the Baron's, that music, which is so admirably fitted to depict the passions, was also capable of portraying objects in the physical world, by

Percussion	8	Trombones.	12
Organ	1	Chorus	563

The effect was very soft: the voices could be heard very distinctly. An odd fact was that the bass parts appeared almost weak.

awakening in the listener's imagination sensations identical with those
which such objects would evoke in reality. Men admire the sun: consequently, by evoking the sensation of admiration in the highest degree,
the concept "sun" would be conjured up in their minds. It may be that
there is some slight flaw to be discerned in this argument; none the less,
Baron van Swieten was firmly convinced of the truth of it. He pointed
out to his friend that, although an occasional trace of this descriptive
method may be met with here and there in the works of the Great
Masters, nevertheless the field as a whole remained still to be explored
and exploited. He proposed that Haydn should become the abbé
Delille of music; and Haydn accepted.

    In Handel's own lifetime, Milton had written expressly for him the
text of an Oratorio entitled *The Creation of the World*—a text which,
for some reason unknown to me, was never set to music. The English
poet Thomas Linley★ derived from Milton's text the words of a second
Oratorio; and finally, when Haydn was leaving London, the impresario
Salomon gave him Linley's version. Haydn took the text with him to
Vienna, without too seriously contemplating making use of it; however, Baron van Swieten, in order to encourage his friend, not only
made a German translation from the English words, but further enriched the text with a number of choruses, arias and duets, in order that
the Master's genius might find more opportunities to display itself in
all its splendour. In 1795 Haydn, who was by this time already sixty-
three years of age, undertook this immense work; and he laboured at
it during two whole years. When people used to urge him to finish it,
he would reply in all tranquillity: "I am spending a long time over it,
because I intend that it should last a long time."

    Early in 1798 the Oratorio was completed, and in the course of the
ensuing Lent was given its first performance in the Appartments of the
Schwarzenberg Palace, the costs being borne by that same Society of
Music-Lovers★ that had originally commissioned it from the composer.

    Who could describe the enthusiasm, the delight, the applause that
echoed and re-echoed throughout that evening? I was there myself, and
I can assure you that never in my life have I been present at so memorable an occasion: the reigning monarchs of the world of Letters, the
cream of polite Society—all were gathered together there in that great
Hall, which was most eminently suitable for music. Haydn himself
conducted. The profoundest of silences, the most reverent attention, an

atmosphere that I could almost describe as *religious* in its deep respect, held sway throughout the entire assembly: such was the mood that held the audience in its grasp when, at long last, the strings struck up the first note. Nor was such expectation disappointed. We beheld, wending its way before our senses, a long procession of wonders, of a beauty unconceived until that instant. Men's minds were taken unawares: drunk with delight and admiration, for two whole hours on end they experienced to the full that which, hitherto, they had known only by fleeting intimations—an existence of bliss, nourished by desires constantly renewed, ever reinvigorated, and yet unfailingly satisfied.

You have the habit, in France, of referring so frequently to the abbé Delille and to his "descriptive manner", that I will make no apology for a brief digression on descriptive music: indeed, digressions and the "descriptive manner" go hand in hand—this unhappy genre would pine away and die, were it deprived of all that is not its own true self.

There is one objection to descriptive music, and that of the most irrefutable sort. In effect, some malicious wit might well take up the charge in Voltaire's line:

> *Mais, entre nous, je crois que vous n'existez pas*★.

Here, however, are the arguments advanced by those who *do* believe in the Real Presence. It is plain to all that music has power to imitate nature in one of two fashions: there is physical representation, and there is emotional representation. You will recall, in the duet:

> *Se a caso madama*
> *La notte ti chiama* . . .

from *Le Nozze di Figaro*, the various ting-tings and dong-dongs by which Susanna contrives so amusingly to suggest the sound of a bell— Count Almaviva's bell, announcing some long, long errand to be entrusted to the husband of this same alluring Susanna. Now this is physical representation. There is a German opera, in which some oaf goes to sleep on the stage, while his wife, from her window, sings a duet with her lover. In this instance, the snoring of the husband, in faithful physical rendering, forms a delightful comic bass to the soft murmurs of seduction that the lover croons to the wife. Here again, you have an exact representation of nature.

Precise imitation of this sort is diverting for a moment or two, but quickly palls. In the sixteenth century, certain Italian *maestri* so developed this facile technique, that often it furnished the basis for an entire opera. Thus we have *Il Podesta di Coloniola*, for which *maestro* Melani composed the following aria:

> *Talor la granocchiella nel pantano*
> *Per allegrezza canta: qua, qua, ra;*
> *Tribbia il grillo: tri, tri, tri;*
> *L'agnellino fa: bè, bè;*
> *L'usignuolo: chiù, chiù, chiù;*
> *Ed il gal: curi chi chi*

—during the course of which, the orchestra proceeds relentlessly to mimic each animal in turn as it is named.

Scholars will tell you that, at a date even slightly earlier, Aristophanes had exploited this same type of mimicry in the drama. But Haydn was extremely sparing in his use of these techniques, both in the *Creation* and in the *Seasons*. To take an instance, he succeeds with wondrous effect when he echoes the cooing of doves; he was, however, adamant in his resistance to our descriptomaniac Baron, who was positively longing to hear the croaking of frogs as well.

In music, the most satisfying of physical descriptions is perhaps that which is content merely to hint at the object which is designated—that which reveals the object as through a veil of mist, and which is most scrupulously careful to avoid any painstaking precision in the delineation of Nature "as she is". Imitation of this sort offers the finest specimens of music in the "descriptive manner". There is a pleasing example by Gluck, in the "Pilgrims' aria" from *Les Pèlerins de la Mecque*, which suggests the murmuring of a brook; Handel has given us the gentle sound of falling snow, as the flakes settle quietly upon the silent earth; but the composer who outdistances all his rivals in this is Marcello, in his cantata *Calisto in orsa*; for here, at the instant when Juno transforms this star-crossed maiden into a snarling beast, the listener is made to shudder by the ferocity and the savagery of the accompaniments, as they portray the great she-bear roaring in paroxysms of anger.

This is the style of mimicry which was perfected by Haydn. You are aware, my dear Friend, that every art is based upon a given degree of *falsehood*—a principle by no means easy to penetrate in spite of its apparent clarity, yet one which is established as the very source and wellhead of the greatest of Truths. In like fashion, from some obscure cavern there issues forth the stream that is destined to water the broad and spreading acres of many a province. We will talk more of this some other day.

Is there not greater pleasure in allowing your gaze to fall directly upon some fine prospect in the Jardin des Tuileries, than in contemplating this identical prospect faithfully reflected in one of the great mirrors of the Château? And yet this mirror-image, this mere reflection of a reality, is far richer and more natural in colour than any painting, were the artist Claude Lorrain himself. The figures therein actually move, while every detail is truer and more faithful—yet, obstinate creature that you are, you continue to prefer the painting. The skilled artist never deviates from that exact measure of falsehood which is allowable to the art that he practises; he is perfectly well aware that, if the Fine Arts afford a source of pleasure, it is not by imitating Nature to the point of producing the "perfect illusion"; and he draws the most careful distinction between those faultless daubs known as *trompe-l'œil* on the one hand, and Raphael's *St. Cecilia* on the other.

The aim of imitation is to convey an impression identical with that which would be produced by the actual object imitated, if that object were to strike us during one of those rare instants of enhanced susceptibility and exaltation which lie at the root of all passionate experience.

So much may be said, then, concerning the physical imitation of Nature by music.

The alternative form of imitation, which may be termed *sentimental*, unless this word should seem too ridiculous in your view, is not concerned to refashion material objects, but rather to re-create the *feelings* that these objects evoke*. For instance, the music of Paolino's aria:

Signor! Deh concedete ...

from *Il Matrimonio segreto*, does not in any precise sense *portray* the misery of a man who sees his mistress carried off by a powerful nobleman; instead, it portrays a profound and wistful melancholy. It is the function of the *words* to particularise this general wistfulness, and to etch in the exact contours of the painting; and this combination of words and music, nevermore to be separated in our hearts if we have heard them but once, forms the most vital, living portrait that ever a passionate nature was inspired to paint of his own most secret emotions.

Music such as this, no less than those impassioned sections of *La Nouvelle Héloïse*, no less than the *Lettres d'une Religieuse portugaise*, may appear merely tedious to many people:

On peut être honnête homme . . .★

and still not appreciate it. One may suffer from this minor disability, and none the less prove a man of remarkable qualities. Mr. Pitt, for instance. . . I would wager that Mr. Pitt had no high regard for the aria:

Fra mille perigli . . .★

as sung by Signora Barilli in *I Nemici generosi*; yet for all that, had *I* a kingdom to govern, Mr. Pitt might sleep sound in the prospect of being Chancellor of the Exchequer.

Will you forgive me a comparison that is not without its absurdity? Will you promise me not to laugh? For it is a Teutonic notion that I have a mind to place before you. In Goethe's *Wahlverwandtschaften*, the following passage meets my eye:

FRAGMENT OF A LETTER
written by Ottilie★

"In the evening, I accompanied the Captain to the theatre: the opera started later than it does at home in our little town, and we could hold no conversation without being overheard. Gradually, we began to look about us and to observe the countenances of our neighbours; I would have given much to have my needlework; I asked the Captain to pass me my bag; he gave it to me, but begged me in a whisper not to take out my embroidery-thread. 'I assure you,' he said to me, 'that in Munich, to do needlework in a box at the Opera would be a most ridiculous *faux-pas*, for all that it may prove good breeding in Lambach!' In one hand, I already held the purse I was embroidering, and in the other the tiny reel of golden thread, and I was just about to begin, when the Captain took fright. 'Listen,' he said, 'I am going to tell you a little tale about a certain reel of golden thread.'

'Is it a fairy-tale?'

'Unhappily, no.'

'Far though it was from my intention,' he continued, 'I have been finding myself comparing the sensibility of each and every individual in the audience about us to that same little reel of yours, with its thread of gold. In the soul of every being who has taken a ticket here tonight, there is a reel, and the reel is wound about with lengths, some long, some short, of golden thread. Now along comes Mozart, the subtle Enchanter; with his magic spells of sound he catches at the end of the golden thread; at that very instant, the being in whom the reel lies hidden begins to respond; all the while the reel is unwinding, his experience continues; yet this emotion that the composer desires to awaken in his breast will endure only so long as the length of the precious thread; as soon as the spell-weaver portrays a degree of feeling that the listener himself has never experienced, then snick! no more thread of gold is left upon the reel, and ere long that listener will begin to feel bored. Only a soul that has been steeped in the fire of passion is rich in recollections, and it is these recollections that furnish the greater or lesser length of thread which is wound upon the reel. And of what use to Mozart is all his genius, if he has to cope with reels all bare of thread?

'Would you take Monsieur Turcaret to hear *Il Matrimonio segreto*? For all the golden braid that he wears upon his coat, there is but little thread of gold upon the reel that (in our image) represents his soul. Too soon it will be exhausted; and so our Monsieur Turcaret will start to yawn at Carolina's lamentations. The reason is so simple. What can *he* hope to find, stored away among his memories? What are the most stirring emotions that *he* has ever felt? Grief at finding himself heavily implicated in some bankruptcy? Or misery at beholding the splendid paint-work of his carriage basely scraped and spoilt by a carter's waggon? These are the woes to which he would respond, were they portrayed. Besides, he has dined well, he is overflowing with good cheer, and what his heart in truth desires is the gay jigging of a merry quadrille. Yet there beside him sits his poor wife who, in the recent campaign, has lost a lover whom she adored; *she* takes no pleasure in an evening at the theatre; for her, it is a social duty, to be borne with bravely; she is pale; her eye lights upon nothing with interest; neither upon any object nor, at the beginning, upon Carolina or upon her situation.

'Old Geronimo's daughter has *her* lover beside her; he is alive, how then should *she* know what true grief is? The music seems almost importunate to this suffering creature, whose only longing is to feel nothing. Not without infinite difficulty may the Enchanter catch at the end of the little thread of gold; but at long last her attention is held, her gaze steadies, her eyes grow moist. The depths of suffering that break through the aria:

Signor! Deh concedere . . .

begin to soften her heart; presently, tears will be coursing down her cheeks—how (this is now her worry) shall she conceal them from her great oaf of a husband who is on the point of nodding off to sleep, and who would consider this display of feeling plainly idiotic? The composer may lead this poor, suffering creature whithersoever he desires; he will demand of her a heavy ransom of tears; the thread of gold will be a long, long time unwinding. Cast your glance upon those who are around you; in their eyes, do you observe. . .?' At this point, the performance began."

When music is successful in evoking images—the silence of a fine summer night, for instance—it is said to be "picturesque". The finest achievement in this manner is the *Creation*, just as *Don Giovanni* or *Il Matrimonio* are the most notable triumphs of expressive music.

The *Creation* begins with an Overture, representing Chaos. A blurred confusion of noise assails the ear; sounds emerge disjointedly, notes cut adrift from all intelligible melody; in a little while, a few scattered fragments of themes appear, attractive enough in themselves, yet still shapeless, still incapable of resolution. These are followed by half-sketched images, now solemn, now tender; everything is jumbled pell-mell together; the *charming* and the *powerful* tread close upon each others' heels, in haphazard sequence, the infinitely great jostles with the infinitely small, austerity is intertwined with laughter. This weirdest foregathering of every *fioritura* known to music—trills, grace-notes, mordents, telescoped phrases, discords—offers, so people maintain, an admirable portrait of Chaos.

It is my *mind* which tells me this. I admire the artist's talent, I can clearly discern in his music everything that I have described; furthermore I would agree that no man, perhaps, could do better. Yet I would still enquire of Baron van Swieten, who first conceived the notion of this symphonic introduction: "Is it *possible* to portray Chaos in music? Would a listener, unless he were already in the secret, actually *recognise* Chaos in what he heard?" Let me, in all candour, make a confession:

there was a ballet, presented in Milan by Salvatore Viganò, in which the choreographer showed Prometheus bringing the gift of souls to human creatures still bound down to the level of the brutish beasts. In this ballet, Haydn's "Symphony of Chaos" received additional commentary from the steps of a trio of delightful ballerinas expressing, with a spontaneous grace that seemed inspired by very Heaven, the first faint stirring in the soul of an awakening to Beauty. Now I will confess that it was this *commentary* which first revealed to my eyes the full ingenuity of the music; and today, I can understand it and derive great pleasure from it. By comparison, the score of all the other sections of *Gli Uomini di Prometeo* seemed merely tedious and insignificant.

Yet before I had seen Viganò's ballet, which caused a *furore* throughout the length and breadth of Italy, I used to tell myself that since, in the "Symphony of Chaos", none of the thematic material is resolved, *therefore* there is no melody, *therefore* no pleasure for the ear, *therefore* no music. It is as though one were to insist that painting should portray the darkness of impenetrable night, depicting a total absence of illumination. Imagine an immense, square canvas, of immaculate blackness, set in a fine frame—would it be a picture?

In Haydn's Oratorio, music proper re-emerges with all its enchantment when the Angels set about telling the great work of the Creation. Before long, we come to the passage in which God is shown, creating Light:

> *And God said,*
> *Let there be Light:*
> *And there was Light.*

It must be acknowledged that music knows no more impressive moment. In anticipation of the Word that the Creator is to speak, the composer gradually reduces the complexity of his chords, resolving them into unison, and hushing his orchestra in a progressive *diminuendo* as he moves towards the long final close; then, with a crash, the hush explodes into a thunderclap of sound at the words:

> *And there was . . . LIGHT!*

At the first performance this outburst from the entire orchestra, in the resounding key of C major, accompanied by all the known resources of harmony, and following upon the silence into which all sound had gradually died away, made an impression upon those of us who were in that audience as though a thousand torches had suddenly shattered the darkness of some gloomy cavern with a great blaze of light.

Next there comes a fugal passage, in which the Angels of the Host of the Lord describe the fury of Satan and of his horde, as they are cast forth into the pit of Hell, and by the very hand of Him whom they abhor. Here, Milton has verily a rival. Haydn's score is lavishly bestrewn with all the barbarous uncouthness of the *enharmonic style**: horrid dissonances, sequences of weird modulations, diminished sevenths of bizarre design. The horrifying effect of this chorus is increased by the harshness of the Germanic text. The audience shudders: but now the music begins to describe the beauty of the new-created world, the heaven-born freshness of the first green things that made fair the earth; and the soul at long last knows relief. The tune that Haydn has selected to portray the flowery groves of the Garden of Eden might, it is true, have been somewhat less commonplace. At this point, the score really required a touch of that celestial melody which characterises the Italian school. None the less, in the recapitulation, Haydn sustains it with so much art, while the harmonies of his accompaniment are so impregnated with nobility, that no one, unless his memory still echoed with the melodies of Sacchini, could sense what might perhaps be less than perfect here.

Soon there comes a storm to disturb the blissful existence of Adam and his fair companion; the gales are heard to roar; thunderclaps rend the ear, at first overhead, then distantly reverberating in prolonged rumbles; sharp showers of hail bounce off the leaves; then finally, gentle and unhurried, comes the snow, falling in great flakes upon the silent countryside.

These musical landscapes are all encompassed in great waves of harmony, than which nothing more glittering nor more majestic can be conceived. The melodies entrusted to the Archangel Gabriel, who is the leader of the chorus, stand out with especial distinctness from the vast assembly of voices by their uncommon energy and beauty.

One aria is devoted to evoking various impressions of water, from the roaring waves of a great ocean lashed to fury, to the tiny brook that quietly murmurs in the meanderings of its valley. The musical rendering of the brook is outstandingly successful; yet in spite of this, I am bound to confess that the idea of assigning a whole aria to the portrayal of *various impressions of water* strikes me as singularly eccentric, nor does it promise much satisfaction for the listener.

It is as though one were to commission Correggio to paint a picture of impenetrable darkness, or else of a sky suffused throughout with light; the very subject is inherently absurd; and yet Correggio, being Correggio, would still contrive, despite all the absurdity, to introduce a multitude of secondary details, each a source of delight in itself, and his work would be a pleasure to behold.

We find several other passages remarkable for their sheer virtuosity in the *Creation*; for instance, there is one theme, of which Haydn was particularly fond, and which he had already used three times in other contexts. Here, it is employed to portray the earth as it comes to be "with verdure clad"—covered with trees and flowers, with every species of plant and with sweet-smelling perfumes. What was needed in such a case was a melody that was tender, light-hearted and in-genuous; and I must confess that I have always felt that this favourite theme of Haydn's held more of simpering affectation than of true simplicity and gracefulness.

This aria is followed by a brilliant fugue, in which the Host of Angels praises the Creator, and where Haydn's genius shines forth once more in all its glory. The constant reiteration of a theme, which is essential to the structure of a fugue, here has the particular advantage of expressing the impassioned urgency of the Angel-Host, driven irresistibly by Love to raise their voices all of one accord and to hymn the glory of their Divine Creator.

And now, behold . . . behold the Sun itself which, for the first time, appears in all the splendour of its wondrous setting: the noblest pros-pect that ever human eyes were privileged to rest upon.

The rising of the Sun is followed by the rising of the Moon, which sails forth soundlessly amid the canopy of the clouds, shedding its silvery gleam over the night-darkened earth. The Reader will have observed that it is necessary to skip an entire day, otherwise the Sunrise can hardly be followed directly by the rising of the Moon; however, this is the realm of descriptive poetry, consequently a simple transition will suffice to save the situation. The First Part concludes with a chorus of Angels.

There is a charming harmonic device to be discovered in the *stretto* section of the finale in this First Part of the *Creation*. On the point of returning to a full and final close, Haydn does not simply stop the orchestra dead, as he does now and then in his Symphonies; but embarks instead upon a series of modulations, rising steadily by semitones. Each transition is sustained by resonant chords which, at every bar, appear to herald this final resolution for which the ear so desperately longs—only to find it yet once again postponed by some new modulation, still more unexpected than the last and of still greater beauty. Our astonishment increases step by step with our impatience; and when at last the long-awaited cadence is achieved, its coming is greeted by a spontaneous burst of applause.

The Second Part opens with an aria which begins in solemn majesty, next grows light-hearted, then finally concludes on a note of tenderness, and which describes the creation of the birds. This aria changes mood distinctly as it progresses, portraying now the fearless Eagle who, scarcely has he left the Creator's hands, seems to quit the earth and to soar away towards the sun; now the joyousness of the Lark:

> *His welcome bids to morn the merry lark . . .*

—now the loving gentle Turtle-Doves and now, finally, the plaintive Nightingale. The liquid voice of Philomel is echoed in all its freshness.

There follows a fine trio, devoted to the Whale, and to the effect that his great body produces as he disturbs the waters, thrusting them asunder with his enormous bulk. A well-constructed recitative shows us the generous Charger whose proud neighing re-echoes through the boundless immensity of the prairies; the Tiger, lithe and fierce, gliding swiftly through the forests and slipping between the trees; in the distance, we hear the roaring of the King of Beasts, while nearby, gentle Ewes, all ignorant of danger, quietly crop the grass.

Then comes an aria announcing, in noble and stirring terms, the creation of Man. The musical conception that corresponds to the phrase:

> *. . . a Man,*
> *The Lord and King of nature all,*

is rendered doubly effective by a happy inspiration in the German text. This language permits the use of an augmentative figure of speech, which would sound quite ridiculous in French, but which has a fine, majestic resonance in the original. In literal translation, the text reads as follows: "Behold Man, *the virile*, King of all Nature." The epithet "virile", following hard upon the word "Man", has the effect of driving out all ignoble and vulgar associations, so that all our attention may dwell upon the highest and the most majestic attributes of that great and joyous Being whom God has just created.

Haydn's music soars upward with ever-increasing power on each of these opening words, and achieves a superb resolution on the phrase "King of nature all". The effect is unforgettable*.

The second section of this aria tells of the creation of Eve, that enchanting and lovely being who, from the moment of her first fashioning, is all love. The conclusion of this aria suggests the joy experienced by Adam. By general consent, it is acknowledged to be the finest passage in the whole of the *Creation*; and I would add—following up my own theories—that this is because Haydn has returned to the realm of *passionate* experience, and that his task was to portray one of the most thrilling moments of joy that the heart of man has ever known.

The Third Part of the *Creation* is the shortest. The text consists of an excellent translation of the pleasanter episodes in Milton's epic. Haydn portrays the ecstasies of the first and most innocent of all loves, the touching conversations between the first man and wife, and their common gratitude, pure and fearless in its inspiration, towards the miraculous Goodness that had created them, and that appeared to have created all Nature to minister to their needs. Every single bar of the Allegro is shot through and through with white-hot shafts of joy. Yet there are also to be found in this Third Part traces of a common-or-garden, church-going piety, mingled with terror.

Finally a chorus, in part fugal, in part melodic in inspiration, concludes this astonishing production; nor are the qualities of the opening —its fiery ardour, its solemn majesty—one whit diminished in the closing bars.

Haydn enjoyed one piece of good fortune, which enabled him to write great music for the human voice. For the soprano part, he had at his disposal one of the finest female voices that existed perhaps in all the world at that particular time: that of Christine Gerardi.

Music such as this needs to be performed with simplicity; with precision; and with expression.[1] The least hint of ornamentation would

---

[1] *Con portamento*, as the Italians would say.

totally transform the characteristics of the style. The type of singer who is indispensable is a Crivelli; the *fioriture* of a Tacchinardi would be completely out of keeping.

LETTER XIX

Salzburg, 2 June 1809.

My dear Friend,

Now it is *I* who will take up the tale once more. The *Creation* enjoyed an immediate success; every gazette throughout the length and breadth of Germany reported the astounding impression that it had created in Vienna; and the score, which appeared in print only a few weeks later, made it possible for music-lovers in every corner of Europe to judge of its quality. The rapid sales of this published score contributed some several hundreds of golden *louis* to the otherwise unimpressive fortune of our composer. Below the staves of music, the bookseller had printed the text both in German and in English; this was immediately translated into Swedish, French, Spanish, Czech and Italian. The French translation is bombastically flat, as may be judged from any performance at the Conservatoire in the rue Bergère; however, it would be unfair to blame its author for the feeble impression that the *Creation* produced on the occasion of its first performance in Paris. A few minutes before it was due to start at the Grand Opéra, the Infernal Machine of 24 December 1800 exploded in the rue Saint-Nicaise*.

There are two Italian versions in existence: the first, which is full of absurdities, was printed in conjunction with the score which was published in Paris; the second was supervised both by Haydn himself and by Baron van Swieten. Since it is the best, it has, of course, only been printed in conjunction with the little piano-arrangement, which is published by Artaria. Its author, Signor Carpani, is a man of considerable intelligence who, in addition, possesses an excellent knowledge of music*. This Italian version was given a performance under the direction of Haydn and of Carpani, at the mansion of one of those uncommon men of parts who, by their absence, rob France of part of her cultural glory—namely, Prince Lobkowitz, whose high-born existence and whose all-but-boundless fortune are both entirely dedicated to the Arts, to their enjoyment and to their protection.

It is to be observed that music such as this, where harmony is all, cannot fittingly be judged unless the harmonic elements are at full strength. A dozen or so singers and instrumentalists—however excellent we may suppose them to be—grouped together about a piano, can give nothing but the most imperfect notion of the work; whereas one competent voice, aided by a slightly less-than-competent pianist, can easily render Pergolesi's *Stabat Mater* in such a fashion as to entrance the listener. Haydn's *Creation*, however, requires not less than twenty-four voices, together with an orchestra of sixty players. Thus appropriately performed, it has been heard in France, in Italy, in England, in Holland and in Russia.

The *Creation* has been criticised on two grounds: for its melodic content, and for its general style. There is no question, but that the melodic standard of the work is well above average; none the less, I am inclined to agree with the critics that some five or six melodies by Sacchini, flung in somewhere amidst this monstrous great mass of harmony, would have contributed a touch of celestial grace, nobility and tunefulness which, as it stands, one may search for in vain. As for the recitatives, perhaps either Porpora or Zingarelli would have done them better.

I am bound to confess that a Marchesi or a Pacchiarotti, a Tenducci or an Aprile would be tearing their hair in despair at having to sing such music, where as often as not the vocal line stops dead, stepping aside so that the orchestra may explain the composer's notions. To take an instance, in the opening Section, in the very first part of the very first tenor aria, the wretched singer is required to stop short after the words:

Let chaos end . . .

so that the orchestra may speak.

With these few reservations, however, it is surely possible to make out a case for Haydn. I would speak up boldly in front of his critics and ask: "What *is* it, then, that constitutes melodic beauty?" To which, if they be honest, they are bound to reply that in music, as in love, nothing is beautiful but what pleases. The Rotunda on the Isle of Capri, the *Apollo Belvedere*, the *Madonna alla Seggiola*, Correggio's *Night*—all these constitute true beauty, and will continue to do so wherever man has raised himself above the level of the savage. By contrast, if the works of Carissimi, of Pergolesi or of Durante are still extolled, it is only because it has become the tradition to do so; in reality, they no longer inspire pleasure to the same extent as formerly —and that, not only in the cold regions of the North, but even in that land of beauty which originally gave them birth. Their names are on everybody's lips; and yet, at every turn, I observe them set aside in preference for some rondo by Andreossi, some scene by Mayr, or some work by even less illustrious composers. I am myself heartily astonished at this revolution in taste, which in effect corresponds in nothing to my *own* manner of feeling, yet which I have observed to be a very real and indisputable fact in Italy. At all events, however, there is nothing more normal than to attribute "Beauty" to that which pleases. Where is that lover honest and true who has never felt the urge to address his mistress in the words of Metastasio:

> *Ma spesso ingiusto al vero,*
> *Condanno ogni altro aspetto;*
> *Tutto mi par difetto*
> *Fuor che la tua beltà?*

It may be that in the graphic arts, beauty is constant; for in arts such as these, the pleasures of the mind by far outweigh the pleasures of the senses. Here, Reason has always had a firmer hold; and every man of sensibility knows perfectly well, for instance, that Guido Reni's faces are more *beautiful* than those of Raphael, while these latter, on the other hand, are more *expressive*. Whereas in music, where at least two-thirds of the pleasure experienced is purely physical, the senses make their own decisions. And the fact is that the senses experience pleasure or pain at a given moment in time; but do not make comparisons. Any man of sensibility may observe from his own recollections, that the intensest moments of experience, whether of pleasure or of pain, leave no distinct memories behind them*.

Mortimer, trembling with uncertainty, was returning home after a long journey abroad; he adored Jenny, yet she had never vouchsafed an answer to his letters. Upon reaching London, he took a horse, and set out for her home in the country. As he reached the gates, he drew rein; she was walking in the park. Thither he ran, his heart beating fast; he came towards her, she held out her hand, blushing as she greeted him. Looking at her, he knew that she returned his love. Side by side, they strolled along the avenues of the park; Jenny's dress caught on the thorns of an acacia-bush. In the times that followed, Mortimer enjoyed Jenny's favours; but then Jenny was unfaithful to him. A score of times I have argued with him, that Jenny never loved him; and on each occasion he has cited, as proof of her love, the manner in which she received him on his return from the Continent; yet never could he give me a single, solitary detail. There is but one indication: whenever his glance falls on an acacia-bush, he begins to tremble; this, in actual fact, is the *only* distinct recollection he has kept of the most delicious moment in all his life.

The first seven or eight times that you listen to the duet from Cimarosa's *I Nemici generosi*:

> *Piaceri dell'anima**
> *Contenti soavi . . .*

the pleasure which you experience will grow. But once you have fully and completely assimilated it, then, at each new hearing, the delight that you take in it will diminish. Now if, in music, pleasure is the sole thermometer by which beauty may be registered, then this duet is destined to grow progressively less perfect, the more often you hear it. And when you have listened to it for the thirtieth time, should the performers now suddenly substitute the duet:

> *Cara, non dubitar . . .*

from *Il Matrimonio*—a duet that you have never heard before—the latter is sure to produce far greater pleasure than the other, by virtue of its very novelty. If now, after this experience, someone were to ask you, which of the two duets was the most beautiful, and if you were resolved to reply in all sincerity according to the promptings of your heart, I am persuaded that you would be in great perplexity.

Now let us suppose that you have appartments in the Palais de Fontainebleau. and that in one of the rooms there hangs the painting of

St. Cecilia, by Raphael. At a given moment, this canvas is returned to the Musée de Paris, and is replaced by Guido Reni's *Rape of Helen*. No doubt you will admire the delightful features of Hermione and Helen; yet for all that, were someone to enquire of you which you thought the more beautiful of these two works, then assuredly the sublime expression of St. Cecilia, lost in ecstasy at the sound of celestial music, while the instruments that she had been playing fall from her hands to the ground—assuredly this expression must tilt the scales in her favour, and you will award her the palm. Now, *why* is this expression so sublime? There are some three or four good reasons, all of which I perceive upon the tip of your tongue, ready to persuade me. Yet it is a rational process of analysis—and one, moreover, that it is easy enough to set down on paper—that convinces you that these three or four arguments of yours are sound; whereas I should deem it impossible to write as many as four lines—unless it were poetic prose, which does not count*—to demonstrate whether the duet *"Piaceri dell'anima"* is better or worse than the duet *"Cara, non dubitar . . ."* or than the duet

> *Crudel! perchè finora*
> *Farmi languir cosi?*

from Mozart's *Figaro*.

It is impossible to experience simultaneously the impact of two separate melodies; and the pleasure which either gives leaves too few traces in the memory for it to be possible to judge them at a distance.

I can perceive but one exception to this law. A man may chance to listen to the aria:

> *Fanciulla sventurata** . . .

from *I Nemici generosi*. Now this experience takes place in Venice, at the Teatro della Fenice; and beside him there sits a woman whom he adores to desperation, but who cannot return his passion. Time passes; he returns to France; and once again he hears this enchanting aria. A trembling seizes his limbs: *his* pleasure is for all eternity associated with these gentle notes; but in this case the aria has been transformed; it is to him what the little thorny acacia-bush was to Mortimer.

Once artists have achieved a certain degree of perfection, the works of the greatest among them have an equal claim upon our admiration; and such preference as we may give, now to one and now to another, depends entirely upon our own temperament, or upon whatever ephemeral mood may happen to possess us. One day, it may be Domenichino who delights me, causing me to give him preference over Guido Reni; on the day following, the celestial beauty of old Guido's heads will triumph, and I shall set his *Aurora*, that hangs in the Palazzo Rospigliosi, above the *Communion of St. Jerome*.

I have often heard it averred, in Italy, that in music an important element of Beauty is constituted by novelty. I am not alluding to the mere mechanics of the art: counterpoint is similar in this to mathematics, that any fool, given enough patience, may grow to be a much-respected scholar. In this domain, there is no *Ideal Beauty*; there is merely an Ideal Regularity, which can be demonstrated by rule-of-thumb. But as for that realm where genius dwells, the realm of melody—ah! melody knows no rules. Of all the arts, there is none so ill-provided with Rules to turn out beauty. All the better, then, for melody; and for us, too!

Genius has stalked on ahead; but the poor critics have managed to take note only of those paths that were trodden by the earliest pioneers; and their task has been confined to warning all those great men who came after that from such paths they must not stray. When Cimarosa was in Prague, conducting a performance of his aria:

Pria che spunti in ciel l'aurora . . .

he refused to listen to certain pedants who kept admonishing him: "Sir, your aria possesses Beauty, because you have followed such-and-such a Rule laid down by Pergolesi in such-and-such an opera; but it would have possessed more Beauty still, had you only respected such-and-such another rule, from which Galuppi ne'er departed."

Was not Domenichino all but persuaded by the other painters of his day that his *Martyrdom of St. Andrew* (which is in Rome) was not a thing of beauty?

I have a fine chance here to bore you with all the so-called Rules that have been invented in order to construct fine melodies; but I am of a generous nature, and I will resist the temptation to inflict on you the boredom from which *I* have suffered, listening to them.

The stronger the element of melody in any piece of music, the more that music is subject to the vicissitudes of all things human; the stronger the element of harmony, the more assured is the basis of its fortune. Those solemn ecclesiastical chants that flourished at the same time as

Pergolesi's wondrous *Stabat Mater* have not passed out of fashion nearly
so swiftly.

In any case, I may perhaps be arguing here utterly at random; for I
would confess to you that this same "old-fashioned" *Serva Padrona*
—provided only that it be sung in Italy—brings me more pleasure, and
above all pleasure of a more intimate quality—than all the operas of
our ultra-modern Signor Paër, all lumped together.

If it be true, however, that we have in fact identified that element of
music which suffers most severely at the hands of time, then Haydn
may expect to survive longer than any other composer. He invested all
his genius in *harmony*, that is to say, in the element that endures the
longest.

Let me quote you a passage from *The Spectator*, that is, from the
opinions of very reasonable persons:

"The Recitative Musick, in every Language, should be as different
as the Tone or Accent of each Language; for otherwise, what may
properly express a Passion in one Language, will not do it in another.
Every one who has been long in *Italy* knows very well, that the
Cadences in the *Recitativo* bear a remote affinity to the Tone of their
Voices in ordinary Conversation; or, to speak more properly, are only
the Accents of their Language made more Musical and Tuneful.

Thus the Notes of Interrogation, or Admiration, in the *Italian*
Musick . . . which resemble their Accents in Discourse on such Occasions, are not unlike the ordinary Tones of an *English* Voice when we
are angry; insomuch that I have often seen our Audiences extreamly
[sic] mistaken as to what has been doing upon the Stage, and expecting
to see the Hero knock down his Messenger, when he has been asking
him a question; or fancying that he quarrels with his Friend, when he
only bids him Good-morrow".

The Spectator, No. 29*.

Music, which calls into play the imagination of every listener, is more
intimately related than, say, painting, to the particular nervous system
of the individual. If it makes him happy, it is by causing his imagination
to offer him certain pictures that afford him pleasure. His heart, already inclined to susceptibility by the immediate and physical satisfaction that is produced by the suavity of the sounds, takes delight in these
visions of the imagination, and rejoices in the contentment that they
evoke in him with a degree of ardour that would be foreign to him at

any other moment. Now, it is evident that the character of these visions will vary in accordance with the different types of imagination that produce them. Is it possible to conceive any two beings more opposite one to the other, than a stout, tow-headed, well-fed, fresh-complexioned German who, from dawn to dusk, drinks nothing but beer and eats nothing but slices of *butterbrot*; and a slender, almost emaciated Italian, with his dark hair, his flashing eyes and his sallow skin, who subsists exclusively on coffee and an occasional austere and frugal meal? How the Devil could you expect that an identical experience should afford pleasure to two such dissimilar creatures, whose very languages are poles apart? For these two beings, there *cannot* be one single and unique concept of Beauty★. If our pedants should insist upon discerning some common Ideal of Beauty that both can agree upon, it will necessarily follow that the degree of pleasure afforded to either by any object that both admire equally will be very slight. They may both profess a certain admiration for the Funeral Games in Book V of the *Aeneid*; but if you should really wish to stir them deeply, you must offer each of them visions which correspond exactly to their radically differing temperaments. Take some poor little Prussian schoolboy from Königsberg, who for eleven months in the year never stops shivering with cold: how in Heaven's name do you imagine that you can induce *him* to respond to Virgil's *Eclogues*, with their visions of the bliss of lying in the shade, beside the dancing waters of a spring, deep in the heart of some cool grotto?

Viridi projectus in antro . . .

If you really wished to offer him a vision that would rejoice his heart, you would have done better to tell him tales of some cosy chamber well-heated by a roaring stove.

This instance may be applied to all the arts. In the eyes of an honest Flemish burgher who has never studied drawing, the shapes of Rubens' women are the finest in all the world. Yet we, who admire nothing so much as contours that are infinitely slender, we who are tempted to criticise even Raphael's women for being somewhat too full in the figure,[1] let us be chary of laughing too heartily at him. For it would

[1] See, for instance, that *Figure of a Woman*, after Raphael, engraved by ★★★, which is to be found in all the print-shops; or equally, *Adam and Eve*, taken from the loggias of the Vatican, and engraved by Müller in 1813.

6

appear that each and every single creature and, in consequence, each and every nation—were we to observe with sufficient attention—would be found to favour its own Ideal of Beauty, which would be the quintessence of all those things that afford it greatest pleasure, drawn from among objects of a similar nature.

Ideal Beauty, for a Parisian, is that which gives greatest pleasure to the majority of those who live in Paris. At the opera, for instance, the voice of M. Garat delights them a hundred times more than that of Signora Catalani. Not all, perhaps, would care to confess to this phenomenon of sensibility—though *why*, I am at a loss to understand. In the Arts, which can sway the fortunes of the State neither one way nor the other, what ill can come of this poor liberty?

A score of times a day you may observe evidence—it suffices but to have eyes to see—that the French nation has been transformed in its whole mode of being during the last thirty years. There is no creature on earth who bears less resemblance to what we were in 1780, than a young Frenchman of the year 1814. We used to be gay and sparkling; whereas these young gentlemen are almost English in their unsmiling austerity. There is more of gravity, more of Reason, less of charm. And since this younger generation, which, twenty years hence, will constitute the race in its entirety, has changed, there is wilder nonsense even than usual in the arguments of our poor pedants, when they insist that Art shall always remain the same.

"Let me confess," a young Colonel said to me recently, "that ever since the Retreat from Moscow, I for one seem to find that *Iphigénie en Aulide* is no longer quite so fine a tragedy as it used to be. That Achilles, now—is he not a trifle *foolish*, or a trifle weak? On the other hand, I feel myself drawn towards Shakespeare's *Macbeth*."

However, I am digressing not a little: the Reader will have discerned that I am not a young Frenchman of the year 1814. Let us return to our enquiry, which is to discover whether, in music, it is conceivable that *Ideal Beauty*, for a Dane, may be the same as for a Neapolitan.

All nations love the nightingale; this is because its song, echoing through the nights of that fine season towards the end of spring which, in every land, is felt to be the most enchanting moment of the year, is both a wondrous thing in itself, and at the same time the symbol of another wondrous thing. For all that I am from the North, the song of the Nightingale never fails to remind me of those homeward strolls through the city of Rome, towards two o'clock in the morning under the fine night-skies of summer, after some *conversazione*. As one passes along the deserted streets, one is all but deafened by the cascade of notes uttered by the nightingales that are bred in every household. The power possessed by this melody to evoke the joyous season of the year is the stronger, in that we cannot listen to the nightingale at will, and consequently, we do not dull the edge of our delight by indulging in the experience at unpropitious times, when our faculties are ill-disposed to appreciate it.

Haydn wrote his *Creation* to a German text, with which Italian melody is incompatible. How then, even had he so desired, could he have aped the tuneful graces of Sacchini? Moreover, being born in Germany, and knowing not only his own soul, but the soul of his compatriots also, it would appear that it was these latter whom, first and foremost, he sought to please. It is lawful to criticise a man when we perceive that he has failed to follow the path that leads to the goal which he has set himself; but is it not unreasonable to quarrel with him about the nature of the goal itself?

Be this as it may, there is one illustrious Italian *maestro* who has attempted the only criticism that is worthy both of himself and of Haydn: he has rewritten the entire score of the *Creation* from beginning to end; but his work will see the light only when he himself is dead and gone. This *maestro* is persuaded that Haydn is a pure genius in the realm of symphonic music. In all other aspects of his art, he judges him to be but a competent craftsman. For my own part I would aver that, when these two *Creations* shall finally see the light of day side by side, the German version will always triumph in Vienna, whereas in Naples the Italian will be crowned with laurels.

A FRAGMENT OF A LETTER
RECEIVED IN ANSWER TO THE PRECEDING

Montmorency*, 29 June 1809.

I was enchanted with your letter, my dear Edward; we share the same ideas, concealed under differing forms. In my opinion, it is in no way the fault of your great composers, if their entrancing melodies are not equally delightful to all men. The reason lies deep in the very nature of the noble art which confers the gift of immortality upon them. For in all matters that touch upon their respective means of pleasing the beholder, sculpture and music lie at opposite poles.

Observe that, whenever men wish to propose an illustration of *Ideal Beauty*, it is to sculpture that they invariably turn. Now, the Ideal of Beauty that is found in sculpture is of a universal application, for throughout the divers nations of the world, the human figure varies in form much less than does the human temperament, which is fashioned by the climate that it inhabits. A handsome young peasant from the neighbourhood of Copenhagen, and a young Neapolitan no less renowned for beauty, are by no means so dissimilar in outward appearance as they are in their passions and their characters. It is therefore much easier to prescribe a universal Ideal of absolute beauty for the art which reproduces these external forms, than it is to do so for those other arts which derive from the many and diverse affections of beings whose inner dissimilarity is so complete.

Over and above the absolute beauty of form and feature, much value attaches, in the graphic arts, to beauty of expression. But arts of this description never rival the art of poetry in the fidelity with which they reproduce the moral nature of man; and consequently, they have no propensity to cause displeasure to the Dane, for having afforded too much pleasure to the Neapolitan. By contrast, there are a thousand and one little incidents in daily life that afford admirable material for faithful copying in a novel or a comedy; and here, that which is felt to be entrancing in Naples will be judged indecent and insane in Copenhagen, while that which is sensed to be exquisite in Zealand will exude an icy chill on the banks of the Sebethus. The poet must needs make his choice and determine whether he will please the one or please the other. Not so Canova: *he* has need to trouble himself with no such awkward calculations. His Helen, his Paris will seem no less divine in Copenhagen than in Rome; the sole divergencies will be individual, each man rejoicing in the beauty of the figures, and admiring the artist who conceived them, to a degree proportionate with his own sensibility. Why should this be so? The answer is, that these delightful figures portray only the lesser of the heart's affections; if it lay in their power to incarnate the more violent passions, the point would soon be reached at which the sensibilities of South and North began to go their separate ways. How perplexing, therefore, the difficulties of the composer!— he who, of all artists, models his work most closely upon the affections of the human heart and who, as though this were not enough, can portray them only by setting in motion the imagination and the sensibility of each and every member of his audience, by inviting their co-operation, as it were, in the fulfilment of his art. How can you expect a man from the North to prove susceptible to Cimarosa's aria:

Come! io vengo per sposarti?

The despairing lover who sings these words cannot appear otherwise to him than as some poor, unhappy wretch escaped from Bedlam. In the reverse instance, however, *God save the King* might conceivably appear somewhat insipid in Naples. Do not be too downhearted, then, over the fate of your beloved Cimarosa; he may fall out of fashion; yet posterity, that holds the scales of justice, will surely recognise his genius, and on that score set him beside Raphael. Only remember that Raphael's genius is accessible to all the earth, or at all events to every land in Europe; whereas in music it is natural that every country should have its own special Raphael. Each of those worlds that sails through the heavens above our heads has its own sun, which for some neighbouring world is but a distant star, dimmer or brighter, depending on the distance. Thus Handel, who is the glorious sun of England, is but a star of the first magnitude in the land of a Mozart or a Haydn; while, descending southward towards the Equator, Handel is no more than a star of very

commonplace dimensions for those fortunate beings who dwell beside
the shores of Cape Posillipo.

Your
Louis

LETTER XX

Hallein*, 5 *June 1809.*

My dear Louis,

Two years after the *Creation*, Haydn, invigorated by success and
urged on by his friend van Swieten, composed another Oratorio, entitled *The Seasons*. Our descriptomaniac Baron had compiled the text
from Thomson's poem*. There is less profundity of feeling here than in
the *Creation*; but in such a subject, there was plenty of room for gaiety,
for the joys of grape-gathering, for the delights of profane love; and *The
Seasons* would be the finest thing the world has ever known in the field
of descriptive music, were it not for the existence of the earlier work.

The music is technically more complex and less spontaneous in
inspiration than in the *Creation*. There is, however, one aspect in which
it outdistances its elder sister, and that is in the quartets. At all events,
what is to be gained by carping at such music? "But it is not *Italian*
music," some protest. "Capital!" say I. I acknowledge that the Symphony is a genre designed to act on sluggish Teutonic constitutions; yet
we also may profit from it. Thus, in the Arts, it is by no means disad-
vantageous that each nation should claim distinct characteristic features.
The stock of pleasure at the disposal of the world as a whole is thereby
augmented. Our sources of delight include both the Neapolitan melodies of Paisiello and the German symphonies of Haydn. When shall we
be able to watch Talma on one day giving us an *Andromaque* and on
the next showing us the wretched Macbeth dragged down into the
morass of crime by the ambitions of his wife? For you must realise that

the so-called Macbeths, Hamlets, etc., that have been given us by Monsieur Ducis*, while they are doubtless excellent plays in their own way, bear about as much resemblance to the English dramatist's originals as they do to Lope de Vega. In the matter of romantic drama, I feel that we have attained a point identical with that which we had reached some half a century ago in relation to Italian music. There will be a mighty outcry; pamphlets will be written, and satires; perhaps there may even be a few stout blows delivered with canes at a moment when the public, becalmed in some deep political doldrums, will imagine itself competent to hold opinions in literature. But at all events, this same public, bored finally to exasperation by dull latter-day disciples of the great Racine, will finally insist on seeing *Hamlet* and *Othello*. The comparison is valid, save at one particular point; for Shakespeare's plays will deliver a death-blow neither to *Phèdre* nor to *Cinna*, while Molière will remain without a rival, for the simple reason that he is unique.

The text of *The Seasons* is poor stuff. As for the music, you must imagine a gallery full of pictures, all different in style, in subject and in colouring. This gallery is divided into four main rooms; and in the centre of each of these there hangs one huge and dominant painting.

The themes of these four main paintings are as follows: for the first snow and the north wind; the cold and all its horrors.

For the second, summer, including a thunderstorm. For the third, autumn, with hunting; finally, winter, and an evening with the villagers.

The first thing that strikes one is that no one who lived beneath more clement skies would have dreamed of including snow and all the horrors of winter in his portrayal of the spring. In my personal opinion, it constitutes a singularly depressing opening. However, in the opinion of those who favour this style of thing, all these uncouth noises form an admirable introduction to the delights which are to follow later.

I have no intention, my dear friend, of taking you step by step through every bar of *The Seasons*.

In his attempt to portray the sun in high summer, Haydn found himself confronted with his own first sunrise in the *Creation*: and this art, which some people insist against all the odds on labelling "descriptive", is in fact so vague, so positively anti-descriptive, that despite the unbelievable amount of effort devoted to the problem by the greatest orchestral writer in the world, he did not wholly avoid the trap of repetitiveness. The exhaustion, the utter prostration of all that lives and breathes, even down to the plants, during the blazing heat of a summer's day, is excellently rendered. This description, in which art adheres closely to nature, fades away into universal silence. This silence is then shattered by the sudden thunderclap that heralds the onset of the storm. Here, Haydn is in his element: a world of fiery flashes, shouting, reverberation and terror. It is a picture that might have been conceived by Michelangelo. However, the storm passes over, the clouds disperse, the sun comes out once more, the raindrops that weigh down the leaves of the trees sparkle in the forest, the storm is followed by a wonderful evening, night comes at length, and all sounds are hushed; only the moaning of some nocturnal bird, and the echo of a distant church-bell,

> *Che paia il giorno pianger che si more,*
>
> Dante, *Purgatorio*, Canto VIII, l.6.

come now and then to disturb the universal silence.

In this section, the art of "physical imitation" is carried about as far as it conceivably can be. Yet this quiet landscape forms a somewhat undramatic ending to the summer, after the terrifying passage of the storm.[1]

---

[1] I beg the Reader to allow me a repetition. I would like to quote a letter, the original of which I posted off to my friend at the same time as the one which is before you. It was written in French by a charming Canoness of Brunswick, whose recent death we now lament.

The passage that I wish to quote formed the conclusion of a letter about Werther, who as everyone knows, was born in Brunswick and was the son of Monsieur l'abbé de Jérusalem.* The Canoness, at my request, was analysing in precise detail the kind of taste in music that Werther had.

". . . music being the art that is the most apt in portraying nuances, the art whose descriptions pursue the hidden stirrings of the soul into its furthest recesses, I believe that it is possible to draw a distinction between sensibility in the manner of Mozart, and sensibility after the fashion of Cimarosa.

"Certain faces, such as that of Wilhelmine von M***, or that of the Angel in the painting by Parmigiano that hangs in my bedroom [a], appear to me to be the outward and visible signs of beings whose strength is overwhelmed by their sensibility, and who, in their instants of emotion, actually *become that emotion personified*. There is no room in them for anything else: courage, concern for their reputation, everything is not merely overwhelmed, but entirely banished. To such a race, as I believe, belongs that adorable *Cherub* to whom I have just alluded, were he to be discovered, like his namesake, reclining at the feet of a godmother whom he worships, and singing

Voi che sapete . . .

(a) It was a copy of the *Madonna al lungo collo*, which may be seen in the *Musée de Paris*. The Angel in question is the one on the Virgin's right, looking at the spectator.

The stag-hunt with which the "Autumn" section begins is a most appropriate subject for music. Everyone will recall the Overture to *Le jeune Henri*.

The grape-gathering, with the topers singing away on one side of the picture, while all the young folk of the village are busy dancing on the other, forms a delightful composition. The drinking-song is interwoven with the tune of a traditional Austrian folk-dance, arranged as a fugue. The impression created by this lively, bustling dance is very

"It seems to me that the peoples of the North are the faithful liege-subjects of such music, 'which is their Queen'.*

"When you have come to know Germany better, and when you have made the acquaintance of two or three of those unhappy maidens who, every year in this land of ours, die of love—I forbid you to laugh, my satirical French *monsieur*!—*then* you will perceive the nature of the power that music wields over our souls. Observe, I pray you, of a Sunday evening, in the *Hollandts Garten*,* amid those romantic wildernesses where all the young folk of these Northern cities go strolling together on holidays, towards nightfall; observe those pairs of lovers, partaking of coffee at their parents' side, whilst troupes of musicians out of Bohemia play on their horns those waltzes of theirs, the slow and moving music of their native land; observe their gaze, as it steadies in each others' eyes: observe them holding hands over the little table, without embarrassment beneath their mother's gaze, since they are here what is called *Verlobte* . . . and now? The boy is carried off without warning by conscription: his *Verlobte* is not plunged headlong into wild despair, yet she is sad; all night long, she reads romances; gradually, her chest grows weaker; she pines away and dies, nor can the finest doctors in the land discover any cure for *that* particular malady. Yet, outwardly, there is nothing to be seen. It was but two weeks since, that you saw her at her mother's house; she served you tea; you thought her sad, but nothing more. Yet today, when you ask for news of her, 'Poor Fraülein ***', you will be told, 'she died of a broken heart.' Here in Germany, such a reply is nothing out of the ordinary. 'And her *Verlobte*, what of him?' 'He is in the army, but we have no further news of him.'

"It is hearts such as these that can be touched by Handel and Mozart, by Boccherini and Benda: it is their secret.

"Whereas your raven-haired women from the South, with all their unflagging energy—women such as these are destined to worship the music of Cimarosa. They would stab themselves for a lover who is alive, but not one would allow herself to pine away and die of regret for an unfaithful swain.

"The arias that Cimarosa, and indeed all Neapolitan composers, give to their women reveal a strain of forcefulness even in their most impassioned moments. Take *I Nemici generosi*, which we saw in Dresden some two years ago—our Mozart would have woven a web of celestial tenderness about the words:

Non son villana, ma son dama . . .

Cimarosa has turned this avowal of love into a sprightly little air, because that was what the dramatic situation demanded; yet no German maiden could have uttered those words without tears in her eyes . . ."

6*

amusing, especially when it is performed in the land of its origin. It is frequently played in Hungary, during the wine-harvest. This, I believe, is the only occasion on which Haydn, in a direct imitation of nature, exploited his recollections of the region where he was born as the basis of a successful musical composition.

The critics accused *The Seasons* of being still more barren of melody than the *Creation*, maintaining that it was "a piece for orchestra, with vocal accompaniment"*. The composer, they said, was growing old. He was further charged—not without some absurdity, in my opinion —with having adulterated a serious subject with a certain admixture of levity. Why serious? Because the composition as a whole was entitled *Oratorio*. It may be that the title is ill-chosen; yet surely, when a piece of symphonic music has nothing to say to the emotions, it is all the better for an occasional sparkle of gaiety. Rather better justified are the remarks of those chilly mortals who accuse Haydn of having put two winters into a single year.

The most penetrating criticism that has been made of this work was that which was formulated by Haydn himself, and which he addressed to me when I went to offer him a report on the performance that had just been given at the Palais Schwarzenberg. The applause had been unanimous. I hurried away from the concert-hall in order to go and congratulate the composer*. But scarcely had I opened my mouth to speak, when Haydn, fair-minded as always, prevented me: "I am delighted that my music should have pleased the public; but from you, I will accept no compliments. I am persuaded that you are yourself perfectly well aware that *The Seasons* is not the *Creation*; and I will tell you the reason for it. In the *Creation*, the *dramatis personae* were Angels; here, they are Peasants." This criticism is most apt, in relation to a man whose genius lies rather in the direction of sublime grandeur than in that of human tenderness.

The text of *The Seasons*, which barely rises above the commonplace even in the original version, has been translated into several languages with monotonous banality. The music has been variously arranged for quartets and quintets, and (much more so than that of the *Creation*) has become popular for use at intimate concerts given by amateur groups. Since the melodic element, such as it is, is to be found mainly in the orchestral writing, most of it remains intact even when the vocal parts are eliminated altogether. But in any case, I am probably a bad judge of *The Seasons*. I have heard it performed only once, and even on that occasion I was only half-listening.

I was involved in an argument with a Venetian seated beside me, concerning the degree of melodiousness that existed in music towards the middle years of the seventeenth century. I was maintaining that melody was almost unknown at that period and that music was, in all likelihood, little more than a series of agreeable noises.

At these words, my companion sat up in his seat as though he had been stung, and began to tell me the story of one of his compatriots, the singer Alessandro Stradella*, who flourished towards the year 1650. He was received by the most distinguished families in Venice, and the highest-born ladies in the city would quarrel over the privilege of taking lessons from him. It was in this manner that he first met Hortensia, a lady of Roman birth who was courted by a noble Venetian. Stradella fell in love with her; nor was he hard-pressed to triumph over his rival. He carried off Hortensia and took her with him to Rome, where they gave themselves out to be man and wife. The Venetian suitor, wild with fury, promptly hired a pair of assassins and set them on their traces; this couple of scoundrels, having vainly scoured a number of Italian cities for their prey, ran them to earth at last, and arrived in Rome one evening, just as Stradella was about to sing in an Oratorio in the fine church of San Giovanni Laterano. The assassins resolved to carry out their task while the congregation was leaving the church; and so they entered in, partly to keep an eye upon one at least of their intended victims, partly to discover whether Hortensia might not also be among the crowded audience.

Scarcely had they been listening for more than a few minutes to the wondrous voice of Stradella, when they began to feel their bowels melted with compassion. Stricken with horror, they began to shed tears of remorse; and by the end, they had no further thought but to rescue those very lovers whose death they had sworn to encompass. They waited for Stradella at the church-door; and at length they observed him leaving together with Hortensia. Going up to him, they thanked him for the pleasure he had just given them, and confessed that he literally owed his life to the impression that his voice had made upon them. They then explained the dreadful aim of their mission, and advised him to escape from Rome without an hour's delay, so that they might convince the jealous Venetian that they had arrived too late.

Stradella and Hortensia were not slow to act upon this advice, and set forth for Turin. The Venetian nobleman for his part, having received the report submitted by his agents, was fired to a still higher pitch of fury. He made his way to Rome and there took counsel with Hortensia's own father. He succeeded in convincing the old man that nothing could wash away the stains of his dishonour, save the blood of his daughter and her seducer. This flinty-hearted progenitor, accompanied by two hired assassins, set out for Turin, having first taken care to supply himself with several letters of introduction to the Marquis de Villars, who was at that time French Ambassador to the Court of Savoy.

Meanwhile, the Duchess-Regent of Savoy, having learned of the adventure that had attended the two lovers in Rome, was resolved to rescue them. She secured Hortensia's retreat into a convent, while Stradella received the title of First Musician to the Royal Household, and thus was permitted to live actually within the precincts of the Royal Palace. These precautions seemed adequate, and so for several months the lovers basked in the warmth of tranquillity and perfect happiness, when one evening Stradella, who was taking the air upon the ramparts of the city, was set upon by three armed men who left him for dead with a stab wound in the chest. The assailants proved to have been Hortensia's father together with his two hired assassins, who all retreated immediately after the crime to seek asylum in the Residence of the French Ambassador. M. de Villars, who wished neither to protect them from the consequences of a murder which was the nine-days' wonder throughout all Turin, nor to hand them over to justice after his own Residence had been invoked as a sanctuary, arranged for them to escape a few days later.

Against all probability, however, Stradella recovered from his wound; and thus for a second time the Venetian saw all his plans frustrated. Nevertheless, he still continued to cherish his schemes for vengeance. Now, however, with a prudence learnt from failure, he determined to take measures that bore the mark of certainty upon them, and for the moment he was satisfied to set a horde of spies to watch over Hortensia and her lover. In this manner, a year went by; at the end of which time, the Duchess of Savoy, who meanwhile had grown ever more deeply interested in their fate, resolved to legitimise their union, and to crown it with the consecration of marriage. After the ceremony was over, Hortensia, who was bored with convent life, had a wish to see the port of Genoa. Thither Stradella took her; and the following morning, both were found dead in bed—stabbed.

This melancholy adventure took place, so it is averred, in the year 1670. Stradella was a poet and a composer, besides being the greatest singer of his century.

I replied to my acquaintance, Stradella's fellow-countryman, that the very quality of harmonious sound, even when bereft of all semblance of melody, affords a pleasure that is anything but illusory, even to men whose souls are still the most profoundly steeped in savagery. In the year 1637, when Murad IV, after the storming of Baghdad, ordered the massacre of every living being within its walls, one solitary Persian found courage enough to raise his voice. He cried out, begging that he might be brought into the presence of the Emperor, since he had secrets of the utmost importance to impart to him before he died.

When he was flung down at the feet of the Emperor, Skackali (for such was the Persian's name) pressed his face against the earth, exclaiming: "Sire, let me perish, but let there not perish with me an art which is worth as much as all thine Empire; first hear me sing, and then ordain my death." Murad, with a sign, gave his consent; from beneath his robes Skackali drew forth a little harp and then and there began to improvise a kind of romance upon the ruin of Baghdad. Murad, grim tyrant that he was, and despite the shame that every Turk experiences at betraying the least sign of emotion, found the tears coursing down his cheeks, and ordered the massacre to cease. Skackali, laden with riches, followed him to Constantinople; and there he introduced the music of Persia, in which no European ear has ever succeeded in detecting the first faint trace of melody.

It is my theory, that Haydn is the Tintoretto of music. In much the same fashion as the Venetian painter, he combines the forcefulness of a Michelangelo with the impassioned ardour, the originality and the abundance of his own inventiveness; and the whole is decked out with a wealth of colour which transforms the least of details into a thing of delight. I would mention, however, that this Tintoretto from Eisenstadt delved deeper into the recesses of his art than did the Tintoretto of Venice; above all, he understood the secret of working *slowly*.

I feel myself growing obsessed with a mania for comparisons★. I will entrust you with my little collection, on condition that you promise not to laugh too heartily. I am of the opinion, then, that

in music,	Pergolesi ⎫ Cimarosa ⎭	correspond to	*Raphael* in painting
	Paisiello	corresponds to	*Guido Reni*
	Durante		*Leonardo da Vinci*
	Hasse		*Rubens*
	Handel		*Michelangelo*
	Galuppi		*Bassano*
	Jommelli		*Lodovico Carracci*
	Gluck		*Caravaggio*
	Piccinni		*Titian*
	Sacchini		*Correggio*
	Vinci		*Fra Bartolomeo*
	Anfossi		*Albano*
	Zingarelli		*Guercino*
	Mayr		*Carlo Maratta*
	Mozart		*Domenichino*

The least imperfect of these correspondences is that of Paisiello with Guido Reni. As for Mozart, Domenichino would have needed a temperament still more profoundly steeped in melancholy for the resemblance to be perfect.

Domenichino possessed the gift of expressiveness; yet the expressions he portrayed rarely transcend the categories of innocence, shyness and respect.[1] Mozart, on the other hand, portrayed the most impassioned and the most sensitive tenderness in the arias:

> *Vedrò, mentr'io sospiro,*
> *felice un servo mio?*

sung by Count Almaviva;

> *Non so più cosa son, cosa faccio . . .*

sung by Cherubino;

---

[1] See his *Two innocent and shy girls*; in this painting it may be observed that gaiety was likewise a quality in which Domenichino was deficient. The Angels, whose faces should be radiant with the Mysteries of Joy, look decidedly unhappy. See also the *Young Woman led before the Tribunal of Alexander*.

> *Dove sono i bei momenti*
> *di dolcezza e di piacer?*

sung by the Countess Almaviva; and in

> *Là ci darem la mano,*
> *la mi dirai di sì . . .*

from *Don Giovanni*; while he portrayed the most exquisite gracefulness in the arias:

> *La mia Dorabella capace non è;*
> *fedel quanto bella il ciel la fe' . . .*

from *Così fan tutte*; and in

> *Giovinette, che fate all'amore,*
> *non lasciate che passi l'età . . .*

again from *Don Giovanni*.

The same beauty and radiance that characterise the features of Raphael's beings, are to be met with again in the melodies of Cimarosa.

One is persuaded that all those beings whom Cimarosa has portrayed in the hour of their affliction are, in normal circumstances, radiant. Take Carolina, for instance, in *Il Matrimonio segreto*. By contrast, the women in Mozart's world bear an affinity with those maidens whom we meet in Ossian, with their fine fair hair and their blue eyes so often brimming with tears. It may be that they are less beautiful than the flashing womanhood of Italy; yet they are far more deeply moving.

Listen to the part of the Countess in *Le Nozze di Figaro*, as sung by Signora Barilli; and now imagine the same part *acted*, portrayed by some actress as passionate as Signora Strinasacchi and as beautiful as Mademoiselle Mars—the being who emerged, it would seem, in Shakespeare's words:

> *. . . like patience on a monument,*
> *Smiling at grief*★.

On days when the earth seems full of happiness, your choice would lie with Cimarosa; but in hours of melancholy, your preference would go to Mozart.

I might have extended my list by including the "mannerist" painters, setting beside them the names of Grétry and of almost all the younger German and Italian composers. Such notions, however, are likely to prove so wholly personal and idiosyncratic, that to you they would merely seem bizarre.

Baron van Swieten had plans for persuading Haydn to write yet a third descriptive Oratorio, and in this he would surely have succeeded, had death not intervened to stop him. And I too will draw to a close, now that we have reached the end of our journey through all that mass of music created by our hero.

Who would have guessed, on that day when I first took up my pen to address you upon the subject of Haydn, some fifteen months ago, that my gossip would run on so far and so fast?

You have been gracious enough not to allow these letters to bore you; and the writing of them has afforded me, on two or three occasions in each week, a most welcome distraction. Keep them. If ever I should visit Paris, I might perchance find some satisfaction in reading them once more.

Adieu.

LETTER XXI

Salzburg, 8 June 1809.

Haydn's musical career came to an end with *The Seasons*. The labour of its composition, together with advancing years, had weakened him. "I am finished," he confided to me a short while after completing this last Oratorio, "my head is no longer what it was; in the old days, ideas came tumbling about me without my ever needing to run after them; but now it is *I* who have to go and seek them out—and I was never one for paying calls at other peoples' houses."

In spite of this, he contrived to compose a small number of quartets; however, it remained beyond his powers to finish that which bears the number 84★, although he struggled with it for three years on end, almost without respite. In his declining years, he kept himself busy arranging a series of ancient Scottish airs. A London bookseller paid him two guineas apiece for these arrangements★, and he completed nearly three hundred of them; but in 1805 he discontinued this work also, on the orders of his doctor. Life was gradually ebbing away from him; nowadays, whenever he sat down to the piano, he was overcome with fits of dizziness.

From this time onwards, furthermore, he stayed at home in Gumpendorf, never once setting foot outside his garden. When he wished to remind his friends of his existence, he would send them a little visiting-card of his own devising. The words ran as follows:

All my strength has left me; old and weak am I.

The musical setting of these words peters out in the middle of the period, and the phrase remains unfinished: a fitting symbol of the composer's declining powers.

Molto adagio

Hin   is al-le mei-ne   Kraft

alt   und Schwach bin ich

Joseph Haydn.

At this very time when I am writing to you, the great man—or rather, that sorry part of him that still remains with us here below—is wholly obsessed by two exclusive ideas: fear of ill-health and fear of poverty. Ever and anon he will swallow a few drops of Tokay; and he knows no greater pleasure than an occasional gift of game which may diminish the expenses of his modest table.

Visits from his friends★ rekindle a faint spark of life in him; and once in a while, he may grasp an idea, and even follow it up a little way. For instance, in the year 1805, the announcement of his death appeared in the Parisian press; and since he was an honorary member of the *Institut de France*, that illustrious company, which is wholly lacking in cautious Teutonic circumspection, ordered a Mass to be celebrated in honour of his memory. This notion caused Haydn vast amusement. "Had the Gentlemen only taken the trouble to let me know!" he kept repeating, "I would have gone there myself, and with my own hands I would have conducted that wonderful Mozart Mass that they performed in my honour." In spite of his joking, however, in his heart of hearts his gratitude was unbounded.

Shortly after this episode, Mozart's widow and son resolved to celebrate Haydn's birthday by giving a concert in the lovely little Theater auf der Wieden. The programme included a cantata, specially written by the younger Mozart in honour of his father's immortal rival. To understand the impression produced by this concert, one needs to appreciate the infinite generosity that reigns in German hearts. I would be prepared to wager that, during the whole three hours that the performance lasted, not a single joke, good or bad, was made in any corner of the hall.

This occasion served as a reminder to the Viennese musical public of the loss that it had already sustained, and of the further loss that it might expect to sustain in the near future.

Arrangements were made for a performance of the *Creation*, to be sung in Carpani's Italian version. An orchestra of 160 players was gathered together in the mansion of His Highness Prince Lobkowitz.

This orchestra was reinforced by three renowned soloists: Frau Fischer, from Berlin*, Herr Weinmüller and Signor Radichi. The audience contained well over fifteen hundred persons. The feeble old man, in spite of his exhaustion, insisted on having a farewell glimpse of this public, for whose delight he had so diligently laboured. He was carried in in an armchair; and at that instant, every heart that was contained within the walls of that noble auditorium was deeply moved. The Princess Esterházy, together with Haydn's friend Magdalena von Kurzböck, went forward to meet him. More impressively even than the fanfare of the orchestra, the common emotion of the audience heralded his coming. He was placed in the centre of three rows of seats, all reserved, either for his personal friends, or else for the highest and

most illustrious society of Vienna at the time. Salieri, who was conducting, came over to Haydn before the Overture, and asked for his instruc-
tions. The two men embraced; Salieri took his leave, ran across to his
stand and then, in an atmosphere of intensest emotion, the orchestra
struck up. The music itself is deeply religious in inspiration; and I leave
you to imagine how sublime it appeared to this audience already moved
to tears by the sight of a noble genius hovering on the very threshold of
death. Surrounded by the Illustrious Great, by his friends, by all manner
of artists, by delightful women all with their gaze fixed upon him, and
listening to the praise of God sounding forth in a voice that he himself
had created, Haydn bade a brave farewell to the world and to life itself.

The *cavaliere* Capellini, a doctor of the highest distinction, chanced to
observe that Haydn's legs were insufficiently covered. He had but to
whisper a word to his neighbours, and all the loveliest shawls quitted the
delightful feminine shoulders that they had hitherto been draping, and
flew to bestow their warmth upon the dearly loved old man.

Haydn, who had been reduced to tears several times by the manifesta-
tion of so much glory and of so much love, began to feel exhausted as
the First Part drew to a close. His chair was carried out; but just as he
was about to leave the hall, he bade the porters stop, bowed his head to
the audience in an acknowledgement of gratitude and then, with a
gesture that was characteristically Germanic, turned his face towards the
orchestra, raised both his arms towards Heaven and, his eyes all shining
with tears, invoked a blessing upon these lifelong friends and companions in his labours.

LETTER XXII

Vienna, 22 August 1809.

Returning once more to the Austrian capital, the news that I bring
you, my dear Friend, is that the mere mortal remnant of Haydn has

now followed his spirit, and left us. This splendid genius now exists no more, save in our memories. I have more than once reminded you that, even before he entered upon his eight-and-seventieth year, which was destined to be his last, he was exceedingly weak. Whenever he took a step towards his piano, fits of dizziness would overtake him, while his fingers would fall from the keys and light instead upon his rosary—his final consolation.

War flared up between Austria and France. This news rekindled a spark of life in Haydn, and sapped the remaining ounces of his strength.

At every instant, he would be enquiring after news; he would sit down at his piano and, with the tiny thread of voice remaining to him, would sing

*Gott erhalte Franz den Kaiser!**

The French armies advanced as though with seven-league boots. Finally, on the night of 10 May, they reached Schönbrunn, scarce half a league from Haydn's little garden; and the following morning, they fired some fifteen hundred cannon-shots not two hundred paces from his house, in order to reduce Vienna, the city that he had loved so dearly. In his imagination, the old man could see it destroyed utterly by fire and steel. Suddenly, four shells burst close beside his house. His two servants, livid with terror, ran to him for protection; life seemed to flow back into his veins; he raised himself out of his deep chair and, with a proud gesture, exclaimed aloud: "Why all this terror? Know that, where Haydn is, disaster cannot strike!" A convulsive shudder cut short the flow of words, and he was carried into bed. On 26 May his strength began perceptibly to ebb. None the less, having ordered his servants to carry him to his piano, he sat down and thrice in succession in a voice as loud as his state would permit him, sang out:

Gott erhalte Franz den Kaiser!

This was his swan-song. Still seated there at the piano, he fell into a kind of coma, and on 31 May, in the early hours of the morning, life finally departed from him. He had lived for seventy-eight years and two months.

At the beginning of the French occupation of Vienna, Frau von Kurzböck had begged him to allow her to have him carried to her house, which was safe in the centre of the town; he thanked her, but showed no desire to leave his beloved retreat.

Haydn was buried at Gumpendorf, like the obscure and unknown peasant that he was. It is rumoured, however, that Prince Esterházy intends to build a monumental tomb in his memory*.

A few weeks after his death, a memorial performance was given at the *Schottenkirche* of Mozart's *Requiem*. On the occasion of this ceremony, I decided to risk a visit into the city*. I called upon a number of generals and civil administrators attached to the French army, and one and all seemed touched by the loss that had been sustained by the Arts. In this, I recognised the true nature of my fellow-countrymen. I spoke with several of these people, and among others with a most courteous gentleman* who, on that particular day, was wearing the uniform of the *Institut de France*—a costume which struck me as the height of elegance.

A similar homage was paid to Haydn's memory, both in Breslau and in Paris, at the Conservatoire. In Paris, the ceremony included a Hymn, specially composed by Cherubini. The text of this work is, as usual, drearily uninspired; but the music is worthy of the great man whom it is designed to honour.

From first to last, Haydn had been profoundly religious. One might almost say, without wishing to make a sermon of it, that his genius received additional inspiration from the sincerity of the faith which he accorded to the Truths of Christian teaching. Each of his scores is headed:

In nomine Domini,

or else:

Soli Deo gloria;

and each and every one concludes with the words:

Laus deo.

Whenever, in the heat of composition, he felt his imagination drying up, or sensed that some insurmountable difficulty was holding him back, he would quit his piano, take up his rosary, and begin to tell his beads. He would maintain that this means had never once failed him. "When I was working on the *Creation*", he used to tell me, "I felt so impregnated with the Divine certainty, that before sitting down to the piano, I would quietly and confidently pray to God to grant me the talent that was needful to praise Him worthily."

Haydn made his will in favour of a blacksmith who, after deduction of the twelve thousand florins that he left to his two faithful domestics, inherited some eight-and-thirty thousand florins in paper money. Haydn's manuscripts were put up to auction, and were bought by Prince Esterházy.

Prince Liechtenstein desired to possess the elderly parrot* that had belonged to our composer. About this bird, the most wondrous of tales were told: in its youth, it was asserted, it used to sing, and could talk in several languages. If popular rumour were to be credited, it had been its master's pupil. The blank look of astonishment that appeared on the blacksmith's face, when he saw the wretched parrot knocked down for fourteen hundred florins, caused a sudden surge of laughter to seize upon all those who were present at the sale. I do not know who bought his watch. Admiral Nelson, passing through Vienna on one occasion*, had paid him a visit and had begged him, as a favour, for one of the quill-pens with which he wrote his music; in exchange, he prayed him to accept the watch that he had worn about his person through the heat of so many battles.

Haydn had composed his own epitaph:

Veni, scripsi, vixi.

He leaves no posterity.

Cherubini*, Pleyel, Neukomm and Weigl may be considered as his pupils.[1]

Haydn suffered from the same weakness as the celebrated Austrian Minister, Prince von Kaunitz: he could never bear to be painted as an old man. In the year 1800 he flew into a temper with a painter who had done his portrait as he then appeared, that is to say, in the sixty-eighth year of his age. "If I was Haydn when I was forty," he stormed at the

---

[1] There are several biographies of Haydn in existence. I am persuaded—as is only right and proper—that mine is the most accurate. I will spare the Reader any elaboration of the many and excellent reasons upon which this certainty is based. None the less, should some learned scholar see fit to cast doubt upon the facts that I have here set down, I am prepared to come to the defence of their exactitude. As for my manner of *experiencing* music—in this, every man has his own, peculiar to himself; or else has none at all. Besides which, there is perhaps no single sentence in all this volume which has not been translated from some foreign work*. There is little to feed the Author's vanity in a few scattered lines of

offender, "why do you desire to pass on to posterity a Haydn who is sixty-eight? Neither you nor I have anything to gain by this exchange!" Such were the life and death of this illustrious man.

Why did all those Frenchmen renowned in the field of *Belles-Lettres* proper—La Fontaine, Corneille, Racine, Molière, Bossuet—arrange to meet together on this earth in the year 1660 or thereabouts?

Why did all the greatest painters appear in the world simultaneously, towards the year 1510? And why, ever since those fortunate epochs, has nature shown herself so parsimonious? These are weighty questions, to which, every decade or so, the public chooses to proffer a different answer, for none has ever yet been discovered that is satisfactory.

One thing is certain: once these epochs have vanished into dust, then there remains precisely nothing. Voltaire possesses a multitude of different talents; Montesquieu employs an inexhaustible store of wit to instruct us in the most useful of sciences; Buffon has described Nature in splendid and reverberating periods. Rousseau, the greatest of them all in literature, is unrivalled among French writers for the perfection of his prose. And yet, considered as "Men of Letters"—that is, as men whose destiny is to give pleasure with the printed word—how many fathoms deep do they not lie, these Great Ones, beneath a La Fontaine, beneath a Pierre Corneille!

The same phenomenon may be observed in painting, if you except that fortunate irruption which, a century after Raphael and Correggio, endowed the world with Guido Reni, the brothers Carracci and Domenichino.

Is music destined to share a similar fate? All things tend to suggest that this is so. Cimarosa, Mozart and Haydn are all recently gone from

meditation upon the general character of Art. This century of ours has a most notable talent for teaching others how to do their job. In happier days, one set about one's tasks oneself; and it must be acknowledged that this last was a directer method of proving that one understood the True Principles:

Optimus quisque facere, quàm dicere, sua ab aliis benefacta laudari, quàm ipse aliorum narrare malebat.

Sallust, *Catilina*

The Author has striven to the best of his ability for the elimination of those countless repetitions which swarmed in the original letters. These letters were addressed to a man whose sensibility predestined him to be a most excellent connoisseur of art, but who had only recently perceived that he had a fondness for music.

among us. And none appears to bring us consolation. "Why so?" you may well ask. And here is my reply: because those artists who are alive today *imitate* those who went before them; whereas they themselves imitated no one. Once they had mastered the pure mechanics of their art, each created only that which afforded pleasure to his own soul. They wrote for themselves, and for those whose temperaments were similar to their own.

A Pergolesi, a Sacchini were driven to write by the imperious tumult of their own passions; whereas today the most distinguished artists work in a light and frivolous vein. What could be more amusing than Fioravanti's *Cantatrici villane*? Compare it with *Il Matrimonio segreto*. *Il Matrimonio* yields a pleasure that is beyond description, when one is in a certain mood; *Le Cantatrici* is invariably entertaining. I would beg you to recall those performances that used to be given at the Tuileries in 1810. Everyone preferred *Le Cantatrici* to any other opera on the Italian repertoire, because to derive amusement from the antics of those gay ladies of Frascati, the audience must be endowed with the least possible dose of sensibility that is required for listening to music at all; and a precisely similar degree of insensibility was exactly what the music had to offer. To be dressed up in full gala uniform; to attend the theatre amid a crowd of courtiers all eaten up with the cares and frets of ambition—there can assuredly be in all the world no circumstances less propitious to a mood for music.

In Art, and further, I believe, in every human action where originality has some part to play, either one is oneself, or one is nothing. We must surmise, therefore, that those composers who work in the light and frivolous vein are persuaded that this vein is indeed the richest of all; and consequently, that they are beings whose souls are ignorant of all true warmth and for whom passion is a word empty of meaning. Yet what are the Arts, when there is no true passion in the artist's heart?

In Rome, in the wake of the angelic purity of Virgil came the intellectual acrobatics of Seneca. We too, in Paris, have our Senecas, who, though they are never weary of extolling the fine simplicity and spontaneity of Fénelon and of the "Golden Age" of Louis XIV, contrive in practice to avoid these virtues like the plague, preferring for themselves a style that is baroque and artificial. In similar fashion, Sacchini and Cimarosa are rapidly vanishing from the Italian stage and their place is stolen by composers who, all fretful with impatience to make their mark, go tumbling headlong into the abyss of erudition, extravagance and sheer nonsensicality, and are more concerned to startle the intellect than to stir up the emotions. The virtuosity and the tediousness of the *concerto* is spreading everywhere, like an infection. And worst of all is this: once you acquire the habit of food that has been cooked with every spice in India, then the soft sweet perfume of the peach seems merely insipid.

It is averred that, in Paris, a man who desires to preserve the purity of his taste in literature will never model his style upon any author, save those who appeared before the end of the seventeenth century, and perhaps the four great writers of the century that followed. Should he so much as glance at books published since that time, should he deign to leaf through the great mass of those that issue from the presses every day, it is exclusively for the *facts* they may contain:

Historia, quoquo modo scripta, placet.

But at all costs he will guard himself against the contagion of their style.

Perhaps our young composers should act in similar fashion. For if not, what protection is possible against this malady of *generalised Senecitis*, that is undermining all the Arts, and to which I know of no living exception, save only Canova; for Paisiello is grown old, and works no more.

AN ABRIDGED CATALOGUE OF
THE WORKS OF JOSEPH HAYDN*

I VOCAL MUSIC

(a) Masses

Missa brevis in F major (*c.* 1749–50)
Great Organ Mass in E flat (?1766)
Missa Sanctae Caeciliae in C major (1769–73)
Missa Sancti Nicolai in G major (1772)
Little Organ Mass in B flat major (1775–8)
Mariazell Mass in C major (1782)
Kettledrum Mass in C major (1796)
Missa Sancti Bernardi de Offida (*Heiligmesse*) in B flat major (1796)
Nelson Mass in D minor (1798)
Theresienmesse in B flat major (1799)
Schöpfungsmesse in B flat major (1801)
Wind-band Mass in B flat major (1802)

(b) Minor Church Music

Te Deum in C major (before 1764)
Te Deum in C major (1799–1800)
Stabat Mater in G minor (1767–8)
3 *Arias* (pro Adventu, etc.)
2 *Ave Regina* (A major, F major)
5 Hymns
1 *Lauda Sion*
Litania de B.V.M. in C major (*c.* 1780)
3 Motets
3 Offertories
1 *Regina coeli*

4 *Salve Regina* (E major, 1756; G minor, 1771; E flat major, *c.* 1760–70; G major, *c.* 1761–70)

(c) Operas in the German Tradition (Singspiele)

Der krumme Teufel (libr. Felix Kurz-Bernardon, *c.* 1751: lost)
Der neue krumme Teufel (libr. Felix Kurz-Bernardon, *c.* 1758: lost)
La marchesa Nepola (1762: 5 arias preserved)

(d) Marionette Operas

Die bestrafte Rachbegierde (1779)
Philemon und Baucis (1773)
Hexenschabbas (1773: lost)
Didone abbandonata (1776: lost)
Genovevens vierter Theil (1777: lost)

(e) Operas in the Italian Tradition

Acide e Galatea (libr. Migliavacca, 1762)
La Canterina (1766)
Lo Speziale (libr. Goldoni, 1768)
Le Pescatrici (libr. Goldoni, 1769)
L'Infedeltà delusa (libr. Coltellini, 1773)
L'Incontro improvviso (libr. Frieberth, based on Dancourt, 1775)
La Vera costanza (libr. Puttini and Travaglia, 1776)
Il Mondo della luna (libr. Goldoni, 1777)
L'Isola disabitata (libr. Metastasio, 1779)
La Fedeltà premiata (1780)
Orlando Paladino (libr. N. Porta, 1782)
Armida (libr. Durandi, 1783)
L'Anima del filosofo (libr. Badini, 1791)

(f) Incidental Music

Alfred oder der patriotische König (libr. Bicknell, 1796)

(g) Cantatas and Oratorios

Wedding Chorus for Prince Anton Esterházy: *Vivan gl'illustri Sposi* (1763)

Birthday Cantata for Prince Nikolaus Esterházy: *Destatevi, o miei Fidi*
   (1763)
Cantata on the Occasion of the Prince's return: *Al tuo arrivo felice* (1764)
Applausus for the birthday of an Abbot (1768)
Il Ritorno di Tobia (Oratorio, libr. G. G. Boccherini, 1774–5, extended
   1784)
The Invocation of Neptune (Oratorio, incomplete, 1794)
Cantata: *Die Erwählung eines Kapellmeisters* (?c. 1795)
Die sieben Worte des Erlösers am Kreuze (various versions, 1785–99)
Die Schöpfung (the *Creation*: libr. van Swieten, after Linley, after
   Milton: 1798)
Die Jahreszeiten (*The Seasons*: libr. van Swieten, after Thomson: 1801)

(h) *Choruses*

Italian Catch (1791)
The Storm (text by John Wolcott, 1792)
What Art expresses (text by Dr Harington of Bath)
9 partsongs (4 voices)
4 partsongs (3 voices)

(i) *Canons*

The Ten Commandments (*Die zehn Gebote Gottes*, 1791–5)
46 secular canons (1790–1800)

(j) *Concerted Solo Works and Concert Arias*

Pietà di me, benigni dei (terzetto, 1791–5)
Dunque o Dio quando sperai (duet, before 1790)
Guarda qui (1796)
Quel Cor umano e tenero (1794)
Saper vorrei (duet, 1796)
Ah, come il cor mi palpita (aria, ?1783)
Ah, tu non senti amico (aria, 1786)
Chi vive amante (1787)
Da che penso a maritarmi (1790)
Dica pure chi vuol dire (1786)
Dice benissimo (c. 1783)

D'una sposa maschinella
Il meglio mio carattere (1790)
Infelice sventurata (1789)
La moglie quando è buona
Or vicino a te mio core (*c.* 1780)
Se tu mi sprezzi, ingrata (1788)
Solo e pensoso
Sono Alcina (1786)
Son pietosa, son bonina (1789)
Tornato per mia bella (*c.* 1780)
Un cor si tenero (1787)

(k) *Solo Cantatas*

Deutschlands Klage auf den Tod Friedrichs des Grossen (1786)
Arianna a Naxos (1789)
Lines from *The Battle of the Nile* (1800)

(l) *Lieder*

47 lieder for voice and piano, including two collections containing 12
lieder each (1781 and 1784); *Der schlaue und dienstfertige Pudel* (*c.* 1790);
Gott, erhalte Franz den Kaiser (1797); and 14 English lieder

(m) *Arrangements*

445 Scottish and Welsh airs, including:
  William Napier, *A Selection of Original Scots Songs* (Vol. II, 1792:
    100 airs by Haydn; Vol. III, 1794, 50 airs by Haydn)
  George Thomson, *A Select Collection of Original Scottish Airs* (1800–
    05: 144 by Haydn)
  George Thomson, *A Select Collection of Original Welsh Airs* (1800–05:
    42 by Haydn)
  George Thomson, *A Select Collection of Irish Airs* (1800–05: 1 by
    Haydn, the rest by Beethoven)
  William Whyte, *A Collection of Scottish Airs* (Vols. I and II, 1800–05;
    65 settings by Haydn)

II INSTRUMENTAL MUSIC

(a) Symphonies

108 Symphonies, including:

No. 6	D major	*Le Matin*	*c.* 1761
No. 7	C major	*Le Midi*	1761
No. 8	G major	*Le Soir et la Tempête*	*c.* 1761
No. 22	E flat major	*The Philosopher*	1764
No. 26	D minor	*Lamentatione*	1767–8
No. 30	C major	*Alleluia*	1765
No. 31	D major	*The Horn Signal*	1765
No. 43	E flat major	*The Mercury*	*c.* 1772
No. 44	E minor	*Mourning Symphony*	*c.* 1772
No. 45	F sharp minor	*Farewell*	1772
No. 48	C major	*Maria Theresia*	*c.* 1772
No. 49	F minor	*La Passione*	1768
No. 53	D major	*L'Imperiale*	*c.* 1775
No. 55	E flat major	*The Schoolmaster*	1774
No. 59	A major	*Fire Symphony*	*c.* 1767–8
No. 60	C major	*Il Distratto*	1774
No. 63	C major	*La Roxolane*	*c.* 1777–80
No. 69	C major	*Loudon*	*c.* 1778–9
No. 73	D major	*La Chasse*	1780–1

Nos. 82–7: 6 "Paris" Symphonies, including:

No. 82	C major	*L'Ours*	1786
No. 83	G minor	*La Poule*	1785
No. 85	B flat major	*La Reine de France*	1785–6
No. 92	G major	*Oxford*	1789

Nos. 93–104: 12 "London" Symphonies, including:

No. 94	G major	*The Surprise*	1791
No. 96	D major	*The Miracle*	1791
No. 100	G major	*Military*	1794
No. 101	D minor/major	*The Clock*	1794
No. 103	E flat major	*The Drum-Roll*	1795
No. 104	D minor/major	*The London*	1795

Also: *Sinfonia concertante* in B flat major for violin, 'cello, oboe, bassoon (1792)

String quartet Op. I, No. 5, in B flat major: original version
scored as symphony with 2 oboes, 2 horns (1757–60)
Partita in B flat major (before 1765)
The famous *Toy Symphony* (actually *Divertimento* No. 47) is now
no longer attributed to Haydn, but is believed to be either by
Leopold Mozart or by Michael Haydn

(b) *Overtures and Miscellaneous Orchestral Works*

16 operatic overtures and other pieces, including overture to the
Oratorio *Il ritorno di Tobia*
Die sieben Worte des Erlösers am Kreuze (orchestral version, 1785)
6 Marches
150-odd minuets
35 German dances

(c) *Concertos for Various Instruments*

1 organ concerto (C major, 1756)
1 concerto for violin and cembalo (F major, before 1766)
9 keyboard concertos
4 violin concertos (before 1770: C major; D major; A major; G major)
2 'cello concertos (C major, D major)
4 horn concertos (2 lost; the other 2 in D major)
1 trumpet concerto (E flat major, 1796)
1 flute concerto (D major)
5 concertos for two *lire organizzate* (1786)

(d) *Divertimenti, Cassations, etc.*

6 scherzandi for flute, 2 oboes, 2 horns, 2 violins and bass (*c.* 1760)
8 nocturnes for 2 *lire organizzate* (or flute and oboe), 2 clarinets, 2 horns,
2 violins and bass (1790)
48 divertimenti for various combinations of instruments
6 Feldparthien for 2 oboes, 2 clarinets, 2 horns, 2 trombones (*c.* 1765)

(e) *Chamber Music*

83 string quartets:
Op. 1, nos. 1–6 (? 1755)

Op. 2, nos. 1–6
Op. 3, nos. 1–6 (1767)
Op. 9, nos. 1–6 (before 1769)
Op. 17, nos. 1–6 (1771)
Op. 20, nos. 1–6 (1772)
Op. 33, nos. 1–6 (1781). No. 3 = "the Bird quartet"
Op. 42 (1785)
Op. 50, nos. 1–6 (1787, dedicated to King Frederick William II of
    Prussia. No. 6 = "the Frog quartet")
Op. 48 (1787: *Die sieben Worte*, arrangement for quartet)
Op. 54, nos. 1–3 (1789)
Op. 55, nos. 1–3 (1789). No. 3 = "the Razor quartet"
Op. 64, nos. 1–6 (1790). No. 5 = "the Lark quartet"
Op. 71, nos. 1–3 (1793, dedicated to Count Apponyi)
Op. 74, nos. 1–3 (1793, dedicated to Count Apponyi). No. 3 = "the
    Rider quartet"
Op. 76, nos. 1–6 (1797, dedicated to Count Erdödy). No. 3 = "the
    Emperor quartet"
Op. 77, nos. 1–2 (1799, dedicated to Prince Lobkowitz). No. 1 =
    "the Compliment quartet"
Op. 103. Unfinished, dedicated to Count Fries.
126 baryton trios (1765–75)
21 string trios (1760–8)
41 piano trios (1759–67 and 1784–97)
8 duets for baryton and another instrument
6 duos for violin and viola
12 divertimenti for 2 barytons and 'cello
17 baryton duos
9 flute trios
1 trio for horn, violin and 'cello

(f) Piano Works
60 piano sonatas (1760–94)
11 minor piano compositions, including:
    Capriccio in G major (1765)
    Theme and variations in F minor (1793)
89 miscellaneous dances
32 pieces for musical clock (1772–93)

The Haydn family making music

Gouache by an unknown artist showing the final scene from
L'Icontro improviso, with Haydn at the harpsichord. Esterházy
Palace Theatre, 1775

Wolfgang Amadeus Mozart

Mozart

LIFE OF MOZART
by Herr Schlichtegroll
(Translated from the German)

A LETTER

Venice, 21 July 1814.

It is your wish, my dear Friend, to possess a sketch of the life of Mozart. I have made enquiries as to the best studies available concerning this celebrated man, and I have further schooled myself to patience and translated for your benefit this biography composed by Herr Schlichtegroll★. It appears to be written with a certain degree of frankness. I offer it to you as it stands, begging that you will forgive its plain simplicity.

CHAPTER ONE

Childhood

Mozart's father exercised the strongest influence over the remarkable destiny of his son, whose natural gifts he developed and perhaps even modified; in consequence, it is necessary that we should begin by saying a few words about him. Leopold Mozart, father to our composer, was the son of a bookbinder from Augsburg; he studied in Salzburg and, in 1743, became a member of the orchestra maintained by the Prince-

Archbishop of that city. In 1762, he became assistant *Kapellmeister* in the Prince's household. Since his official duties did not occupy the whole of his time, he used further to teach musical composition and to give violin lessons to the good people of Salzburg. He even published a book, entitled *Versuch einer gründlichen Violinschule,* or *Treatise concerning a rational Method of Instruction in Violin-Playing,* which became very popular. He had married a certain Anna-Maria Pertl and it has been recorded, as a circumstance worthy of the attention of an exact observer, that this couple, who were destined to engender an artist whose disposition was so favourable to the creation of musical harmony, were themselves a very byword in Salzburg for the unusual comeliness of their persons.

Of the seven children that were born of this marriage, two alone survived: a daughter, Maria Anna, and a son, Johann Chrysostom Wolfgang Amadeus Mozart, who forms the subject of this study. Mozart was born at Salzburg on 27 January 1756. A few years later, Leopold Mozart abandoned his practice of giving private lessons and resolved to devote all the time that his official duties permitted to supervising in person the musical education of his two children. Maria Anna, who was slightly older than Mozart, profited greatly from his instruction and, in the years that followed, whenever she accompanied her family on tour, she was not lacking her share of the applause evoked by the genius of her brother. In the end, however, she married a Counsellor of the Prince-Archbishop of Salzburg, preferring simple domestic happiness to the renown that accompanies great artistic gifts.

The young Mozart was about three years old when his father began to teach his sister—then aged seven—to play upon the harpsichord. From that moment onwards, Mozart began to give evidence of his astonishing predisposition for music. His greatest pleasure lay in trying to pick out major thirds on the piano, and nothing would equal his delight when he succeeded in discovering this harmonious chord. Here I propose to relate a number of insignificant details which, in my opinion, may none the less prove to be of interest to the Reader.

When he was four years old, his father began, almost as a game, to teach him some little minuets and other musical pieces—a pastime that afforded as much pleasure to the teacher as to the pupil. It would take Mozart about half an hour to learn a minuet; and little more than twice that amount of time to master considerably longer pieces. As soon as he had learnt them, he would perform them with the utmost precision and in perfect time. In less than a year he made such rapid progress that, by the time he was five years old, he was already composing little pieces of his own, which he would play to his father; and the latter, in order to encourage his son's dawning genius, would give him pleasure by writing them down. Even before the time when the boy began to display his aptitude for music, he would become so intently absorbed in any of the little games which were suited to his age that, as soon as the pastime to any extent caught hold of his fancy, he would happily give up even his meals in order to indulge in it. On all occasions he betrayed a warm heart and a loving nature. He would often enquire, not once but ten times in a day, of those who were looking after him, "Do you really love me?"—and if ever, even in play, the answer came as "No!" immediately the tears would be seen rolling down his cheeks. However, from the very first moment when he discovered music, his pleasure in the sports and pastimes of his age evaporated; or rather, such amusements held no attraction for him, unless they were mingled with music. A friend of his parents used frequently to enjoy playing with him; one of their games was to carry toys in procession from one room to another; and on such occasions, the one who had nothing to carry would sing a march, or play one on the violin.

At one point, Wolfgang took such all-absorbing pleasure, for a number of months, in the common studies of childhood, that he forsook all else, even music, in order to master them. While he was learning his arithmetic, the tables, the chairs, the walls and even the floor might have been seen to be constantly covered with figures, written by Mozart in chalk. His intelligence was so alert that he would readily develop a passionate interest in whatever novel ideas might be offered to him. Before long, however, music regained its place as the preferred object of his studies; and his progress in the field was so rapid that his father, for all that he stood constantly beside him and was able to observe him step by step, was none the less tempted to consider his development, on more than one occasion, as nothing less than miraculous.

The following anecdote, which is told by one who witnessed the occurrence with his own eyes, will serve to bear out the foregoing assertions. Leopold Mozart was returning from church one day in the company of one of his friends and discovered his son busily writing something down on paper.

"What are you up to there, young fellow?" he asked.

"I'm composing a concerto for the harpsichord. I have almost finished the first movement."

"That's a splendid bit of scribbling! Let's have a look."

"No, please, not yet, I haven't finished."

In spite of the boy's objections, Mozart's father picked up the piece of paper and showed it to his friend: it was covered with a scribbled mess of notes, scarcely distinguishable one from the other on account of the numerous blots of ink. At first the two friends laughed long and heartily over this nonsensical rigmarole; after a while, however, Leopold Mozart began to look at it more closely; his eyes dwelt fixedly upon the paper, and then, at long last, began to fill with tears of admiration and delight.

"Yet look, look, my friend," he exclaimed, his voice filled with emotion, and at the same time smiling, "see how every bar of the piece is composed in accordance with the rules; the only pity is, that no one can use it; it is too difficult; no one would be able to play it."

"But it's a *concerto*!" protested young Wolfgang. "It has to be practised until it can be played properly. Listen, I'll show you how it should be done."

Whereupon he sat down and began to play; but he only managed to give a general notion of what his ideas had been. At this period, Mozart was firmly convinced that to play a concerto and to perform a miracle were one and the same thing; in consequence, the composition to which we have referred was a very jungle of notes, all accurately placed in relation to each other, yet bristling with such difficulties that not even the most proficient of harpsichordists would have possessed the skill to perform them.

The boy Mozart was a source of such amazement to his father, that the latter conceived the notion of travelling abroad, of visiting Courts both in Germany and in foreign lands, and of inviting others to share his own admiration for his son. In these parts, there is nothing extraordinary in such an idea. Thus no sooner had Wolfgang attained his sixth year, than the whole Mozart family, consisting of father, mother, Maria-Anna and Wolfgang, set out upon a journey to Munich. There, the Elector listened to the two children, who were showered with infinite compliments. Their first excursion proved an unqualified success. Back once more in Salzburg, the two young prodigies, delighted

with the welcome they had received, settled down to study with renewed eagerness and soon achieved a degree of technical proficiency on
the piano that no longer required the particular circumstance of their
youth to be remarkable. In the course of the autumn of the year 1762
the whole family paid a visit to Vienna, and there the children gave
concerts in the presence of the Court.

It was on this occasion that the Emperor Francis I remarked jokingly
to little Wolfgang:

"It is not *very* difficult to play, if you use *all* your fingers: but if you
could play using one finger only, and on a keyboard that you couldn't
see—now *that* would be something worth admiring!"

The child showed not the slightest hint of surprise at this somewhat
bizarre suggestion, but promptly sat down and began to play with one
finger only, producing passages of unbelievable clarity and precision.
He then asked for a scarf to be placed over the keyboard of the harpsichord, and when this was done, continued to play on unperturbed, as
though for many years he had been accustomed to practise just this
style of performance.

From his earliest years, Mozart, inspired by the truest pride in his art,
never allowed his personal vanity to be flattered by the eulogies that he
received from the Great. When his audience consisted of persons
ignorant of the subtleties of music, he consistently refused to play anything save inconsiderable trifles. By contrast, he would display all the
ardour and play with all the care of which he was capable, as soon as he
knew himself in the company of genuine connoisseurs; and his father
was frequently obliged to resort to subterfuge and to pretend that the
noble gentlemen, before whom he was to appear, were in fact notable
experts in the art. On one occasion, when he was six years old, the boy
sat down at the harpsichord to play in the presence of the Emperor
Francis; before starting, however, he turned to the sovereign and enquired: "Is not Herr Wagenseil present? He is the person who should
be sent for; *he* understands." The Emperor commanded that Wagenseil
should be fetched, and made him take his own place beside the harpsichord. "Sir," said Mozart to the composer as the latter took his seat,
"I am going to play one of your concertos; you must turn the pages
for me."

So far Wolfgang had confined himself to the harpsichord, and the
extraordinary aptitude that he displayed for this instrument appeared

to contradict the very notion that he should be encouraged to practise on some other. Yet the genius that inspired him led him onwards to achievements greater by far than any might have dared to hope for; he had no need even of lessons.

When he returned with his parents to Salzburg from Vienna, he brought with him a miniature violin with which he had been presented during his visit to the capital; and with this instrument he used to amuse himself. Not long after this homecoming, Wenzl, a noted violinist who, at that time, was just beginning to compose, came to call upon Leopold Mozart, in order to ask for his advice and criticism concerning a set of six trios that he had written during the Mozarts' absence in Vienna. On this occasion, Schachtner, who played the trumpet in the Archbishop's orchestra, and who was one of those persons to whom the boy Mozart was the most deeply attached, happened to be present in the house, and it is he who shall be allowed to relate the incident. "Mozart's father," writes Schachtner, "was to play the bass, Wenzl the first violin, while I myself was to take the second violin. At this point, the boy came up and asked to be allowed to take this latter part himself; his father, however, scolded him for this childish request, explaining to him that, since he had never received any regular tuition in the violin, he obviously could not hope to play it properly. The boy replied that, to him, it appeared by no means essential to have taken lessons, merely in order to play a part written for second violin. Half angered by this retort, his father told him to run away and stop interrupting us. At this, Wolfgang was so upset that he began to cry piteously; and as he was walking away, holding his little violin, I begged that he should be allowed to play in unison with us. His father raised numerous objections, but in the end gave way. 'Very well then,' he said to Wolfgang, 'you may take the part together with Herr Schachtner, but only on condition that you play so softly that no one can hear you; otherwise, out you go straight away.' We began the trio, and little Wolfgang played beside me; nor had we proceeded far before I observed, to my greatest amazement, that I was completely superfluous. Without a word, I set my own violin aside, meanwhile keeping my eyes fixed upon the boy's father, who in effect was moved to tears by this scene. In this fashion, the child played through all six of the trios. At the conclusion, the congratulations which we freely bestowed upon him emboldened him so far as to claim that he could play the first violin part just as well. Good-humouredly, we resolved to try the experiment, nor could we help laughing as we listened to him valiantly struggling with the part, in a fashion which, it is true, scarcely corresponded with the composer's intention, yet none the less never once failing to supply a note."

Every day brought fresh proofs of Mozart's extraordinary aptitude for music. He was able to discern and to analyse the minutest distinctions between various sounds; and any wrong note, or indeed any note which was harsh, unsoftened by some appropriate harmony, was true torture for him. Thus it came about that, in his earlier childhood, and even as late as his tenth year, he was affected with an insurmountable horror of the trumpet, save when its sole function was to accompany a melody entrusted to other instruments; at the very sight of one, he would be dismayed much as other children may be dismayed by the appearance of a loaded pistol which, for a joke, is suddenly aimed straight at them. His father thought to cure him of this aversion by himself playing the trumpet in his presence, despite his son's prayers and entreaties that he be spared this torment; at the first note, however, he turned pale and fell prostrate on the floor, and in all probability he would have fallen straight away into a fit of convulsions, had not the playing been interrupted then and there.

From that day forward, after he had proved his mettle upon the violin, he would occasionally play upon the instrument belonging to Herr Schachtner, that family friend of whom mention has been made already: he was wont to speak of it with great enthusiasm, since he was able to coax from it sounds of a surpassing softness. One day, Schachtner called on the Mozarts and found the boy amusing himself by playing tunes on his own little violin. "What's the matter with *your* violin?" came the child's peremptory question; whereupon he continued executing his own musical fancies. At length, after a few moments' reflection, he turned again to Schachtner. "Couldn't you have your violin tuned again the way it was last time I used it? It is pitched a quarter of a semitone lower than mine here." At first, this scrupulous exactitude was greeted with a burst of laughter; however, Leopold Mozart, who already, on several earlier occasions, had had the opportunity to observe his son's singular propensity for remembering precise degrees of pitch, caused the violin to be sent for; and indeed, to the astonishment of all those present, it proved to be tuned exactly one quarter of a semitone lower than that which Wolfgang was holding.

7*

Although the boy was daily greeted by fresh proofs of the amazement and of the admiration that his gifts aroused, he grew up neither headstrong nor conceited; an adult in genius, in all other respects he never ceased to be the best-behaved, the most obedient of children. Not once did he protest or grumble about what his father told him to do. Even when he had been practising the whole day long without a rest, he would start playing again without the least display of temper, as soon as his father desired it. He could interpret his parents' wishes at the slightest hint, and would obey them in a flash. Indeed, he carried the virtue of obedience to the point at which he would even refuse to accept sweets, when he had not specifically been granted permission to accept them.

In July 1763, consequently when Mozart was seven years old, his family set out upon their first journey beyond the frontiers of Germany; and it is at this period that the name of Mozart first begins to acquire celebrity throughout Europe. The tour began in Munich, where the young virtuoso executed a violin concerto in the presence of the Elector of Bavaria, after having extemporised a prelude of his own imagining. In Augsburg, in Mannheim, in Frankfurt, in Coblenz and in Brussels the two children either gave concerts in public, or else performed in the presence of the reigning Sovereign; and everywhere they went, they were showered with unstinted praise.

In November they arrived in Paris, where they remained for five months. They were granted an audience at Versailles and, in the presence of the whole Court, Wolfgang played the organ in the Chapel Royal. In Paris itself, they gave two grand Public Concerts, and from every side they received the most enthusiastic welcome. It was here, moreover, that they were even granted the honour of having their portrait engraved and distributed; the engraving, taken from a sketch by Carmontelle*, showed the father with his two children, one on either side of him. And it was in Paris that Mozart composed and published his first two works*. The first of these he dedicated to Madame Victoire, the second daughter of Louis XV; the other, to Madame la Comtesse de Tessé.

In April 1764 the Mozarts crossed the Channel and visited England, in which country they remained until about the middle of the year following. The children performed in the presence of the King and here, as at Versailles, Wolfgang played the organ in the Chapel Royal.

In London his playing of the organ was esteemed more highly than his performance upon the harpsichord. While in that City, he and his sister together gave a Grand Concert, in which all the orchestral pieces* were of his own composition.

It may well be conceived that the two children, and notably Wolfgang, were unable to remain content with that degree of proficiency which daily earned them such flattering applause. Despite their continual journeying, they practised with unrelenting regularity. It was in London that they started to play concertos for two harpsichords. Wolfgang also began to sing full-scale concert-arias, to which achievement he brought a remarkable wealth of expression. Both in Paris and in London certain incredulous persons had procured various difficult pieces by J. C. Bach, Handel and other masters, and set them before him; he would play them straight off at sight, with unfailing precision and accuracy. On one occasion, in the presence of the King of England, he extemporised a passage full of the most striking melody, while working exclusively from a figured bass. On another, Johann Christian Bach, who was then Master of the Queen's Music, took the boy on his knees and played a few bars on the harpsichord. Mozart picked up the passage where he had left off, and thus alternating one with the other, they played through an entire sonata, with such perfect precision, that all those who could hear but not see them were convinced that the whole sonata had been played by a single person. During his sojourn in England, and consequently when he was in his eighth year, Wolfgang composed a set of six Sonatas*, which he caused to be engraved in London and which he dedicated to the Queen.

In July 1765 the Mozart family crossed the Channel once more, landing in Calais, then pursuing the journey through Flanders, where the young virtuoso frequently played the organ in various monastic churches and in cathedrals. At The Hague, both children succumbed, one after the other, to an illness which endangered their lives; and it was four months before they were on their feet again. During his convalescence, Wolfgang composed six Sonatas for the piano*, which he dedicated to Princess Caroline of Nassau-Weilburg. At the beginning of 1766 they spent a month in Amsterdam, whence they returned to The Hague, in order to take part in the ceremonies attendant upon the coming-of-age of the Prince of Orange. For this solemn occasion, the young Mozart composed a *quodlibet**, or pot-pourri on popular airs for full orchestra, together with divers sets of variations and a small number of arias for the Princess.

After several performances given in the presence of the Stadtholder, they returned to Paris, where they spent a further two months. Finally they returned home to Germany by way of Lyons and Switzerland. In Munich, the Elector presented young Wolfgang with a theme and asked him to develop it and to write it down on the spot. This exercise he carried out then and there, using neither harpsichord nor violin. After he had completed the score, he played it straight through—a feat which evoked the highest degree of astonishment both in the Elector and in all his Court.

After an absence which had lasted for more than three years, the family reached Salzburg once again towards the end of November 1766, and there they remained until the autumn of the year following. In these less disturbed circumstances, Wolfgang's genius seemed to grow by leaps and bounds. In 1768, the children performed in Vienna, in the presence of the Emperor Joseph II, who commissioned the boy Mozart to compose the music for an *opera buffa*. This was *La finta Semplice*; it won the approval, both of Hasse, the Court *Kapellmeister*, and of Metastasio; but it was never actually performed*. On several occasions, in the company of *Kapellmeisters* Giuseppe Bonno and Hasse, of Metastasio, of the Duke of Braganza or of Prince von Kaunitz, Leopold Mozart would give his son the first Italian aria that happened to come to hand, and Wolfgang would then score in all the different instrumental parts in the presence of all those assembled. For the inaugural ceremony of the Waisenhauskirche, he composed the music for the Mass, as well as that for the Motet, together with a trumpet duet*; and although he was even now but twelve years of age, he conducted the solemn concert in the presence of the full Imperial Court.

He returned to spend the year 1769 in Salzburg. In December of that year, his father took him to Italy. Wolfgang had just been appointed *Konzertmeister* to the Archbishop of Salzburg. It is not difficult to conceive the warmth of the welcome that was accorded in Italy to this celebrated prodigy who already excited so much admiration in other parts of Europe.

The stage which served as the setting for his finest hours of glory was the Residence of Count Firmian, the Governor-General of Lombardy. In March 1770, as soon as he had received the libretto for the opera which was to be given during the Carnival Season of the year 1771, and for which he had undertaken to compose the music, Wolfgang left Milan. In Bologna, he made the acquaintance of a passionate admirer whose enthusiasm knew no bounds, in the person of the illustrious Father Martini—the same from whom Jommelli had once requested lessons*. Father Martini, and with him all the music-lovers of Bologna, were overwhelmed at the sight of this child of thirteen, who was small for his age and who indeed scarcely appeared to have reached the age of ten, developing each and every one of the fugal subjects proposed by Martini, and performing them upon the piano without an instant's hesitation, and with impeccable accuracy. In Florence, he caused similar amazement by the faultless precision with which he was able to play at sight the most complex of fugues and themes that were set before him by the Marquis de Ligniville, a celebrated connoisseur. Concerning this interlude in Florence, there has survived an anecdote which has nothing to do with music. In the course of his sojourn in this city, he made the acquaintance of a young English boy named Thomas Linley, who was about fourteen years old, or in other words about the same age as Wolfgang. Linley was a pupil of Nardini, the celebrated violinist, and himself was able to perform upon this instrument with a wondrous degree of grace and skill. The friendship that sprang up between the two boys rapidly developed into a passionate attachment. On the day when they were to part company, Linley presented his friend Mozart with a poem on the subject of separation—a valedictory sonnet composed at his request by the celebrated poetess Maddalena Morelli. He accompanied Wolfgang's travelling-coach as far as the limits of the city; and the two children bade farewell to one another amid torrents of tears*.

Leopold Mozart and his son took up their quarters in Rome for Holy Week. It may well be conceived that, on the Wednesday evening, they did not fail to attend the service in the Sistine Chapel, in order to hear the celebrated *Miserere*. As it was at that time currently reported that the Papal musicians were forbidden, upon pain of excommunication, to disclose the score of this work, Wolfgang resolved to commit it to memory at a hearing. And indeed, as soon as he returned to the inn where he was lodged, he wrote it down. This same *Miserere* was to be repeated on Good Friday; Mozart was again among the congregation with his manuscript concealed in his hat, and thus he was able to make a few corrections. This incident was the sensation of the city. The people of Rome, a thought dubious as to the veracity of the tale, proposed that the boy should sing this *Miserere* at a concert. His performance was a delight to hear. The castrato Cristofori, who himself had sung the part in the Sistine Chapel, and who was present among the audience, brought the final touch to the completeness of Mozart's triumph by the extent of his amazement.

The difficulty involved in Mozart's feat of memory is much greater than one might imagine at first glance. But I entreat the Reader to allow me to supply a few details concerning the Sistine Chapel and the *Miserere*.

In normal circumstances, the Choir of this Chapel consists of not less than thirty-two voices, with neither organ nor instruments of any sort to accompany or sustain them. This *ensemble* reached its peak of perfection—a peak which, in all its later history, it never surpassed—in the early years of the eighteenth century. Since that time, salaries paid to choristers in the Papal Chapel have remained nominally unchanged, in consequence of which their real value has considerably diminished; by contrast, the opera was gradually gaining in popularity and singers of merit were being offered salaries hitherto undreamed-of to accept engagements on the stage. In consequence, as the years went by, the Sistine Chapel found ever greater difficulty in attracting the finest talents.

The *Miserere**, which is performed in the Sistine only on two occasions during Holy Week, and which produces so overwhelming an impression upon newcomers, was composed some two centuries ago by Gregorio Allegri, one of the descendants of that Antonio Allegri who is universally renowned under the name of Correggio. As the first notes begin to fill the Chapel, Pope and Cardinals prostrate themselves before the altar; the gleam from the candles falls upon that *Last Judgement* which Michelangelo painted in fresco on the wall which serves as reredos to the altar. As the *Miserere* proceeds, the candles are extinguished one by one; and the faces of the countless Damned, portrayed with such terrifying violence by Michelangelo, grow but the more awesome in the half-light shed by the pale flicker of the last candles that still retain their flame. As the *Miserere* moves towards its final close, the choirmaster, who is conducting, imperceptibly decreases the tempo; the choristers let their voices die away; the harmonies are gradually extinguished; and the Sinner, confounded in the presence of God in all His majesty, prostrate before His high Throne, seems to await in silence the coming of the Voice that is to judge him.

The awe-inspiring impression produced by this canticle is due, in my opinion, both to the manner in which it is sung, and also to the place in which it is performed. Tradition has taught the Papal choristers certain techniques of *portamento* which are indescribably effective, yet which it is impossible to convey in the written score. Moreover, the melody which they sing represents the perfect fulfilment of that primary condition, without which no music can stir the depths of the human soul. The same theme is repeated in each versicle of the psalm; yet the musical structure, repetitive in general outline, is none the less subtly varied in detail. Thus it is easily grasped, and yet it avoids anything that might tend towards monotony. It is the practice of the Sistine Chapel to mark an accelerando or rallentando on certain words, to increase or to hush the volume of sound according to the sense of the text, and to sing certain verses as a whole more vivaciously than others.

Now, here is an anecdote which goes to show the difficulty involved in that extraordinary feat performed by Mozart when he sang the *Miserere*. The story is told of the Emperor Leopold I, who was not only fond of music, but himself no inconsiderable composer, that on one occasion he instructed his Ambassador to request from the Pope a copy of Allegri's *Miserere* for use in the Imperial Chapel in Vienna. The request was granted. The Choirmaster of the Sistine ordered the copy to be made, and it was dispatched forthwith to the Emperor, in whose service, at that time, there were to be found the finest singers of their generation.

In spite of all their talents, however, Allegri's *Miserere*, when it was performed at the Court of Vienna, produced no impression other than that of a relatively commonplace passage of plainsong; and in consequence, the Emperor and all his suite were convinced that the Papal Choirmaster, jealously cherishing his *Miserere*, had eluded his master's command, and had sent instead some banal composition of worthless inspiration. Forthwith, the Emperor dispatched an envoy to the Pope to complain of this instance of *lèse-majesté*; and the Choirmaster was dismissed, the Pope refusing, in a fury of indignation, even to listen to his pleas of innocence. The wretched creature, however, managed to persuade one of the Cardinals to plead his cause and to convince the

Pope that the secret of actually performing the *Miserere* could not be conveyed by the written score, nor could it be learnt, save with much time and perseverance, and by dint of countless lessons from the choristers of the Papal Chapel, who alone had inherited the tradition. His Holiness, who knew nothing whatsoever of music, found it well-nigh impossible to conceive that the identical notes on paper should possess a different value in Vienna and in Rome. None the less, His Holiness commanded the wretched Choirmaster to set down the arguments in his defence, for eventual transmission to the Emperor; and at long last, with the passage of time, he was restored to favour.

It was this story, well-known in Rome, that struck the imagination of the Roman audience when they beheld a mere child who was able to give a faultless rendering of their *Miserere* after no more than two lessons; and, in the domain of art, there is nothing more difficult than to excite astonishment in Rome. The mightiest of reputations shrivel and grow small as they pass through the gates of this illustrious city, where men are accustomed to nothing less than the noblest and the finest in every province of art.

I cannot tell whether it was on account of the personal triumph which it procured him, but it appears that the solemn and melancholy music of the *Miserere* made a deep impression upon Mozart's soul; and ever after, he showed a marked predilection for Handel and for the haunting tenderness of Boccherini.

CHAPTER TWO

Childhood—continued

From Rome, the Mozart family set out for Naples, where Wolfgang played the piano at the Conservatorio della Pietà. When he had reached the middle of his Sonata, the audience suddenly decided that there must be a magic charm in his ring; he was forced first to stop, then to try and make out what all the shouting was about, finally to remove the so-called magic ring. It is not hard to imagine the effect produced among

an audience of this singular quality when they realised that, even without the ring, the music was still as beautiful as ever. Wolfgang gave a
second Grand Concert in the Residence of Count von Kaunitz, the
Emperor's Ambassador; after which he returned to Rome. The Pope
expressed a desire to see him, and on the occasion of this audience conferred upon him the Cross and the patents of a Knight of the Order of
the Golden Spur (*auratae Militiae eques*). In Bologna, he was unanim-
ously elected a Member and a Master of the Accademia Filarmonica.
In accordance with the traditional customs, he had been locked in a
room all alone, and in less than half an hour he had composed an antiphon for four voices★.

Leopold Mozart was in haste to return to Milan, so that his son might
begin work upon the opera that he had agreed to compose. Time was
growing short. The month of October 1770 was already drawing to a
close when they arrived. Had it not been for this earlier promise,
Mozart could have obtained what is considered in Italy to be the greatest
honour that any composer can aspire to—namely, the commission to
write an *opera seria* for the Roman stage.

On 26 December, in Milan, there took place the *première* of the opera
Mitridate, with music by Wolfgang, who was now fourteen years of
age. This work enjoyed more than twenty successive performances. As
evidence of its popularity, this single fact is worth recording: the
impresario promptly signed a written contract with the young musician, commissioning him to write the first opera for the year 1773.
Mozart now left Milan, which was still ringing with his praise, in order
to spend the final days of the Carnival in Venice, in the company of his
father. In Verona, where he merely passed through without stopping,
he was presented with a diploma conferring upon him the membership
of the local Philharmonic Society. Wherever he travelled in Italy, he
was welcomed with the most flattering attentions; and his true name
was forgotten in preference for his nickname: *il cavaliere filarmonico*.

In March 1771, when Mozart, accompanied by his father, eventually
returned to Salzburg, he discovered there awaiting him a letter from
Count Firmian, in Milan, commissioning him, in the name of the
Empress Maria Theresa, to write a dramatic Cantata for the marriage
of the Archduke Ferdinand. The Empress had nominated the renowned
Johann Adolph Hasse, by virtue of his seniority among the Court
Kapellmeisters, to compose the opera for this occasion; and it was her

wish that the youngest composer within her dominions should have the honour of the Cantata, whose subject was to be *Ascanio in Alba*. Mozart promised to undertake this commission and in August set out for Milan, in which city, during the time of the wedding celebrations, the Opera* and the Serenade were performed alternately.

In 1772, on the occasion of the election of the new Archbishop of Salzburg, he composed a Cantata entitled *Il Sogno di Scipione*; the winter of the year following he spent in Milan, where he wrote an *opera seria*, entitled *Lucio Silla*, which was honoured with twenty-six consecutive performances. A number of journeys undertaken in the company of his father in the course of this year and the year following afforded him the opportunity to compose a variety of excellent works, such as an *opera buffa* entitled *La finta Giardiniera*, two High Masses for the Chapel of the Elector of Bavaria, and so on. In 1775, the Archduke Maximilian stayed for a while in Salzburg, and it was on this occasion that Mozart composed the Cantata entitled *Il Re Pastore*.

The most extraordinary part of Mozart's life was his childhood; and the details of this period may furnish agreeable matter for reflection, both to the philosopher and to the artist. We shall deal more briefly with the remaining portion of his all-too-short career.

CHAPTER THREE

At the age of nineteen, Mozart might well have been persuaded that he had scaled the very summits of his art, since every voice, from London to Naples, was constantly asserting that this was indeed the case. In so far as he was concerned to make his fortune and to secure a permanent position in the world, he was free to make his choice among all the capitals of Europe. In every land, his own experience was there to teach him that he might rely upon a universal degree of admiration. His father, however, came to the conclusion that Paris was the city best suited to his needs, and so, in the month of September 1777, he set out for the French capital, whither he was accompanied only by his mother.

There is no doubt whatever but that it would have been immensely to his advantage to take up his permanent residence in this city; a first objection, however, was that French music, at that time, was distinctly foreign to his taste; a second was that the state of vocal music as it then was would have made it all but impossible for him to work, save in the field of instrumental music; and a final one was that, in the course of the year following, he experienced the sorrow of his mother's death. From that day onwards, further residence in Paris became unbearable to him. After composing a Symphony* for one of the *Concerts Spirituels*, together with a number of other pieces, he hurriedly got together his belongings and, at the beginning of 1779, returned to his father.

In the month of November of the year following, he journeyed to Vienna, whither he had been summoned by his sovereign lord, the Archbishop of Salzburg. He was by now twenty-four years of age. Life in Vienna appealed to him, and even more so, it would seem, the beauty of the ladies of that city. One thing at all events is certain: namely, that he made his home there, and that nothing thereafter could weaken his attachment to this capital. The forces of passion had by now made themselves felt in the heart of this being who was at once so exquisite in sensibility and so admirably fashioned for the pursuance of his art; and it was not long before he became the favourite composer of his century, thus furnishing the very first instance of an infant prodigy who was later to grow into a great man.[1]

It would be too tedious, and above all too difficult, to attempt an individual analysis of each and every work that Mozart wrote; in any

---

[1]Mozart composed the music for his opera *Idomeneo* under the most favourable of auspices. The Elector of Bavaria, who had consistently bestowed favours on him and treated him with unfailing kindness, had entreated him to write this opera for his company in Munich, whose orchestra was one of the best-furnished with talent in the whole of Germany. At that period, Mozart was in the full flower of his genius: he was twenty-five years of age, and head over heels in love with Fraülein Constanze Weber, a renowned virtuoso, who was later to become his wife. The family of his beloved, however, taking into consideration the fact that he held no permanent position, that he was constantly travelling from one city to another, and that his morals had, up to that point in his career, been anything but unimpeachable, set its face against the marriage. Mozart took it upon himself to prove to this recalcitrant family that, despite his lack of an assured social standing, he none the less was endowed with certain talents that might merit him distinction; and the power of his love for Constanze served to fashion in his imagination those themes around which he built the impassioned arias that he needed for his work. Love and self-love, both fanned to the fiercest blaze of intensity, combined to inspire the young composer to produce an opera which he himself invariably considered as the finest thing that he had written, and from which he frequently borrowed for his later compositions.

case, the true music-lover will already be familiar with them all. The majority of his operas were composed in Vienna, and enjoyed immense popularity in that city; yet none brought more enjoyment to its audience than did the *Magic Flute*, which was honoured with a hundred performances in less than a single year.

As with Raphael, so also with Mozart: his genius extended over the whole range of his art. One aspect alone appears to have eluded Raphael, namely the art of painting fore-shortened figures on a ceiling. He invariably resorts to a subterfuge, pretending that the canvas of the painting is fastened to the vault of the roof, or else supported by allegorical figures.

In the case of Mozart, I can perceive no single genre in which he failed to achieve an absolute mastery: operas, symphonies, songs, dance-tunes—he was great in everything he touched. Baron van Swieten, who was Haydn's friend, would go so far as to assert that, had Mozart lived, he would have robbed even Haydn of his undisputed sovereignty in the realm of orchestral music. In *opera buffa*, he lacked a certain vein of merriment; and in this respect he is inferior to composers such as Galuppi, Guglielmi and Sarti.

Independently of his genius, the purely *physical* qualities in his music that strike the listener include a quite novel manner of using the orchestra, and in particular the wind-section. He scores for the flute—an instrument that Cimarosa rarely used at all—with wonderful effect. And in his arias, the accompaniments are enriched with all the wealth of beauty borrowed from the most sumptuous symphonic writing.

Mozart has been accused of taking no interest in any music save his own, and of knowing no works other than those which he himself had written. Such accusations bear the hallmark of petty wounded vanities. Mozart's entire life was occupied with setting his own inspirations down on paper; nor, it is true, did he have time enough to peruse all the notions of others. For all that, he was unstinting in his praise of everything he met with that seemed good, approving the simplest little song, provided only that it showed originality; less politic, however, than the great Italians, he was ruthless in his contempt for mediocrity.

Composers whom he respected included most notably Porpora, Durante, Leo and Alessandro Scarlatti; yet Handel he placed on a pinnacle above them all. He knew by heart all the major works of this great master. "There is not one among us," he was wont to say, "who understands as well as Handel how to produce a great effect. When he wishes it, off he goes and strikes at you like a thunderbolt!"

He used to say of Jommelli: "He is a composer who is brilliant within certain limits and who, within these limits, will always be brilliant; but he should never have ventured forth beyond them, nor should he have attempted to write Church Music in the antique style." He had no high opinion of Vicente Martin y Soler, whose opera, *Una Cosa rara*, was very popular during that period. "It contains a number of excellent things," he used to say, "but twenty years from now, no one will bother to notice them." He has left us nine operas based on Italian texts:

La finta Semplice, an *opera buffa*, which represents his first venture into dramatic music;
Mitridate, an *opera seria*;
Lucio Silla, an *opera seria*;
La finta Giardiniera, an *opera buffa*;
Idomeneo, an *opera seria*;
Le Nozze di Figaro
Don Giovanni } both written in 1787;
Così fan tutte, an *opera buffa*;
La Clemenza di Tito, an opera based on a libretto by Metastasio, performed for the first time in 1792.

He wrote only three German operas*:

Die Entführung aus dem Serail;
Der Schauspieldirektor; and
Die Zauberflöte, dating from 1792.

He left seventeen symphonies* and a variety of instrumental pieces of every description.

As a performer, Mozart was one of the leading pianists in Europe. His prestissimo playing was extraordinary; in particular, he was admired for the dexterity of his left hand.

As early as 1785, the celebrated Joseph Haydn had asserted to Mozart's father, who at that time happened to be in Vienna: "I do declare to you, before God and as I am an honest man, that I consider your son to be the greatest composer of whom I have ever heard."

Such, then, was Mozart, considered as a *musician*. Yet he who has some acquaintance with human nature will evince no surprise on learning that a man who, in respect of his artistic gifts, was the object of a universal admiration, betrayed something less than greatness in other situations. Mozart was remarkable neither for the handsomeness of his features nor the manliness of his body, for all that his father and mother had both been renowned for their unusual beauty.

Cabanis writes:

"It would appear that sensibility behaves as though it were a fluid whose total quantity is limited, and which, in consequence, whenever it flows in abnormal abundance through one of the channels open to it, diminishes proportionately in the others."*

As he grew to maturity, Mozart's physical development remained below normal standards; his whole life long, his health was uncertain; he was thin and pale; and although the actual shape of his face was extraordinary, his expression was memorable in nothing save in its extreme variability. His features would alter from one instant to another, yet never revealing anything save the pleasure or the distress that he happened to feel in that immediate instant. He had one tic or idiosyncrasy which, as a general rule, is a symptom of stupidity: his body was perpetually in motion; he would play incessantly with his hands, or tap restlessly on the floor with his feet. Nothing noteworthy, moreover, in his general way of life, if one excepts his passionate love for the game of billiards. He had a table of his own at home, upon which, almost daily, he would continue to play alone, after his last partner had left. Mozart's hands were so specifically and categorically fashioned for the keyboard, that they were, if anything, clumsy when directed to any other task. At table, he would never cut the food that lay in front of him; or else, on the rare occasions when he did attempt this operation, he succeeded only at the cost of infinite difficulty and awkwardness. As a general rule, he would entreat his wife to perform this office in his place.

This same being who, considered as an artist, had reached the highest stage of development even from his very earliest years, remained to the end of his life completely childish in every other aspect of existence. Never, until he died, did he learn to exercise the most elementary forms of self-control. The ordering of his domestic affairs, the proper husbanding of money, temperance, or the rational choice of pleasures—these were never virtues with which he had the least acquaintance. Invariably it was the pleasure of the moment that swept away all other considerations. His mind being constantly preoccupied with a host of ideas that excluded all manner of reflection upon what we are wont to call the serious side of life, he stood everlastingly in need, during the whole span of his existence, of some guardian to watch over his temporal affairs. His father was keenly aware of this weakness; and it was this consideration which persuaded him, in the year 1777, to have his wife follow his son to Paris, since his own employment at Salzburg did not allow him, at that time, to absent himself from that city.

Yet this same man, eternally absent-minded, eternally preoccupied with childish amusements, appeared to grow in stature and to take his place among beings of a superior race, as soon as he sat down before a piano. On such occasions, his soul would take wings, and the whole power of his being was able to concentrate upon that single object for which he had been born: namely, the *harmony of sound*. The largest orchestra held no difficulties for him, nor did it prevent him, even in the heat of performance, from observing the least note misplaced; and he would point his finger then and there, with an accuracy that was well-nigh uncanny, at the instrument which was guilty of the fault, and demonstrate which note should have been played instead.

On one occasion, when Mozart was visiting Berlin, it was already very late in the evening when he arrived. Hardly had he clambered down from his travelling-coach, when he was enquiring of the pot-boy from the inn, whether there was any performance at the Opera that night. "Yes, *Die Entführung aus dem Serail*. It's excellent." Scarcely were the words out of the lad's mouth, when Mozart was off like a shot in the direction of the theatre, where he stood on the threshold of the doorway leading to the pit, so as to be able to listen incognito. At one instant, however, he would be so delighted with the ingenious interpretation of certain passages, at the next, so upset by the incompetent rendering of others, or annoyed by the tempo, or vexed by the superfluous vocal embroideries invented by the singers, that imperceptibly he found himself up against the rail separating the audience from the orchestra-pit, every shade of satisfaction or displeasure meanwhile being plainly manifested on his features. The conductor having taken a number of liberties with one of the arias, Mozart, as soon as he came within range, was verily beside himself with anger, and before long was almost shouting aloud at the orchestra, indicating the proper manner in which the passage should be played. Heads began to be turned in consternation towards this stranger in a travelling-cloak who was causing such a disturbance; whereupon some of those present recognised Mozart, and in a flash the news spread among orchestra and singers alike that the great man himself was in the audience. Among the cast there were not a few, including an admirable prima-donna, who were so overwhelmed by this piece of information, that they refused to continue with the performance. The conductor approached Mozart, and told him of the awkward situation in which he was now placed as a consequence of this refusal. Like a flash, Mozart vanished into the wings, and there succeeded, by dint of flattery freely bestowed among the singers, in inducing them to carry on with the show.

Music was both the business of his life, and at the same time his most enjoyable distraction. Never, not even in the earliest years of his childhood, did he need to be told to sit down to the piano. On the contrary, he had to be watched lest, once there, he should grow oblivious of all passage of time and so do injury to his health. From his boyhood onwards, he showed a marked preference for making music at night. At nine o'clock in the evening he would sit down to his harpsichord, nor would he rise from it again before midnight, and even then he had to be literally prised away from it, otherwise he would have continued all night long extemporising and inventing his own fancies. In the normal round of daily life, no man ever betrayed a gentler disposition; yet the slightest noise that came to interrupt his playing would cause him to fly into an uncontrollable passion. He had no share of that affected or misplaced modesty which causes the majority of virtuosi to refuse to perform until they have been wooed with numerous entreaties. Indeed, certain Great Persons of Vienna were wont to accuse him of playing with disproportionate enthusiasm before any Tom, Dick or Harry who took a genuine pleasure in listening.

CHAPTER FOUR

There was a certain music-lover in one of the many cities visited by Mozart in the course of his journeyings, who had gathered together at his residence a numerous assembly of friends and acquaintances, in order that they might enjoy the pleasure of listening to this renowned musician; for the latter had promised to honour him with his presence. Mozart arrived, spoke no more than a word or two here and there, and sat down at the piano. Being under the delusion that the company in which he found himself consisted wholly of connoisseurs, he began to play, molto adagio, a prelude which, while rich in the most agreeable harmonies, was at the same time extremely simple; for he wished by this means to prepare his listeners, so that they might appreciate the emotions that he intended to express later. The assembled company found this music exceedingly commonplace. Gradually his playing assumed a more lively turn; the company was of the opinion that it was quite pretty. Now his tone became severe and solemn, while his harmonies grew more striking, more exalted, and at the same time less familiar; a number of the ladies present began to find him decidedly tedious, and to whisper in each others' ear a hint or two of criticism, a word of complaint; and so, before long, half the *salon* was chattering away merrily. The host could hardly contain his embarrassment; but eventually Mozart himself began to have an inkling of the impression that his music was making on the audience. He adhered notwithstanding to the principal theme that he had started to develop; but now he began to clothe it in all the fire and impetuosity of which he was capable. Still the company as a whole paid not the least attention. Whereupon he began to tell his audience exactly what he thought of it, and in no uncertain terms; yet all the while he never ceased to play; and since, luckily, his imprecations were in Italian, hardly a soul present understood a single word he said. For all that, the noisy chatter gradually died away; and when Mozart's anger had subsided likewise, he could not but laugh himself at his own impetuous behaviour. He began to give his themes a more popular twist, and finished the recital by taking a commonplace tune that everybody knew and by playing it in ten or a dozen charming variations. The entire company declared itself enchanted; and only a tiny number among those present had observed the dramatic incident that had occurred. Mozart none the less left the house immediately, meanwhile inviting his host, together with a select gathering of connoisseurs, to call upon him that very same evening at the inn where he was staying. He engaged them to stay to supper; and at the first hint expressed that they would care to hear him play, he began to extemporise on the harpsichord, where, to the extreme amazement of his audience, he remained, oblivious of all else, until well past midnight.

An ancient harpsichord-tuner had called upon him, in order to replace some of the strings of his travelling pianoforte*. "Now, my good man," said Mozart, "how much do I owe you?" The poor, decrepit creature gazed at him as though he were the living image of his God, he was dazed, crushed, annihilated, and in reply he could only stammer: "Oh your Imperial Majesty . . .! Oh Sire, Oh Most-Highest Kapellmeister to his Imperial Majesty . . .! I cannot . . . I know, for it is true, that I have called upon you more than once . . . Give me . . . Well, give me a single crown."

"A single crown!" exclaimed Mozart. "Why, that is absurd! No honest artisan, such as yourself, should take such pains and trouble for a single crown." Whereupon he made him accept a whole handful of ducats. The decent old fellow took his leave with deep, sweeping bows, still muttering over and over again: "Ah! Your Imperial Majesty!"

Among all his operas, *Idomeneo* and *Don Giovanni* were those which he esteemed most highly. He was not fond of talking about his own works; or, if he did so, he would invariably dismiss them in a few words. On the subject of *Don Giovanni* he once declared: "This opera was not written for Viennese audiences; it was much more to the taste of those of Prague; in the last resort, however, I composed it exclusively for my own satisfaction and for that of my friends."

His favourite time for composing was in the morning, from six or seven o'clock until ten. After which he would get out of bed. Not a line more would he write during all the rest of the day, unless he had some urgent work on hand that must be finished by a specified time. Once an idea had taken possession of him, nothing could drag him away from his scores. If he was forced to quit his piano, he would continue to compose in the company of his friends; and later he would spend night after night with his pen in his hand. Yet at other times, the labour of composition was so repugnant to him that he was utterly unable to complete a piece of music until the very last minute before the performance. On one occasion, when he had been commissioned to write a piece for a concert that was to be given at Court, he left it so late that he had not even time to score in the part that he himself was to play. The Emperor Joseph, whose inquisitive nature could leave nothing alone, came by chance to let his eye fall upon the sheet of music which, apparently, Mozart was following, and was amazed to see nothing but blank staves. "Where," he enquired, "is *your* part?" "There!" replied Mozart, tapping his forehead with his finger.

He came within a hair's-breadth of a similar mishap on the occasion of the Overture to *Don Giovanni*. It is fairly generally agreed that this is the finest of his Overtures; yet it was not until the night preceding the opening performance, when the dress-rehearsal had already been held, that he set to work on it. That evening, towards eleven o'clock, as he retired to his study, he entreated his wife to make him a bowl of punch, and to remain beside him in order to keep him awake. She agreed, and started to tell him a series of fairy-stories and of singular adventures, which caused him to laugh so heartily that the tears ran down his cheeks. The punch, on the other hand, tended to make him drowsy; with the result that he could work only so long as his wife persisted with her story-telling, and closed his eyes as soon as she stopped. In the end his efforts to keep awake, this continued alternation of wakefulness and dozing, left him so exhausted, that his wife persuaded him to snatch a short sleep, giving her word that, in an hour's time, she would arouse him. He promptly fell asleep, and slept so deeply that she left him for two hours. When she finally awakened him, it was five o'clock in the morning. Seven o'clock was the hour for which he had summoned his music-copyists; and when they arrived, the Overture was finished. In the time remaining, they were forced to write at top speed in order to have the necessary parts copied ready for the orchestra; and the instrumentalists were obliged to give their first performance without rehearsal*. There are indeed certain persons who claim that they can identify, in the Overture, those passages that Mozart wrote just as he was dozing off, and those which he composed just as he came back with a start to consciousness.

Don Giovanni was not particularly well-received in Vienna when it was first produced. Shortly after the *première*, discussion was raging away among a numerous company containing most of the true connoisseurs of the capital including, among others, Haydn. Mozart himself was not present. Everyone was in complete agreement that it was a work of great merit, the product of a brilliant imagination and rich in genius; yet at the same time, everyone found something or other to criticise. Each in turn had expressed his opinion, save only the ever modest Haydn. They begged him to give his verdict. "I have no competence to decide this issue," said he, with his accustomed self-effacement. "I know but one thing, which is that Mozart is the greatest composer who exists in the world today." The conversation turned hurriedly to other matters.

Mozart for his part had the deepest respect for Haydn. He dedicated to him a set of quartets* which may be numbered among the finest achievements in the genre. A certain Viennese composer, who was by no means devoid of merit, but whose talents were very far from rivalling those of Haydn, used to take a malicious pleasure in searching through the latter's compositions, meticulously picking out all the tiny inaccuracies that, by some oversight, had been allowed to creep in unperceived. He would frequently call on Mozart, invariably bringing with him a collection of Haydn's Symphonies or Quartets, in which he had put all the separate parts together to form a full score, and gleefully pointing out the passages in which, by following this method, he had discovered a few instances of stylistic carelessness. Unfailingly Mozart would attempt to change the subject; at long last, however, he could no longer restrain his irritation. "Sir," he declared on one occasion, impatience evident in his voice, "if you and I together were both rolled into one, there would still not be enough material to fashion a single Haydn."

There was once a painter who, desiring to flatter Cimarosa, declared to him one day that he considered him superior to Mozart. "*I*, Sir?" retorted the composer. "Tell me, Sir, what would *you* say to a man who came and told you that you were a greater artist than Raphael?"

CHAPTER FIVE

Mozart used to judge his own works, not only with impartiality, but frequently with a degree of severity that he would not gladly have suffered in another. The Emperor Joseph II was fond of Mozart and had made him his *Kapellmeister*; this same sovereign, however, had some pretentions to be thought a connoisseur and a devotee of the Italian style. His travels in Italy had left him infatuated with Italian music; and the small coterie of Italians whom he kept about him at his Court could hardly fail to encourage him in this particular prejudice, which, when all is said and done, appears to me to be reasonable enough.

In their discussions concerning Mozart's earlier works, jealousy tended to predominate over justice; and the Emperor, who rarely attempted any independence of judgement, was easily convinced by the verdicts of these musical enthusiasts. On one occasion, after he had been listening to a rehearsal of an *opera buffa* (*Die Entführung aus dem Serail*), which he himself had commissioned from Mozart, he addressed the composer: "My dear Mozart, it is too exquisite for *our* ears; there are far too many notes in it."

"I humbly beg to disagree with your Majesty," retorted Mozart, very drily indeed. "It contains exactly the number of notes that are necessary." The Emperor said nothing, and indeed appeared somewhat embarrassed by the reply; but when the opera was performed, he had no words of praise too lavish for it.

Subsequently, however, Mozart himself was less than satisfied with his achievement; he introduced a considerable number of cuts and alterations; and on a much later occasion, happening to play on the piano one of the arias which, originally, had been more enthusiastically applauded than any other, he remarked: "As chamber-music, that's fine; but for the stage, it's too garrulous. In the old days, when I wrote this particular opera, I used to be as pleased as Punch with anything I turned out, and thought nothing too long-winded."

Mozart was completely disinterested in money-matters; on the contrary, generosity was the very corner-stone of his nature. He would frequently give his money away to those who deserved it little; and even more frequently spend it senselessly, without a thought for the morrow.

In the course of a visit to Berlin, Frederick-William II, King of Prussia, offered him a regular salary of three thousand crowns (11,000 francs), if he would elect to reside at his Court and take charge of his orchestra. Mozart's reply was categoric: "Am I, then, to abandon my good Emperor?" Yet at this period, Mozart had no fixed pension in Vienna. One of his friends subsequently reproached him for having rejected the King of Prussia's offer. "I like living in Vienna," replied Mozart. "The Emperor appreciates me, nor do I care a fig for money."

None the less, exasperated by a series of vexations stirred up by his enemies at Court, he was driven to entreat the Emperor to grant him his discharge; yet a single word from His Imperial Majesty, who dearly loved our composer, and more still his music, caused him then and there to alter his resolve. He was not politic enough, however, to take advantage of this favourable opportunity and to solicit a regular pension; it was the Emperor himself who finally had the notion of establishing him on a firm material footing; unhappily, however, in his attempt to discover the most appropriate arrangement, he consulted an individual★ who was anything but well-disposed towards Mozart, and who proposed the sum of eight hundred florins (rather less than 2,200 francs). In all his life, Mozart never drew a salary higher than this. It was awarded to him as chamber musician to the Emperor; yet on no occasion did he write anything in this capacity. It happened once, in consequence of one of those general Orders in Council that are of such frequent occurrence in Vienna, that he was required to submit a statement containing the particulars of all the moneys that he received from the Court Treasury. His reply was enclosed in a sealed note: "Too much for what I have done, too little for what I might have done."

Music-sellers, theatrical managers and other such worshippers of Mammon, took almost daily advantage of his almost proverbial lack of interest in money-matters. Thus it came about that the vast majority of pieces that he wrote for the piano brought him literally not a penny. He would compose them in order to make himself agreeable to those whose society he frequented, whenever they chose to hint that they would be greatly obliged if they might have something from his own pen for their own private use and enjoyment. In cases such as these, he was obliged to match his composition precisely to the degree of skill that any individual had managed to acquire on the instrument of his choice; and this is the reason why, among his collected writings for the harpsichord, there are a great many which appear singularly unworthy of his genius. Artaria, the principal music-publisher of Vienna, together with a number of his colleagues in the trade, soon discovered how to get hold of copies of these pieces; whereupon they would promptly publish them without so much as asking permission from the composer, still less with the idea of offering him a remuneration.

CHAPTER SIX

One day a certain theatrical manager*, whose business had fallen into a deplorable state and had brought him to the very brink of despair, sought out Mozart and poured forth all the sorry details of his misery. "You, Sir," he added at the conclusion of his lament, "are the only man in all the world who can save me from utter ruin."

"I?" demanded Mozart. "How do you mean?"

"By writing an opera for me, an opera conceived exactly in accordance with the tastes and preferences of those who patronise my theatre. Of course you may at the same time contribute something, within limits naturally, for the connoisseurs and for your own reputation; but the essential thing to remember is that you are writing for a popular audience, to whom good music means absolutely nothing. I shall see to it that the libretto reaches you without delay, and that the décor is appropriately sumptuous—in a word, that everything is properly staged, just the way people like it nowadays."

Mozart was touched by the poor wretch's entreaty, and promised to take the business in hand.

"What sort of a fee will you require?" continued the theatre-manager.

"But you haven't a penny in the world," said Mozart. "However, listen. Here is an arrangement which will get you out of your difficulties and which, at the same time, will take care that I do not entirely lose all profit from my labours. I will give the score to you, and to you only; you can pay me what you think it is worth; but I will give it to you only on the express condition that you shall allow no single copy to be made of it. If the opera proves popular, I shall then proceed to sell it elsewhere."

The manager was overjoyed at Mozart's generosity, and promised and promised until he was forced to stop for breath. Mozart for his part hastily sat down and composed the music, contriving it exactly in the style which had been described to him. The opera was performed;

night after night the auditorium was filled to bursting-point; throughout the length and breadth of Germany the critics were full of it—and within a few weeks it was being produced on five or six different stages —naturally, without any of them having obtained their copies from the manager in financial difficulties.

This was not the only occasion on which Mozart encountered nothing but ingratitude at the hands of those whom he had obliged; yet nothing could cure him of his willingness to help those who were in trouble. Every time some needy virtuoso happened to pass through Vienna and, having no previous acquaintances in that city, appealed to Mozart, the composer would begin by making him free both of his house and of his board, would then introduce him to anyone who might prove useful to him, and would rarely allow him to depart before he had composed a concerto or two for his benefit; nor would he so much as keep a copy of these productions, esteeming that, if this particular performer and no other was able to play them, he would be able to display his talents to greater advantage.

On Sundays, Mozart would frequently give concerts in his own house. Now there was a certain Polish Count who was introduced on one of these occasions; and he, no less than all the rest of the assembled company, was delighted by a Quintet which, that very day, received its first performance. He openly declared to Mozart how enchanted he had been by the piece, and begged him to compose a flute trio for his own use, whenever he might find the leisure to do so. Mozart gave his promise, but only on condition that there should be no hurry over the matter. As soon as he had returned to his lodgings, the Count sent the composer the sum of a hundred golden half-sovereigns (rather more than 2,000 francs), together with a note conceived in the most courteous terms, thanking him for the pleasure which he had enjoyed that day. In return, Mozart sent the Count the original score of the Quintet which apparently had so delighted him. After which, our Count left Vienna. A year went by; at the end of which time he returned, called on Mozart and asked for news of his trio. "Sir," replied the composer, "I have not yet felt myself in the mood to compose something worthy of your Lordship."

"Nor, I suppose," rejoined the Count, "would you feel in the mood to repay the hundred golden half-sovereigns that I paid you for the piece in advance?" Mozart indignantly paid him back his sovereigns

Bust of Mozart by Rodin

The Hour of Music, a red chalk drawing by T. Gainsborough

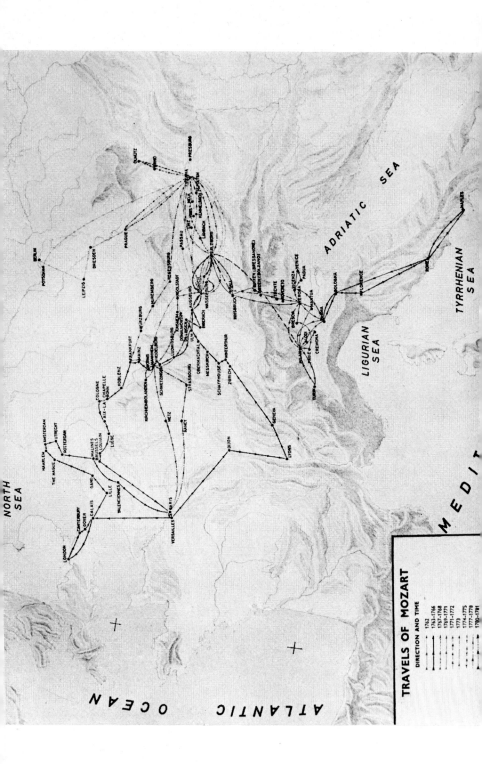

TRAVELS OF MOZART

DIRECTION AND TIME

1762
1763–1766
1767–1768
1769–1771
1771–1772
1773
1774–1775
1777–1778
1780–1781

then and there; but not a word did the Count breathe concerning the original score of that Quintet; and before long it was published by Artaria in the form of a Quartet for harpsichord, with accompanying parts for violin, viola and 'cello.

It was often observed that Mozart showed great promptness in adopting unfamiliar habits. The health of his wife, whom he never ceased to love passionately*, was exceedingly uncertain; and, during a long illness from which she suffered, he took to meeting everyone who came to call upon her, running up to them with his finger held to his lips, and signalling to them not to make a noise. In time, his wife recovered; yet for a long while still to come, he continued to welcome everyone who came to call on him with his finger held against his lips, and himself addressing them in a voice which scarcely rose above a whisper.

While this illness lasted, he would occasionally go out riding on horseback, alone in the early dawn; yet before he left the house, he never failed to leave a note, couched in the style of a doctor's prescription, beside his wife's pillow. Here is a sample of these prescriptions:

"Good morning, dearest one, I trust that you slept well, that nothing disturbed you.
Take good care:
　—not to catch cold,
　—not to hurt yourself by stooping,
　—not to fly into a temper with the servants.
Avoid anything that might upset you before I return.
Take good care of yourself.
I shall be back at nine o'clock."

Constanze was an admirable helpmeet for Mozart, and on more than one occasion she gave him invaluable advice. He had by her two children*, whom he loved most dearly. Mozart's income was considerable; yet his unbridled passion for pleasure, together with the wild disorder that reigned in the housekeeping accounts, resulted in the fact that, at his death, he bequeathed nothing to his family save the glory of his name and the benevolent concern of the Viennese musical audiences. After the great composer's death, the Viennese strove to manifest towards his children their deep gratitude for the pleasures that he had so many times afforded them.

During the closing years of his life, Mozart's health, which had always

8

been delicate, began to deteriorate rapidly. As with all those who are endowed with a high degree of imagination, he was frightened by the prospect of evil days to come and the idea that he had not long to live was a recurrent torture to him. When such a fit was on him, he would work so hard, with such rapidity and with such intense concentration, that he would sometimes grow oblivious to all that was not his art. Frequently, in the very heat of his enthusiasm, his strength would desert him, he would collapse from sheer exhaustion and have to be carried to bed. Everybody was fully aware that this insensate urge to work was destroying his health. His wife and his friends did all that lay in their power to distract him; so as not to distress them, he would accompany them on the walks and visits where they chose to take him; yet his mind was elsewhere. If, now and then, he was enabled to escape from this customary state of silent melancholy, it was only thanks to forebodings of his fast-approaching end—an idea which left him prey to a terror ever-renewed. We may discern here a type of madness similar to that which took possession of Torquato Tasso, or to that which afforded such perfect bliss to Rousseau in the vale of Les Char-mettes, revealing to him, under the influence of the fear of approaching death, the only true philosophy, which is to wrest enjoyment from the present instant and to draw the blinds against all sorrows. It may be that, without this exaltation of the nervous sensibility which borders close on madness, there can be no superior genius in those arts that require a most delicate susceptibility. Mozart's wife, distressed by this bizarre state of mind, made it her business to arrange for those persons whose society her husband enjoyed, to call upon him and to arrive "unexpectedly", as though by chance, just at the very moment when, after several hours of labour, he should, in the natural course of events, have been thinking of taking some rest. He took pleasure in these visits; yet for all that, he would not set aside his pen. There would be talk, and attempts would be made to involve him in the conversation; but he would not respond. If a remark were addressed to him, he would answer with a couple of disconnected words and promptly resume his writing.

Extreme concentration of this nature, moreover, is not infrequently the concomitant of genius, but is not invariably proof and evidence of it. Consider Antoine Thomas: who can digest his vast, bombastic accumulation of superlatives? And yet there were times when he was so profoundly absorbed in his meditations pertaining to the principles of eloquence that on one occasion, at Montmorency, it happened to him, when his lackey brought the horse upon which he was accustomed to take exercise, to offer the beast a pinch of snuff. Raphael Mengs likewise, in this present century of ours, contrived to be a very model of absent-mindedness, and yet he is no more than a decidedly third-rate painter; whereas Guido Reni, whose passion for gambling exceeded that of any normal mortal and who, towards the end of his life, would sometimes paint as many as three pictures in the course of the day in order to redeem those debts contracted during the course of the night, has left us works, the feeblest of which affords us greater pleasure than the proudest masterpieces of Mengs or of Carlo Maratta, who was the most industrious of God's creatures. A certain lady once confided to me: "Mr. So-and-So swears that until Doomsday I shall have dominion over his soul; ceaselessly he takes his oath that I and none but I alone shall be mistress of this soul of his. And indeed, I do verily believe him; but to what purpose, if this soul of his displease me?" And to what purpose likewise, all the industry of a being devoid of genius? Mozart furnishes what is perhaps the most striking instance in all the eighteenth century of the happy combination of *both* these qualities. Georg Benda, the composer of *Ariadne auf Naxos*, is another of those whose absent-mindedness is proverbial.

CHAPTER SEVEN

It was in this state of mind that Mozart composed *Die Zauberflöte*,[1] *La Clemenza di Tito*, his *Requiem* and many other less familiar pieces. It was while he was writing the music for the first-named of these operas

[1] At the time when *Les Mystères d'Isis* was being given in Paris, at the Grand Opera, a letter concerning this production, written by a German lady, was published in the press. Here follows an extract:

"I have seen *Les Mystères d'Isis*.* The décor, the ballets, the costumes—all these are excellent; but have I seen *Mozart's* opera? Have I received the faintest impression of his music? Categorically, no.

"*Die Zauberflöte*, in the original, is what in France is known as an 'opéra comique', that is to say, a comedy interspersed with lyrics. The libretto is based on the well-known

that he began to suffer, while in the very throes of composition, from those fainting-fits to which we have already referred. He was much

novel, *Séthos*; the dialogue is alternately spoken and sung. This is the general pattern that Mozart used as a framework for his delightful music, which corresponds so perfectly with the text.

"How could anyone fail to perceive that to transform such a work into a 'Grand Opera' is to distort its nature utterly and beyond recall? In order to give it a *dignity* acceptable to the Académie de Musique, it was necessary, first of all, to transform the spoken dialogue of the libretto into a species of recitative entirely foreign to it; it was necessary to intercalate a variety of arias and melodies which, just because they happen to be by the same composer, belong neither to the same opera, nor to the same style; finally it was necessary to inflate the original with a vast quantity of heterogeneous material, exclusively in order to introduce the sumptuous ballets with which it has gratuitously been enriched. The outcome of all this is a production which has nothing to do with Mozart; the musical unity is disturbed, the artistic intention of the whole is obscured, the enchantment vanishes.

"And yet all might have been well, had we only been allowed to hear Mozart's music as he himself originally wrote it! Far from it: many of the most striking passages, in this derisive parody, have been robbed of all their uniqueness, all their most characteristic features: tempo, pitch, significance—all these have been altered.

"In the German version, Bochoris* is a young bird-catcher who is merry, simple-minded and slightly clownish, and who, all unknowingly, carries about with him a magic flute; when he makes his entrance, he is dressed in a costume made of birds'-feathers; upon his back he bears the cage in which he secures his catch; and in his hand he holds the flute with which he inveigles his prey. He is heralded by a ritornello brimful of gaiety; and as he enters, he sings:

> *Der Vogelfänger bin ich ja,*
> *Stets lustig, heissa! hopsassa!*
> *Ich Vogelfänger bin bekannt*
> *Bei alt und jung, im ganzen Land.*
> *Weiss mit dem Locken umzugehn,*
> *Und mich auf's Pfeifen zu verstehn.* (Scale on the flute)
> *Drum kann ich froh und lustig sein;*
> *Denn alle Vögel sind ja mein.* (Scale on the flute)

"These are the lines which Mozart was given by his librettist, and which were transmuted through his imagination, emerging in the musical version that he deemed appropriate. In the place of these cheerful and simple phrases, the French librettist has forced his poor Bochoris to spout stanzas of high-flown sentiment. We heard of 'fond Nature's dam', of the 'faithful Graces', of

> Cupid who about them darts
> On ae'ry wing . . .*

—all of which may appear very pretty in France; but Mozart's tune tends to sound somewhat out-of-place.

"Our German Bochoris has a tune which he uses to express his anxious longing to chance upon some maiden who may return his love; to the strains of this same tune, his French equivalent utters a string of solemn moral platitudes a thousand leagues removed from the true spirit of the young Bird-Catcher:

> *La vie est un voyage:*
> *Tachons de l'embellir . . . etc.*

attached to *Die Zauberflöte*, although he was somewhat dissatisfied with a number of passages that the public loved most dearly, and which it

"This is *not* what Mozart wanted to say.

"Nor is it what Mozart wanted to say, when the stanzas of the charming duet that is sung by the Bird-Catcher and Princess Pamina are transformed into the following trio by some drawing-room poetaster:

Je vais revoir l'amant que j'aime . . . * etc.

In the original German, this episode constitutes a hymn to love, sung by two young beings, a Princess and a Bird-Catcher, who have met all alone in the middle of a forest; the melody is extremely beautiful in itself; and it becomes deeply moving when one recalls the innocence, the naïveté and the undefined emotions of the two creatures who are together on the stage.

"Similarly with the Nymphs of the Night, who appear to rescue the Prince from the threat of a venomous serpent that is making ready to attack him while he sleeps; these maidens have never beheld a man; their surprise and their terror are portrayed in their voices; yet of all this there is not a hint in the trio sung by the 'Ladies of Myrrhinus'.

"Again and again, a situation which is moving in itself, and whose dramatic development follows so simple and so natural a plan, is eliminated and in its place we find one of those dramatic platitudes, those everlasting artificialities, for the lack of which the French theatre would pine away and die.

"I will not insist upon those various passages which, to their considerable disadvantage, have been transposed into other keys, nor upon a number of other alterations; but I must voice my complaint, when I find that a quantity of the finest items have been suppressed altogether. In particular, I missed a charmingly simple little duet, sung by the two children; and a second duet, sung by the Prince and the Princess, after they have passed together through the ordeals by fire and by water. This dramatic situation, involving two lovers who together endure the perils of initiation, is one of the factors which persuade me to prefer the original German libretto, however baroque it may appear in other respects.

"In honour of Mozart's memory, therefore, it behoves me to declare to the people of France: your opera, *Les Mystères d'Isis*, is a striking piece of work, noble in sentiment, noble in style, and infinitely superior, perhaps, to our poor *Zauberflöte*: but it is *not*, it is not in the least, Mozart." *Wilhelmine**

Those who can recall both the original and the imitated versions will, I believe, find exemplified in this contrast the whole conflict between the *Classical* and the *Romantic* manners. The French versifier, of whom I know nothing, not even his name, in all probability was as proud as a turkey-cock at having produced something that smacked distantly of cousinship with the masterpieces of Racine and Quinault. What he failed to observe was that he had sacrificed every trace of natural simplicity, every suspicion of grace, every hint of originality; and that nothing is better calculated to lull the audience quietly into a doze than a play in which every spectator who has followed his course of lectures on the "Elements of Literature" at the Athénée is able to predict, during the course of each and every scene, exactly which incidents will follow. Given no greater element of genius on one side or the other, the Romantic manner may be held to have this advantage if no other: that of causing us a start of mild surprise. Would you learn the real truth concerning this famous quarrel which is destined to fill the literary columns of the press for half a century to come? It is this: that the Romantic manner—which is the manner of *true* poetry—will not countenance mediocrity. No Romantic drama, contrived with a measure of genius equal to that which inspired the latest eight or ten tragedies which you have

was never weary of applauding. This opera enjoyed a considerable number of performances; however, the enfeebled state of Mozart's health made it impossible for him to conduct the music, save on the first nine or ten occasions. On evenings when he was too ill to go to the theatre, he would place his watch beside him, while his mind appeared to be following the orchestra. "End of Act I," he would say; or else, "Now they are singing this, or that"; whereupon, once again, he would fall a prey to the idea that soon he would be forced to leave all this for ever.

At this point there occurred a somewhat curious incident, which greatly hastened the effect of this fateful mood. I beg the Reader's forbearance while I relate this incident in all its detail, since we owe to it the celebrated *Requiem* which is reputed, and with good reason, among the finest works that Mozart ever composed.

One day, while he sat buried deep in his thoughts, he heard a carriage drawing up before his door. A stranger* was announced, who desired to speak with him. The visitor was shown in; and Mozart beheld in front of him a man of mature years, dressed in the best of taste, whose manners spoke of much noble breeding and even held a suggestion of authority.

"I am commanded, Sir, by a man of great influence, to seek you out."

"What man is that?" interrupted Mozart.

"He desires not to make himself known."

"Splendid! And what does he want?"

"He has recently suffered bereavement of one who was very dear to

---

dispatched to me from Paris—contrived, I mean, with a measure of genius equal to that which produced, say, *Ninus II*, or *Ulysse*, or *Artaxerce*, or *Pyrrhus*—could have hopes to survive beyond the second scene. These reverberating alexandrins may be cloaks to hide the puffed-up emptiness of fools, but they offer no safe refuge against the Enemy of Enemies. A style, you call it? What sort of style is it, that cannot even quote the most characteristic saying of that most characteristically French of all great Frenchmen . . .?

It was King Henri IV who declared that he could wish that the poorest peasant in the Realm of France might have at least a fowl to stock his pot of a Sunday. In order to make this good King, this King who was such fountain of wit, acceptable on the stage, Legouvé makes him say:

> Je veux enfin qu'au jour marqué pour le repos,
> L'hote laborieux des modestes hameaux,
> Sur sa table moins humble, ait, par ma bienfaisance,
> Quel ques uns de ces mets réservés à l'aisance;
> Et que, grâce a mes soins, chaque indigent nourri,
> Bénisse avec les siens la bonté de Henri.

him, and whose precious memory he will cherish eternally; he desires each year to commemorate the death by a solemn service, and he requests you to compose a *Requiem* for this occasion." Mozart was vividly impressed by this speech, by the note of gravity on which it was spoken, by the aura of mystery that appeared to hang over the entire incident. He promised to undertake the *Requiem*.

"Place all your genius at the service of this work," pursued the stranger. "He who employs you is a true connoisseur of music."

"So much the better."

"How much time will you require?"

"Four weeks."

"Good. Then in four weeks' time I shall return. How much do you propose to ask for your labours?"

"A hundred ducats." The stranger counted them down on the table then and there, and vanished.

For the space of some instants, Mozart remained lost in deepest thought; then, suddenly, he called for pen, ink and paper and, despite the protests of his wife, began to write. This furious spate of exertion continued for several days on end; all day and all night, he composed without pause, and with an urgency that seemed to increase the further he advanced. But his body, already weakened, was unable to endure this trance-like concentration of effort; and one morning he collapsed in a coma and was forced to call a halt to his labours. Some two or three days later, in reply to his wife, who was attempting to distract him from the sombre thoughts that occupied his mind, he snapped back: "I know one thing at least: I am writing this *Requiem* for myself; it will come in handy at my own funeral service." Nor could anything clear his mind of this obsession.

The longer he worked, the more he felt his strength ebbing away from him day by day; and his score was desperately slow in taking shape. The four weeks that he had stipulated drew to a close; and one day he beheld the same anonymous caller on his doorstep.

"I have failed," said Mozart, "to keep my word."

"Don't worry," replied the stranger. "How much more time do you need?"

"Another four weeks. I have become much more deeply involved in the work than I had foreseen, and it has far outgrown the bounds of my original conception."

"In that case, it is only right that the fee should be increased proportionately; here are fifty ducats more."

"Sir," said Mozart, whose astonishment had never ceased to grow, "who are you?"

"That makes no matter. I shall return again in four weeks' time."

No sooner had he vanished, than Mozart called one of his servants, and ordered him to follow the stranger and to ascertain his identity; but the servant, whose skill in such exercises was limited, came back to report that he had lost all trace of him.

Poor Mozart now became obsessed with the idea that this mysterious caller was no ordinary mortal; that beyond question he entertained relations with the Other World, and that he had been sent to announce his own impending death. In consequence, his sense of urgency grew only more intense, as he laboured over that *Requiem* which he now conceived as the most lasting memorial to his genius. On several occasions as he worked, he collapsed with alarming fits of fainting. At length, however, before the four weeks were ended, the work was finished. At the expiry of the agreed term, the stranger reappeared; but Mozart was no more.

His career was as brief as it was brilliant. When he died, he was scarcely six-and-thirty years of age; yet in this short span of time he made himself a name that is destined never to perish, while men still live whose souls respond to the ineffable.

A LETTER CONCERNING MOZART

Monticello, 29 August 1814.

My dear Friend,

It is clear, from the letter which I have quoted above and which, in my opinion, gives an extremely accurate analysis of the situation, that Paris has no real knowledge of Mozart's operas, with the exception of *Le Nozze di Figaro*, *Don Giovanni* and *Così fan tutte*, which have been given by the Italian company at the Théâtre de l'Odéon★.

If we consider *Figaro*, the first observation that springs to mind is that the composer, whose soul lay ever at the mercy of his sensibility, has transmuted all those sentimental attachments—rarely more than skin-deep in Beaumarchais' original—with which the charming inhabitants of the Castle of Aguas-Frescas are wont to while away their leisure hours, into urgent and heart-felt passions. In the play, Count Almaviva wants to make love to Suzanne, but nothing more; he knows nothing of the passionate longing that echoes through the aria:

> *Vedrò, mentr'io sospiro,*
> *Felice un servo mio?*

and similarly inspires the duet:

> *Crudel! perchè finora*
> *Farmi languir così?*

Assuredly, the voice that we hear in these passages belongs to a being who has little or nothing in common with the man who, in Act III, scene 4 of the French play, speaks the following lines:

"Who is it, whose power reduces me to the slavery of this caprice? A score of times I have resolved to tear myself free. . . . Strange indeed are the effects of irresolution! Did I but desire her without desiring not to desire her, I should desire her a thousand times less!" Now how on earth could the composer have encompassed a notion such as this, which none the less embodies a great deal of truth? How can music be expected to convey a pun?

In the comedy, the audience has the impression that the Countess' inclination for Chérubin, her little page, *might* grow into something more serious; yet her secret soul with all its hesitations, the tender melancholy that possesses her, her musings upon the portion of happiness that destiny allots us, the divers and manifold heart-searchings that precede the birth of intense passion—all this is portrayed in infinitely subtler detail by Mozart than by the French comic dramatist. This secret landscape of the soul almost eludes the power of words to describe it; the situation is perhaps one of those that music can portray far better than language. Consequently, the arias sung by the Countess serve to characterise her in a manner that is completely new; and the same thing is true of the character of Don Bartolo, which is so admirably delineated in the great aria:

8*

> *La vendetta, oh, la vendetta*
> *È un piacer serbato ai saggi . . .*

Figaro's dark jealousy, in the aria:

> *Se vuol ballare*
> *Signor Contino . . .*

is a thousand leagues removed from the light-heartedness of his French predecessor. In this sense, one might argue that Mozart has distorted the sense of the original as much as possible. I am more than a little doubtful, whether music could in fact sustain those typically French moods of gallantry and gaiety over four whole acts and in every character; I fear it would be difficult; music requires clear-cut passions, exaltation or disaster. The subtle cut-and-thrust of repartee leaves the soul unmoved, the musing heart unsatisfied. Figaro, alluding to Chérubin's leap through the window, observes: "The urge to jump may at times become infectious; don't forget Panurge's sheep!" The idea is delicious, but the delight lasts only for about three seconds; if you dwell on it too long, if you say it over slowly, all the charm evaporates.

I would dearly love to hear a version of *Le Nozze di Figaro* with music by that most pleasing of composers, Fioravanti. In Mozart's interpretation, I can discover only one passage which conveys the true feeling of the original comedy, and that is in the duet:

> *Se a caso madama*
> *La notte ti chiama . . .*

sung by Susanna and Figaro; and even here, Figaro's jealousy has far too serious a ring about it, when he comes to the line:

> *Se udir brami il resto . . .*

Finally, to make the disguise impenetrable, Mozart concludes his *Folle Journée* with the most beautiful piece of church-music that can be heard anywhere: the passage occurs after the word:

> *Perdono!*

in the Finale of the whole opera.

Mozart has entirely transformed the picture that was painted by Beaumarchais. The wit has evaporated, surviving only in the actual dramatic situations; the characters have grown tender and passionate. Chérubin is the merest sketch in the original comedy; by contrast, the very depths of his soul are laid bare in the arias:

Non so più cosa son, cosa faccio . . .

and

Voi che sapete
Che cosa è amor . . .

and in the concluding duet with the Countess, when they meet together amid the darkened pathways of the garden, hard by the clump of towering chestnut-trees.

Mozart's opera is a sublime fusion of wit and melancholy, and as such is unique, for there exists no other example. The consistent portrayal of sadness and tenderness may, in the long run, threaten to be tedious; but here, the provocative wit of the French comic dramatist, which sparkles through every situation, categorically eliminates the only possible flaw that might be implicit in the style.

In order to retain the spirit of the original, the music should have been written in collaboration by Cimarosa and Paisiello. Alone among composers, Cimarosa might have endowed Figaro with all the scintillating gaiety and self-confidence that we associate with the character. I know of nothing that corresponds more nearly to such a personality than the aria:

Io quand'ero un fraschettone
Sono stato il più felice . . .*

and it must be confessed that this aspect of Figaro is but feebly portrayed in the one and only light-hearted aria that Mozart has given us:

Non più andrai farfallone amoroso . . .

It might even be asserted that the tune of this aria holds a hint of banality; its charm derives wholly from the manner in which, gradually, it becomes more and more expressive.

As for Paisiello, it is enough to recall the Quintet from *Il Barbiere di Siviglia*, in which Basilio is told:

Andate a letto . . .

to appreciate that he was pre-eminently capable of depicting purely comical situations, in which no warmth of feeling is involved.

Considered as a masterpiece of the purest tenderness and melancholy, entirely unadulterated by any unwanted ingredient of solemnity, whether tragic or majestic, there is nothing in all the world that can be compared to *Le Nozze di Figaro*. One of my delights is to imagine a production with one of the Mombelli sisters in the part of the Countess; with Bassi as Figaro; with Davide or Nozzari as Almaviva; with Signora Gafforini as Susanna; with the other Mombelli sister as Cherubino; and with Pellegrini as Dr. Bartolo.

If you have ever heard these wonderful voices, you will be able to share in my daydream; yet it is impossible to talk significantly to people about music, save in terms of what they themselves remember. I might, by dint of superhuman effort, succeed in conveying to you some impression of Guido Reni's *Aurora*, that is to be seen in the Palazzo Rospigliosi, even though you had never set eyes upon it in all your life; but I should be as tedious as the perpetrator of some effusion of *poetic prose*, were I to attempt to speak to you of *Idomeneo* or of *La Clemenza di Tito*, with any such profusion of detail as I have given in respect of *Figaro*.

It may be asserted as a plain, unvarnished truth, and without fear of succumbing to those magnifying mirages which offer such a constant temptation whenever one is discussing a genius such as Mozart, that there is absolutely nothing that will bear comparison with *Idomeneo*. I will readily confess that, contrary to the opinion that is held throughout the length and breadth of Italy, the greatest *opera seria* that has ever been written is not, for me, *Gli Orazi e Curiazi*; it is *Idomeneo*, or perhaps *La Clemenza di Tito*.

In music, the majestic manner soon becomes the manner tedious. Music is utterly incapable of expressing Horace's line:

Albano tu sei, io non ti conosco più;

still less the high-minded patriotic spirit that inflames the part from beginning to end. By contrast, the characters of *La Clemenza* are motivated one and all by tenderness and tenderness alone. Is it possible to conceive a more tender inspiration than that of Titus saying to his friend:

Confidati all' amico; io ti prometto
Che Augusto nol saprà?

And in the final scene, that of the pardon, when Titus says to him:

Sesto non più; torniamo
Di nuovo amici . . .

the situation is calculated to bring tears to the eyes of the most rhinoceros-hided of tax-collectors. I have observed this phenomenon with my own eyes, at Königsberg, at the conclusion of the terrible Retreat from Moscow. Coming at long last safe again ashore on the coasts of the civilised world, we discovered an excellent production of *La Clemenza di Tito* in progress in that city, where the Russians were courteous enough to allow us twenty days' respite, of which, to tell the truth, we stood in no little need.

To have the least conception of *Die Zauberflöte*, it is absolutely essential to have seen it*. The libretto, which seems to have much in common with the irresponsible fantasies of a tender imagination run riot, harmonises as though by some special dispensation of Providence with the genius of the composer. I am convinced that Mozart himself, had his genius lain in the literary field, would have immediately sketched out the situation of the blackamoor Monostatos, as he approaches by moonlight, deep in the silence of the night, and steals a kiss from the lips of the sleeping Princess. Here, chance contrived a unity of which music-lovers hitherto had known but one example: Rousseau's *Le Devin du Village*. The same man, one might almost say, created both words and music.

Molière's wholly romantic imagination at work in his *Don Juan*, with its portrayal of such an immense variety of fascinating situations, varying from the murder of Donna Anna's father to the invitation issued to the Statue, addressed in person, and the Statue's terrifying answer—all this, yet once again, harmonises in the most miraculous fashion with Mozart's genius*.

His terrifying accompaniment to the Statue's reply is a masterpiece, completely untainted by the slightest suspicion of false grandeur or of classical bombast; it is the equivalent, in music, of "terror" as conceived by Shakespeare.

Leporello's fright, in the scene where he is desperately searching for an excuse not to have to address the Commendatore, is depicted in a vein of pure comedy—an achievement which, in itself, is rare enough in Mozart; on the other hand, those whose souls are susceptible to such things may carry away from this same opera memories of a score of details steeped in purest melancholy—and this, even in Paris, where the average spectator will, by curtain-fall, have kept no recollection even of the lines:

> *Ah! rimembranza amara!*
> *Il padre mio dov'è?**

Don Giovanni had no success in Rome; it is conceivable that the orchestra simply failed to master the extremely difficult score; yet I would wager that the day will come when Roman audiences will applaud it heartily.

The libretto of *Così fan tutte* would have been ideal for Cimarosa; it was totally unsuited to the genius of Mozart, for whom love was never a laughing matter. Love, for him, was at all times the passion that could make or mar his life*. His interpretation revealed only one side of the characters, their tenderness of heart; he failed altogether with the humorous part of the sardonic old Sea-Captain. However, here and there he redeemed himself by virtue of his supreme skill in harmony, as towards the end, in the Trio:

> *Tutte fan così . . .*

Mozart is even more remarkable taken as a subject for philosophical speculation than considered as the creator of immortal masterpieces. Never before did chance contrive to offer us the spectacle of the very soul of genius as it were stripped naked. In no combination of circumstances could the physical being have played a lesser part than in that astonishing duality of soul and body that the world was to know as *Mozart,* and whom our present-day Italians like to call *quel mostro d'ingegno.*

Metastasio

LETTERS CONCERNING METASTASIO

LETTER I

Varese, 24 October 1812.

My dear Friend,
   The common run of mortals too readily disdain the quality of *grace*.
It is a characteristic of vulgar minds, to revere only that which inspires
in them a certain element of fear. This is the reason why, in human
society, the Soldier is an object of universal admiration; and why, on
the stage, the tragic manner enjoys the highest esteem. The herd will
applaud only where there is unmistakable evidence of obstacles surmounted; and this explains why Metastasio enjoys so unremarkable a
reputation, if we compare that reputation to his true deserts. There is
no man so dull that he cannot comprehend Titian's *Martyrdom of St.
Peter*, where it hangs in the Musée de Paris; but there are few indeed
who are able to appreciate Corregio's *St. Jerome*. The majority
needs to be taught that this latter style of beauty, so filled with charm
and grace, is none the less beauty for all that. In this domain, women,
so infinitely less bowed down beneath the habitual burden of calculat-
ing egoism than are their men-folk, enjoy a marked superiority.
   The purpose of music is to inspire physical pleasure; and Metastasio
was the musician's poet *par excellence*. His gentle inspiration drove him
to eschew anything that might cause the audience the least distress, be
it never so remote. He draws a veil over the anguish of the heart, whenever it threatens to become too painful; his endings are never unhappy;
his world knows none of the dreary realities of life; he reveals nothing

of those chilly suspicions which instil their venom into the tenderest of human passions.

He realised that, so long as the music of his operas was good, it would distract the spectator from his sorrows by causing his mind to dwell upon the object that he loved; consequently, at every step, he reminds us of all that we need to know about his characters, if we are to grasp the import of what they are singing. He seems to be saying to his audience: "Surrender to pleasure; even your faculty of attention will not be taxed; follow your natural bent, and forget all about the play and its dramatic structure; be happy, there, deep in the recesses of your box; listen to my character and feel what he feels, in all its tenderness." His heroes retain scarcely a trace of the drabness of reality. He has invented beings shot through and through with flashes of *joie de vivre* and inspiration, such as real creatures, even those born beneath the most propitious of stars, have encountered only in the rarest, most blessèd instants of their existence: a Saint-Preux, setting foot in Julie's bedroom.

Strictly reasonable people—people who can read Tacitus and Alfieri unrepelled by their embittered irony; whose musical sensibility, being developed hardly or not at all, is infinitely far even from suspecting the true object of this entrancing art; who, insensitive to the thousand pricks and stabs that, in real life, come ever and anon to wound the tender heart or, worse still, to drag it down once more to the level of flat and stale reality—such people, say I, on reading Metastasio, have affixed the label "*Not True*" to that which, in effect, is the very summit of art. "Falsehood" of this type is indeed a deliberate contrivance of art, since it represents the condition necessary to produce a specific category of enjoyment. It is as though one were to criticise the sculptor who created the *Apollo Belvedere* for having omitted all those tiny details of muscular structure which may be observed in the *Gladiator*, and in various other statues which represent, not Gods, but merely men. The truest thing that one can say is that the particular brand of pleasure which is afforded by one of Metastasio's operas is simply not appreciated in that land which lies encompassed by the Rhine, the Alps and the Pyrenees. I behold in my mind's eye a typical Frenchman—a man of intellect and culture, well-versed in the correctest comment to make on any matter that may worthily occupy the attention of a man of the world—setting foot in the Vatican Palace, and there discovering its entrancing *loggie*, decorated by Raphael with those charming arabesques which are perhaps the purest and most celestial inspirations that ever human genius, urged on by love, was prompted to create. Our good French friend, however, is shocked: shocked at the improbability of it all; his reason cannot assimilate those womens' heads borne high on lions' bodies, those cupids riding horseback on chimaeras. "But it's not *natural*," he protests, his voice dogmatic. Indubitably true. And likewise indubitably true is this: that *you*, you who live in France, can have no inkling of that species of delight that a man born beneath happier skies may find while savouring ices in the Villa d'Albano*, during the cool of the evening that follows a scorching day. He is in the company of charming women; the heat, now at last retreating, induces a mood of sweetly sensuous languor; he reclines upon a horsehair couch; and thence his gaze, travelling over a ceiling embellished with a glorious wealth of colour, is caught, caught and compelled to follow the entrancing contours that Raphael has bestowed upon those creatures which, since they bear no resemblance to anything we may have encountered elsewhere, can awaken in us none of those dreary, commonplace ideas which, in such rare and magical instants, destroy felicity beyond recall.

I am further persuaded that the darkened theatres of Italy*, and those boxes, which are drawing-rooms in miniature, have much to do with the impression created by the music. Are they not well-nigh innumerable, all those delightful women who, in France, have learnt English, and for whom the word *love* possesses a fascination that the word *amour* has lost for ever? The reason? Simply that the word *love* has never been uttered in their presence by one of those sorry, low-born creatures, whose hearts are ever unworthy to sense its meaning. The word *love*, in all its virgin purity, remains unsmirched; whereas the word *amour* lies muddy and bedraggled in my mind, soiled by the memory of every popular lyric and dance-tune that was ever written.

And it is beings sensitive to nuances such as this who are destined to appreciate Raphael's arabesques; nor will they appreciate any less those glittering creatures, whose hearts are pure and free from all base human instincts, that Metastasio invites us to behold.

He excludes everything that might recall the dismal and realistic side of life, driving it far hence into outer darkness. From the welter of the passions he has selected only so much as he needs to awaken sympathy; nothing bestial, nothing that leaves a bitter taste in the mouth; upon the rough violence of physical desire, he bestows a patent of nobility.

He never conceived his poetry, save in the context of music. Now music, his most beloved art, is excellently suited to the expression of the passions, whereas individual dramatic characterisation lies quite outside its scope. Consequently, in Metastasio's operas, the Enamoured Roman and the Persian Prince afflicted with a similar passion will speak, through his libretti, an identical language, for the simple reason that Cimarosa, in setting these libretti, will give each of these beings an identical language through his melodies. Patriotism, faithful friendship, filial devotion, the honour of chivalry—all these, too, are passions with which history or society have made us familiar; yet in Metastasio they acquire an unfamiliar charm; you will find yourself gently wafted towards lands unknown, the country of the Houris of the Prophet.

To such inaccessible peaks of idealism are his dramas transported; and it is fatal to *read* them; they must never be heard, save in the context of the music. Yet it is *such* pieces that the chilly critics of a certain country have analysed as though they were Racinian tragedies. These poor devils, with a blindness not dissimilar to that which possessed the legendary Crescimbeni, one of their illustrious Italian predecessors, who, in his *Studies in Literature*, took the *Morgante maggiore*, one of the most hilarious (and, in places, rather more than hilarious) epics in the language, for a piece of serious writing; these poor boobies, say I, who would have been better advised to apply themselves to some less hazardous trade, failed even to notice that Metastasio was so far from seeking to inspire "pity and terror", that he even categorically refuses to portray anything which is unpleasant: and this alone is reason enough why he should lavishly have been patronised by such Governments as desire to lull their subjects into submission with physical pleasures. What! Would you suggest that this world of ours might be better ordered? Would you criticise the *status quo*? Shame upon you! You will make us hate each other; you will, if you have your way, succeed only in breeding discontent among us: besides, Sir, it is damned bad manners!

These miserable critics were well and truly scandalised by the frequency with which Metastasio chose to violate that sacred law decreeing *Unity of Place*; nor did they for one instant suspect that the Italian poet, instead of abiding dutifully by this Rule, in fact was following a precept of his own devising, and which decreed the very opposite— namely, to change the location of his scenes as frequently as possible, so that the splendour of the *décors* which, in Italy, rise to such heights of magnificence, might afford a pleasure constantly renewed to the eyes of his delighted audience.

It was Metastasio's intention to waft us, for our enjoyment, ever further away from the realities of life; on the other hand, if he were to show us, in his characters, beings similar to ourselves, for whom we might feel sympathy, it was essential for him to adhere to an unfailing *truth to nature* in his portrayal of details. This is the feature of his work that raises it to a level of equality with Shakespeare and Virgil, and exalts it infinitely far above Racine and the rest of the world's great poets.

I must rush to arms, for I perceive that I have given cause for scandal; my arms shall be quotations.

Yet into what language could you hope to translate the following?

> *Un pauvre bûcheron, tout couvert de ramée,*
> *Sous le faix du fagot aussi bien que des ans*
> *Gémissant et courbé, marchait à pas pesants,*
> *Et tâchait de gagner sa chaumine enfumée.*
> *Enfin, n'en pouvant plus d'effort et de douleur,*
> *Il met bas son fagot, il songe à son malheur.*
> *Quel plaisir a-t-il eu depuis qu'il est au monde?*
> *En est-il un plus pauvre en la machine ronde?*
> *Point de pain quelquefois, et jamais de repos.*
> *Sa femme, ses enfants, les soldats, les impôts,*
>   *Le créancier, et la corvée*
> *Lui font d'un malheureux la peinture achevée.*
> *Il appelle la Mort. Elle vient sans tarder,*
>   *Lui demande ce qu'il faut faire.*
>   *"C'est, dit-il, afin de m'aider*
> *A recharger ce bois; tu ne tarderas guère."*

It is with Metastasio as it is with our own La Fontaine: they are perhaps the two most untranslatable poets in the world.

Let us glance at one or two of his dramatic situations. In *L'Olimpiade*, which is Pergolesi's masterpiece, Clisthenes, Tyrant of Sicyon, is to preside over the Olympic Games. His daughter Aristea* is to be the trophy awarded to the victor; she for many years has been in love with Megacles, by whom her love is returned; yet this young Athenian, renowned for his triumphs at the Olympic Games, has been rejected by

the Tyrant, who abominates the very name of Athens. Forced to flee
from Sicyon, he has taken refuge in Crete, where Lycidas, Prince of
that country, had occasion to save his life at the peril of his own. The
two friends arrive together at the Games, which are presided over by
Clisthenes. Lycidas beholds Aristea, and falls in love with her. He calls
to mind the triumphs that his friend has previously secured at these
celebrated Games; and, there being no tradition of such exercises in
Crete, he begs Megacles to enter the lists in his stead, under his name,
and thus to win for him the beautiful Aristea. Megacles emerges vic-
torious from the contest; but he has been recognised by Aristea, all
a-tremble with emotion. For an instant, he contrives an excuse to draw
Lycidas away, and to remain alone with his beloved: her happiness
knows no bounds.

SCENA NONA
Megacle, Aristea.

Aristea:
    Alfin siam soli:
    Potrò senza ritegni
    Il mio contento esagerar; chiamarti
    Mia speme, mio diletto,
    Luce degli occhi miei . . .

Megacle:
                No, principessa,
    Questi soavi nomi
    Non son per me: serbali pure ad altro
    Più fortunato amante.

Aristea:
             E il tempo è questo
    Di parlarmi così? . . .
    . . . .
    . . . .

Megacle:
              Tutto l'arcano
    Ecco ti svelo. Il principe di Creta
    Langue per te d'amor. Pietà mi chiede,
    E la vita mi diede. Ah! principessa,
    Se negarla poss'io, dillo tu stessa.

Aristea:
> E pugnasti . . .

Megacle:
> > Per lui.

Aristea:
> > > Perder mi vuoi . . .

Megacle:
> Sì, per serbarmi sempre
> Degno di te.

Aristea:
> > Dunque dovrò . . .

Megacle:
> > > Tu dèi
> Coronar l'opra mia. Sì, generosa,
> Adorata Aristea, seconda i moti
> D'un grato cor. Sia, qual io fui fin ora,
> Licida in avvenire. Amalo. È degno
> Di sì gran sorte il caro amico . . .
> . . . .

Aristea:
> Ah! qual passaggio è questo! Io dalle stelle
> Precipito agli abissi. Eh no: si cerchi
> Miglior compenso. Ah! senza te la vita
> Per me vita non è.

Megacle:
> > Bella Aristea,
> Non congiurar tu ancora
> Contro la mia virtù. Mi costa assai
> Il prepararmi a sì gran passo. Un solo
> Di quei teneri sensi
> Quant'opera distrugge!

Aristea:
> > E di lasciarmi . . .

Megacle:
> Ho risoluto.

Aristea:
> > Hai risoluto? E quando?

Megacle:
>Questo (*morir mi sento*)
>Questo è l'ultimo addio.

Aristea:
>   *L'ultimo! Ingrato* . . .
>*Soccorretemi, o Numi! il piè vacilla:*
>*Freddo sudor mi bagna il volto; e parmi*
>*Ch'una gelida man m'opprima il core!*
>   (S'appoggia ad un tronco)

Megacle:
>*Sento che il mio valore*
>*Mancando va. Più che a partir dimoro,*
>*Meno ne son capace.*
>*Ardir. Vado, Aristea: rimanti in pace.*

Aristea:
>*Come! già m'abbandoni?*

Megacle:
>   *È forza, o cara.*
>*Separarsi una volta.*

Aristea:
>   *E parti* . . .

Megacle:
>   *E parto*
>*Per non tornar più mai.*
>   (In atto di partire.)

Aristea:
>*Senti. Ah, no!* . . . *Dove vai?*

Megacle:
>*A spirar, mio tesoro,*
>*Lungi dagli occhi tuoi*
>   (Parte risoluto, poi si ferma.)

Aristea:
>*Soccorso* . . . *Io* . . . *moro.*
>   (Sviene sopra un sasso.)

Megacle:
>   (Rivolgendosi indietro)

Misero me, che veggo!
Ah! l'oppresse il dolor! Cara mia speme,
(Tornando.)

Bella Aristea, non avvilirti; ascolta:
Megacle è qui. Non partirò. Sarai . . .
Che parlo? Ella non m'ode. Avete, o stelle,
Più sventure per me? No, questa sola
Mi restava a provar. Chi mi consiglia?
Che risolvo? Che fo? Partir? Sarebbe
Crudeltà, tirannia. Restar? Che giova?
Forse ad esserle sposo? E'l re ingannato,
E l'amico tradito, e la mia fede,
E l'onor mio lo soffrirebbe? Almeno
Partiam più tardi. Ah! che sarem di nuovo
A quest'orrido passo! Ora è pietade
L'esser crudele. Addio, mia vita: addio,
(Le prende la mano, e la bacia.)

Mia perduta speranza. Il ciel ti renda
Più felice di me. Deh, conservate
Questa bell'opra vostra, eterni Dei;
E i dì, ch'io perderò, donate a lei.
Licida . . . Dov'è mai? Licida!

SCENA DECIMA
Licida, e detti

Licida:
Intese

Tutto Aristea?

Megacle:
Tutto. T'affretta, o prence,

Soccorri la tua sposa.
(In atto di partire.)

Licida:
Ahimè! Che miro!

Che fu?

Megacle:
Doglia improvvisa
Le oppresse i sensi.

Licida:

         E tu mi lasci?

Megacle:

                 Io vado . . .
Deh! pensa ad Aristea. (Che dirà mai
Quando in sè tornerà! Tutte ho presenti,
Tutte le smanie sue.) Licida, ah! senti!
    Se cerca, se dice:
    L'amico, dov' è?
    L'amico infelice,
    Rispondi, morì.
    Ah no! sì gran duolo
    Non darle per me:
    Rispondi, ma solo:
    Piangendo partì
    Che abisso di pene
    Lasciare il suo bene,
    Lasciarlo per sempre,
    Lasciarlo così!

           (Parte.)

It was in 1731, to the best of my belief, that Pergolesi journeyed to Rome in order to write *L'Olimpiade*; the opera was a fiasco. Since, in Italy, Rome is the capital city of all the Arts, and since it is beneath the gaze of this Roman audience, at once so exquisite in its taste and so skilful in its connoisseurship, that every artist must prove his worth, this fiasco caused Pergolesi great distress. He returned crestfallen to Naples, where he composed a number of pieces of sacred music. Meanwhile, his health was deteriorating from one day to the next; for four years he had been afflicted with a vomiting of blood that was gradually undermining his whole constitution. His friends persuaded him to rent a cottage at Torre del Greco, a village situated on the seashore, at the foot of Mount Vesuvius. In this locality, those who suffer from maladies affecting the chest are reputed, either to recover more speedily, or else, if the disease will admit of no alleviation, to succumb more rapidly than elsewhere.

Pergolesi, from his solitary retreat in this cottage, would sally forth to Naples once a week to conduct performances of the pieces that he had composed in the interim. It was at Torre del Greco that he wrote his famous *Stabat Mater*, the cantata *Orfeo*, and the *Salve Regina*, which was the last of all his works.

Early in the year 1733, his last remaining strength being entirely exhausted, he quitted this life; and the obituary notice which appeared in the *Gazette*, on the occasion of his death, was at the same time the signal that heralded his immortality. Not an *impresario* in the whole of Italy, but would give his operas, and none but his; whereas only a short while before, they had neglected them utterly. Rome demanded to behold once more his *Olimpiade*, which was revived in a production of untold splendour. The greater the indifference shown by one and all towards this incomparable masterpiece, while its author yet lived, the greater the enthusiasm with which its beauties now were greeted.

In this opera, which is the unrivalled masterpiece of dramatic expression in the whole repertory of Italian music, there is no scene in which this quality more markedly prevails than in that which we have just quoted. The aria:

Se cerca, se dice . . .

is known by heart throughout the length and breadth of the Peninsula and is perhaps the principal reason why *L'Olimpiade* is no longer revived. No manager would be prepared to risk producing an opera, whose most significant aria is already familiar to every member of the audience.

In *L'Olimpiade*, music constitutes a second language, whose powers of expression are exploited by Pergolesi to reinforce the expressiveness of that normal language which is spoken by Metastasio's characters. But Pergolesi's language, which is capable of portraying the very faintest of nuances in the fluctuations of a heart possessed by passion— nuances which are far too subtle to lie within the scope of any literary language—loses all the power of its enchantment as soon as it is forced to move at speed. In consequence, the composer has reduced the encounter between Megacles and Aristea to the status of a simple recitative, reserving the full intensity of that divine language that he spoke so well for the aria:

Se cerca, se dice . . . ,

which is perhaps the most deeply-moving piece that he ever wrote.

It would have been contrary to the most elementary principles of the musical art to have interpreted the entire scene in terms of singing. The melody which could depict the *reasons* that make the unhappy Megacles in duty bound to sacrifice his mistress to his friend, simply does not exist.

On the other hand, the greatest dramatic actor in the world, speaking the lines:

Se cerca, se dice:	If she should look for me, if she
L'amico, dov' è?	should ask, "Where is my love?"
L'amico infelice,	You are to answer thus:
Rispondi, morì	"My unhappy friend is dead."
Ah no! sì gran duolo	Ah! No, you must not cause her
Non darle per me:	such suffering on my account;
Rispondi, ma solo:	Tell her rather this, and this alone:
Piangendo partì.	"He went forth from here weeping."
Che abisso di pene	What an abyss of sorrow!
Lasciare il suo bene,	To quit the object of one's love,
Lasciare per sempre,	To quit it for ever,
Lasciarlo così!	and to quit it thus!

—no matter what degree of tenderness he, with all the skill at his command, might contrive to instil into his manner of utterance, he could declaim them but once; he could portray but a single one among the thousand different ways in which the soul of the ill-fated Megacles is torn asunder. There is not one among us but must sense, however obscurely, that at the moment of so cruel a separation, there would be a score of ways, all equally impassioned and all distinct, in which, addressing the friend who is destined to remain beside a mistress so dearly cherished, one could utter the words:

> *Ah no! sì gran duolo*
> *Non darle per me:*
> *Rispondi, ma solo:*
> *Piangendo partì.*

The unhappy lover might speak these lines, now with extreme emotion, now with resignation and courage; now perhaps with some faint glimmering of hope that Destiny might relent and now with unrestrained despair in the face of irremediable misfortune.

It is inconceivable that he should speak to his friend of the sorrow that lies in wait for Aristea the moment she regains consciousness without his imagination leaping forward to his own impending plight; consequently the lines:

Ah no! sì gran duolo
Non darle per me . . .

which are repeated five or six times by Pergolesi, are endowed with five or six different intonations in the language in which he clothes them. In the portrait which the great composer has given us of Megacles' unhappy plight, the uttermost limits of human sensibility have been attained. Such a state of anguish, we feel, cannot endure; a few minutes of such music are enough to leave both singer and audience emotionally exhausted; and this, my dear Friend, explains why, in Italy, a well-sung aria will be applauded with such delirious intoxication. For the great singer is one of the noblest of human benefactors: he has plunged an entire audience into the very wellhead of divine delight—a delight, of which the listeners would instantly have been deprived by the minutest lapse or the tiniest careless blemish on his part. Never did any man, perhaps, afford greater pleasure to his fellow-mortals than did Marchesi, when he sang the rondo:

*Mia speranza! io pur vorrei . . .**

from Sarti's *Achille in Sciro*.[1] This pleasure was a reality; its existence is an historical fact. To discover its equal, we must quit the narrow confines of real life, and resort to that realm of imaginary situations, the novel: we must visualise the instant when the Baron d'Étange took Saint-Preux by the hand and gave consent to his marriage with his daughter.

What will be plain is that the composer requires no more than six or seven short lines of verse provided for him by the librettist; and once

---

[1] On 29 August 1774, a lady of sensibility, who was far from suspecting that one day her correspondence would be published, wrote these words to her lover:
"Could it perchance have slipped my memory, to tell you that I have listened to Millico? He is Italian. Never, no never has such perfection in the art of singing been married to such a degree of sensibility and expression. What tears did he cause to start forth from the eye! What tempests did he stir up in the soul! My senses swam; never did anything make so deep, so heart-rending, indeed so agonising an impression upon my soul; yet I could have wished never to cease listening to his voice, until I had died from excess of it." (*Letters of Mademoiselle de Lespinasse*, 1809, Vol. I, p. 185.)

the latter has properly developed and elucidated a genuinely dramatic situation, he is able to bring tears to the eyes of a whole crowded theatre. His music will illustrate not only the primary force of the passion that possesses his hero, but in addition not a few among the hundred different variations of mood to which this hero's soul is subject while he is actually addressing the mistress of his heart. Is there any man living who, at the instant of separation that is to tear him from the being whom he adores, will not reiterate the words: *Adieu! Adieu!* and then again, and still again, *Adieu!* The actual word that passes his lips is always the same; yet what being is so utterly benumbed by his misery as to be unable, later, to recall that the syllables, at each and every repetition, were uttered with a different intonation? The reason is evident: for, in all such instants of joy or anguish, the heart is in a constant state of flux and varies from one second to the next. Yet it stands to reason that our everyday vernacular tongues which, after all, are nothing but a series of conventional symbols designed to express a number of generally familiar concepts, should include no special symbols to express such subtle nuances, which no more than twenty people, perhaps, out of every thousand have ever experienced. As a result, those rare beings endowed with true sensibility were unable to communicate their impressions one to the other, nor to portray them. And then, close on a century ago, in Italy, there arose some seven or eight men of genius who finally discovered this language, for want of which such difficulties had arisen. This language, however, has one defect: it remains unintelligible to all those nine-hundred-and-eighty beings out of every thousand who have never experienced the phenomena that it describes. Such people, confronted by a Pergolesi, behave as we ourselves should do, were we confronted by some savage redskin of the Miami tribe who, in his uncouth tongue, should tell us the name of some American tree which grows in the trackless forests through which he passes as he hunts, and yet which we ourselves have never seen. The word that strikes our ear is nothing but mere sound; nor can it be denied that if our savage were to prolong his disquisition, the same sound would very soon grow singularly tedious.

Since we are being frank, let us not stop half-way. If, even as we stifle our own yawns, we perceive in our neighbours every sign of the intensest pleasure, we shall instinctively strive to throw a wet blanket over this insolent enjoyment, which we ourselves possess no means of

sharing; and it is only natural that, judging others according to ourselves, we should deny the reality of their preposterous emotions, and
do our best to ridicule the delight that they absurdly claim to feel.

It follows, then, that there is nothing in the world more futile than
arguing about music. Either one feels it, or one does not; and that is the
end of the matter. Unhappily for the cause of Truth, however, it has
nowadays become *fashionable* to cherish a passion for this gentle art.
Even old Duclos, than whom no man was wittier and whose wit was
so satirical and dry—even he, setting out on his *Italian Journey* at the
age of sixty, must needs inform us that he has "a passionate fondness"
for music. The devil he has! What an idea!

Now this language, which nowadays it is so fashionable to cherish so
passionately, is of its nature exceedingly imprecise. It required a poet
endowed with powers to act as guide to our imagination; and it was
the good fortune of a Pergolesi, a Cimarosa, to discover precisely such
a poet in Metastasio. The language of music penetrates directly to the
heart, as it were without passing through the mind; it acts directly,
producing *pleasure* or *pain*; in consequence, the first quality of our
composers' poet must of necessity be that of endowing his characters
with unfailing clarity in their discourse; and this, precisely, was
Metastasio's achievement.

Every character who is touched, be it ever so lightly, by the wand of
music is thereby raised to an ideal degree of beauty. Beaumarchais portrays Chérubin in a light and airy style; Mozart, using a language that
possesses infinitely greater power, had only to give *his* Cherubino the
arias:

> *Non so più cosa son, cosa faccio . . .*

and

> *Voi che sapete*
> *Che cosa è amor . . .*

to leave the charming mannerisms of French comedy a thousand
leagues behind. Molière wrote scenes which, to any man of taste, are a
sheer delight; yet could even such a genius as his—a genius, moreover,
that created so many things that music cannot even aspire to—could
even the genius of a Molière contrive to paint comic portraits as rich in
their effect as those realised by Cimarosa in the arias:

Io quand'ero un fraschettone,
Sono stato il più felice . . .

and

Sei morelli e quattro baj . . .

and

Le orecchie spalancate . . . ?

It is to be observed that Cimarosa's comic arias one and all produce their effect *in spite of* the words which, three times out of four, descend to indescribable depths of banality. On the other hand, it is worth noting that these words nearly always manage to depict, through the characters, either a clearly-defined emotional state, whether of happiness or unhappiness, or else a comico-satirical situation which is lively in pace and rich in absurdity; and that these are precisely the qualities that music demands above all others. Music shies away in terror from those intricate and at times truly touching subtleties that we find so enchanting in Marivaux. To illustrate my point, I would gladly quote the whole of Pergolesi's *Serva Padrona* . . . were it but known in Paris. Since, however, this bewitching music has never yet been heard on the banks of the Seine*, and therefore cannot be called to mind by words, let me be allowed instead to quote from one of the most delightful men that was ever nurtured by our gentle land of France.

In the year 1740, being then in Bologna, the Président de Brosses* addressed to a friend of his in Dijon a letter which contains the following passage—a passage which he assuredly never thought to see in print:

". . . however, among all his many duties (alluding to Cardinal Lambertini, Archbishop of Bologna and later Pope, under the name of Benedict XIV), one of the most imperative and inescapable is that of appearing in person thrice a week at the Opera. Now, this Opera is not to be discovered here in the city of Bologna; in truth, were that the case, no one would be seen there, for such a mean employment of time would appear to lie beneath a Gentleman's attention; since, however, it is to be found in a village that lies some four leagues distant from the city, fashion decrees a most punctilious attendance. Dear God! It is a wonder to behold how all the fops and fashionable ladies do bestir

Stage set by Alessandro Sanquirico for Metastasio's *Alessandro nelle Indie*

Pietro Metastasio

themselves, congregating thither as fast as a quartet of post-horses, hurriedly harnessed to a travelling-coach, may convey them, as though they were bound for some amorous assignation! At this season of the year, there is scarce another opera to be found in the whole of Italy. For a country troupe, the performance is by no means despicable; nor is it only that choruses, ballets, libretti, singers even, are far from devoid of talent; but rather, that these Italian arias are of such surpassing beauty that, do they but fall upon the ear, all other desires are stilled upon the instant. In particular there are two players, both masters of the comic manner, a *buffo* and his partner who, during the intervals in the *opera seria*, offer a *farsa* which they perform with such spontaneous mimicry and with such a wealth of comic expression, as can neither be overpraised nor yet imagined. Were it true that a man might die of laughter, then should I assuredly be dead beyond recall, and that despite the irritation that I felt at the distension of my spleen, a phenomenon that occasioned me some distraction and hindered me from attending as appreciatively as I had wished to the heaven-inspired melodies of this operatic farce. The music is by Pergolesi. Then and there, from off the conductor's music-stand, I purchased the original score, which I intend to carry with us back to France. To complete the picture, the feminine portion of the audience makes itself decidedly at home in the theatre, converses loudly, or, to adhere more closely to the truth, shouts at the top of its voice from one box to another across the intervening space, stands up and claps its hands with piercing shrieks of *Bravo! Bravo!* As for the men, their behaviour is a degree more restrained. They confine themselves, when the curtain falls on an act that they have fancied, to shouting and applauding without remission, until the players shall have begun it all over again; after which, the clocks now striking midnight, all go their various ways, dispersing homeward by pairs of couples cross-linked by mutual inclination—unless they should vote rather to sup before returning, here on the spot in some local tavern or eating-house."

In these delightful *opere*, comic no less than tragic, the arias and the full flow of melody begin only with the onset of passion. At the first hint of passion in the libretto, the composer will seize upon it; but all the rest, all that serves but to prepare these outbursts, is reduced to recitativo secco.

As soon as the character shows signs of being possessed by the beginnings of some intense emotion, the recitative will be enriched by an

9

orchestral accompaniment, written in by the composer himself—as in that wonderful recitative which is sung by Crivelli, in the second act of *Pirro*:

> *L'ombra d'Achille*
> *Mi par di sentire . . .*

or as in that which is given to Carolina, in Act II of *Il Matrimonio Segreto*:

> *Come tacerlo poi, se in un ritiro*
> *Ad entrar son costretta!*

And if and when the character becomes *wholly* possessed of the passion that afflicts him, at that precise moment the aria will begin.

There is one singular feature that calls for comment: namely, that the librettist, if he wishes to develop intricate conceptions in eloquent language, must of necessity confine himself to the recitatives. At the first suggestion of passion, the composer will require nothing further from him save the barest minimum of words; he and he alone must bear responsibility for all emotional expression.

Let us examine one or two other dramatic situations as they were conceived by our charming friend Metastasio. Were I to disclose this letter of mine amid that agreeable company that is wont to foregather at Madonna del Monte*, and whose society, my dear Louis, I presently propose to join, there is not one among these delightful persons but would be familiar with all the melodies which go with the lines that I am about to set down here; nor would he refrain from singing them softly to himself. How different, how singularly different, from the situation that prevails in those distant lands where you are fated to dwell!

> *Oh! fortunatos nimium, sua si bona norint!*
> Virgil, *Georgics*, II—458.

Alack, wretched creatures that ye are, know yet happiness while still there is time! Is this not madness? We tremble with indignation; we work ourselves up into frenzies of hatred; we busy ourselves eternally with all these *Weighty Interests* of politics which, if the final truth be told, interest us not one jot! That the King of Spain should go a-hunting after Philosophers and hang the lot; that Norway should propose for itself a Constitution, a sound, well-reasoned one, maybe, or else, maybe, absurd—what matters it to *us*? Are we such fools, then, that we must assume the cares that go with greatness, and *only* the cares? These days and hours that you daily throw away in futile debate and argument: these hours are precious in your lives; old age draws nigh, and youth will soon be gone:

> *Così trapassa al trapassar d'un giorno*
> *de la vita mortale il fiore e' l verde:*
> *nè perchè faccia indietro april ritorno,*
> *si rinfiora ella mai, nè si rinverde . . .*
> *. . . amiamo or quando*
> *esser si puote riamato amando.*

Tasso, *Gerusalemme liberata*, canto XVI, octave xv.

LETTER II

Dante was endowed by nature with the gift of mature reflection; Petrarch, with a host of attractive ideas; Boiardo and Ariosto, with vivid imaginations; yet none of these can lay claim to a style of thought as lucid and as precise as Metastasio's; none of these, in his own particular field, succeeded in achieving a degree of perfection as unique as did Metastasio in the genre that was his own.

Dante and Petrarch, Ariosto and Tasso—all these bequeathed to their successors some fleeting glimpse of a chance, on rare and happy occasions, to imitate their style. Here and there some singular and fortunate mortals of exceptional talent have arisen, and even contrived to write a line or two that these great men might not perchance have disavowed.

There is more than one sonnet by Cardinal Bembo that can stand comparison with Petrarch; Monti, in his *Bassvilliana*, fashioned not a few *terzine* which are not unworthy of Dante; while Boiardo found, in Agostini, if not an imagination rival to his own, at least a tolerable imitator of his style. I could quote you a little handful of octaves which, at first glance, by the richness and the ingenuity of their rhymes, suggest the hand of Ariosto. I can call to mind a greater number still, whose harmonious and majestic ring might conceivably have deluded even Tasso himself; whereas, despite the thousands of attempts which, for nigh on a century now, have been made to produce even a single aria in the manner of Metastasio, the whole of Italy has not yet beheld two lines together that, by the furthest stretch of the imagination, could foster the illusion for an instant.

Among all the poets nurtured by the soil of Italy, Metastasio is unique in that, until the present day, he has remained quite literally inimitable.

Who has the patience to count up the *Replies*—wellnigh innumerable —that have been written to his *Canzonetta a Nice?* Yet not a single one is readable; nor, to the best of my knowledge, does anything comparable exist in any other tongue; not even in Anachreon, not even in Horace.

LA LIBERTÀ

A NICE
CANZONETTA

Grazie agl'inganni tuoi,
Al fin respiro, o Nice!
Al fin d'un infelice
Ebber gli Dei pietà!

FREEDOM
To Nice
A CANZONET

Thanks to your falsehood, O Nice, at last I draw breath again! At last the Gods have shown mercy to a mortal wretch!

Sento da' lacci suoi,
Sento che l'alma è sciolta;
Non sogno questa volta,
Non sogno libertà.

Mancò l'antico ardore,
E son tranquillo a segno,
Che in me non trova sdegno
Per mascherarsi amor.

Non cangio più colore
Quando il tuo nome ascolto;
Quando ti miro in volto,
Più non batte il cor.

Sogno, ma te non miro
Sempre ne' sogni miei;
Mi desto, e tu non sei
Il primo mio pensier.

Lungi da te m'aggiro
Senza bramarti mai;
Son teco, e non mi fai
Nè pena, nè piacer.

Di tua beltà ragiono,
Nè intenerir mi sento;
I torti miei rammento,
E non mi so sdegnar.

I feel that my soul is loosed from its bondage; no, this time it is no vision, no vain dream is my freedom.

The fires which so long did consume me now are cold and dead; and once more I am calm, so calm that not even anger remains in my heart, to serve as a mask for love.

No longer do I change colour nor blush at the sound of your name; my heart no longer beats wildly whenever I gaze on your face.

Dreams may I have now that are not unfailingly of you; nor, when I awaken, are my first waking thoughts of you alone.

When I am parted from you, I no longer yearn unceasingly for your presence; and when I am close by your side, it causes me neither pleasure nor pain.

I can speak of your beauty, and yet remain unaffected by it; I can recall the wrong that you have done me, and yet be free from anger.

Confuso più non sono
Quando mi vieni appresso;
Col mio rivale istesso
Posso di te parlar.

Volgimi il guardo altero,
Parlami in volto umano;
Il tuo disprezzo è vano,
E vano il tuo favor.

Che più l'usato impero
Quei labbri in me non hanno;
Quegli occhi più non sanno
La via di questo cor.

Quel che or m'alletta o spiace,
Se lieto o mesto or sono,
Già non è più tuo dono,
Già colpa tua non è.

Che senza te mi piace
La selva, il colle, il prato;
Ogni soggiorno ingrato
M'annoia ancor con te.

Odi, s'io son sincero:
Ancor mi sembri bella;
Ma non mi sembri quella
Che paragon non ha.

When you draw near me, I am no longer troubled; I can discuss you, even with him who is my rival.

Dart your disdainful glances at me, or favour me with kindly words; vain is your contempt and vain your generosity.

Your lips no longer hold me in their ancient thrall; your eyes no longer discern the road that leads to my heart.

Today my delight or distress, today my joy or despair reside no longer in your gracious gift, depend no longer on your guilt.

Forest, hill and meadow delight me now, even when you are absent; while cheerless abodes depress me, even despite your company.

Hearken, if I be not sincere! For even now you seem beautiful to me; but no longer do I behold you as the One who has no peer.

E (non t' offenda il vero)
Nel tuo leggiadro aspetto
Or vedo alcun difetto,
Che mi parea beltà.

Quando lo stral spezzai,
(Confesso il mio rossore)
Spezzar m'intesi il core
Mi parve di morir.

Ma per uscir di guai,
Per non vedersi oppresso,
Per racquistar sè stesso
Tutto si può soffrir.

Nel visco, in cui s'avvenne
Quell'augellin talora,
Lascia le penne ancora,
Ma torna in libertà.

Poi le perdute penne
In pochi dì rinnova,
Cauto divien per prova,
Nè più tradir si fa.

So che non credi estinto
In me l'incendio antico,
Perchè sì spesso il dico,
Perchè tacer non so.

And more (if I speak truth, be not offended!): for now I observe in the grace of your features some slight defects which once I deemed perfections.

At the instant when I snapped my chains (I do now confess my shame), it seemed to me my heart would break, I thought that I should die.

Yet to escape from the thraldom of misery, to earn release from oppression, to be master once more of my own soul—for this, no suffering is too great.

So it may chance with some small bird that falls into a snare; not a few feathers may remain behind, and none the less he will regain his freedom.

. . . and then, within a space of days, the lost feathers will grow again; experience will have made him wise, nor will he ever again be deceived.

Well do I know that you will not believe these fires of old to be extinct in me, because I speak so constantly of what befell me, because I cannot hold my peace.

Quel naturale istinto,
Nice, a parlar mi sprona,
Per cui ciascun ragiona
De' rischi che passò.

Dopo il crudel cimento
Narra i passati sdegni,
Di sue ferite i segni
Mostra il guerrier così.

Mostra così contento
Schiavo, che uscì di pena,
La barbara catena,
Che strascinava un dì.

Parlo, ma sol parlando
Me soddisfar procuro;
Parlo, ma nulla io curo
Che tu mi presti fè.

Parlo, ma non dimando
Se approvi i detti miei,
Nè se tranquilla sei
Nel ragionar di me.

Io lascio un' incostante;
Tu perdi un cor sincero;
Non so di noi primiero
Chi s'abbia a consolar.

That which urges me to speak, O Nice—it is the natural instinct which impels us one and all to celebrate the dangers which we once encountered.

Thus does the warrior, once the bloody battle is over, retell the tale of his by-gone fury and show the scars of his wounds.

Not otherwise, nor with less pleasure, does the sometime slave, now set at liberty, display the cruel chains which, in days gone by, he used to drag at his ankles.

I speak, 'tis true; and yet in speaking I seek for nothing but my own satisfaction; I speak, yet caring nothing, whether you should believe me or not.

I speak, yet without enquiring whether *you* approve of my thoughts, nor whether your heart is at peace, should you chance to speak of me.

I have quitted a faithless mistress, whereas you have lost a true lover; nor can I tell which of us two will earliest find consolation.

So che un sì fido amante
Non troverà più Nice;
Che un' altra ingannatrice
È facile a trovar.[1]

The clarity, the precision, the sublime facility which, as may be seen, characterise the style of this great poet, and which are such indispensable qualities in any lyric that is destined to be sung, possess the further, unexpected advantage of making his works extremely easy to get by heart. It needs no conscious effort for the memory to retain these inspired stanzas which, while they display implicit obedience to the minutest precepts of versification, contrive none the less to silence the least suspicion of constraint.

The *Canzonetta a Nice* appeals to a particular aspect of the sensibility; to that same element which responds with such delight to *La Maddelena*, that little painting by Correggio which hangs in Dresden and which has been so excellently reproduced in Longhi's engraving.

It is no easy matter to read *La Clemenza di Tito*, or *Giuseppe riconosciuto*, and to remain dry-eyed the while; nor does the Italian stage offer many speeches able to rival in sublimity certain passages from the roles of Cleonice and Demetrio, Temistocle and Attilio Regolo.

I can see nothing in any language that may fittingly be compared to Metastasio's *Cantatas*. I would be sorely tempted to quote them all at length.

Alfieri excelled above all other poets in his gift for depicting the

---

Yet this I know: that Nice will never discover so constant a lover again; whereas such another false mistress is easy enough to be found.

[1] An excellent instance of love *à l'italienne*, in the manner of Cimarosa: its sorrows, in truth, diminish its joys, yet never destroy the sentient being. A German would have left us a description of the ravages that the anguish of love has occasioned in his mortal body; he can admit no evidence of the intensity of a passion, save the unlovely portrait of the maladies that it produces. Compare, in French, the novels of Madame Cottin.

The translation that has been provided here serves no purpose other than to facilitate the Reader's understanding of the original text. As one translates this famous *Canzonetta*, the inherent *naïveté* of the Italian language, compared with our own, can be felt at every line. Repeated infidelities to the original are essential, if an intolerable degree of banality is to be avoided; spontaneous expressions of feeling must be transmuted into epigrams; epithets must be added to words which, without this accompaniment, would ring too harsh and denuded in French ears. Yet the fifteen or twenty *Studies in Literary History* which, during the past few years, have been published in France, give us a *very* different picture of the Italian language.

9*

minds of tyrants and the reason, I believe, is this: had he himself been endowed with fewer moral qualities, he was likely, had he ever been elevated to the throne, to have proved a tyrant of sublimest stature. There are scenes from his *Timoleone* which are superb: the style, I am perfectly well aware, bears no resemblance to that of Metastasio; yet I am not convinced that posterity will inevitably label him the greater poet. Alfieri's style, as one reads him, thrusts itself too readily upon the attention. Style is like the transparent varnish that covers a canvas: spread over all the colours equally, its function is to intensify their brilliance without distorting them; in Alfieri, however, style claims a part of the attention to itself.

Who, reading Metastasio, has ever a thought to spare for style? The verse simply sweeps one along, unresisting. Metastasio is the only poet outside France whose manner has given me a delight equal to that which I discover in the poetry of La Fontaine.

For fifty years, not a birthday, not a wedding occurred at the Court of Vienna, unless it were duly celebrated in an *Occasional Ode*, supplied upon request by Metastasio. Is it possible to conceive of drearier material? In France, in such circumstances, all we ask of a poet is that he should prove himself slightly less than execrable; Metastasio is sublime; the more barren the soil, the richer the harvest.

Observe moreover, my dear Friend, that Metastasio, with his opera-libretti, has cast a spell not only over Italy, but over the cultivated minds of every Court in Europe; and that this singular victory was achieved by faithful adherence to the following convenient and simple little rules:

Every libretto must contain parts for six characters, all diversely in love, so that the composer may begin by having contrasts to exploit. The leading castrato, the prima donna and the tenor, being the three principal participants in the opera, are to be allotted five arias apiece: an outburst of passion (*l'aria patetica*); a display of technical virtuosity (*aria di bravura*); a piece in sustained and homogeneous style (*aria parlante*); an exercise in *demi-caractère*; and finally, an outpouring of unrestrained joy (*aria brillante*). The drama must be divided into three acts, and must not exceed a given number of lines; each scene must conclude with an aria; the same character may never sing two arias in succession, nor may two arias belonging to the same category come one upon the heels of the other. Acts I and II must conclude with arias of a more impressive type than are found elsewhere in the opera. In Acts II and III respectively, the librettist must contrive a pair of neat little niches, the first to contain a recitativo obbligato followed by an aria in the Grand Manner (*di trambusto*), the second to accommodate a heroic duet—not forgetting, however, that this latter must invariably be sung by the leading pair of lovers. These are the rules of the genre—without them, no music! It goes without saying that, in addition to the above, the librettist must provide as many opportunities as possible for the stage-manager and the scene-painter to display their skill and ingenuity. However bizarre they may appear, these "rules"—of which a number were formulated by Metastasio himself—have been vindicated by experience; nor, as practice has consistently proved, may they be disregarded without endangering the effectiveness of the opera.

As a final point, let it be noted that this great lyric poet, to help him in his task of producing one miracle after another, had at his disposal no more than a seventh part, approximately, of the total number of words available in the Italian language. This language possesses in all some four-and-forty thousand, according to a modern lexicographer, who has actually taken the trouble to count them; whereas the language of the opera will admit no more than six or seven thousand at the very most.

At the very end of his life, Metastasio wrote the following lines to one of his friends:

". . . His Majesty was so delighted by the female roles in *Il Re Pastore* that, for my sins, he has commanded me to contrive, between now and next May, another libretto in a similar manner. With my poor head in its present state of confusion, thanks to the constant state of nervous disorder wherein I live, it is a desperate business indeed to have to meddle with such hoydenish creatures as the Muses. Yet my labours are rendered a thousand times more distasteful still, in consequence of all the divers impediments to which I am subjected. To begin with, all Greek or Roman subjects are ruled out of court, since our chaste nymphs will in no wise countenance such improper costumes! I am obliged to resort to Oriental history, in order that all the noble ladies playing male parts may be duly and decently swaddled from head to foot in Asiatic draperies. Anything so bold as a contrast between vice and virtue is of necessity excluded from these dramas, because none of the ladies is prepared to play the part of a villainess. I may employ but five characters, for the excellent reason once given by the Governor of a certain stronghold, that it is impolitic to allow one's superiors to get lost in the crowd.[1] The length of the performance, the number of scene-changes, the arias, everything, almost down to the precise and actual number of words in the text, is laid down by immutable decree. Tell me, is this not sufficient to drive the most tractable of men into the pit of distraction? Conceive, then, the effect that all this has on me, who am the High Priest of all the evils that befall us in this Vale of Sorrows!"

The most ironical of circumstances—one which proves, moreover, that Chance enters into everything, even into the verdicts of that fearsome old scarecrow, *Posterity*—is that it was commonly felt to be a sort of generous concession when such a man was eventually promoted to a status of equality with Laura's chilly lover, who left us nothing but half a hundred sonnets, not lacking, I grant you, in a certain suavity.

By the time he was ten years old, Metastasio, born in Rome in 1698, was already famous for his improvisations. A wealthy Roman lawyer named Gravina, who, as a cure for boredom, used to write atrocious tragedies, fell victim to the child's charm: for a start, inspired by his *admiration for the Hellenic tongue*, he changed his name from Trapassi to Metastasio; he then adopted him, took infinite pains to ensure his proper education—which, by a miracle, was destined to be excellent—and finally, in his will, left him an independence.

In the year 1724, when Metastasio was twenty-six, his first opera, *Didone abbandonata*, was performed in Naples. In writing it, he had scrupulously followed all the advice offered to him by the beautiful Marianna Romanina, whose memorable performance in the part of Dido was directly inspired by her passionate devotion to the poet—an attachment, it appears, which was to prove durable. Metastasio, who became an intimate friend of Marianna's husband, for several years lived as a member of the household, surrendering to the pleasures of sweet music and tirelessly studying the Greek poets.

In 1729, the Emperor Charles VI, that notable music-maker who never laughed and who, in his youth, had played so despicable a role in Spain, summoned him to Vienna as resident librettist to his private opera-house. Metastasio hesitated for some little while, but in the end agreed.

Once in Vienna, Metastasio was destined to remain there for the rest

[1] These operas were performed by Archdukes and Archduchesses.

of his life. In that same city he survived to an extreme old age, surrounded by all the luxuries pertaining to a refined and aristocratic sensuality, and having no other care nor concern save to express, in noble verse, the emotions that were engendered in his noble soul. Dr Burney, who saw him when he was two-and-seventy years of age, deemed him to be still the handsomest man of his century, and found him also the merriest. He constantly set his face against all orders, decorations and titles, hid his life in deep obscurity, and was happy. To none of the tenderer emotions did this sensitive creature remain a stranger.

In the year 1780, having attained the venerable age of eighty-two, and being now on the point of receiving the Last Sacraments, he gathered together the remaining ounces of his strength and sang this final hymn to his Creator:

> *Eterno Genitor,*
> *Io t'offro il proprio figlio*
> *Che in pegno del tuo amor*
> *Si vuole a me donar.*
>
> *A lui rivolgi il ciglio,*
> *Mira chi t'offro; e poi*
> *Niega Signor, se puoi,*
> *Niega di perdonar.*

It was on 2 April 1782 that Metastasio, a man who had been both great and happy, passed away; having been acquainted, during the course of his long career, with every one of those great composers whose music charmed the world.

A LETTER CONCERNING THE PRESENT STATE
OF MUSIC IN ITALY

Venice*, 29 August 1814.

And so, dear Friend of mine, you still recall those letters that I addressed to you from Vienna some six years since? And now you would be obliged if I would furnish you with a sketch of the present state of music in Italy? Since those earlier days, my ideas have developed in quite a new direction. Today I am both wealthier and happier than I was then in Vienna; and all my leisure, when it is not devoted to the circle of my acquaintance, is sacrificed to studying the history of painting.

You are familiar with the extent of my delight, when at last I recovered an independence, albeit one barely sufficient to answer my daily needs. It would seem, however, that I was misled by my ambitions; for, out of this so-called "bare sufficiency", I daily contrive to set aside enough to purchase excellent small pictures—works which the great collectors have disdained, or rather whose merit they failed to recognise. Only a few days ago, at the house of a sea-captain, the most courteous of mortals, whose lodgings lie on the Riva degli Schiavoni, I was privileged to contemplate some charming little sketches by Paolo Veronese, filled with that same wondrous shimmer of golden colour which gives so much life to his large canvases. Well, believe it or not, but I already entertain the hope that I may succeed in acquiring for myself one or two similar sketches by this great painter, whose masterpieces, along with so many others, lie well and truly buried in your cavernous Musée de Paris. In France, you pride yourselves on being civilised; yet, by robbing Italy of her finest treasures, you have behaved no better than barbarians. Vandals that you are, you failed to perceive, when you carried off the paintings, that of necessity you left behind the atmosphere which is essential to their enjoyment. You have diminished the quantity of pleasure that exists in the world. Not a few fine canvases that now hang solitary and as it were forgotten in some remote corner of your gallery, were once the pride and glory of a whole city, and daily furnished matter for endless conversation. The traveller who arrived in Milan would hear about Titian's *Crown of Thorns*, ere he had scarcely climbed down from his coach; in Bologna, your hired guide would begin by enquiring whether you wished to visit Raphael's *St. Cecilia*; and even this menial would have got by heart some half-dozen ready-made phrases touching the masterpiece of his city.

Now, none knows better than I how utterly, intolerably tedious is the sound of such guide-book phrases to the genuine amateur of the Arts, whose only desire is to experience and to judge for himself; again and again, his ears are veritably deafened by the roar of Italian superlatives; yet this raging torrent of hyperbole is in itself a symbol of the general attitude of the country towards the Fine Arts. These same superlatives that *I* find tedious, may yet chance to awaken a love of Art in the breast of some young tailor of Bologna who, one day, is destined to become an Annibale Carracci. They bear, perhaps, some resemblance to those marks of deference which daily greet the Marquis of Wellington as he passes through the streets of Lisbon; for assuredly the little attorney's clerk who cries *e viva!* is utterly incapable of appreciating the military genius and the inspired prudence of this rarest of mortal men; yet no matter: for the hero himself, such shouting constitutes the due reward of all his merits; and meanwhile, as the applause rings in the ears of that young Captain who is his aide-de-camp, it may serve further to inspire and mould a second Wellington.

No man in Rome is better known, nor yet more highly esteemed, than Canova; whereas, in Paris, the Great Personage who will be familiar to the common people of any given district is Monsieur le Duc de ✱✱✱, whose mansion stands at the corner of the next street. This simple contrast will suffice to show that you have gained precisely nothing by carrying off to Paris the *Transfiguration* and the *Apollo Belvedere*; you have gained precisely nothing by transferring on to canvas that *Descent from the Cross* which Daniele di Volterra originally painted in fresco, and by carrying that work likewise off to Paris; one and all, these masterpieces are *dead*; you have the art, but where's the audience?

An Italian Opera-House is an excellent thing, and so is an Art Gallery

—if you want such institutions, then have them: I approve. By such means you may at long last manage to acquire, in Art, in Opera, a smattering of taste, a rooted passion for the mediocre; yet never hope for greatness. *Your* field of genius lies not in art or music, but rather in comedy, in the satirical ballad, in books of ethics spiced with irony:

Excudent alii spirantia mollius æra
Virgil, VI, v. 847.

O People of France! *Your* destiny is to produce men such as Molière: another Collé France may hope to see, another Pannard, another Hamilton; a second La Bruyère, more Dancourts, further *Lettres Persanes*. In this delicious genre, no rival nation will ever threaten your supremacy; cultivate it therefore, pour all the richness of your talents into it, encourage writers whose abilities lie in this direction; for greatness springs unbidden from the very soil that you trample heedlessly under foot. The orchestra* that plays at your Théâtre-Français is a torture to the ear; replace it: refurbish the stage; deck it out with those spectacular sets which may be seen at the Teatro alla Scala in Milan—sets whose colour is changed every two months, yet which cost no more than does a similar area of common-or-garden canvas*. When this is done, there is not a cultivated mind in Europe, from Stockholm in the North to Naples in the South, but will foregather in the Place du Carrousel and make a bee-line for the Théâtre-Français, to see *Tartuffe*, to watch *Le Mariage de Figaro*. We who have travelled abroad, *we* know that plays such as these can be performed nowhere in all the world, save only in Paris.

And in similar fashion, the paintings of Lodovico Carracci may be considered invisible, outside Lombardy. Among all those delightful women who frequent your society, can you name me one who ever managed to look at certain paintings without yawning her pretty head off—at the *Christ calling St. Matthew*, for instance, or at that *Entombment of the Virgin*, whose shades have blackened imperceptibly with time? There is not a man or woman of fashion in the whole of France—of this I am persuaded—who could for an instant tell the difference between these original masterpieces on the one hand, and the crudest of copies on the other, provided that the latter were placed in the right frames. Yet in Rome, this same fashionable society will talk and argue two whole weeks on end, discussing the manner in which that fresco, painted by Domenichino for the Convent of St. Nilus, is destined to be transferred to canvas. No one, in Rome, is esteemed more highly than the great Artist; in Paris, it is the successful General or the Privy-Councillor who has the Royal favour, it is the Maréchal de Saxe or Monsieur de Calonne who attracts the admiring glances of the public. I am not arguing that this is either right or wrong; I am merely pointing out the bare facts of the case. And the great Artist who cherishes his reputation and who knows full well the foibles of the human heart, must of necessity choose to live where his merits will be best appreciated and where, in consequence, his defects will be most severely criticised. In Rome, the painters X and Y and Z—I have never met them, mark you, but I am familiar with their delightful works—will assuredly keep their reputations intact even if they choose to live in a fourth-floor garret; the whole metropolis, high and low, from the nephew of the Pope himself to the humblest of parish priests, will clamber up the narrow stairs to seek them out, wrapped in reverent admiration; and a fine canvas will win them much greater renown than a witty retort. This is the climate that an artist needs to live in; for the artist, no less than any ordinary man, has his moods of depression.

Whenever I set foot in an unfamiliar city, I hire a carriage in order to make the rounds and deliver my letters of recommendation; and one of the most interesting conversations for me is always that which I hold with the saddler whose carriage I am to hire. I start by enquiring which are the curiosities that should be visited, and who are the notables in the region; he invariably preludes his reply with some mild abuse directed against the Excise; but, once he has paid this customary tribute to his own rank in society, he gives me an excellent notion of the current trends in public opinion.

Last time I re-visited Paris, that prima donna of yours, Signora Barilli, was still alive; yet, when I took those excellent furnished lodgings in the rue Cérutti*, Heaven forfend that the landlord should have mentioned her in so much as a passing word! Indeed, it would be a miracle if he so much as knew the names of Mademoiselle Mars or of Fleury. Yet the visitor to Florence has but to set foot in Schneider's Hotel, and the most ignorant kitchen-lad will speak up straight away: "Giovanni Davide arrived in town three days ago; he is going to sing with the Mombelli sisters; the opera will be a *furore*; everyone is coming into Florence to see it."

You will be more than a little shocked, my dear Louis, if ever you journey into Italy, to discover that many of the orchestras are decidedly inferior to that which plays at the Théâtre de l'Odéon; and to find innumerable operatic companies that can boast but one or two tolerable voices. You will think me as great a liar as the proverbial teller of travellers' tales. Nowhere throughout the length and breadth of Italy will you behold such a veritable galaxy of talents as that which provides the daily fare of Paris, where, in the same opera, you may hear Signora Barilli, with Signora Neri and Signora Festa as supporting cast; and, among the men, Crivelli, Tacchinardi and Matteo Porto. Yet do not despair for your evening's entertainment; for, here in Italy, those same singers whom you judge, and rightly, to be mediocre, will be transformed, electrified by the presence of an audience that is born with an instinctive feeling for music and that will respond with heart-felt enthusiasm; the trail of fire darts back and forth, from audience to stage, from stage to audience; suddenly the company comes to life as an *ensemble*; and now the singing glows with such warmth, such brio, as you did never so much as dream of. There will be those instants o trance-like ecstasy, when actors and audience alike are utterly possessed, oblivious to everything, save to the beauty of some Finale by Cimarosa. Paris is prepared to pay Crivelli thirty thousand francs for an engagement, yet this is nothing; Paris must further be prepared to purchase an audience fit to appreciate him, and also to encourage the love that he bears to his art. In one passage, he will invent some stroke of genius, perfect in its absolute simplicity . . . not a soul in the audience responds. In another, he will contrive one of those commonplace *fioriture*, accessible to the crudest of untrained ears . . . promptly each member of the audience, overjoyed to demonstrate his connoisseurship, deafens his neighbour with a thunderstorm of idiotic clapping. Yet even *this* applause is devoid of real warmth: it is not the soul that has been transplanted into some seventh Heaven of delight, it is merely the intellect which approves of what it hears. An Italian will surrender unreservedly to the pleasure of listening to some glorious melody, even when he is hearing it for the first time; a Frenchman will clap, yet only with illassured anxiety, for he is scared of seeming to applaud something which may prove mediocre; nor is it until the third or fourth performance, by which time he will finally have decided that this aria is *delicious*, that he will dare shout *bravo!*, carefully stressing the first syllable of the word, of course, to show that he knows Italian. Observe him now: it is a *première*, and he is in the foyer, greeting his friend. "Divine, divine!" say his lips; but his eyes hold a question-mark. If his friend replies with another superlative, well and good; if not, he will promptly send his idol toppling off its pedestal. In consequence, the verdicts of Parisian musical audiences admit of no discussion; a work is never anything but *delicious* or *execrable*; whereas, southward of the Alps, since each individual is certain of what he personally feels, arguments about music are endless.

Every one of the great singers whom I have heard at the Théâtre de l'Odéon has struck me as being cold and uninspired: even Crivelli is no longer the artist he is in Naples. Tacchinardi alone contrived to hint at perfection in *La Distruzione di Gerusalemme*. This is a true catastrophe, nor can it be repaired with money alone; it stems from the inherent nature of French audiences.

Take this same Frenchman, so ill at ease whenever the discussion turns to music, so timid and touchy, so eager to save his vanity from danger; and now observe his lightning response to some shaft of wit, to some ingenious flash of repartee. Admire his intelligence; consider the quicksilver subtlety, the skill, the wealth of ingenuity with which he analyses every detail of its irony and humour! You must of necessity conclude, if you are an idealist, a dreamer: "Such a land as this will surely nourish a Molière or a Regnard; never a Galuppi or an Anfossi."

The typical young Italian aristocrat is a *dilettante*; he has composed a line or two, inspired or otherwise, and he is passionately in love with the local prima donna; let him but set foot at Court, he scarcely knows where to put himself, so awkward is his embarrassment. By contrast, the scion of any French ducal family will trot cheerfully up to the very threshold of the Royal Bedchamber, strutting as elegantly as a peacock; to the most casual observer, he appears pleased with himself, he is in full possession of his faculties; humming a cheerful ditty, he wanders across the room, and leans against the very balustrade that separates the Royal Bed from the rest of the appartment. Whereupon an Usher, a dismal being in black, advances towards him and informs him that *common* mortals are forbidden to seat themselves, and that he is *profanifying* His Majesty's Balustrade.

"Sir," retorts our young Duke, "How right you are. Have no fear; throughout the land I will proclaim your *un*common zeal in *defensifying*

His Majesty's Seat!" At which he whirls on tiptoe like a ballerina, amid a burst of laughter.

This much I will confess, my dear Louis: that I have in no wise modified the opinion that I held six years ago, when I wrote to you about the greatest Composer for Orchestra that the world has ever known. It is the fashion for instrumental composition that has brought the art to ruin. There are more violinists, more pianists than there are singers; and it is easier to play than to sing. This is the reason why instrumental music possesses such an unhappy tendency to corrupt the taste of all true admirers of *bel canto*; which work of corruption it has now pursued effectively for half a century and more.

There remains, in the whole of Italy, but one solitary master of the art of *bel canto*: Domenico Mombelli. And assuredly his two charming daughters have enjoyed no greater advantage than to have profited from such a master.

This is the true and original method of singing, nor shall I ever cease to extol its virtues until my dying day. Here in Vienna we used to have an example of the style in the person of Signora Martinez, a sometime pupil of Metastasio, who was an incomparable mistress of the art. Together with the celebrated Marianna Romanina, she spent her youth, at the beginning of the eighteenth century, in Rome and Naples; consequently, none knew better than she the secret that the human voice must learn if it is to cast its magic spell on every heart.

And this secret is simplicity itself: it must have beauty, and it must display it.

Nothing more. In order that this miracle may come to pass, however, the accompaniment must be soft and unobtrusive; the strings should preferably play pizzicato;[1] and, as a general rule, the singer should select passages marked andante. Nowadays, the finest voices take refuge in recitative; both Signora Catalani and Velluti have obtained their greatest triumphs in such passages. This was the style that used to flourish,

---

[1] Signor Paganini, of Genoa, is in my opinion the finest violinist in Italy; his pianissimo playing is unrivalled; his repertory includes a multitude of concertos which are as miserably insignificant as those which bore us to tears in Paris; yet even here, his wonderful pianissimo marks him as a being apart. Personally, I enjoy nothing so much as his "Variations on the G string". For your further information, this Genoese violinist is but thirty-two years of age; in time, perhaps, he will learn to play more rewarding music than concertos; perhaps he may even have enough common sense to grasp that his talents would be better employed, were he to interpret some noble aria by Mozart.

eighty years ago, in those old cantatas which were once the fashion; today, the orchestra starts by charging like a regiment of cavalry straight through a polonaise; this is followed by some grandiloquent aria, in the course of which the orchestra braces itself for a battle royal with the voice; or else, if by a miracle it manages to quell its noisy ardour, the blessèd silence is filled with melodramatic holding-notes, while the singer warbles his way through a series of interminable trills; and *this* cascade of rubbish calls itself an opera! It tickles the fancy for quarter of an hour at most, and has never been known to call forth a single tear.

The finest prime donne that it has been my pleasure to discover in Italy (here let me observe, to keep my conscience clear, that the *very* greatest singers may conceivably have missed the privilege of performing in my presence)—the finest prime donne, I repeat, that it has been my good fortune to come across in recent years have been Fräulein Häser and the Mombelli sisters. Fräulein Häser has recently married a delightful poet and no longer sings in public; the other two, however, are the most brilliant of daystars now rising in the firmament of Italy. Would you fashion some idea of them? Conceive, then, an unrivalled mastery of method, an incomparable suavity of tone, an untold richness and variety of expression; recall poor Signora Barilli; endow her with a voice still finer than that which she possessed while yet alive, and grant her that warmth which now and then she lacked. As far as I am aware, the Mombelli sisters confine themselves strictly to *opera seria*; in consequence, Signora Barilli would still have held the advantage over them, in that she could render so divinely the aria:

Fanciulla sventurata . . .

from *I Nemici Generosi*, and portray the Countess in *Le Nozze di Figaro*, Donna Anna in *Don Giovanni*, etc. On the other hand, you should have been in Milan that season when the two Mombelli sisters were singing in Metastasio's *Adriano in Siria*; the occasion was unforgettable, and the occasion created a *furore*. Fortunately, my dear Friend, neither is scarcely more than a girl; and so you may hope one day to hear at least the younger of the two, Marianna, who usually sings the hero's part and dresses as a man.

The music-loving public of Milan lacked nothing for its pleasure on this occasion, save only the satisfaction of seeing two other notable singers in the same cast: Velluti*, that admirable artist, who, to the best of my knowledge, is the only remaining first-class male soprano in the castrato tradition now left in Italy; and Davide the younger. The latter possesses an excellent natural voice; yet he is still greatly inferior to the Mombelli sisters in technique and training. His speciality lies in the inexhaustible and exquisite profusion of his *fioriture*; he is a true concert-virtuoso, of the type that is adored in Paris; I am persuaded that, were he to visit the latter city, his fame would quickly rival that of Monsieur Garat. As for my poor little Signorine Mombelli, with one accord our connoisseurs would echo: "Is *that* all?" Whereas in Italy, they have every quality required to lift them to the very summit of renown. May Heaven grant one prayer, one prayer only: *please* let them not run off and marry★ some rich fellow who will deprive us of their talents.

Signora Manfredini would afford you immense satisfaction in the title-part of Paër's *Camilla*; her voice is unusually resonant; however, in this opera, which I saw in Turin, the artist who really swept me off my feet was the *buffo* Bassi, without a doubt the finest master of the comic style who is to be heard today in Italy. You should listen to him, in this same opera *Camilla*, addressing his master, a young officer who is determined to spend the night in a hideous castle of evil aspect:

> *Signor, la vita è corta;*
> *Andiam, per carità . . .*

He has warmth, he is a polished actor, and he is passionately devoted to his art. In addition to all these qualities, he possesses a profound understanding of the comic genius, and himself has written comedies that are by no means devoid of merit. All this unstinted admiration of mine dates from the occasion when I watched him singing in *Ser Marcantonio*, in Milan. As to his present whereabouts, I have no idea★. Over and above what I have described, he possesses quite a passable singing voice; did he but boast a basso profondo as remarkable as that of Matteo Porto, who sings in Paris, he would be perfect.

But what would you? According to my system of philosophy, a given degree of passion will necessarily damage the voice in the case of a man, just as, in the case of a woman, it destroys that characteristic bloom of freshness which is so attractive. You will grumble, that this is just another of my bizarre speculations; "All the better, say I," in the words of César de Senneville★.

Nozzari you have seen in Paris. His interpretation of the part of Paolino (*Il Matrimonio segreto*) is finer than that of any other tenor in the world. The range of the part, I felt, lay slightly too high for your admirable Crivelli.

Pellegrini possesses a superb basso profundo; he could well profit, however, from a course of lessons in the art of acting. As instructors, I would recommend Baptiste the younger, Thénard and Potier; or better still, the ingenious Dugazon★, if this delightful comic actor, whose inspiration, O solemn and self-satisfied race of grocers that you are, you never appreciated, still lives among you.

With *le Signore* Grassini, Correa, Festa, Neri and Sessi, all of whom have sung in Paris, you are better acquainted than I. Nor, even now, are you easily consoled for the departure of Signora Strinasacchi, who was so inimitable in the part of Carolina (*Il Matrimonio segreto*), and whom your regular theatre-goers, not without some justification, used to call "the Mademoiselle Dumesnil of the Théâtre Louvois".

Recently, in the splendid new opera-house in Brescia, I derived immense enjoyment from listening to Signora Carolina Bassi; her outstanding characteristic as a singer is her ardent temperament. A similar quality accounts for the success of Signora Malanotti. By contrast, Vittoria Sessi★ enjoys the advantage of unusually handsome features, together with an extremely powerful voice.

I have never watched Signora Camporesi, who by now must be in Paris, and whose reputation is particularly high in Rome.

There is no point to my adding anything to what you already know about Tacchinardi, who is so excellent once he really works himself up in the part; the tenor Siboni is not lagging far behind him. Parlamagni and Ranfagna are still much as they were when you knew them, that is to say, excellent in comic character-parts. De' Grecis and Zamboni are both notable actors: De' Grecis in particular was perfect in the opera *I Pretendenti delusi*, which was a great success in Milan some three years ago. This is a version of our own opera, *Les Prétendus*, admirably adapted for the Italian stage, and most amusingly set to music by Mosca. I was particularly delighted with the trio:

Con rispetto e riverenza . . .

with its passage for the flute at the conclusion.

There is nothing I can tell you, either of Signora Catalani, or of

Signora Gafforini. The former I have not seen ever since her début in Milan some thirteen years ago; as for the latter, she, tragically, has got married. In her, the comic genius flowered in all its glory. Her performances in *La Dama soldato*, in *Ser Marcantonio* and in *Il Ciabattino* were unforgettable. Never again shall there be born into the world, solely for the purpose of ministering to the frivolous pleasures of sophisticated people, another living being that so shone and sparkled, whose wit was more irrepressible, nor whose merriment was more irresistible. Signora Gafforini represented for Lombardy what Signora Barilli represented for Paris: and neither one nor the other will ever be replaced. Knowing the temperament of the two races concerned, you may be tempted to conclude that Signora Gafforini, in many respects, must have been the very opposite of Signora Barilli; and were you so to conclude, you would be right.

Some three months since, I visited the Milan Conservatorium, and there I listened to a most impeccable voice. My neighbours, as I overheard, were whispering to each other: "Is it not ridiculous that Signor ★★★, that incomparable *buffo* with all his temperament and ardour, should be left to vegetate in some forgotten corner of Milan? Why don't they make him Professor at the Conservatorium? He might be able to put some life into this marble statue!" The statue's name escapes my memory.

Travellers returning from Naples are full of unbounded enthusiasm for the *buffo* Casacciello. I have also heard a great deal about Signora Paër and the tenor Marzocchi.[1] This, however, brings to an end the list of those whom I personally know as outstanding in the Italian theatre.

[1] At this point, the Reader will be struck by a very considerable omission. However, the Author, rather than propound his own cloudy judgements upon a number of composers who, one and all, possess excellent qualities, even where it might be argued that they have been led grievously astray by the passing whims of fashion, proposes here to do no more than outline the relevant facts in each instance.

Paisiello and Zingarelli do not belong to the present-day school; they are the last surviving contemporaries of the group that included Piccinni and Cimarosa.

Valentino Fioravanti, whose name is so familiar in Paris thanks to his *Cantatrici villane*, comes from Rome, and is still quite young. His *opere buffe* are exceedingly popular. The following are his principal works: *le Pazzie a vicenda*, first performed in Florence in 1791; *Il Furbo* and *Il Fabbro parigino*, both performed in Turin in 1797.

Simone Mayr, born in Bavaria but educated in Italy, is perhaps the composer who enjoys the highest reputation; yet at the same time, there is none of whom I personally am less fitted to speak. His style is precisely that which, in my opinion, is thrusting us headlong towards the total ruin of dramatic music. This composer lives in Bergamo; nor

I would add Signora Sandrini, whom I heard with pleasure once in Dresden. I shall say nothing about our own theatres back in Vienna; once I started, I should never stop. Ask any French officer who was stationed in that city in 1809; I will warrant that he has not yet forgotten the tears that were shed at the *Crusaders*, a melodrama whose effectiveness need fear no comparison from the best of Romantic tragedies; nor the unquenchable gales of laughter that rocked the audience at the antics of that splendid dancer Rainoldi—if I remember right—who was so outstanding in the ballet *Les Vendanges*. A similar high standard prevailed in other works given at the same period: *Don Giovanni*, *Il Matrimonio segreto*, *La Clemenza di Tito*, Paër's *Sargino*, Cherubini's *Eliska*, a certain *Lisbeth folle par Amour**, together with a number of other operas in the German tradition, all of which deserved the reputation they enjoyed.

Must I repeat what I have said before, that in all probability there are a number of considerable figures whose reputation, in Italy, is both

have the most fabulous offers ever succeeded in tempting him to any other city. He is exceedingly industrious. I have seen at least a score of operas from his pen. Paris knows him through his *opera buffa*, *I finti Rivali*, which was given with Signora Correa as prima donna. The general verdict was that the work contained a reasonable amount of melody, marred by an occasional lapse into vulgarity, but was lavish to the point of profusion in the orchestral scoring. His *Pazzo per la Musica* is a pretty piece; *Adelasia ed Aleramo*, an *opera seria*, was a great success in Milan. Mayr gives us the full benefit of all that stupendous progress which orchestral music has made since the days of Pergolesi; yet at the same time he fills us with regret for those wonderful melodies which were the glory of that period.

Ferdinando Paer, who, I most regretfully confess, ranks no higher in my opinion than does Mayr, was born in Parma in 1774. His wit is such that I have heard it praised to the skies by some of the most brilliant minds in Paris, As a composer, he has already given us some thirty operas. Two years ago, *Camilla* and *Sargino* were being performed simultaneously in Naples, Turin, Vienna, Dresden and Paris.

Pavesi and Mosca, both composers who are very popular in Italy, have given us between them a considerable number of *opere buffe*. These contain a quantity of pleasing melodies; nor are these melodies completely smothered by the orchestra.

Farinelli, who was born near Padua, writes music that usually attracts an audience. He is a product of the Conservatorio de' Turchini, in Naples; and he has already some eight or ten operas to his credit.

Certain persons hold out the highest hopes for Signor Rossini*, a young man of five-and-twenty, who is just beginning to make himself a name. It must be confessed that his melodies, as rendered by the enchanting Mombelli sisters, are extraordinarily graceful. The most successful work to date by this young man, whose features are unusually prepossessing, is *l'Italiana in Algeri*. It seems, however, that he already shows a tendency to repeat himself. *Il Turco in Italia* was recently given in Milan and proved a failure; I could find no trace of originality in it, and not a spark of fire.

high and well-deserved, and yet whose names I have not even mentioned, for the simple reason that I do not know them? I have never
been to Sicily; and it is many years now since I last saw Naples. Naples
is the happy land, the land engendered by volcanic fire, which is the
cradle of the finest voices. In days gone by, when I was there, I was
struck by a number of habits that are very different from our own, and
rather merrier. It is not the custom, in those regions, to denounce a
plagiarist by printing a pamphlet; the thief is detected in the very act.
Consequently, if the composer whose work is being performed has
robbed another, stealing an aria, say, or even an inconspicuous passage
here and there, perhaps no more than a bar or two, the whole audience,
having no sooner caught the first notes of the "borrowed" episode, will
burst into a thunder of *bravo!* -ing, each *bravo!* being accompanied by
the name of the true and legitimate owner. If Piccinni is the villain and
Sacchini, say, the victim, the former will be deafened with an unremit-
ting roar: *Bravo, Sacchini!* And if, as the opera proceeds, the audience
should come to discover that he has borrowed a bit here, there and everywhere, the ironical applause will proliferate: "Excellent! Bravo,
Galuppi! bravo, Traetta! bravo, Guglielmi!"

Had we but this same tradition in France, I wonder how many operas
at the Théâtre Français would have been greeted by this special brand
of *bravo?* Hush, though; not a word about those still living!

Nowadays, everyone knows that the famous aria, *"Enfant chéri des
Dames"*, from *Les Visitandines*, is in fact by Mozart.

Duni would have heard shouts of *Bravo, Hasse!* at the beginning of
the aria:

> *Ah! la maison maudite . . .*

whose opening fifteen bars are also the first fifteen bars of the aria:

> *Priva del caro bene . . .*[1]

Monsigny would have been greeted with a *Bravo, Pergolesi!* for the
beginning of his duet:

> *Venez, tout nous réussit . . .*

which is absolutely identical with that of the aria:

> *Tu sei troppo scelerato. . . .*

[1]See Roland's *Italian Journey.*

And yet another *bravo!* for the aria:

> *Je ne sais à quoi me résoudre.* . . .

Philidor likewise would have recognised the words *Bravo, Pergolesi!* in the roar that greeted his aria:

> *On me fête, on me cajole* . . .

whose accompaniment may be found note for note in the aria:

> *Ad un povero polacco* . . . ;

he would have discerned the words: *Bravo, Cocchi!* in that which arose at the aria:

> *Il fallait le voir un dimanche,*
> *Quand il sortait du cabaret* . . .

which is nothing but the aria:

> *Donne belle che pigliate* . . .

repeated bar for bar; and *Bravo, Galuppi!* for the cavatina:

> *Vois le chagrin qui me dévore.* . . .

Nor would Grétry have escaped some such instances of mockery and derision.

Indeed, what could be simpler than to make a little journey into Italy —in which country, as a general rule, music is not printed—to take down a copy of anything that catches one's fancy, either because it is good in itself, or else because it echoes the current trend of popular taste in Paris, which trend is easily discernible in any one of the hundred-odd lyric theatres that open their doors year in, year out, on the banks of the Seine; to string the bits together with a dozen bars of harmony; and then to come back home to France and be a famous composer! There is absolutely no danger; no French score ever crosses the Alps.

Just imagine the success that the Théâtre Feydeau holds in store for Mosca's aria:

> *Con rispetto e riverenza* . . .

from *I Pretendenti delusi.* Or for the quartet:

> *Da che siam uniti,*
> *Parliam de' nostri affari* . . .

from the same opera. And who, I ask you, would ever recognise them? As for those fine Italian voices. . . . Those petty pedants of ours, those upstart, would-be Voltaires, among their other imbecilities, have perpetrated one which will probably endanger the fullness of our pleasure for many years to come. These philosophising gentry have got up on their hind legs to tell us, in pompous professorial tones, that a certain minor operation performed upon an insignificant number of choir-boys was threatening to turn the whole of Italy into a desert; the population was menaced with extinction; already grass was growing in the via di Toledo; and then . . .! Think, gentlemen, think! The Sacred Rights of the Human Race! For Heaven's sake! These creatures must have fine, hard, rationalising heads, to judge by their chilly insensitivity to the Arts! Unhappily for them, another hard and rationalising head, this time of rather higher quality—a certain Englishman, a Dr. Malthus—has been inspired to compile an *Essay on Population**, which is a work of veritable genius, and which yet may serve to counteract to some extent the shrill, thin sermonising of MM. Roland, O'Alembert and other honest folk, who had been better advised to heed the precept *Ne sutor*, and hold their tongues for good and ill alike whenever they felt tempted to talk about the Arts.

Now, Dr. Malthus demonstrates most sapiently to our squeamish philosophising friends that the population of any given country will invariably increase in direct ratio to the quantity of food available. To this he adds, that the chief cause of distress and poverty, which is so widespread in the world, is the tendency shown by any population—a tendency encouraged by human improvidence as well as by human instincts—to increase beyond the limits of available production. He frequently expresses the opinion, that governments should cease to lavish upon marriage a degree of encouragement which, in respect of that singular institution, is and always will be entirely superfluous. Develop some new product, open up some new country, inaugurate some new industry, and marriages and children will come into being of their own accord; drive people into marriage without fulfilment of these necessary conditions, and you will, admittedly, still have children; but either they will fail to grow to maturity, or else they will hinder the birth of further children.

Whenever reason takes a hand in these matters, the number of marriages will inevitably correspond to the means available for raising a family. In those Dutch villages which were studied by Dr. Malthus, whenever a man died, this meant an inheritance, capital free for use, an industry lying fallow, waiting for exploitation; promptly, you might observe a marriage; no death, no wedding. Even the most terrible sources of mortality, plague or war or a transitory famine, have no power to bring about the permanent depopulation of a country whose industry and fertility are on the increase.

Without wishing to embark upon a learned disquisition, nor to produce an impressive display of statistics, I would maintain, along with Dr. Malthus, that if the Monastic Orders, to whom our friends the *Philosophes* owe such a debt of gratitude for having furnished them with so many limitless topics to discourse upon—if the Monastic Orders *were* detrimental to the population, it is not because they themselves took no direct part in ensuring its increase, but rather because they contributed nothing to the general level of production. Even so, it would be hardly fair to compare the monks to our enchanting Neapolitans; in any case, their numbers were considerably greater.

Any mortal being who possesses but the least shadow of sensibility will appreciate that Italy is the very homeland of Beauty, in every domain. *You*, my dear Friend, have no need that I should furnish proof and warrant for this assertion; and yet there are a thousand little details which would appear to suggest that it is especially propitious to music. The intense heat of noon, followed at nightfall by a refreshing coolness which fills the heart of every living thing with joy—all this has the effect of making the hour at which people wend their way towards the theatre the most delicious instant of the day. Almost everywhere throughout the Peninsula, this instant occurs between nine and ten o'clock in the evening, or in other words, at least four hours after the evening meal.

It is customary to listen to music wrapped in a mantle of propitious darkness. Except on high feast-days, the Teatro alla Scala, in Milan, which is vaster even than the Grand Opéra in Paris, receives no illumination save that which is reflected from the footlights; in a word, the audience can relax completely, remote and hidden in the darkened boxes, which are like miniature drawing-rooms.

I could be disposed to believe that a certain languor must be induced before the mind can truly begin to enjoy the music of the human voice. It is a patent fact that a month's residence in Rome will affect the gait even of the most restless and quicksilvery of Frenchmen. The impatience that marked his step during the first few days gradually vanishes; nothing any longer makes him hurry. In cold climates, work is essential to keep the circulation going; in countries where it is warm, the *divino far niente* is God's sweetest gift to man.

In Paris. . . .[1]

Are you going to blame me, in my attempts to discover the present state of music in France, for having mentioned only Paris? In Italy, one may refer to Leghorn, Bologna, Verona, Ancona, Pisa and a score of other cities that are most certainly not capitals; in France, however, the provinces are utterly barren of originality; Paris, and Paris alone, in all this great kingdom, counts for anything in music.

The provinces are possessed by a disastrous spirit of *imitation*, which makes them worthless in the Arts, as indeed in many other things. In Bordeaux, in Lyons, in Marseilles, it is impossible to tell that you are not in the Quartier du Marais, in Paris. When will these cities take the great resolve to be themselves, and learn to voice their disapproval of what is sent to them from Paris, when what is sent to them from Paris happens not to suit *their* taste? As things stand at present, that which is feather-light in Paris is ponderously imitated in the provinces; simplicity becomes a sign of affectation; one is studiously unstudied, pretentiously unpretentious.

In Toulouse no less than in Lille, the most pressing concern of any young man who desires to appear well-dressed, or of any young woman who wishes to attract admirers, is to imitate that which is fashionable in Paris; with the result that, even in these frivolous matters where pedantry is inconceivable, the land is swarming with pedants. Such creatures seem to have none but the vaguest notion of what causes them pain, what causes them pleasure: to find out, they must first enquire what Paris has decided. I have often heard it maintained by foreigners, not without some semblance of reason, that France consists of Paris and a lot of villages. An intelligent man who happens to have been born in the provinces will for many years display less simplicity in his manners than would have been the case had he been born in Paris; and there is

[1]At this point, the Author has preferred to suppress everything that he wrote, in the course of a purely private correspondence, concerning those composers and singers who are at present living in Paris. He is more than a little distressed, however, that this common act of courtesy should have prevented him from restating all the admiration that he feels for Mesdames Branchu and Regnaut, no less than for Elleviou.

nothing in the world that he can do about it. Simplicity: "That upright-ness of soul, that will admit no second thoughts, neither touching itself, nor concerning its acts",[1]—is perchance the rarest of all qualities that may be encountered in France.

He who is familiar with Paris will discover nothing new in Marseilles or in Nantes—nothing, that is, except the Loire or the harbour, purely physical phenomena; the prevailing mentality is identical; whereas fine cities such as these, cities of eighty thousand souls and so diversely situated, might furnish much instructive material for the curious obser-ver, had they but the slightest trace of originality. Geneva, which is not one quarter the size of Lyons, yet where, despite a touch of pedantry in the atmosphere, foreign travellers tend to stay much more frequently than they do in the larger city, and not without good reason—Geneva should be an example for Lyons. In Italy, it is hard to imagine anything more different, in some cases more signally and diametrically contrast-ing, than certain cities built not thirty leagues apart. Signora Gafforini, the idol of Milan, was almost whistled off the stage in Turin.

In order to consider the present state of music in Italy, there is no point in comparing Paris with Rome; the evidence would seem to point once more in favour of the gentle land of France, and that evi-dence would be thoroughly misleading. The fact to be borne in mind is that, in Italy, little townships with a population of some four thousand souls all told, such as Crema and Como—two instances chosen at ran-dom from among a hundred—possess well-equipped theatres and even, from time to time, excellent singers. Last year we used to drive over to Como all the way from Milan to hear the Mombelli sisters; it is as though you were to drive out of Paris in order to go to the theatre in Melun or in Beauvais. The traditions of the two countries are utterly dissimilar; it would require no effort to believe oneself a thousand leagues away.

In France, even in the greatest cities, there is not a note to be heard, save for the thin, shrill squeak of the current opéra-comique fetched down from Paris. Should an opera prove popular at the Théâtre Feydeau, you may safely wager that within two months it will be running to dutiful applause in Lyons. When, oh when will the wealthy citizens of a town that holds a hundred thousand people and lies at the very gates of Italy—

[1]Fénelon. The Author has not made an exact note of every single idea that he has borrowed. This pamphlet is scarcely more than a scrap-book of extracts and quotations.*

when will these people at last grasp the notion that they might summon a composer of their own, and enjoy an opera created for themselves?

The fair skies of Bordeaux, the quickly-mounting fortunes that are made there, the sea-trade that constantly fosters new ideas—all these things, combined with the fiery Gascon temper, should logically breed a type of comedy far sprightlier, far richer in incident, than that which flowers in Paris. Yet there is not the slightest trace or hint of such a development. The student, here as elsewhere, pores over his Laharpe; nor does it once occur to him to cast aside his book and wonder: "But do I *really* enjoy this sort of stuff?"

The only trace of originality that may be found in France is to be discovered among the common people, too ignorant to have a model to imitate; in France, however, the common people are not concerned with music; no wheelwright's son this side of the Alps will ever grow up to be a Joseph Haydn.

In all matters pertaining to politics and literature, the wealthier classes are duly told each morning in their newspapers exactly what they are expected to think during the rest of the day. And there is one last factor which, in France, contributes to the decadence of the Arts: namely, that grim English spirit of seriousness with which people endowed with the finest minds and the most exquisite sensibility nowadays apply themselves to politics. I confess that I find it a notable convenience to live in a land that is endowed with a liberal constitution; on the other hand, unless one happens to be burdened with a species of pride that is uncommonly touchy, and to be cursed with a sensibility that is singularly ill-adapted to the pursuit of happiness, I fail to see what pleasure one may hope to derive from constantly fretting oneself to a shadow over constitutional and political problems. Given the contemporary pattern of pleasures and habits that preoccupy a man of fashion, the degree of happiness that one may hope to obtain from the specific manner in which power is distributed within the body politic of which one happens to be a member, is scarcely considerable; one may suffer from its abuse, yet hardly profit from its amelioration.

I like to compare the state of mind of those patriotic souls who are forever worrying away about the *Law of the Land*, or the *Balance of Power*, with that of a man who is everlastingly obsessed with the structural soundness of the house in which he lives. Now I consider it perfectly reasonable to select my appartment, once and for all, in a house

Scene from Act III of Metastasio's *Didone abbandonata*, an engraving by Giuliono
Zuliani, from a drawing by Pietro Antonio Novelli

"Porto con Sbarco magnifico", a sketch by Allessandro Bibiena, intended for a
stage-setting of Metastasio's *Issipile*

that is solid and well-constructed; but, after all, this house was built in order that people might live in it and peacefully enjoy there all the pleasures of life; and I cannot help feeling that a man must be singularly maladapted if, finding himself in a drawing-room surrounded by pretty women, he can do nothing better than worry about the state of the roof:

Et propter vitam, vivendi perdere causas.

You will observe, my dear Friend, how promptly I have obeyed you, answering your summons literally by return of post. I have given you a summary of all those passably superficial ideas which occur to me at the moment concerning the present state of music in Italy. It is rushing headlong towards decadence—or at least, so one might believe if one were to pay any attention to public opinion which, by a miracle, happens in this instance to be right. Personally, this *decadence*, evening after evening, fills my very soul with rapture; during the daytime, however, I dwell in the company of a different Art.

It follows that everything that I have written will necessarily be ill-informed and painfully incomplete: for instance, it is only now, at this late hour, that it occurs to me that Mosca has a brother who, like the other, is a very pleasing composer.

I would very much have preferred to talk to you about the *Last Supper*, painted in Milan by Leonardo da Vinci, and about the wonderful copy that has been made of it by *il cavaliere* Bossi; to discuss the fine paintings which were sketched by this notable painter—who is also the most agreeable company—for the late Count Battaglia, and which are based upon the character of the four great Italian poets; to tell you of the Appiani frescoes that may be seen in the Royal Palace, or of the Villa built by Signor Melzi on the shores of Lake Como . . . and so on and so forth. All this would have been much better suited to my present preoccupations than to describe for you the finest of modern operas.

In music, as in many other things, alas, I belong to a bygone century.

Madame de Sévigné, ever faithful to her old loves, entertained a fondness for none but Corneille and used to say that Racine, like coffee, was but a passing fashion. It may be that I am no less unjust towards Mayr and Paër, Farinelli, Mosca and Rossini, whose reputation in Italy is very high indeed. The aria:

Ti rivedrò, mi rivedrai . . .*

10

from *Tancredi*, by Rossini, who is popularly reported to be exceedingly young, none the less gave me an intense and real pleasure. And I still hope, one day, to hear a particular duet by Farinelli, which begins with the words:

No, non credo quel che dite . . .

and which, on not a few stages, is customarily inserted into Act II of *Il Matrimonio segreto*.

I will confess to you, my good and patient Louis, that ever since the year 1809, when I used to write to you from my refuge in Salzburg, there is one problem that I have been trying to solve, and which I have still failed to answer to my satisfaction: namely, the strange lack of enthusiasm which is shown in Italy for Pergolesi and for those Great Masters who were his contemporaries. The phenomenon is no less puzzling than if *we* were to prefer the paltry little scribblers of our own day and age to the generation that gave us Racine and Molière. I am perfectly aware that Pergolesi was born before music had fully perfected all the various means at its disposal; it is only since his death, apparently, that orchestral writing has made those vast strides which have carried it forward to the very limits of its possibilities; yet the art of *chiaroscuro* similarly made immense strides forward after Raphael— but for all that, Raphael still remains the greatest painter in the world.

It was Montesquieu who once wrote so judiciously:

"If Heaven one day saw fit to endow men with the piercing sight of the Eagle, who can doubt but that the Rules of Architecture would be altered overnight? A more complex system of Orders would be needed."

It is evident that the Italians have changed since the days of Pergolesi.

The peoples of Lombardy were the first to be awakened from their slumbers, in response to the conquest of Italy, which was brought about by a series of exploits that reverberated with the true ring of greatness; in more recent times, the heroic adventures of the Italian brigades in Spain and in Russia, the linking of the fortunes of the Peninsula with those of a great Empire—no matter that this Empire should have been doomed to ultimate disaster—the genius of Alfieri, whose clarion-call to the new generation opened the eyes of this generation to the vanity of those studies on which the ardent enthusiasm of its youth was being frittered away—all these things combined to engender in this land of Beauty—

Il bel paese
Ch' Apennin parte, e' l mar circonda e l'Alpe
Petrarch, *Sonnet* 146

—the burning desire to grow into a nation.

In Spain★, so I have heard, Italian troops were reputed to have proved more valorous, in certain conflicts, even than the battle-hardened brigades of France. In the ranks of this untried army, not a few fine characters soon made their mark. To judge by one young general, whom I saw wounded in the neck at the battle of the Moskowa, its officers are no less remarkable for the nobility of their character than for their abilities in the field. Their manners, in my experience, were plain and unaffected, their reasoning straightforward and penetrating; and they were free from vain bravado. Such things were inconceivable in 1750.

Now all this represents a profound transformation at work among the peoples of Italy. This transformation has not yet had time to make its influence felt on the Fine Arts. The subjects of the sometime Kingdom of Italy have not yet been privileged to enjoy any of those long periods of tranquillity, in the course of which Nations eager for new experience are wont to turn their attention towards the Arts.

For several years now I have been highly satisfied to observe, in Lombardy, a phenomenon which may not appear equally desirable in the eyes of all our fellow-countrymen: namely, a suspicion of coolness towards France. This attitude originated with Alfieri; and it was accelerated by that levy of twenty or thirty millions which the Kingdom of Italy paid annually out of its budget to Imperial France.

An ardent young man poised on the very threshold of his career, burning to make his mark, will feel himself constrained, oppressed even, by the admiration to which he is compelled by those who have preceded him in this same career, and who have already reaped the finest laurels. Were the Italians to admire us more, they would resemble us less in our finer qualities. It would surprise me little to learn that, today, they had begun to discover that there is no true greatness in the Arts without originality, and similarly no true greatness in a Nation without a liberal constitution on the English model. Perhaps I may still live long enough to see Machiavelli's *La Mandragola*, the *Commedia dell'Arte*★ and the operas of Pergolesi once more revived in Italy. Sooner or later the Italians themselves will come to realise that herein lie their truest claims to glory; and when they realise this, other nations will respect them the more for it. Personally, I will confess that I was miserably disappointed, on a recent occasion, when I strolled into a theatre in Venice, only to discover that the play that was billed for performance was *Zaïre*. There was not a dry eye in the audience, even the corporal on guard at the entrance to the stalls had tears streaming down his cheeks; and the actors were not devoid of merit. But, if I wanted to see *Zaïre*, I should go to Paris and watch it at the Théâtre Français. I derived infinitely more pleasure on the following day from watching *L'Ajo nell'imbarazzo*, a comedy written by a Roman gentleman, and played to perfection by a great barrel-shaped actor who immediately reminded me of Iffland from Berlin, and at the same time of Molé in those semi-serious parts that he made his speciality towards the end of his career. This fat Italian actor struck me as every bit deserving to join the other two, and form with them a notable triumvirate. Yet, even so, I scoured Venice in vain for a trace of Gozzi's comedies, or of the *Commedia dell'Arte*; instead, day after day almost without respite, the playbills announced French drama in translation. Only the day before yesterday I slipped out of that dreary production, *La Femme jalouse*, and fled to the piazza San Marco, to laugh my fill a while in front of the *teatro di polichinello*. And, if the truth be told, I found nothing in the whole of Venice—outside the opera—that gave me greater pleasure. The explanation, I believe, is simple enough: for Polichinello and Pantalone were born and bred in Italy; nor is there any way, in any genre, of being great—if one is destined to be great—except by being oneself. The rest is waste of breath.

Appendices

DEDICATION TO MADAME D'OLIGNY

London*, 13 October 1814.

It is the most natural thing in all the world, Madame, that I should humbly offer you this little work, the first indeed that I have ever written. It was composed at a time when sorrow was likely to have eaten my life away, had I not provided myself with some distraction. On occasions you deigned to enquire what might be my occupation and how it befell, that I was not more grievously affected by that which was happening to me. Know, then, my secret: for I was living in another world. Yet never would I have quitted this more familiar world, of which you, Madame, are the brightest ornament, had I but encountered in these regions some other being whose sensibility was worthy to match your own, or else had it been conceivable that She who formed the object of my admiration might have felt towards me something other than simple friendship.

I take my leave of you, Madame, filled with regret at having seen a cloud come between us in these latter days; and since, where friendship is involved, it is the instant of parting that often determines an enduring coldness for the future, I am afraid that, in the days to come, we may find ourselves strangers to each other. I have found consolation in setting down, here in this secret, hidden spot, this simple formulation of the feelings that stir within me and for which I ask no gratitude; I love, because I take pleasure in loving.

I am aware, moreover, of that which you resolved to do on my behalf. That you *did* resolve it, I am certain; and this resolve, albeit doomed never to come to fruition, allows me the pleasure of laying at your feet my undying gratitude.

Adieu, Madame. The empty pride that Fashion imposes on its subjects may perchance oblige me to address you as though my heart were cold and indifferent; yet this, towards you, I can never be, no matter to what distant lands my destiny may lead me.

I am,

with profound respect,
THE AUTHOR

A CATALOGUE OF MOZART'S DRAMATIC WORKS

(Compiled from Köchel's list, revised by Dr. Alfred Einstein)

Köchel Number	Date	
35	1766–7	*Die Schuldigkeit des ersten Gebotes.* Sacred play with music. Libretto by Jacobus Antonius Wimmer.
38	1767	*Apollo et Hyacinthus seu Hyacinthi Metamorphosis.* Latin comedy. Intermezzo to Rufinus Widl's *Clementia Croesi.*
50	1768	*Bastien und Bastienne.* German operetta. Libretto by Weiskern, based on *Les Amours de Bastien et de Bastienne,* by Madame Favart and Harny. The latter is a satire of Rousseau's *Le Devin du Village* (1752).
51	1768	*La finta Semplice.* Opera buffa. Libretto by Marco Coltellini, based on Goldoni.
87	1770	*Mitridate, Re di Ponto.* Opera seria. Libretto by Vittorio Amadeo Cigna-Santi, based on Racine.
111	1771	*Ascanio in Alba.* Serenata. Libretto by Giuseppe Parini.
126	1772	*Il Sogno di Scipione.* Serenata. Libretto by Metastasio.
135	1772	*Lucio Silla.* Dramma per musica. Libretto by Giovanni da Gamerra.
196	1774–5	*La finta Giardiniera.* Opera buffa. Libretto by Raniero da Calzabigi(?).
208	1775	*Il Re Pastore.* Dramatic Festival play. Libretto by Metastasio.
344	1779	*Zaide.* German opera (unfinished). Libretto by Schachtner.
345	1779	*Thamos, König in Aegypten.* Incidental music and choruses to play by Tobias von Gebler

10*

366   1780   *Idomeneo, Re di Creta*. Opera seria. Libretto by
               Giambattista Varesco.
384   1782   *Die Entführung aus dem Serail*. German musical play.
               Libretto by Gottlieb Stefanie.
422   1783   *L'Oca del Cairo*. Opera buffa (unfinished). Libretto
               by Giambattista Varesco.
430   1783   *Lo Sposo deluso, ossia La rivalità di tre donne per un
               solo amante*. Opera buffa (unfinished). Libretto by
               Lorenzo da Ponte(?).
486   1786   *Der Schauspieldirektor*. Comedy in one act. Libretto
               by Stefanie.
492   1786   *Le Nozze di Figaro*. Opera buffa. Libretto by
               Lorenzo da Ponte.
527   1787   *Il Dissoluto Punito, ossia Il Don Giovanni*. Dramma
               giocoso. Libretto by Lorenzo da Ponte.
588   1790   *Così fan tutte, ossia La Scuola degli amanti*. Opera
               buffa. Libretto by Lorenzo da Ponte.
620   1791   *Die Zauberflöte*. German opera. Libretto by
               Emmanuel Schikaneder.
621   1791   *La Clemenza di Tito*. Opera seria. Libretto by
               Metastasio, adapted by Caterino Mazzola.

TRANSLATOR'S NOTES

Page

3 ... *I was in Vienna.* Stendhal's only visit to Vienna occurred between April and November 1809 when, as a "Commissaire des Guerres", he formed part of Napoleon's army of occupation during the campaign that culminated in the Battle of Wagram. The "I" who writes these supposed letters is sometimes Carpani, sometimes Stendhal, sometimes imaginary, and varies in nationality from French to Austrian via Italian.

3 ... *certain devouring sorrows.* The fall of Napoleon, the invasion of Paris, the loss of his position in the Civil Service. The "distraught passion" that Stendhal claimed to feel for Madame Beugnot was largely make-belief.

3 ... *of Haydn, Mozart and Metastasio.* This description of the origins of the book is nonsense. Cf. Foreword.

4 ... *Isle of Wight.* On 16 Sept. 1817, Stendhal was in Paris. He had, however, spent a few days, from 3–16 Aug., at the Tavistock Hotel, London, where probably he had heard the name of the Hampshire island.

7 ... *Dear Friend.* Louis de Bellisle. Concerning this, and all other personalities mentioned in the text, see Biographical Index.

7 ... *small and humble house.* . . . Now one of the three Haydn-Museums in Austria, situated in the Haydngasse. The other two are at Rohrau and at Eisenstadt.

8 ... *Tasso. Canto ii.* Stendhal not only misquotes, but gives an inaccurate reference. The correct version is as follows:

> *Muoiono le città, muoiono i regni,*
> *copre i fasti e le pompe arena ed erba,*
> *e l'uom d'esser mortal par che si sdegni* . . .
> *Gerusalemme Liberata*, canto **XV**, st. **xx**, ll. 3–5.

9 ... *a clear space* . . . The famous *glacis* surrounding the old city of Vienna. The fortifications were demolished by a decree of Franz Joseph on 31 Dec. 1857; the *glacis* now contains the Ringstrasse and various public buildings: Rathaus, Parliament House, University, Museums, etc.

9 ... *The Prater Island* . . . In 1814, the present Donau-Kanal was the main channel of the Danube, and thus the Prater was in fact an island. It ceased to be so when the new course of the Danube was cut between 1868 and 1881.

10 ... *the Pálffys* . . . Stendhal uses the name "Countess Palfy" as his secret way of referring to the Countess Daru.

10 ... *for those who govern.* One of the earliest formulations of an essential element in Stendhal's philosophy: namely, that democratic politics and great art are incompatible. Cf. *The Charterhouse of Parma*, where the idea is worked out.

10 ... *the North of Germany* . . . Stendhal had lived for something over two years in Brunswick. His theory of national temperaments, although oversimplified, is essential to his concept of a relative aesthetic.

10 ... *the Musical Society.* From 1807 until 1813, the complex of Court Theatres in Vienna (including opera, drama and ballet) was under the general direction of a

group of noble amateurs, the Gesellschaft der Cavaliere, which included Franz-Joseph Lobkowitz, Ferdinand Pálffy von Erdödy, Hieronymus zu Lodron, Stefan Zichy and three members of the Esterházy clan, under the presidency of Joseph von Schwarzenberg.

11 ... *the two Martinez ladies* ... "le signore Martinez", in Carpani. Stendhal translates: "monsieur Martinez" (!).

11 ... *his faithful music-copyist.* Johann Florian Elssler. See Biographical Index.

12 ... *a conscientious harmonist.* In few passages does Stendhal reveal so blatantly the limitations of his musical sensibility. For an analysis of this sensibility, see Foreword.

13 ... *in the Musée de Paris* ... Here and elsewhere, I omit the catalogue-numbers given by Stendhal. During his Italian campaigns, Napoleon stole many hundreds of Italian masterpieces and lodged them in the Louvre; after 1815, many, but not all, of these were returned to their original owners. The Veronese *Wedding-Feast of Cana* (which Stendhal describes misleadingly as *la cène de Saint-Georges*) came originally from Venice. Today, it still hangs in the Louvre (Salle des États)—possibly on account of its size (some 11 yards by 7), which made it difficult to transport.

14 ... *this very virtuosity* ... Stendhal himself had failed lamentably when he tried to learn to play an instrument. This accounts (partly at least) for his contempt for "virtuosity".

14 ... *continually gives pleasure.* But this pleasure will vary in relation to the temperament of the listener. Another element in the theory of a relative aesthetic.

17 ... *at Rohrau.* ... Haydn's father, Mathias Haydn, came from Hainburg and had settled in Rohrau in 1727. His mother was Anna Maria Koller. Haydn was the second child. The quotation at the head of the chapter is used by Carpani.

17 ... *the office of sacristan.* ... To be exact, the office was known as *Marktrichter*, and involved organising certain communal activities in the village (e.g., fireguard rota, etc.)

17 ... *at Hainburg.* ... A small town on the Danube, north of Rohrau and about forty miles east of Vienna.

18 ... *a pair of tympanis.* ... Stendhal mistranslates the Italian *timpani* = kettledrum. What Haydn actually discovered was a flour-bin, on which he practised before playing the drums in a local Rogation-Week procession (Ascension Day, 1738).

18 ... *his young relative.* ... It was in fact Father Palmb, the parish priest of Hainburg, who sent for Haydn and introduced him to Reutter.

19 ... *two hours a week.* Inexact. Reutter himself was a casual man who did not take his work at the choir-school seriously; he only gave Haydn two lessons in the whole of his career. But Haydn learnt singing from Finsterbusch and the violin from Gegenbauer, besides latin, arithmetic, writing, etc.

22 ... *Baden.* ... Baden bei Wien is a popular spa some twenty miles south of Vienna. Carpani addresses his Letters 3–5 from the same town; however, Stendhal's later letterheadings (Salzburg, etc.) are his own invention. The Emperor Franz I made Baden his summer residence after 1800. The "pretty new Baden Concert-Hall" was the Stadt-Theater, designed by Joseph Kornhaksel and opened in 1812 (demolished, 1908).

22 ... *the boredom of concertos.* See Foreword.

23 ... *composed a Mass.* ... In fact, a twelve-part *Salve Regina*.

25 ... *Mannersdorf.* ... A popular Spa, about twenty miles from Rohrau.

25 ... *died in 1792.* Stendhal's dates, here and elsewhere, are frequently inaccurate. See Biographical Index.

26 ... *at the age of nineteen*. .... Haydn was expelled from St. Stephen's in November 1749, at the age of seventeen and a half; his voice had begun to break some eighteen months earlier. He had previously refused to become a castrato. The immediate offence which was the excuse for his expulsion was to have snipped the pigtail off the wig of the choirboy in front of him.

26 ... *of keeping him clothed*. Inaccurate. Haydn's first rescuer was not Keller, but one Spangler, a tenor from the Michaelerkirche, who lodged him for several months until the birth of a new baby to Frau Spangler left no more room for Haydn. Haydn did not meet the Keller family until some six years later.

27 ... *for the Redoutensaal*. Stendhal writes *Ridotto*. The *Redoutensäle* are two large ballrooms forming part of the Hofburg complex, and used for fashionable dances. In the nineteenth century they also served as concert-halls, and Beethoven conducted his own symphonies there.

29 ... *never laughed in all his life*. .... It was Leopold I (1658–1705) who had this gloomy reputation, not Charles VI. All four of the "Baroque" Emperors of Austria were first-rate musicians.

30 ... *with two horns added*. .... Stendhal (copying Carpani) writes "son premier quatuor en B *fa* à sextuple". Here and elsewhere, the Stendhal–Carpani notation for key-signatures is frankly baffling; it is clear that Carpani knew as little about harmony as his imitator, Griesinger dates the first set of Quartets as early as 1750 (Op. I, No. 1 is in B flat major); but most scholars date this early experiment from 1755. A number of the early Quartets were originally symphonies, sextets or divertimenti (e.g., II, 3 and II, 5); but the "à sextuple" could equally refer to a movement in sextuple time.

30 ... *of his friend Keller*. .... See note to p. 26.

30 ... *near the Michaelerkirche*. .... The house still stands, almost unchanged since Haydn's time.

31 ... *taught him something of Italian*. Stendhal's chronology is misleading. It was Metastasio who was in charge of the education of Marianna and Antonia Martinez; and it was he who proposed Porpora as their singing-master. Porpora required an accompanist and so Haydn was engaged. This is the origin of Haydn's association with the great teacher, described on pp. 24–25.

31 ... *musical soirées*. .... Morzin lived at Lukaveč, in Bohemia, near Pilsen. His orchestra contained sixteen players.

31 ... *another word spoken of the matter*. It is Griesinger who asserts that the symphony heard by Esterházy was that now known as No. 1 in D major. The rest of the story is fantasy. Morzin disbanded his orchestra for financial reasons; and Haydn, being out of a job, applied to Esterházy in the normal way and with the normal recommendations.

31 ... *Frieberth*. .... Stendhal writes "Friedberg", and lands himself in a hopeless muddle. The Esterházy *Kapellmeister* was Gregor Joseph Werner, who, in 1761, was near to retirement, which was why Prince Anton was looking for a successor. Karl Frieberth was a young tenor who had just joined the Esterházy opera-company, and who was to sing parts in Haydn's early operas (esp. *Il Ritorno di Tobia*); later he gave Carpani much information about Haydn's early career. But there was also a composer named Joseph Frieberth, a friend of Werner, who was visiting him at this time, and who may have encouraged the old *Kapellmeister* to nominate his successor. It was Joseph Frieberth who later contrived unsatisfactory libretti for Haydn.

31 ... *on the occasion of his birthday*. Haydn was already in the service of the Esterházy

family when he wrote (in 1761 or 1762) the "birthday-symphonies", commonly
known as "Le Matin," "Le Midi" and "Le Soir et la Tempête" (Nos. 6–8).

32   ... *Assistant Master of the Music.* ... Haydn's contract as *Vizekapellmeister* is
     extant. See Leopold Novak, *Joseph Haydn*, pp. 152–5.

32   ... *lost in a fire.* ... Much of the baryton-music has in fact survived, including
     126 baryton-trios, 9 divertimenti and a number of duos.

34   ... *Helenental.* ... A deep valley running through the Vienna woods, from
     Baden bei Wien towards Mayerling. In the nineteenth century, it was a favourite
     haunt of artists, writers and musicians.

34   ... *the House of Esterházy.* ... The present heir to the title, Dr. Paul Esterházy, is still
     an immensely wealthy landowner, and is in constant conflict with the Austrian
     government over questions such as admitting the public to the Eisenstadt Palace
     (1967).

35   ... *120 symphonies.* Modern catalogues list 83 quartets (including the unfinished
     B flat major/D minor) and between 104 and 108 symphonies. It is worth recalling
     that, when Haydn began his career, the borderline between the quartet, the
     symphony and the divertimento was only very sketchily drawn.

36   ... *from one of his symphonies.* ... From Symphony No. 94 in G major (1791). See
     Tovey, *Essays in Musical Analysis*, V, p. 151.

36   ... *the great shadows in Rembrandt.* ... This typically "Stendhalian" comparison
     between Haydn's orchestration and Rembrandt's chiaroscuro is taken from
     Carpani (see also below, p. 49).

40   ... *the pains of melancholy.* An idea which Stendhal will develop at length in *Rome,
     Naples and Florence* and in the *Life of Rossini*. It contains the essence of his Romantic
     sensibility in relation to music.

41   ... *in the café de Foy.* ... A café situated in the Galleries of the Palais-Royal, and
     famous for the political discussions which took place among its habitués. It sur-
     vived until 1863.

42   ... *some two or three millions.* ... Probably a reference to Colonel Andrea Corner, a
     Venetian officer whom Stendhal had met during the retreat from Moscow. He
     frequently refers to Corner's simplicity, bravery and contempt for money. Later,
     Corner lived in melancholy poverty in Paris.

42   ... *Volney.* ... Stendhal had copied this passage out into his diary on 20 Sept. 1811
     See *Journal* (ed. Pléiade), pp. 1114–15 and notes.

44   ... *that same flippancy.* ... The *Edinburgh Review* used the word "flippant" to
     categorise Stendhal's *Rome, Naples and Florence*. Stendhal was offended.

45   ... *a History of Painting.* ... The experience described is that of Stendhal himself,
     while working on his *Histoire de la peinture en Italie*.

47   ... *Signora Contessina.* ... This aria is in fact sung by Geronimo. Stendhal has
     muddled it with the aria "*Contessa garbata*" ..., sung by Carolina.

47   ... *this tune.* The chant is taken from *Sixty Chants Single and Double* (1785), by John
     Jones (1728–96), organist of St Paul's Cathedral from 1755. It was among those
     sung annually by the Charity Children, and was heard by Haydn in 1791. He
     noted it in his diary, but improved the last line slightly in so doing.

49   ... *to chiaroscuro.* ... An important article on this subject will be found in the
     Proceedings of the *Sixième Congrès du Stendhal Club*: "Stendhal et le clair-obscur",
     by Philippe Berthier.

49   ... *the original date of these letters.* See note to p. 200.

50   ... *at Eisenstadt.* ... Haydn's modest house, some 200 paces from the Esterházy
     Palace, is now another "Haydn-museum".

51 . . . *more agreeable than the first.* I am indebted to Dr. Basil Deane, Professor of Music in the University of Sheffield, for the elucidation of this passage. The original Stendhal/Carpani description of these harmonic progressions is, as it stands, meaningless.

52 . . . *all is merriment and laughter.* All this description, including the odd technical terms (". . . dal cromatico al patetico . . .", etc.) is taken direct from Carpani. I have not identified the Symphony referred to.

53 . . . *the composer's inward soul.* Not all these fanciful titles have survived. Cf. the list at the end of this section, pp. 58.

54 . . . *the celebrated Misliviček.* These concerts were held in the College of the Barnabite Fathers. They were given in the morning, not in the evening. Cf. Translator's Foreword.

55 . . . *the composer Weigl.* . . . Joseph Weigl, resident composer to the Court Theatres of Vienna, and a close friend of Carpani, to whom he gave much information. He was Haydn's godson.

65 . . . *the only competitor.* Inaccurate. Haydn wrote the original version of the *Seven Words* in response to a straightforward commission (perhaps suggested by Boccherini) from the Cathedral Chapter at Cadiz.

65 . . . *sublime orchestra music.* Inaccurate. The oratorio-version of the *Seven Words* was originally fashioned by Joseph Frieberth (see note to p. 31), who was by now *Kapellmeister* to the Cathedral at Passau. Haydn heard it in 1794, and was so displeased that he invited Van Swieten's collaboration, and produced his own version, performed in 1799.

66 . . . *These include the Symphonies.* . . . This note contains the most baffling passage in the whole book. The Stendhal/Carpani text is as follows: "Elles sont en G *sol re ut*, D *la sol re*, C *sol fa ut* mineur." Not only are these key-signatures impossible to identify with certainty, but Haydn is not known to have written any of his symphonies specifically for religious occasions. On the other hand, a small number of early symphonies contain identifiable Gregorian plain-chant themes (Nos. 26 and 49 are the best-known)—yet none of these corresponds to the key-schemes suggested. An alternative explanation, suggested by Professor Basil Deane, is as follows: "It is *just* possible that symphonies with a slow introduction might have been regarded in France (or Italy) as 'church' symphonies, because of the parallel with the early sonata or concerto 'da chiesa', which began with a slow section. Certainly the Italian *sinfonia* never had a slow introduction." However, I have followed H. Robbins Landon and Rosemary Hughes in opting for the most obvious solution.

69 . . . *A certain Augustinian Father.* . . . Reputedly, Father Franz Aumann (1728–97), choir-master to the Abbey of Sankt-Florian, near Linz. The "comic Mass" is said to have been entitled *Bauernmesse*: however, according to Professor Karl Rehberger, archivist of the Foundation, there is no trace of such a composition among the ten Masses and nine Requiems by Aumann which are still preserved. But further researches (at Kremsmünster or at Lambach, for instance) might still bring it to light.

70 . . . *all by himself.* The Symphony referred to is No. 45 ("The Farewell").

70 . . . *the whole Court of Eisenstadt.* Stendhal has spoilt this version of the story in the retelling. It appears rather that the members of the Esterházy orchestra had got into the bad habit of getting up and leaving their desks as soon as their own particular part was over. The gradual leaving of *all* the players was designed to teach them a lesson.

70 . . . *the third and final version*. It is most uncharacteristic of Stendhal to be overcome with such coyness! The third version is the best: owing to shortage of accommodation at Eisenstadt, Prince Nikolaus had refused to allow the members of his orchestra to bring their wives with them. So, as each part ended, the frustrated young men were to leap away from their desks and rush down towards certain accessible young ladies in the village!

71 . . . *provided by the cuckoo*. The "Toy Symphony" is now attributed, either to Michael Haydn, or else to Leopold Mozart.

71 . . . *with a start*. Symphony No. 94 in G major ("The Surprise").

73 . . . *his successors*. . . . The anecdote refers to Rossini.

74 . . . *On two or three occasions only*. . . . Strangely, Stendhal does not mention the one Haydn comic opera which has recently been revived with considerable success: *L'Infedeltà delusa* (1773).

78 . . . *over the tomb of Admetus*. A slip. Admetus does not die in Gluck's *Alceste*.

78 . . . *Qu'il mourût!* From *Horace*.

79 . . . *orchestral accompaniment*. Part of the attraction of eighteenth-century Italian opera was the considerable use made of recitativo secco. Rossini's use of orchestrally-accompanied recitative, together with his extension of the arias into complex finales, was an important part of the revolution that he was to bring about.

81 . . . *parchment-skinned priest*. Pure fantasy. The following description of Neapolitan musical life is taken from a guide-book: *Napoli e suo contorno con un appendice*, published in 1803 by a lawyer called Luigi Galanti. Stendhal had copied out the musical passages into his diary in October 1811.

82 . . . *Cimarosa in Naples*. Cimarosa had sided with the republican revolutionaries in 1799 and was condemned to death by the reaction in 1800. He was reprieved, but died shortly after in exile.

86 . . . *un tenebroso velo*. From the *Orlando Furioso*, canto XVIII, octave 142.

89 . . . *at home in Hungary*. . . . Eisenstadt (like Rohrau) was, and still is, just on the Austrian side of the boundary.

89 . . . *as a result of this loss*. . . . Stendhal has romanticised the truth. Haydn was decidedly unlucky with his women, and Luigia Polzelli was to prove as mean-minded, as stupid and as avaricious as Maria-Anna Keller. In any case, she was still alive and grasping during Haydn's trip to London. But Prince Nikolaus Esterházy had died on 28 Sept. 1790, and his successor, Prince Anton II, had no interest in music. He disbanded the orchestra and Haydn, who retained his title and a small pension, was free.

89 . . . (1,200 *francs*) *per concert*. Salomon's terms in fact were as follows: £300 for an opera; £300 for six new symphonies, together with another £200 for the copyright; £200 for twenty miscellaneous pieces, to be conducted at so many concerts; and £200 guarantee for a benefit-concert.

92 . . . *the music of Handel*. . . . Haydn knew little of Handel before the English visit. He attended the series of Commemoration Concerts given in Westminster Abbey on 23, 26, 28 May and on 1 June—at which last he heard the *Messiah*. On his second visit, he heard *Joshua*.

92 . . . *the "Society for Ancient Music"*. There were two rival groups with this aim: the *Academy of Ancient Music*, patronised by the merchants, and the *Concerts of Ancient Music*, patronised by royalty and the aristocracy. The rules of both decreed that no work could be performed until the composer had been dead for twenty years.

93 . . . *Gallini ran into difficulties*. . . . There were two Italian opera companies then in London; Gallini's at the Haymarket, and another at the Pantheon. The Prince of

Wales supported the first, the King the second; and His Majesty, not on the best of terms with his son, contrived to hold up Gallini's licence, thus depriving the world of what might have been Haydn's operatic masterpiece.

93 ... *commissioned Reynolds.* ... It was the Duke of York who commissioned Hoppner to paint Haydn's portrait (now in Buckingham Palace). Haydn was also painted by Hardy (at the Royal College of Music).

94 ... *sent him the Degree of D.Mus.* It was Dr. Burney who persuaded the University to award the Degree. Haydn went to Oxford in July 1791, conducted concerts on the 6th and 7th, and was ceremonially awarded the Degree on the 8th. He was slightly puzzled at having to pay half-a-guinea to hire the gown!

94 ... *with its correct accompaniment.* In fact, a three-part *canon cancrizans*, to the words: "Thy voice, O Harmony, is divine."

95 ... *Such is his whole fortune.* Haydn's notorious avarice, which emerged in his later years, was clearly due to the effect of the mean and grasping attitudes of both his wife and of Luigia Polzelli, which made his life an unending misery for some thirty years.

97 ... *the paintings of Guido Reni?* In considering Guido Reni as one of the supreme masters of European painting, Stendhal is reflecting the taste of the eighteenth-century connoisseurs.

99 ... *I was in Vienna.* ... Needless to say, Stendhal was *not* in Vienna in 1799. The "I" in this paragraph is Carpani's.

99 ... *the Mass in B flat major.* ... Possibly the *Theresienmesse,* which dates from 1799. However, the *Heiligmesse* (1796) and the *Missa brevis Sancti Joannis* (1775) are also in B flat major.

101 ... *in Lombardy.* The story is Carpani's, but Stendhal has altered the geographical location.

104 ... *of one of his Masses.* ... The musical quotation given in the text is taken direct from the Stendhal/Carpani version. It would appear to be a variant of the following, which is reproduced from the *Dona nobis pacem* of Mass No. 2 in E♭ major (Missa in honorem Beatissimae Virginis Mariae, or Great Organ Mass, 1766), bars 34–38 (Joseph Haydn: *Kritische Gesamtausgabe,* ed. Jens Peter Larsen, Series XXIII, vol. I, Masses 1–4, ed. Carl Maria Brand, Boston, Haydn Society Inc., 1951). It will be noted that the key-signature is wrong, and that the last three bars are significantly different. The implications of these differences will be discussed in the following note. The passage quoted, however, does not constitute a "principal theme", and is not used in the vocal line at all. It belongs to a short passage of intermezzo for solo organ inserted after the first main vocal statement:

As a general comment, it is to be observed that nineteenth-century critics tended commonly to disapprove of Joseph Haydn's (and of Michael Haydn's) habit of using the *Dona nobis pacem* as a deliberate, cheerful contrast to the usually solemn and minor-mode *Agnus Dei.*

104 ... *a Benedictus.* ... Again, I have given the musical quotation as reproduced by Stendhal/Carpani. Here, the variations from any traceable published text are

much more emphatic. The reference would seem to be to the *Benedictus* of Mass No. 10 in B♭ major (Missa Theresienmesse, 1799). In this movement, there are two passages which bear some relationship to the passage quoted: the first comes from the first violin part, bars 12–16 (Joseph Haydn, *Werke*, ed. Joseph-Haydn Institut, Köln, Reihe XXIII, Bd. 3, *Messen 9–10*, ed. Günther Thomas, München-Duisburg, G. Henle-Verlag, 1965):

The second from the same movement, bars 81–84, equally from the first violin part:

In this movement, the "much orchestral heralding" turns out to be no more than twelve bars of introduction from first and second violins, accompanied by viola and by two bars on the bassoon; the tempo is moderato, not allegro; and the key-signature is one sharp, not two (although this mistake could be accounted for by the accidentals). Here, the variations are so considerable, that there seem to be only two possible explanations. Firstly, that Carpani was quoting entirely from memory, without reference to the original score—but there is little evidence elsewhere that Carpani was enough of a musician himself to have produced such a transposition without impossibly glaring errors. Secondly, and more rewardingly, that Carpani had noted down a variant version that Haydn himself, in his extreme old age, had remembered inaccurately from what he had written in his maturity. If the latter supposition is true, then these two musical quotations are of the greatest musicological interest.

105   . . . *a truly martial ardour.* . . . Haydn's "martial" Mass, the *Missa in tempore belli*, or *Paukenmesse* ("Kettledrum Mass") in C major was written, not during the Seven Years' War, but in 1796, when the Napoleonic armies were advancing on Leoben.

105   . . . *Heinrich Josef von Collin.* Collin's "sublime songs" include such productions as *Östreich über Alles, Wachfeuer* and *Schlachtruf.* The latter begins as follows:

Zur Schlacht, zur Schlacht!
Östreicher beugen nicht ins Joch:
Die alte Kraft—sie lebet noch.
Ob's ernst euch war mit eurem Bund,
Macht nun die ernste Stunde kund!
Zur Schlacht, zur Schlacht!

106 ... *among these mountains.* Stendhal's handling of the imaginary background to these last letters gives us a first glimpse of the future novelist in action.

108 ... *will keep it faithful company.* .... This list is Carpani's; but (with the exception of Piccinni) perfectly reflects Stendhal's own musical taste at this time.

108 ... *the father of us all.* Haydn was overwhelmed with emotion on first hearing the *Messiah* in London, crying out "He is the master of us all." Later he repeated the remark to Carpani in Vienna.

108 ... *in Westminster Abbey.* See Index: Handel Commemoration Festivals. In 1791, the total number of performers in the *Messiah* was listed as 1,068; the actual number, however, was probably about 550—the published figure being made up by including *alternative* members of orchestra and chorus.

109 ... *sometimes given in Paris.* .... The operatic version of the *Distruzione* was given its Paris première on 4 May 1811.

110 ... *The English poet Thomas Linley.* .... I accept D. F. Tovey's argument that the "Lindley", to whom the libretto-version of Milton's *Paradise Lost* is usually ascribed, is a mis-spelling of Linley. In which case, the present reference is to Thomas Linley the Elder (1732–95), the composer who, from 1774, was Manager of the Drury Lane Oratorios. Among his twelve children were Elizabeth Ann, later Mrs. R. B. Sheridan, and Thomas Linley the Younger, for whom the boy Mozart developed such a friendship in Florence (see p. 173). The chronological howler in the preceding sentence of the text is Carpani's.

110 ... *Society of Music-Lovers.* .... The Society had been organised by van Swieten. Twelve of its members had subscribed 50 ducats each, thus guaranteeing the expenses of the first performance and an honorarium of 500 ducats for Haydn himself.

111 ... *que vous n'existez pas.* A misquotation from Voltaire's satire, *Les Systèmes* (1772), in which Spinoza addresses God:

> "*Pardonnez-moi,*" dit-il, *en lui parlant tout bas,*
> "*Mais je pense, entre nous, que vous n'existez pas.*"

113 ... *the feelings that these objects evoke.* Carpani attributes this idea to Etienne de Lacépède.

114 ... *On peut être honnête homme.* .... Molière, *Le Misanthrope*, IV, i:
On peut être honnête homme, et faire mal des vers.

114 ... *Fra mille perigli.* .... The aria is sung by Faustina at the beginning of the opera.

114 ... *written by Ottilie.* This letter is all Stendhal's own invention; it amused him to produce a mild parody of Goethe's style, and then to attribute the result to Goethe himself.

118 ... *the enharmonic style.* .... To be more precise, the A major of Uriel's "Let chaos end . . ." is brought into violent contrast with the C minor of the opening "Symphony of Chaos" on the words: "So Hell's black spirits seek the realms below."

121   . . . *The effect is unforgettable.* In the aria "In native worth and honour clad", Haydn achieves his effect by modulating from his tonic C major, *first* to the dominant G major, and then, unexpectedly, to A flat major.

122   . . . *in the rue Saint-Nicaise.* Napoleon was to have been in the audience at the first Paris performance of the *Creation.* On his way to the Opera House, however, he narrowly escaped when a bomb was thrown at his carriage.

123   . . . *an excellent knowledge of music.* This belated and oblique acknowledgment of Carpani's talents was scarcely calculated to appease the outraged critic. Carpani's Italian text of the *Creation* is still in use.

124   . . . *leave no distinct memories behind them.* Concerning the development of this idea in Stendhal's later thought, see the Translator's "Stendhal and the Art of Memory", in *Currents of Thought in French Literature*, Oxford (Blackwell) 1965, pp. 145–63.

125   . . . *Piaceri dell'anima.* . . . Duet from scene 5, between Faustina and the Marchese Astolfi.

126   . . . *which does not count.* . . . An attack on Chateaubriand, whose style Stendhal detested.

126   . . . *Fanciulla sventurata.* . . . The aria is sung by Faustina in scene IV of *I Nemici generosi*:

> *Fanciulla sventurata,*
> *Son vittima d'amore;*
> *Fuggo la sorte irata,*
> *Cerco il mio caro ben . . .*

128   . . . *The Spectator, No.* 29. Stendhal has simply copied Carpani, who quotes verbatim from *Le Spectateur, ou le Socrate Moderne*, Paris (Brocas) 1754, Discours xxiii, Vol. I, pp. 169–76. The original is one of Addison's contributions, and is dated Tuesday, 3 April 1711.

129   . . . *unique concept of beauty.* The idea, originally Carpani's, is later developed by Stendhal into one of the cornerstones of his theory of Romanticism.

132   . . . *Montmorency.* . . . A village just north of Paris, much frequented by writers and artists in the eighteenth and nineteenth centuries; similar to Hampstead Village in relation to London.

134   . . . *Hallein.* . . . The salt-mining area a few miles south of Salzburg. It was after seeing twigs encrusted with salt after immersion in the subterranean salt-lakes of Hallein that Stendhal evolved his "theory of crystallisation".

134   . . . *from Thomson's poem.* . . . Van Swieten's compilation bears no more than a remote resemblance to Thomson, and Haydn himself found it sententious and lacking in loftiness and nobility.

135   . . . *by Monsieur Ducis.* . . . Stendhal describes a visit to Ducis' *Macbeth* in his diary for 12 Dec. 1804: "C'est une des plus détestables manières dont on pût gâter la superbe pièce de Shakspeare."

136   . . . *l'abbé de Jérusalem.* Another typical Stendhalian muddle. In *Dichtung und Wahrheit*, Goethe describes the adventure which inspired the story of his *Werther*. A young diplomat named Herr Jerusalem, son of a learned theologian ("der Sohn des frei und zart denkenden Gottesgelehrten"), committed suicide out of frustrated love for a colleague's wife. Stendhal's knowledge of German was elementary.

137   . . . *"which is their Queen".* In English in the original.

137 ... *Hollandts Garten.* .... Stendhal writes "Hantzgarten", having probably mis-heard the word during his stay in Brunswick (1806–08). The Hollandts (or Krausescher) Garten was a park attached to the villa "Salve Hospes", built in 1805.

138 ... *with vocal accompaniment.* This criticism is attributed to the composer and theor-ist, Karl Friedrich Zelter (1758–1832), a long-standing friend of Haydn.

138 ... *congratulate the composer. The Seasons* was performed under Haydn's own direc-tion for the first time on 24 Apr. 1801. Stendhal's anecdote therefore (as Carpani pointed out) makes nonsense.

139 ... *Alessandro Stradella.* .... Stendhal retells the story of Stradella in rather more detail in the *Life of Rossini.*

141 ... *a mania for comparisons.* .... See Translator's Foreword, pp. xxiii–xxiv; also Carpani, *Haydine,* pp. 126–7.

143 ... *Smiling at grief.* Stendhal misquotes even more disastrously than usual.

145 ... *the number 84* .... In modern catalogues, the last Quartet is numbered 83. It was one of a set of six for Count Fries, begun in 1803 and abandoned in 1806. Two movements were completed: the key of the whole work would probably have been in D major or D minor.

145 ... *for these arrangements.* .... In fact, between 1800 and 1805, Haydn worked simultaneously for two rival music-publishers, George Thomson and William Whyte. In all, he arranged some 250 Scottish and Welsh songs during this period.

145 ... *Visits from his friends.* .... It was above all Cherubini whose visits caused Haydn the greatest pleasure.

146 ... *from Berlin.* .... An error by Stendhal. Josepha Fischer(-Vernier) appears never to have sung outside Vienna. It was her mother, Barbara Fischer-Strasser, who retired to Berlin in 1796, and gave lessons at the Singakademie in that city. More-over, the famous "farewell performance" of the *Creation* took place, not in the Palais Lobkowitz, but in the Aula Magna of the Old University of Vienna (27 Mar. 1808).

148 ... *Franz den Kaiser!* The celebrated Austrian National Anthem, composed by Haydn, was abandoned when the Germans appropriated the tune to the words: *Deutschland, Deutschland über Alles.*

149 ... *tomb in his memory.* When Haydn's remains were eventually transferred from the Hundstürmer Cemetery at Gumpendorf to Eisenstadt, the skull was found to be missing. Much macabre mystery surrounds the incident.

149 ... *a visit into the city.* The Memorial Service took place on 15 June 1809, and the *Requiem* was conducted by Joseph Eybler. Stendhal, as a member of the Napo-leonic army of occupation in Vienna, managed to be present. See his letter to his sister Pauline of 25 July 1809.

149 ... *a most courteous gentleman.* .... Dominique Denon.

150 ... *the elderly parrot.* .... The bird had been among the many gifts that Haydn had brought back from his second season in London.

150 ... *on one occasion.* .... Nelson, together with Sir William and Lady Hamilton, visited Eisenstadt in September 1800. Griesinger's story about the quill-pen and the watch is not confirmed.

150 ... *Cherubini.* .... Although an ardent admirer of Haydn, Cherubini had not been his pupil, but Sarti's.

150 ... *some foreign work.* In view of the blatant plagiarism involved in the *Life of Haydn,* this comment is slightly less than ingenuous.

154 ... *Works of Joseph Haydn.* See Translator's Foreword, pp. xxxi–xxxii.

163 ... *by Herr Schlichtegroll.* A blatant lie. Adolf Schlichtegroll's *Nekrolog* was translated

into French by Winckler, and simply copied out without acknowledgment by Stendhal. See Translator's Foreword, pp. xii–xv.

170 ... *a sketch by Carmontelle.* ... The original is preserved in the Louvre.

170 ... *his first two works.* Four sonatas (in two groups) for clavier with violin accompaniment (K. 6–9).

171 ... *all the orchestral pieces.* ... Including the two symphonies, K. 16 and 19, but not K. 17 (spurious) or K. 18 (by Abel). Mozart's scoring at this stage was certainly revised by his father and by J. C. Bach.

171 ... *a set of six Sonatas.* ... For clavier with violin or flute (K. 10–15). The dedication is dated 18 Jan. 1765.

171 ... *six Sonatas for the piano.* ... K. 26–31, for clavier with violin.

171 ... *a quodlibet.* ... The "Galimathias musicum", K. 32.

172 ... *never actually performed.* ... The shelving of *La finta Semplice* is the first instance where we find Mozart the victim of a series of court intrigues. It is not impossible that the opposition may have been led by Gluck.

172 ... *a trumpet duet.* ... The trumpet duet (or Concerto) has not survived. The "Motet" is the Offertory: *Veni sancte Spiritus* (K. 47). The Mass *may* be the Mass in C minor/major (K. 139), but the identification is not certain. All three works were commissioned by Father Ignaz Parhammer, sometime confessor to Francis I, and a friend of Leopold Mozart.

173 ... *had once requested lessons.* See p. 56.

173 ... *amid torrents of tears.* The incident is told by Dr. Burney. Concerning Linley, see above, note to p. 110.

174 ... *The Miserere.* ... When Stendhal actually heard the famous Sistine *Miserere*, he was woefully disappointed: "*Non, jamais charivari ne fut plus exécrable*". See *Rome, Naples and Florence* (1 Aug. 1817) and *Vie de Henry Brulard*, Ch. xxxviii.

177 ... *an antiphon for four voices.* The test was held on 9 Oct. 1770; Mozart composed the *Quaerite primum Regnum Dei*, for four voices on a *cantus firmus* (K. 86).

178 ... *the Opera.* ... Hasse's *Ruggiero*, staged on 16 Oct. 1771. The Archduke Ferdinand and his bride, Princess Beatrice of Modena, were later to be Carpani's patrons.

179 ... *a Symphony.* ... The "Paris" symphony in D major (K. 297). First performed on Corpus Christi Day, 1778.

181 ... *only three German operas.* ... See Appendix.

181 ... *seventeen symphonies.* ... Köchel's catalogue lists 53 symphonies, wholly or partly by Mozart.

182 ... *in the others.* Stendhal copied this quotation from Cabanis into his Diary on 24 Sept. 1813, having found it already quoted in *Le Moniteur*, No. 259. It is taken from the *Rapports du Physique et de la Morale*.

186 ... *his travelling pianoforte.* Mozart's early clavier works were written for the cembalo; but the *forte-piano* began to become popular after 1770, and most of his mature keyboard compositions are for this instrument.

187 ... *without rehearsal.* According to Constanze, it was on the last night *but one* before the *première* that Mozart scored the Overture to *Don Giovanni*; consequently, it was only at the dress-rehearsal that the orchestra was obliged to sight-read.

188 ... *a set of quartets.* ... Mozart's "Haydn set" includes the Quartets in G major (K. 387); in D minor (K. 421); in E flat major (K. 428); in B flat major (K. 458); in A major (K. 464); and in C major (K. 465). They were composed between 1782 and 1785.

190 ... *he consulted an individual.* ... There is little evidence for this. Gluck, the previous

"Chamber-Musician to the Court", died on 15 Nov. 1787, and Mozart was appointed to the vacant post at the regular salary on 7 Dec.

191 ... *a certain theatrical manager.* . . . This anecdote can only be an extremely garbled account of Schikaneder's approach to Mozart with the libretto of *The Magic Flute* for the popular Theater auf der Wieden. All the details are wrong.

193 ... *whom he never ceased to love passionately.* . . . The relationship between Mozart and Constanze was much more complex than this simplified and over-romanticised account would suggest.

193 ... *He had by her two children.* . . . Constanze bore Mozart several children, but only two, Carl Thomas and Franz Xaver Wolfgang, survived their father.

195 ... *Les Mystères d'Isis.* See Index; also Translator's Foreword. This letter is copied from Winckler, with minor alterations. Most reputable music-critics were relentless in condemning *Les Mystères d'Isis*; however, Cramer (Stendhal's other source for the *Life*) attempts to defend it.

196 ... *Bochoris.* . . . Nothing is more inept than the renaming of Schikaneder's Papageno with the name of an antique Oriental philosopher!

196 ... *on ae'ry wing.* . . . The French Bochoris/Papageno is required to sing, on his first entrance:

> *Voyez les Grâces fidelles*
> *En folâtrant suivre vos pas,*
> *L'Amour qui vole autour d'elles*
> *Vous sourit et vous tend les bras . . . etc., etc.*

197 ... *l'amant que j'aime.* . . .

> Pamina: *Je vais revoir l'amant que j'aime,*
> *Pour moi, quelle félicité*
> Bochoris: *Je trouve enfin celle que j'aime,*
> *Pour moi, quelle félicité* (Act II, sc. 2)

197 ... *Wilhelmine.* The original letter (which was addressed to *Le Moniteur* No. 337) was signed "D.R.S." The rest of the note is Stendhal's own addition.

198 ... *A stranger.* . . . The story is authentic, although it has a ludicrously banal explanation. The "stranger" was the steward of Count Franz von Walsegg, an amateur composer, who had hit on the idea of commissioning a *Requiem* from Mozart, paying for it generously, and then passing it off as his own. Mozart's feverish state made him take the episode as an evil omen.

200 ... *at the Théâtre de l'Odéon.* The Théâtre de l'Odéon was the home of the Opéra Bouffe in Paris from 1808 until 1819, when it was transferred to the Théâtre Louvois. *Le Nozze di Figaro* was given for the first time in Paris on 23 Dec. 1807; *Così fan tutte* on 1 Feb. 1809; and *Don Giovanni* on 12 Oct. 1811. Stendhal's mistress, Angelina Bereyter, had played Cherubino in *Le Nozze* and Despina in *Così fan tutte.*

203 ... *il più felice.* An aria by Cimarosa inserted in Anfossi's *Gli Artigiani.*

205 ... *essential to have seen it.* All the evidence suggests that Stendhal himself had *not* seen *Die Zauberflöte* in any version save the abominable French adaptation called *Les Mystères d'Isis*. All the details of the description (including that of the "blackamoor Monostatos", who does not appear in *Les Mystères*) are taken from Winckler.

205 ... *with Mozart's genius.* The Mozart/Da Ponte *Don Giovanni* is in fact not based on Molière, but on an earlier opera on the same theme by Gazzaniga.

206 ... *Il padre mio dovè?* Part of the duet from Act I scene 3. Stendhal gives an impressionistic condensation of the libretto:

> Anna: *Ah! il padre mio dovè?*
> Ottavio: *Il padre ... lascia, o cara,*
> *la rimembranza amara:*
> *hai sposo e padre in me.*

206 ... *make or mar his life.* Eric Blom, after a lifelong study of Mozart, reaches the following conclusion: "I have come to feel certain that this close sympathy with his women characters was his compensation for his lack of that complete understanding between him and any real woman that was one of the afflictions of his life. He became its supreme poet because he was deprived of it by fate. . . ."

211 ... *in the Villa d'Albano.* ... This appears to be one of Stendhal's more singular muddles. (i) There is a villa of this name, not in Rome, but near Lake Albano; but it contains no frescoes. (ii) The Villa Albani in Rome (built by Cardinal Alessandro Albani in 1759) does admittedly contain a fresco by a Raphael: but unfortunately it is the *Parnassus*, by Raphael ... Mengs. (iii) Outside the Vatican, the most famous Raphael frescoes which correspond with the description given are those of the Villa Farnesina: the twelve panels of the *Cupid and Psyche* sequence, which decorate the ceiling of the vestibule. Stendhal is probably half-remembering the latter.

211 ... *the darkened theatres of Italy.* ... La Scala was the first European theatre to adopt the modern practice of darkening the auditorium during performances.

213 ... *His daughter Aristea.* ... In classical history, Clisthenes' daughter was called Agarista. Metastasio changed the name for poetical effect.

221 ... *Mia speranza! io pur vorrei.* ... One of the great concert-arias of the eighteenth century. For score and words, see François-Auguste Gevaert, *Chefs-d'œuvre de la musique vocale italienne au XVIIe et XVIIIe siècles*, Paris 1868, No. 54.

224 ... *on the banks of the Seine.* ... It was precisely Pergolesi's *Serva Padrona* which, in Paris in 1752, sparked off the famous "war" between the partisans of Italian and those of French opera. It is true, however, that the opera had not been performed in Paris since the re-establishment of the Italian Opera after the Revolution.

224 ... *the Président de Brosses.* ... One of Stendhal's favourite authors. The quotation is from his *Lettres d'Italie*, No. xxi; but Stendhal has somewhat altered the sense of the original.

226 ... *at Madonna del Monte.* ... The current letter is assumed to be written from Varese. Madonna del Monte is a village some ten miles out of Varese, on the road to Lake Maggiore. Stendhal spent two nights there (26–7 Oct. 1811), at the Hotel Bellati, next to the church, at the height of his melodramatic and disastrous love-affair with Angela Pietragrua. See the *Journal* for these dates.

238 ... *Venice.* ... As a matter of curiosity, Stendhal was in Milan on 29 Aug. 1814. He had arrived on the 10th, and had immediately started serious work on his *Histoire de la peinture en Italie*, which explains the reference at the end of the first paragraph.

240 ... *the orchestra.* ... Berlioz, in his treatise on instrumentation, gives some details of the weaknesses of the Théâtre-Français orchestra. According to him, the main failing lay in the viola section, owing to the habit of entrusting the violas to superannuated violin-players, who simply restrung their ordinary violins with viola strings.

240 ... *of common-or-garden canvas.* I am grateful to Dr. Giampiero Tintori, Director of the Museo Teatrale alla Scala, for his help in elucidating this extremely obscure passage. In early nineteenth-century theatres, where the stage was still lit by

candles, a deposit of soot was rapidly formed on the set, obscuring its brilliance. At La Scala it was therefore the practice to construct the sets in such a way that, every two months or so, the surface-material could be removed and replaced at a minimum of expense.

241 ... *in the rue Cérutti*. ... Stendhal never actually had lodgings in the rue Cérutti (nowadays the rue Laffitte); but in 1810–11 he was a habitué of the Café Hardy on the corner of the rue Cérutti and the boulevard des Italiens.

245 ... *Velluti*. ... In the *Life of Rossini*, Stendhal devotes a whole chapter to Velluti and to his apparently over-free interpretation of the music that Rossini wrote for his voice.

246 ... *please let them not run off and marry*. ... Ester Mombelli (who was twenty in 1814) did in fact not marry until 1827; but Marianna (aged nineteen in 1814) disappeared from the stage in 1817.

246 ... *I have no idea*. Bassi in 1814 was in Vienna, in the service of Prince Lobkowitz. The libretto of *Camilla* (quoted above) is by Carpani.

246 ... *in the words of César de Senneville*. A reference to Book III, ch. i, of Picard's novel, *Les Aventures d'Eugène de Senneville*. ...

247 ... *the ingenious Dugazon*. ... Stendhal had taken lessons from Dugazon in 1804–05. It was there that he met Mélanie Guilbert.

247 ... *Vittoria Sessi*. ... Stendhal mistakes the name: it was Marianna Sessi who was engaged in Paris, and who, among other parts, sung Romeo in Zingarelli's opera in 1812.

249 ... *a certain Lisbeth folle par amour*. A discreet allusion to Stendhal's mistress in Vienna in 1809, Babet Rothe. See the translator's article, "Lisbeth folle par amour" in *Stendhal-Club*, April and July 1968.

249 ... *Rossini*. ... Stendhal knew little of Rossini at this stage, although he had probably seen *Demetrio e Polibio* and, more recently, *Il Turco in Italia*, which had its Milanese *première* at La Scala on 14 Aug. 1814, four days after Stendhal's arrival in the city.

251 ... *an Essay on Population*. ... Stendhal was copying passages from Malthus into his diaries in April 1810.

255 ... *a scrap-book of extracts and quotations*. The guileless naïveté of this "confession" seems to have been inspired by Tartuffe!

257 ... *Ti rivedrò, mi rivedrai*. ... In the *Life of Rossini*, Stendhal makes a point of the fact that the sentiment is *not* expressed in this order, but that the phrases are reversed: *mi rivedrai, ti rivedrò*.

259 ... *In Spain*. ... It is noteworthy that, in *The Charterhouse of Parma*, Stendhal characterises Count Mosca by having him see service in the "Italian Brigades" in Spain before becoming a courtier.

259 ... *the Commedia dell'Arte*. ... In *Rome, Naples and Florence*, Stendhal again laments the death of the *Commedia dell'Arte*, slain by Goldoni's realist drama. He also describes in detail the marionette-theatres which alone carried on something of the old tradition.

263 ... *London*. ... Needless to say, Stendhal was not in London on 13 Oct. 1814, but had just arrived in Milan after a trip to Bologna and Parma.

Recent research by Professor Del Litto (1970) has uncovered two further sources "exploited", often word for word, by Stendhal: (1) Choron et Fayolle, *Dictionnaire historique des musiciens, artistes et amateurs, morts ou vivants, qui se sont illustrés en une partie quelconque de la musique* ... (2 vols., Paris 1810–1811); and (2) Edmund Burke, *A Philosophical Enquiry into the Origin of our Ideas of the Sublime and the Beautiful* (1757).

BIBLIOGRAPHY OF THE WORKS OF
GIUSEPPE CARPANI
including
The Lives of Haydn, Mozart and Metastasio
in Stendhal's adaptation

GIUSEPPE CARPANI
1752–1825

This Bibliography is based on the summary checklist which is to be
found in C. Baseggio: *Biografia degli Italiani illustri nelle Scienze, Lettere
ed Arti del secolo XVIII* (Venice, 1845). I have followed this list, even
when some of the items have proved impossible to trace; on the other
hand, a number of additional works have come to light, which
Baseggio does not mention.

Allievo (l') dell'Orsa. "Dramma".

Amore (l') alla persana. "Dramma", 2 acts.

Amore vince pregiudizio. Comedy.

*Anacreontica. A S.M. l'Imperatrice Maria Luigia d'Austria, per le sue
augustissime Nozze coll' Imperatore Francesco II. L'anno 1808.
Anacreontica in dialetto milanese.* Milan (Giovanni Pirotta) 1816.

*Antiquari (gli) in Palmira. Commedia per musica da rappresentarsi nel
Teatro Grande alla Scala, l'autunno 1780 . . . Musica di Giacomo
Rust, poesia di Giuseppe Carpani.* Milan (Gio. Battista Bianchi), n.d.

Bagni (i) di Baden. Poem.

Bellezza, la. Poem.

CAMILLA

Libretto, based on the three-act comedy, *Camille ou le Souterrain*, by Benoît-Joseph Marsollier des Vivetières (1750–1817), music by Dalayrac, given at the Comédie Italienne, Paris, on 19 March 1791:

(i) Carpani's first Italian adaptation, published in Italy:

Camilla, ossia Il Sotterraneo. Dramma serio-giocoso in 2 atti. Musica di Ferdinando Pär . . . Milan, 1794. Eight other editions of this version are published in various Italian cities between 1794 and 1837.

(ii) Carpani's second Italian adaptation, made in collaboration with G. Caravita:

Camilla. Dramma per musica in 3 atti. Musica di Valentino Fioravanti. Milan, 1810.

(iii) Bilingual French–Italian version, as performed by the Théâtre-Italien in Paris:

Camilla. Dramma eroicomico in 3 atti, tradotto dal francese di Marsollier des Vivetières, da G. Carpani/Camille ou le Souterrain, opéra en 3 Actes. Paris, Théâtre de l'Impératrice, 14 brumaire An XIII. Paris (Métayer) 1804. At least three other editions published.

(iv) German adaptation of Carpani's Italian version, as performed in Vienna:

Arien und Gesänge aus der Oper: Camilla, in drey Aufz. Aus dem Italienischen übers. von Johann Jacob Ihler. Frankfurt-am-Main, 1799.

Camilla, oder: Das geheime Gewölbe. Eine Oper in 3 Aufz. Die Musik ist von Ferdinand Paër. Vienna (J. B. Wallishauser) 1808.

Carovana (la) del Cairo. Grande opera in 3 atti e per musica. Musica di Grétry e Pichel, tradotta e ridotta da G. Carpani. Milan, 1795. (Based on *La Caravane du Caire*, by Boutet de Monvel.) Performed at Monza, 1795.

Concia (la) disturbada. Poem in 3 cantos.

Conti d'Agliate, i. Commedia patria in tre atti in prosa scritta da un' erudita penna milanese stata rappresentata la prima volta in Lorentecchio Villa

de' PP. Olivetani nell' anno 1785. Milan (G. Pirola), n.d.
— another edition. Milan (Bettoni) 1830.

CREAZIONE DEL MONDO, LA

La Creazione del Mondo. Oratorio posto in musica di Giuseppe Haydn e dal tedesco originale recato in versi italiani. Vienna (J. B. Wallishauser) 1801.
— subsequent editions. The first Italian-printed edition appears in Rome, undated (?c. 1807). There are at least a dozen further editions printed in various Italian cities between 1808 and 1893.

Davide, il. Opera sacra posta in musica per ordine dell' I. e R. corte di Vienna dal maestro Giovanni Liverati . . . ed eseguita nell' I. e R. Teatro Italiano nella quaresima dell' 1811, poi riprodotta l'anno 1844, nella chiesa di S. Giovanni Evangelista dei RR. PP. delle scuole Pie di Firenze, dalla Congregazione di Maria SS. Addolorata e S. Giuseppe Calasanzio . . . Florence (tip. Calasanziani) 1844.
— another edition. Florence (tip. Calasanziani) 1855.

Descrizione della Festa da Ballo dato in Vienna dal marchese di Marialva all' occasione delle Nozze di S.A.R. il Principe del Brasile colla S.A.R. Arciduchessa Leopoldina d'Austria. Vienna 1817.

Descrizione delle Pitture della Cupola di S. Celso in Milano.

Didone in America. "Dramma buffo".

Dissertazione intorno alla Maniera e lo Stile manierato.

Dote, la. Translation of la Dot, comedy in 3 acts by Desfontaines, music by Dalayrac, given at Fontainebleau, 8 Nov. 1785.

Effetto (l') dell' Amore e del Caso.

Figlia (la) del Sole. "Dramma", translated from the German (?from Kotzebue), with one act added.

Formosa. "Dramma buffo".

Ginoco (il) delle Reti. Poem.

Giudizio (il) di Febo. Cantata a tre voci, per giorno natalizio di S.M.J. . . . musica di Steffano Pavesi. Venice (Gio. Andrea Foglierini) 1804.

Gott erhalte Franz den Kaiser. Inno popolare, trad. liberamente dal tedesco, colla musica di Giuseppe Haydn. Vienna (J. B. Wallishauser), n.d.

HAYDINE, LE

(i) *Editions and translations:*

Le Haydine, ovvero Lettere sulla vita e le opere del celebre maestro Giuseppe Haydn. Milan (Candido Buccinelli) 1812. viii + 298 pp.

Le Haydine, ovvero lettere sulla vita e le opere del celebre maestro Giuseppe Haydn, di Giuseppe Carpani. Dedicate al R. Conservatorio di Musica di Milano. Edizione seconda riveduta ed accresciuta dall' autore. Padova (tip. della Minerva) 1823. xii + 308 pp.

Haydn, sa vie, ses ouvrages, ses voyages et ses aventures... par Joseph Carpani. French translation by D. Mondo. Paris (Schwartz et Gagnot) 1837. 362 + 32 pp.

(ii) *Stendhal's adaptation:*

Lettres écrites de Vienne en Autriche, sur le célèbre compositeur Haydn, suivies d'une Vie de Mozart, et de Considérations sur Métastase et l'Etat présent de la musique en France et en Italie, par Louis-Alexandre-César Bombet. Paris (Didot) 1814. 468 pp.

Vies de Haydn, de Mozart et de Métastase. Paris (Didot) 1817. 468 pp.

Vies de Haydn, de Mozart et de Métastase, par de Stendhal (Henri Beyle). Nouvelle édition... Paris (Michel-Lévy) 1854. 343 pp.

Vies de Haydn, de Mozart et de Métastase... (as for preceding). Paris (Michel-Lévy) 1872.

Vies de Haydn, de Mozart et de Métastase. Texte établi et annoté par Daniel Müller. In *Œuvres complètes de Stendhal,* vol. XV. Paris (H. and E. Champion) 1914. Introduction by Romain Rolland. lxxv + 495 pp.

Vies de Haydn, de Mozart et de Métastase. Ed. Henri Martineau, in *Œuvres complètes de Stendhal,* vol. XXXI. Paris (Le Divan) 1928. xxvii + 421 pp.

Vies de Haydn, de Mozart et de Métastase. Ed. Georges Eudes, in *Œuvres complètes de Stendhal,* vol. I. Paris (Editions du Mouflon) 1946.

Vies de Haydn, de Mozart et de Métastase. Ed. Vittorio Del Litto and Ernest Abravanel, in *Œuvres complètes de Stendhal*, vol. XLI, Geneva (Cercle du Bibliophile) 1970. lxxv+535 pp.

The Life of Haydn, in a Series of Letters written at Vienna. Followed by the Life of Mozart, with Observations on Metastasio, and on the present State of Music in France and Italy. Translated from the French . . . with notes by the Author of the *Sacred Melodies* [William Gardiner]. London (John Murray) 1817. xv+496 pp.

The Lives of Haydn and Mozart, with Observations on Metastasio, and on the present State of Music in France and Italy . . . Second edition. London (John Murray) 1818. xiv+496 pp.

The Life of Haydn . . . followed by the Life of Mozart . . . with Observations on Metastasio . . . Translated from the French [by Robert Brewin] . . . with notes by the Author of *The Sacred Melodies*. Providence (Miller & Hutchins, and Samuel Avery) 1820.

The Life of Haydn . . . followed by the Life of Mozart . . . with Observations on Metastasio . . . Translated [by Robert Brewin], with notes by William Gardiner. Boston (J. H. Wilkins & R. B. Carter) and Philadelphia (Thomas, Cowperthwait & Co.) 1838.

(iii) *The Carpani–Bombet polemic:*

Carpani. *Lettere due dell' autore delle Haydine . . . al Sig. Luigi Alexander Cesare Bombet sedicente autore delle medesime.* Vienna (stamp. dei PP. Mechitaristi) 1815. Text of two letters sent to, but not published by, *Le Constitutionnel*: dated Vienna, 18 and 20 Aug. 1815, and including the "Declaration" signed by Salieri, J. Weigl, C. Frieberth, Griesinger and Magdalena von Kurzböck.

— [Another edition of the preceding] *Giornale dell' Italiana Letteratura* (Padua), 2nd series, vol. X, pp. 124–40.

Editorial Letter in *Le Constitutionnel*, 13 Dec. 1815, referring to, but not publishing, previous correspondence.

[Stendhal] Letter signed "L. A. C. Bombet", accusing Carpani of plagiarism. *Le Constitutionnel*, 26 May 1816.

Carpani. Letter, dated Vienna, 20 June 1816, replying to Stendhal's accusation. *Le Constitutionnel*, 20 Aug. 1816.

[Stendhal] Letter signed "H. G. C. Bombet" (supposed brother of

L. A. C. Bombet), dated Rouen, 26 Sept. 1816, counter-
attacking Carpani. *Le Constitutionnel*, 1 Oct. 1816.

Carpani. Letter addressed to *Le Constitutionnel*, but not published
by that paper. Dated Vienna, 30 Oct. 1816. Published in
Italian in the *Biblioteca Italiana*, vol. V, Feb. 1817, p. 178.

Carpani. *Correspondence* with Giuseppe Acerbi, editor of the
Biblioteca Italiana, on the subject of "Bombet". MSS in Mantua
Library. Partly published in the 3rd edition of the *Majeriane*
(see below), including the *Dichiarazione dell' Autore contro il
Signor Bombet*, which threatens to reveal "Bombet" as
"Signor E. . . . B. . . . di Grenoble" (1824, p. 214).

In questa Tomba oscura. Poem. Vienna (T. Mollo) 1808. This volume
dedicated to Prince Lobkowitz, contains 63 separate musical settings of the poem by 46 different composers, including Carpani
himself, Beethoven, Czerny, Dalberg, Eberl, Gelinek, Gyrowetz,
Mozart jun., Paër, Righini, Salieri, Wanhall, D. Weber, Weigl,
Zelter and Zingarelli.

Incontro, l'. Cantata pel giorno natalizio di S.M. l'Imperatore nostro
graziosissimo sovrano. Music by Ignazio Gerace. N.p., n.d. (?Vienna,
c. 1805).

Indovinel, l'. Poem in Milanese dialect.

Lettera del Professore Giuseppe Carpani sulla musica di Gioacchino Rossini.
Rome (tip. di C. Puccinelli) 1826.

Lettera di Giuseppe Carpani all' anonimo Autore dell' articolo sul Tancredi
di Rossini *inserito nella* Gazzetta di Berlino *No. 7, 1818. Estratta dal
tome X, anno 30, della* Biblioteca Italiana. Milan (G. Maspero) 1818.

*Lettera di Giuseppe Carpani in difesa del maestro Salieri calunniato di
avvelenamento di Mozard* [sic]. Milan, n.d.

Lettera di Giuseppe Carpani su i giardini di Monza.

Lezion (la) d'on dì. Comedy in Milanese dialect.

Lodoïska. Italian translation of *Lodoïska, ou les Tartares*, by J.-E. Bédéno
Dejaure, originally given, with music by R. Kreutzer, in Paris on
15 Feb. 1791. Carpani's version first performed at Monza, Autumn
1793.

MAJERIANE, LE

Le Majeriane, ovvero Lettere in confutazione delle opinioni del Cavaliere Andrea Majer intorno alla Imitazione pittorica *e le opere di Tiziano.* In Biblioteca Italiana, Milan, Nov. and Dec., 1819.

Le Majeriane, ovvero Del bello ideale e delle opere di Tiziano. Lettere. Ed. 2; riv. ed accresciuta. Padua (tip. della Minerva) 1820.

Le Majeriane, ovvero Lettere sul Bello ideale, in riposta al libro della Imitazione pittorica, *del Cavaliere Andrea Majer. Ed. 3, riv. ed accresciuta.* Padua (tip. della Minerva) 1824. Contains only known portrait of Carpani.

Memorie per servire alla vita di un celebre Cane Mastino vivente in Venezia nel 1802. Venice (Soc. Letteraria e Tipografica), n.d.

Miglior Dono, il. Court cantata, Vienna; music by Weigl.

Nina pazza per amore. Opera libretto, based on Marsollier des Vivetières' *Nina, ou la Folle par Amour* (Paris, 15 May 1786, music by Dalayrac). Translated by Carpani, with spoken dialogue and additions by G. B. Lorenzi: *Nina, o sia La Pazza per Amore.* Music by Paisiello. This famous opera was first given at the Royal Palace, Caserta, on 25 June 1789. Numerous editions.

Ode. Pel faustissimo arrivo in Milano delle L.A.R. l'Imperatore Francesco Primo e l'Imperatrice Maria Lodovica . . . Ode in dialetto milanese di Giuseppe Carpani. Milan (Giovanni Pirotta) 1815.

Passione (la) di Nostro Signore Gesù Cristo. Grande oratorio diviso in quattro parti. Music by Joseph Weigl, later set by Stefano Pavesi and others. First performed in Vienna, 1804. Vienna (J. B. Wallishauser) 1804.

— another edition, Milan (G. Bernardoni) 1824.

— (German translation): *Das Leiden Jesu Christi: ein grosses Oratorium in 4 Abtheilungen. Die Musik ist von Joseph Weigl.* Vienna (J. B. Wallishauser) 1811.

Patriotische Gesundheiten, welche bey einem Mittagessen gebracht wurden, das mehrere Italiäner . . . miteinander hielten. Von Giuseppe de Carpani, einem Mayländer. Aus dem Ital. übers. N.p., n.d. (= ?Vienna, 1810).

11

Piano generale di tutte le Pitture del Palazzo Serbelloni.

Pilade e Oreste. "Dramma".

Principe invisibile, il. "Dramma buffo". Libretto set by Luigi Caruso(?).

Raollo Signore di Créqui. Italian translation of *Raoul Sieur de Créqui*, by Boutet de Monvel, originally given, with music by Dalayrac, in Paris on 31 Oct. 1789. Carpani's version first performed at Monza, Autumn 1791. Later set by (?)Fioravanti. Published Milan, 1791.

Ricciardo Cuor-di-Leone. Italian translation of *Richard Cœur-de-Lion*, by Sedaine, originally given, with music by Grétry, in Paris on 21 Oct. 1784. Carpani's version first performed at Monza, autumn 1787.

Rinaldo d'Aste. Italian translation of *Renaud d'Ast*, by J.-B. Radet and P.-Y. Barré, originally given, with music by Dalayrac, in Paris on 19 July 1787. Based on a story by La Fontaine: *L'Oraison de Saint-Julien.* Carpani's version (in one act) first performed at Monza, autumn 1789. A ballet-version was given at La Scala in 1791. Published Milan, 1789. Further editions: Milan, 1790, 1791; Venice, 1794 (performed at San Moisè).

Rossiniane (le), ossia Lettere musico-teatrali principalmente sulla musica di Rossini. Padua (tip. della Minerva) 1824. 230 pp.
    — *Le Rossiniane, ossia Lettere musico-teatrali di Giuseppe Carpani.* Padua (tip. della Minerva) 1824. 328 pp., with illustrations.

Scuola (la) della Maldicenza. Italian one-act libretto based on Sheridan's *School for Scandal.*

Sei Sonetti milanesi sul soggetto della commune tristezza (i.e., on the death of Maria Theresa). Milan, 1780.

Sestine. Per le acclamatissime Nozze di S.A. il signor principe Vincenzo Auersberg [sic] *con S.A. la signora principessa Gabriella Lobkowitz: Sestine, di Giuseppe Carpani.* Vienna, 1811.

Spazzacamino principe, lo. Original libretto by Carpani, given apparently at Monza in 1789 with music by Tarchi. A second setting by Portogallo (1794) was very successful; but there is some doubt as to whether Portogallo's libretto may not have been wholly or partly by Foppa: *Commedia con musica d'un atto solo, da rappresentarsi nel nobilissimo teatro Giustiniano in San Moisè, il Carnovale dell' anno 1794.* Venice, 1794.

Spiegazione drammatica del monumento della Reale Arciduchessa Cristina, opera del Cavaliere Antonio Canova. A trilingual guide, in French, German and Italian, to the famous statue in the Augustinerkirche, Vienna. Vienna (J. V. Degen) 1806.

Sul Freischütz del maestro Weber: Lettera di Giuseppe Carpani. MS dated Vienna, 1 Dec. 1821; published in *Die Wiener Zeitschrift*, Nos. 96–101, 1824.

Uniforme, l'. Original Italian libretto, translated into German by Georg Friedrich Treitschke, music by J. Weigl: *Die Uniform.* Date of original Italian performance not known.

— *Die Uniform. Frei (nach dem italienischen) übertragen von G. F. Treitschke.* Vienna (J. B. Wallishauser) 1805.

— another edition. Vienna (J. B. Wallishauser) 1806.

— *L'Uniforme. Melodramma giocoso in due atti da rappresentarsi nel Teatro alla Scala in Milano la primavera dell' anno 1809.* Milan (Soc. tip. de' Classici Italiani) s.d.

— another edition. Milan (Stamp. di G. Pirola) s.d. [= 1821].

BIOGRAPHICAL INDEX

(iii) Conservatorio della Pietà de' Turchini. Founded in 1583 by the Confraternity of Santa Maria della Incoronatella. The uniform was a long blue garment described as *color turchino*. Musical instruction was given only after 1680. Pupils included Carapella, Cafaro, Sala. 82, 176, 249 note.

In 1808, all three institutions were united into a single body, the Real Conservatorio di Musica, today known as San Pietro a Masella.

Achille in Sciro (dramatic poem). See Metastasio.

Achille in Sciro (*opera seria*). See Sarti; Marchesi.

"Adam and Eve" (frescoes). See Müller; Raphael.

Adelasia ed Aleramo (*opera seria*). See Mayr.

Admetus (Admeto), King of Pharae; husband of Alcestis. Character in Gluck's *Alceste*. 78

Adriano in Siria (dramatic poem). See Metastasio.

Aeneid, the (epic poem). See Virgil.

Agostini, Niccolò degli. Very minor Italian poet who flourished in Venice in the early years of the sixteenth century. Apart from translations from Ovid, he published (*c.* 1520) a continuation in three books of Boiardo's *Orlando Innamorato*, in which he attempted to fuse classical and romance elements with allegory and philosophy. 228

Agujari (Aguiari), Lucrezia (b. Ferrara 1743; d. Parma 1783). Italian soprano, nicknamed *La Bastardella*, a reference to her origins as the illegitimate daughter of a nobleman. Pupil of abbate Lambertini; début, Florence 1764; sang in Milan and London, and ended her career in Parma. Although weak in expression, she was a supreme bravura singer, and impressed Mozart (in 1770) as the most formidable coloratura he had ever met. 15

Ajo nell' imbarazzo, l' (social comedy). See Giraùd.

Albano (Albani), Francesco (b. Bologna, 1578; d. Bologna, 1660). Italian painter, co-pupil of Guido Reni at the school of the Carracci. Preferred mythological subjects on small scale: "the Anachreon of painting". Despised by his contemporaries as "effeminate". 142

Albano, Villa d' (Rome) = Villa Farnesina(?). 211

Alcaforada, Marianna. Presumed author of the celebrated *Lettres d'Amour d'une Religieuse portugaise, écrites au Chevalier de C***, officier français en Portugal. . . .* First translated into French in 1669.

Recent research, however, has proved that the attribution is spurious, and that the *Lettres* are in fact one of the earliest novels in epistolary form, by Gabriel-Joseph de Lavergne, Vicomte de Guilleragues (1625–85).	114*

Alceste (*opera seria*). See Gluck.

Alembert, Jean le Rond d' (1717–83). French writer, philosopher and mathematician, illegitimate son of Madame de Tencin. Founder-collaborator of the *Encyclopédie*, and author of the famous *Discours Préliminaire*.	67, 252

Alfieri, Vittorio (b. Asti 1749; d. Florence 1803). Poet and political figure, and Italy's greatest tragic dramatist. Stendhal was at first a great admirer of A.; later, his enthusiasm cooled. On 8 May 1803 however, he copied out a long passage of *Timoleone* (1785) in a letter to his sister Pauline, and urged her to learn it by heart.	51, 210, 233, 234, 258, 259

Allegri, Gregorio (*c.* 1580–1652). A relative of Correggio, he was appointed to the Apostolic Chapel by Pope Urban VIII in 1629. His works include *concertini* and *motetti*, and the famous *Miserere* for nine voices in two choirs, sung in the Pontifical Chapel during Holy Week.	173–176

Alsinda (*Alcinda*) (*opera seria*). See Zingarelli.

Andreossi (Andreozzi), Gaetano (b. Aversa 1775; d. Paris 1826). Italian composer, a relative and pupil of Jommelli, consequently sometimes known as Jommellino. He left some 45 operas and 3 oratorios. Popular for a short while, his fame was totally eclipsed by that of Rossini.	124

Andromaque (tragedy). See Racine.

Anfossi, Pasquale (b. Taggia 1727; d. Rome 1797). Italian composer. Studied at Santa Maria di Loreto under Piccinni and Sacchini. Début with *La Serva spiritosa* (Rome 1763). Best known for his *La Vera costanza* (1776) and *Il Curioso indiscreto* (1777). His reputation did not survive the turn of the century. Carpani calls him "the Francesco Albano of music".	85, 85 note, 104, 142, 243

Anfossi, Signor. Brother of the preceding. Untraced.	88

Angiolini, Niccolò (b. 1765; d. Vienna 1815). Italian ballet-dancer, who settled in Vienna in 1794, together with his wife Fortunata, also a dancer of note. Appointed leading character-dancers to the Imperial ballet-company, he and his brother Pietro were responsible for much of the choreography in the company after the departure of Salvatore Viganò (1806). *Die Weinlese* (*Les Vendanges*), "a pantomimic farce" was given in 1809 at the Burgtheater (later at the Kärnthnertor), danced by Franzeska de' Caro and Giulio Viganò. 249*

Angiolini, Pietro. Italian dancer, younger brother of the preceding. After his brother's death, he returned to Italy, and was for a while choreographer to La Fenice (Venice)—e.b. with *Camma, Regina di Galazia*, in 1817.   249*

Apollo.   8, 66, 96

Apollo Belvedere. Celebrated antique sculpture, fourth cent. B.C. Now in the Museo Pio-Clementino, in the Vatican. In 1800, this statue was stolen by Napoleon, and placed in the Louvre in Paris. 66, 124, 210, 239

Appiani, Andrea (b. Milan 1754; d. Milan 1817). Milanese painter greatly favoured by Napoleon who, in 1796, made him "commissario superiore" for procuring works of art for Paris. He was a competent fresco-painter; but is best known for his portraits. The frescoes from the Palazzo Reale die Milano (including the *Apoteosi di Napoleone*, etc.) are now in the Villa Carlotta, Cadenabbia. 257

Aprile, Giuseppe (b. Martina 1732; d. Martina Franca 1813). Italian male soprano and teacher, pupil of the Conservatorio della Pietà. Début *c.* 1763. Renowned all over Italy: Burney notes his "weak and unequal voice, but great taste and expression". Author of a system of *solfeggi*.   123

Ariadne auf Naxos (*opera seria*). See Benda.

Arianna a Naxos (cantata). See Haydn, J.

Ariosto, Ludovico (b. Reggio d'Emilia 1474; d. Ferrara 1533). Major Italian poet, employed by the House of Este. His *Orlando Furioso*, a continuation of Boiardo's *Orlando Innamorato* (*q.v.*, also Agostini), was begun in 1506, published in 1516, and revised in 1522. *The Tempest* is to be found in Canto XVIII, stanza 142. 17, 37, 86, 227, 228

Aristaenetus. Reputed author of two books of love-letters, taken almost entirely from Plato, Lucian, Philostratus and Plutarch. Of the author, nothing is known.   128

Aristophanes (b. Athens *c.* 445 B.C.; d. Athens *c.* 386 B.C.). Greatest of the Greek comic dramatists. His *Frogs* (405 B.C.) is a literary satire directed against his contemporaries, Aeschylus and Euripides. 112

Armida (*opera seria*). See Haydn, J.

Armida abbandonata (*opera seria*). See Jommelli.

Artaria, Dominik (b. Como; d. Vienna 1842). Most famous member of a great family of art-dealers and publishers, whose founders, Cesare, Domenico and Giovanni settled in Vienna *c.* 1750. Franz, son of Domenico, obtained a Royal Privilege in 1770, and extended his activities to music-publishing in 1780. His "discoveries" included Mozart, Beethoven, Hummel, Pleyel, Rossini, etc. Dominik, son of Franz, brought the firm to its highest point of fame in 1802.   190, 193

Artaserse (*opera seria*). See Bertoni.

Artaserse (dramatic poem). See Metastasio.

Artaserse (*opera seria*). See Vinci.

Artaxerce (tragedy). See Delrieu.

Ascanio in Alba (*serenata teatrale*). See Mozart, W. A.

Athénée, l'. Institute founded in Paris towards the end of the eighteenth century for the dissemination of new knowledge to a non-specialist public. In Stendhal's time, lectures by famous authorities on scientific and literary subjects were attracting large and fashionable audiences.   197 note

Attilio Regolo (dramatic poem). See Metastasio.

Augustine, St (= Aurelius Augustinus) (b. Tagasta A.D. 354, converted 387, d. Hippo 430). Author of the *Confessions* and of the *City of God.*   103

Auman (Aumann), Father (b. Bohemia *c.* 1745; d. *c.* 1800). Austrian composer of church music, reputed to have been the teacher of Albrechtsberger. Supposedly the composer of a "comic Mass", the *Bauernmesse.*   69*

Aurora (fresco). See Guido Reni.

Bach, Carl Philipp Emanuel (b. Weimar 1714; d. Hamburg 1788). Fifth son of Johann Sebastian and Maria Barbara Bach. Composer and teacher, who worked mainly for Frederick the Great at Potsdam, before succeeding his godfather Telemann as *Kapell-*

meister at Hamburg. Besides oratorios and *sinfonie*, he left numerous arias, including *Se mai più sarò geloso*. Known in Stendhal's times as "Bach the Elder". Most of the references to C. P. E. Bach would apply more accurately to J. C. Bach.   16, 53, 54, 66, 84, 85 note

Bach, Johann Christian (b. Leipzig 1735; d. London 1782). Youngest son of Johann Sebastian and Anna Magdalena Bach; known as "Bach the Younger" or "Bach the Italian". Studied with Padre Martini (*q.v.*) in Bologna, then settled in London. Founder of the Bach–Abel Subscription Concerts. Most graceful and melodious composer of the family, with a weakness for the *style galant*. 16★, 53★, 54★, 66★, 84★, 85 note★

Baptiste *cadet* (= Eustache-Anselme B., known as). (b. *c.* 1770; d. Paris 1839). Younger brother of the famous Nicolas-Anselme B. (= Baptiste *aîné*). Début, Théâtre-Français, 1792, in Fabre d'Eglantine's *L'Amour et l'Intérêt*. Comic actor, often at his best in minor plays. A favourite of Napoleon. Retired 1822.   247

Barbiere di Siviglia (il), ovvero la Precauzione inutile. Opera buffa. See Paisiello.

Baretti, Giuseppe (b. Turin 1719; d. London 1789). Italian literary critic, friend of Carlo Gozzi. In trouble all his life with the censorship. Under pseudonym Aristarco Scannabue, edited the periodical *Frusta Letteraria* (Venice, 1 Oct. 1763–15 Jan. 1765), which was banned after No. 25. One of Stendhal's sources for the *Letters on Metastasio.*   Intro., pp. xii, xv

Barilli, Marianna, *née* Bondini (b. Dresden 1780; d. Paris 1813). Soprano who made her reputation in Paris; début 1807, in Guglielmi's *Le due Gemelli*. She brought the *opera buffa* to the highest peak of perfection it had yet reached between 1811 and her sudden and tragic death in 1813.   47, 74, 76, 114, 143, 241, 242, 245, 248

Bartolomeo, Fra (= Bartolomeo di Paolo di Jacopo del Fattorino), known as. (b. Suffignano 1475; d. Florence 1517). Major Italian painter of the Florentine school.   66, 142

Bassano, Franceso (= Francesco da Ponte), known as. (b. Bassano 1550; d. Venice 1591). Major Italian painter of the Venetian school.   13, 142

Bassi, Carolina ("La Napolitaine") (b. Naples *c.* 1780; retired *c.* 1821).

11*

Italian soprano, début Naples 1798; sang in Venice, Genoa and, after 1820, at La Scala. Rossini wrote *Bianca e Faliero* for her and Signora Camporesi (1819); but by then her voice was already going.   247

Bassi, Luigi (b. Pesaro 1766; d. Dresden 1825). An eminent Italian *buffo* baritone, who spent the best part of his career in Prague, until 1806, when he entered the service of Prince Lobkowitz in Vienna. Mozart wrote the part of *Don Giovanni* for his voice. Finished his career as manager of the Dresden opera-house.   204, 246

Bassi, Niccolò (b. Naples 1767; d. Vicenza 1825). Minor singer and writer of comic ariettas, etc. Stendhal appears to confuse him with Luigi, as a "writer of pleasant comedies".   246*

Bassvilliana, la (epic poem, dedicated to Pope Pius VI). See Monti.

Battaglia, Count.   257

Bavaria, Maximilian-Joseph III, Elector of (1745–77). Ruler who spent most of his brief career attempting the reconstruction of Bavaria after the War of the Austrian Succession. He commissioned *La finta Giardiniera* from Mozart for the Munich Carnival, 1774–5.   166, 170, 172, 178, 179 note

Beaumarchais, Pierre-Augustin Caron, Sieur de (b. Paris 1732; d. 1799). French watchmaker, inventor, musician, diplomat, intriguer, poet, playwright, financier, etc. His greatest plays, *Le Barbier de Séville* (1775: see Paisiello) and *Le Mariage de Figaro* (1784: see Mozart) are not only comedies, but also political satires—an aspect which is lost in the libretti which have been derived from them.   201–3, 223, 240*

Beethoven, Ludwig van (1770–1827). German composer, who worked in Vienna. Part of the Ninth Symphony was written in Baden. Stendhal had no appreciation for his music.   16

Bellisle, Louis Pépin de (b. 1788; d. Eaux-Bonnes 1823). French administrator, Auditeur au Conseil d'Etat under Napoleon, later Préfet under the Restoration. Intimate friend of Stendhal, with whom he shared a flat in the rue Neuve-du-Luxembourg from 1810 to 1814. Bellisle is the "Cher Louis" to whom the letters in this book are addressed.   7, 8, 11, 22, 53, 66, 72, 81, 106, 226, 242, 244, 257

Bembo, Cardinal Pietro (1470–1547). A celebrated Renaissance humanist and latinist with a European reputation. Secretary to

Pope Leo X. His best-known work is the *History of Venice* (1487–1537). 227

Benda, Jiří Antonín (b. Stáre Benátky 1722; d. Köstritz 1795). Most famous of a large family of Czech musicians, who spent much of his career as *Kapellmeister* to the Thuringian Court at Gotha. The inventor of a new form, the "duo-drama", which exercised a profound influence on the development of German opera. The best example of this form is *Ariadne auf Naxos* (libretto by Brandes), first performed at Gotha, 27 Jan. 1775. 85 note, 93, 137 note, 195

Benedict XIV, Pope. See Lambertini.

Benedictus (church music). See Jommelli.

Bertoja (. . .). Two brothers of this name from Venice (*fl.* 1760–1820) were renowned virtuosos on the 'cello, and reached the height of their reputation *c.* 1800. 11

Bertoni, Ferdinando Giuseppe (b. Salò 1725; d. Desenzano 1813). Italian composer, pupil of Padre Martini. Début with *La Vedova accorta* (Florence 1745). His greatest success was *Quinto Fabio*, which inaugurated a partnership with Pacchiarotti lasting many years, and much appreciated in London (1779–83). *Artaserse* (libretto by Metastasio) was first given at Forlí in 1776; revived at the Haymarket Theatre, 1779. 21

Beugnot, Comtesse (*née* Marguerite Morel: b. Choiseul 1769; d. Paris 1825). Wife of the statesman and administrator Jacques-Claude Beugnot (1761–1835), who was at various times Conseiller d'Etat, Directeur de la Police and Minister. Stendhal half-persuaded himself that he was in love with the Countess (whom he refers to as "Madame d'Oligny"), and dedicated the *Lives* to her. It was her daughter Clémentine-Marie-Amélie, Comtesse Curial, who later became one of the great loves of his life. 263

Beyle, Henri. Real name of Stendhal. His *Histoire de la peinture en Italie* was written at the same time as the *Lives*, and published in July 1817. 45*

Billington, Elizabeth (*née* Weichsel: b. London *c.* 1765; d. Venice 1818). Celebrated English soprano, pupil of J. C. Bach. Début, Dublin 1786; then went to Italy to study under Sacchini. 1794, San Carlo, Naples (a friend of Lady Hamilton); 1796–1800,

Milan (a friend of Joséphine Bonaparte). Retired 1811 with her voice still intact. 15, 93

Boccherini, Luigi (b. Lucca 1743; d. Madrid 1805). Italian 'cellist and composer, who made his reputation at the *Concerts Spirituels* in 1768. In 1769, he unwisely accepted an invitation to Madrid, where the general neglect depressed his talent; he died in poverty and complete neglect. A major figure in chamber-music, rival and sometimes equal of Haydn. 137 note, 176

Boiardo, Matteo Maria, Conte di Scandiano (b. Scandiano 1441; d. Reggio 1494). Italian poet of noble birth; favourite of Ercole I, Duke of Ferrara. Translator from the Greek and Latin. His major work is the *Orlando Innamorato* (1476–92), based on popular epics of the Middle Ages. Ariosto's *Orlando Furioso* was originally conceived as a sequel to Boiardo. See also *Agostini*. 227, 228

Boileau-Despréaux, Nicolas (1636–1711). French poet and critic of the classical period, friend of Racine. His work was later taken as a model by Alexander Pope. 58 note

Bonno (Bono), Giuseppe (b. Vienna 1710; d. Vienna 1788). Austrian composer of Italian origins. Son of an Imperial footman, he was sent by Karl VI to study in Naples. Court composer, 1739; Court *Kapellmeister* 1774. Typically a Court musician, whose output consisted mainly of serenades, cantatas, etc., for ceremonial occasions. Metastasio's *Giuseppe Riconosciuto* was set by Bonno as well as by Porsile and Hasse. 172

Bononcini, Giovanni (b. Modena 1670; d. Vienna 1755). Italian composer, who worked mainly in Bologna, Rome and Venice before settling in Vienna in 1699. Imperial Court Composer from 1700. Apart from operas, B. wrote madrigals, motets, oratorios and symphonies. For a while he was considered the rival of Handel. 16.

Bossi, Giuseppe (b. Busto Arsizio 1777; d. Milan 1815). Lombard painter, pupil of Appiani. Secretary of the Brera Academy, and responsible for the opening of the first four rooms of the Brera gallery in 1806. In 1807, commissioned by Eugène de Beauharnais to copy Leonardo da Vinci's *Last Supper*; the preparatory work for this task led to an important study: *Del Cenacolo di Leonardo da Vinci* (Milan 1810). His last murals may be seen in the Villa Melzi (Bellagio). 257

Bossuet, Jacques-Bénigne (1627–1704). Born at Dijon, Bishop of Condom, later of Meaux. French theologian, historian, preacher and stylist.   151

Braganza, Don Juan, Duke of Lafoens (b. Lisbon 1719; d. Lisbon 1806). Scion of the reigning house of Portugal, nephew of King John V. Losing interest in politics, he made a name for himself as a poet and satirist, later as a patron of the sciences. Elected Honorary Fellow of the Royal Society in London. After the Seven Years' War, Don Juan settled in Vienna, becoming a friend of Maria Theresa and Joseph II. He was also a scholar, soldier, traveller, patron of the arts, and founder of the Portuguese Royal Academy of Sciences. 172

Branchu, Alexandrine-Caroline (*née* Chevalier de Lavit: b. Cap-Français 1780; d. Passy 1850). Great French soprano, a pupil of the Conservatoire. 1801, début at Académie Royale de Musique; later a pupil of Garat. Sang in *opera seria* only. At her best in parts written by Gluck (*Alceste*) and Spontini.   75, 254 note

Brifaut, Charles. Bad French dramatist, *fl.* 1790–1830, whose only claim to fame is to have written the libretto for Spontini's *Olympie*. His *Ninus II* (tragedy in verse, 5 acts) was given at the Théâtre Français on 19 Apr. 1813, and is a perfect example of the depths to which the great classical tradition had sunk by the nineteenth century. 197 note*

Brosses, Président Charles de (1709–77). One of the wittiest minor writers of the eighteenth century; Stendhal admired both his style and his perceptive comments on Italy. His *Lettres historiques et critiques sur l'Italie* had recently been republished (Paris, 3 vols., An VII).   224–5

Brunswick, Canoness of (=Philippina von Bülow, b. 1777. A sister of Amalia von Bülow, Baroness Strombeck, with whom Stendhal had been in love during his stay in Brunswick, 1806–08).   136–7 notes

Buffon, Georges-Louis Leclerc de (1707–88). French naturalist, philosopher and writer. His great work was the *Histoire Naturelle* (1749–89). Stendhal admired him, both as a scientist and as a stylist. 36, 51, 57, 151

Buona Figliuola, la (*opera buffa*). See Piccinni, *La Cecchina*.

Burney, Dr. Charles (b. Shrewsbury 1726; d. Chelsea 1814). English organist, composer, scholar and musical historian. Best known for his *General History of Music* (4 vols., 1776–89). Previously he had published a *Present State of Music in France and Italy* (1771)—a work which Stendhal knew and admired, and which inspired the title of the last chapter of the *Life of Metastasio*. It was Burney who procured Haydn his Oxford D.Mus. during his visit to London. 237

C***, Monsieur de. 21

Cabanis, Pierre-Jean-Georges (b. Cosnac 1757; d. Meulan 1808). French doctor, physiologist and philosopher, leader of the *idéologues*, whose "theory of temperaments" so deeply influenced Stendhal. Later, Stendhal was to frequent the *salon* of Madame Cabanis. The *Rapports du Physique et du Moral de l'Homme* had appeared in 1802. 105, 182

Caesar, Julius. 78

Calisto changed into a she-bear (cantata). See Marcello, *Calisto in Orsa*.

Calonne, Charles-Alexandre de (b. Douai 1734; d. 1802). French administrator, appointed *Contrôleur Général des Finances* by Louis XVI in 1785. His policies were so disastrous that national bankruptcy became inevitable, and he was forced to summon the *Assemblée des Notables* (1787)—the first step that led to the Revolution. In 1788, he fled to England. 241

Camilla, ossia il Sotterraneo (opera). See Paër; Carpani.

Camporesi, Violante (b. Rome 1785; d. Rome c. 1860). Well-known Italian soprano, originally an amateur, later a professional. A pupil of Crescentini, she was a friend of Paër and at one time gave private concerts for Napoleon. From 1816 to 1824 she sang mainly at La Scala. Her reputation was made in operas by Mozart (Donna Anna) and Paër, and in Rossini's *Otello* and *La Gazza ladra*. 247

Canova, Antonio (1757–1822). Leading Italian sculptor of the nineteenth century. His reputation today is reviving, after a period when his works were considered too sweet and graceful for modern taste. Stendhal admired him unreservedly. In 1815, C. was one of the leading figures in the campaign to have the art-treasures stolen by Napoleon returned to Italy. His *Helena* dates from 1812, and is in the Palazzo Abruzzi in Venice; it was a gift to Contessa Isabella Teotochi-Albrizzi. He also made a bust of Carpani, which he presented to the poet. 133*, 153, 239

Cantatrici Villane, Le (*opera buffa*). See Fioravanti.

Canzonetta a Nice (poem). See Metastasio.

Capellini, Dr. Untraced. According to Stendhal, the Viennese doctor who looked after Haydn in his old age. In fact, Haydn's doctor in these years was Dr Franz Edler. 147

Capriccio (set of burlesque madrigals). See Marcello, *Il Flagello dei Musici*.

Caravaggio (=Michelangelo Merisi, known as: b. Caravaggio 1573; d. Porto d'Ercole 1610). Important Italian painter whose reputation was at its height at the end of the eighteenth century. The first major painter to move towards a frankly naturalistic style. His use of chiaroscuro, which influenced both Rembrandt and Rubens, was unreservedly admired by Stendhal. His *Christ laid in the Tomb* is in the Pinacoteca of the Vatican. 63, 142

Carcano, Giuseppe (b. Crema 1703). Minor Italian composer who, in 1742, succeeded Hasse as *maestro di capella* to the Conservatorio degli Incurabili, Venice. Remembered for one opera, *Hamleto* (1740), and one cantata, *La Concordia del Tempo colla Fama*. 16

Carissimi, Giacomo (b. Marino 1605; d. Rome 1674). Major Italian composer; *maestro di capella* at Sant' Apollinare, Rome, from 1630. C. developed the form of the oratorio, and is associated with the beginnings of operatic monologue. Important link between Palestrina and eighteenth-century opera. 124

Carmontelle (=Louis Carrogis, known as: 1717–1806). French caricaturist and draughtsman, also dramatist. One of the wittiest and liveliest observers of the period. Best known for his *Proverbes*, a form later developed by Alfred de Musset. 170

Caroline, Princess of Nassau-Weilberg: sister of William V, Prince of Orange. 171

Carpani, Giuseppe (b. Milan 1752; d. Vienna 1825). Italian poet, librettist, translator and critic, whose book, *Le Haydine* (Milan, Buccinelli, 1812) was unscrupulously plagiarised by Stendhal. Author of the Italian version of Haydn's *Creation*; also of a number of libretti, some of which were extremely popular—e.g. *Camilla, ossia il Sotterraneo* (see Paër). For further details, see Introduction and Bibliography. 122–3, 146

Carracci, Agostino (b. Bologna 1557; d. Parma 1602). Painter. In 1589, he opened the "Eclectic School" in Bologna, in the company of Lodovico and Annibale. 63, 151

Carracci, Annibale (b. Bologna 1560; d. Rome 1609). Painter, brother of the preceding; pupil of his cousin Lodovico. His main work is the ceiling of the gallery in the Palazzo Farnese, Rome (1600–08). 63, 151, 239

Carracci, Lodovico (b. Bologna 1555; d. Bologna 1619). Painter, cousin of Agostino and Annibale. Moving spirit in the foundation of the "Eclectic School", whose pupils included Domenichino and Guido Reni.   63, 75, 142, 151, 240
Works referred to:
> Christ calling St. Matthew. Bologna, Pinacoteca.   75, 240
> Entombment of the Virgin (=The Apostles bearing the body of the Virgin to the Tomb). Painted in 1608 for the Cathedral at Piacenza. Now in Parma Gallery.   240

Casaciello (Casacciello = Casaccia, known as). Popular Neapolitan singer and actor, descendant of a long line of artists. Stendhal will describe his art in Rome, Naples and Florence.   248

Castelli. Milanese banker. Untraced.   54

Catalani, Angelica (1780–1849). Italian soprano and flamboyant operatic tyrant. Trained under Marchesi and Crescentini; début in Mayr's Lodoïska, La Fenice, 1795. In 1815, she took over the direction of the Italian Opera in Paris and, in the space of four years, ruined a fine tradition by her tastelessness and avarice.   130, 244, 247–8*

Catherine the Great, Empress of Russia (b. Stettin 1729; d. St. Petersburg 1796). Catherine II was not only a patron of the Encyclopédistes, but also an enthusiastic dilettante who made the Italian Opera of St. Petersburg into one of the finest companies in Europe. Paisiello wrote his Barbiere di Siviglia for her.   103

Catilina (history). See Sallust, Catilinae Coniuratio.

Catone in Utica (dramatic poem). See Metastasio.

Cervantes Saavedra, Miguel de (b. Alcala de Henares 1547; d. Madrid 1616). Spanish soldier and writer, author of Don Quixote. Stendhal particularly admired his Novelas Ejemplares (1613).   24

Champein, Stanislas (b. Marseille 1753; d. Paris 1830). French composer of Greek origin; début in Paris about 1775. Left about 26 operas, of which the best is La Mélomanie, opéra comique, 1-act in

verse, libretto by Grenier, given at the Opéra Comique 23 Jan.
1781.   47*

Charles V (1500–58): King of Spain, 1516; Holy Roman Emperor,
1519; abdicated, 1555. Most powerful of all Renaissance sovereigns.   79

Charles VI (1685–1740): Emperor of Austria from 1711, father of Maria
Theresa. Stendhal's portrait of him is unfair. He had been trained
for the throne of Spain, and therefore introduced much Spanish
etiquette (and also the Spanish Riding-School) into Vienna; but he
was a first-rate violinist and composer, and epitomises the full
flowering of Austrian baroque.   29, 30, 69, 70, 236

Charlotte-Sophia, née Mecklenburg-Strelitz (1744–1818), consort of
George III and Queen of England. A dull and domesticated lady.
94

"Charmante Gabrielle" (song). See Collé.

Chateaubriand, Vicomte François-René de (1768–1848). One of the
greatest French prose-writers of the Romantic period, and also a
major political figure in his time. Stendhal detested both his style
and (at this period) his royalist politics.   49 note*

Cherubini, Maria Luigi Carlo Zenobio Salvatore (b. Florence 1760;
d. Paris 1842). Italian composer, later naturalised French. Director
of the Conservatoire from 1822 and one of the greatest teachers in
France. Though not primarily a composer of operas, he has a number to his credit, and was influential in the development of the
French operatic tradition.   102, 149, 150, 249
  Works referred to:
    Deux Journées, les. Libretto by J.-N. Bouilly; Théâtre Fey-
    deau, 16 Jan. 1800. C.'s best comic opera, with a remark-
    able overture; a strong influence on Beethoven's *Fidelio*.
    102
    Eliska. No such opera exists. Stendhal's allusion is to *Faniska*
    (1806), which he had seen in Vienna performed by his
    mistress, Babet (=*Elisa*beth) Rothe.   249
    Hymn on the Death of Haydn. 1809.   149

Christ calling St. Matthew (painting). See Carracci, Lodovico.

Christ laid in the Tomb (painting). See Caravaggio.

Ciabattino, Il (*opera buffa*). There are various operas which may be the

composés dans le goût de Haydn, Mozart, Koveluch, Sterkel, Wanhal et Clementi, Op. 9, *c.* 1788. 69

Clemenza di Tito, La (dramatic poem). See Metastasio.

Clemenza di Tito, La (*opera seria*). See Mozart, W. A.

Cleonice: character in *Demetrio* (dramatic poem). See Metastasio.

Cocchi, Gioacchino (b. ?Naples *c.* 1715; d. Venice 1804). Italian composer. Début in Rome, 1743, with *Adelaide.* Left about 35 other operas. *Maestro di capella* at the Incurabili, Venice; one of the many collaborators of Goldoni. 1757–62, resident composer-conductor to King's Theatre, London; succeeded by J. C. Bach. 251

Collé, Charles (b. Paris 1709; d. Paris 1783). French poet, satirist, songwriter and dramatist. His masterpiece, *La Partie de Chasse de Henri IV* (1774) was one of the most popular plays of its period, whose success rivalled that of *Le Barbier de Séville.* It contains the lyric "*Charmante Gabrielle*", with music by Du Cauroy. Collé's other major success, *La Vérité dans le Vin* is also a masterpiece of mildly indecent comic gaiety. 12 note, 43, 50, 240

Collin, Heinrich Joseph von (b. Vienna 1771; d. Vienna 1811). Austrian lyric poet and ballad-writer, dramatist and patriot. Violent opponent of Napoleon; friend of Haydn and of Beethoven. Besides the patriotic poems to which Stendhal refers, his works include the celebrated ode: *Haydns Jubelfeyer* (1807), and a play, *Coriolan,* for which Beethoven wrote his overtures. 105

Commedia dell' Arte. Italian dramatic form originating in the medieval farce, in which the actors wore masks and improvised their parts. The genre was finally killed by the realistic drama of Goldoni. 259, 260

Communion of St. Jerome (painting). See Domenichino.

Concerts Spirituels (or, more correctly, *Concert Spirituel*). Musical institution founded in Paris by André Philidor in 1725 for the production of sacred vocal works. Soon enlarged to include symphonies and concertos. Concerts were normally held in the Tuileries when other theatres were closed. The series ended in 1791. 89, 179

Conservatoire (de Paris). Founded by Decree of the Convention, 3 Aug. 1795; reorganised in 1800 and again in 1812. Its directors included Sarrette (1795–1815); Cherubini (1822–42); Auber (1842–71). Situated in the rue Bergère. 48, 63, 122, 149

St. Jerome (=*Madonna of St. Jerome*: c. 1528).   62, 63 note, 66, 209

Correr (Corraro), Pietro (1707–68). Member of an ancient Venetian family, appointed Ambassador to Imperial Court of Vienna in March 1753, and returning to Venice on 4 June 1757. Patron and protector of Porpora, who was teacher to his mistress, a singer called Wilhelmine.   25, 25

Così fan tutte (*opera buffa*). See Mozart, W. A.

Cottin, Madame Sophie, *née* Ristaud (b. Tonneins 1773; d. Paris 1807). French novelist and moralist, of a sentimental and virtuous persuasion. Very popular in revolutionary France. Her novels include *Claire d'Albe*; *Malvina*; *Amélie de Mansfeld*; *Mathilde*; *Elisabeth, ou les Exilés de Sibérie*. A Jane Austen without the genius.   233 note

Creation, The (oratorio). See Haydn.

Credo (church music). See Perez.

Crescimbeni, Giovan-Mario (b. Macerata 1663; d. Rome 1728). Italian critic and man of letters, principal founder of the Roman literary academy known as *l'Arcadia* (1690). His ideal was a kind of classicism united with a rationalist aesthetic, and a certain *dolcezza di vita* expressed in terms of elegance, lucidity and grace. His ideal was realised by Metastasio. His works include the *Rime* (1695); an *Istoria della volgar poesia* (1698: the first general history of Italian poetry); and *La Bellezza della volgar poesia: commentarj intorno alla storia della volgar poesia* (1700–11).   212

Cristofori (. . .). One of the countless castrati produced by the Sistine Chapel Choir in the eighteenth century.   174

Crivelli, Gaetano (b. Bergamo 1774; d. 1836). A well-known tenor, pupil of Aprile. Début Brescia, 1793; in 1811, he succeeded Garcia as principal tenor to the Italian Opera in Paris and remained until 1817. His talents as an actor matched the quality of his voice.   47, 50, 59, 122, 226, 242, 243, 247

Crown of Thorns, The (painting). See Titian.

Crusaders, The (=*Die Kreuzfahrer*: melodrama). See Kotzebue.

Dama Soldato, La (*opera buffa*). See Naumann; Orlandi.

Dancourt, Florent (b. Fontainebleau 1661; d. Paris 1725). French comic dramatist, one of the most successful of Molière's successors.

Delrieu, Etienne-Joseph-Bernard (1761–1836). Schoolmaster at Versailles and amateur poet-dramatist. Author of some twenty verse-dramas. His reputation today rests wholly on the tragedy *Artaxerce*, given at Saint-Cloud, 11 March 1808. Napoleon admired and appreciated his talents. 197 note.

Demetrio (dramatic poem). See Metastasio.

Demetrio e Polibio (*opera seria*). See Rossini.

Demofoonte (*opera seria*). See Leo.

Demofoonte (dramatic poem). See Metastasio.

Denon, Dominique Vivant (b. Châlons-sur-Saône 1747; d. Paris 1825). Director of Museums under Napoleon, and thus Stendhal's superior during the last part of his administrative career. D. had had an adventurous youth as artist, dramatist and traveller; later he had become a diplomat; and only his wit saved him from the guillotine under Robespierre. An enlightened amateur in many fields, whose ideas for the state development of the arts seem in many ways to have foreshadowed those of M. Malraux. 149*

Descent from the Cross (fresco). See Volterra.

Desforges, Pierre-Jean-Baptiste (b. Paris 1746; d. Paris 1806). French poet and dramatist, friend and pupil of Delille and Thomas. A fertile writer, who provided a number of libretti for Grétry, Philidor, etc. His comedy *La Femme jalouse* (15 Feb. 1785) remained on the repertoire of the Théâtre Français up to 1815: it is typical of the attempt to replace traditional comedy by a socially and morally committed *drame sérieux*. 260

Deux Journées, Les (opera). See Cherubini.

Deviène, François (b. Joinville 1759; d. Charenton 1803). French composer, flute and bassoon virtuoso. Bassoonist at the Théâtre de Monsieur. Left some 12 operas, of which the best is *Les Visitandines* (libretto by Picard: Théâtre Feydeau, 7 Jul. 1792). It was revived in Paris in 1920. In his time, D. was best known as a composer for flute. 250*

Devin du Village, Le (operetta). See Rousseau.

Dictionnaire de Musique. See Rousseau.

Dido. Tragic heroine of the *Aeneid*. 80

Didone Abbandonata (dramatic poem). See Metastasio.

Didone Abbandonata (*opera seria*). See Piccinni.

Distruzione di Gerusalemme, La (oratorio/opera). See Zingarelli.

Dolce Compagna, La (aria). See Sarti.

Dom Juan (comedy). See Molière.

Domenichino (=Domenico Zampieri, known as: b. Bologna 1581; d. Naples 1641). Bolognese painter, pupil of the Carracci, contemporary of Guido Reni and Francesco Albano. In the eighteenth century, his reputation was second only to Raphael; it is now much lower.   49, 127, 142, 241

Works referred to:

    Communion of St. Jerome. In the Vatican Pinacoteca.   49, 127

    Legend of St. Nilus (1609–10). Scenes from the legendary life of the saint. At Grotta Ferrata, near Rome.   241

    Martyrdom of St. Andrew (1608). At San Gregorio Magno, Rome.   127

    Two Shy and Innocent Girls (unidentified).   142 note

    Young Woman before the Tribunal of Alexander (=*Timoclea led before Alexander*). Paris, Louvre.   142 note

Don Giovanni (opera). See Mozart, W. A.

Drunkard's Round, The (*canon énigmatique*). See Martini.

Ducis, Jean-François (b. Versailles 1733; d. Versailles 1816). French dramatist, whose importance in the history of the theatre is far greater than the actual value of his work. He was the first seriously to attempt to adapt Shakespeare to the conditions of the French stage; the result today seems ludicrous, but in the eighteenth century was a revelation. His main adaptations are as follows: *Hamlet* (1769); *Roméo* (1772); *Léar* (1783); *Macbeth* (1784); *Othello* (1792). 135

Duclos, Charles Pinot (b. Dinan 1704; d. Paris 1772). French novelist, wit, scholar and philosopher, author of a number of gossipy histories. In 1766, as a result of his incautious intervention in the "Affaire du duc d'Aiguillon et de La Chalotais", he was advised to take a hurried holiday in Italy. As a result, in 1767, he wrote his *Considérations sur l'Italie*, published posthumously in 1791.   223

Du Deffand, Marie de Vichy-Chamrond, marquise du D. (b. Château de Chamrond 1697; d. Paris 1780). Eighteenth-century *femme d'esprit*, whose *salon* was frequented by Voltaire, Montesquieu and many of the *philosophes*. In 1765, when she had been blind for twelve years, she developed a passion for Horace Walpole, from which resulted an amazing correspondence. 41

Dugazon (=Jean-Baptiste-Henry Gourgault, known as: b. 1741; d. Orléans 1809). French comic actor, Sociétaire of the Comédie Française from 1772. He specialised in the roles of valets, and had been an active revolutionary. Stendhal took lessons from him in 1804. 247

Dumesnil, Marie-Françoise (b. Paris 1713; d. Boulogne-sur-mer 1803). French tragic actress specialising in Racinian heroines; rival of Mlle. Clairon. An ugly woman, who was Sociétaire of the Comédie Française from 1737; friend of Voltaire. 247

Duni, Egidio Romoaldo (b. Matera 1709; d. Paris 1775). Italian composer, a pupil of Durante at Santa Maria di Loreto and the Turchini. Début 1735, in Rome, with *Nerone*. In 1757, settled in Paris, and changed his style: counts with Monsigny, Philidor and Grétry as one of the founders of French comic opera. His best works include *La Fille mal gardée* (1758); *Le Milicien* (1762); *La Clochette* (1766). 250

Durante, Francesco (b. Frattamaggiore 1684; d. Naples 1755). Major Italian composer and teacher of the Neapolitan school. 1710, appointed second-master at Sant' Onofrio; first-master in 1728. His compositions are mainly in the field of church music. Admired by Rousseau as a masterly harmonist. 83, 84, 85 note, 92, 98, 124, 142

Dussek (Dušek, Dusík, Jan Ladislav (b. Čáslav 1760; d. Saint-Germain-en-Laye 1812). Bohemian pianist and composer; a pupil of C. P. E. Bach in Hamburg. After a variegated career, he finished his life in the service of Talleyrand. One of the earliest to exploit the new possibilities of the pianoforte; forerunner of Beethoven, Schumann and Liszt in the development of the piano-sonata. 12 note

Eclogues (poems). See Virgil.

Eliska (non-existent opera). See Cherubini; Rothe.

Elleviou, Jean (b. Rennes 1769; d. Paris 1842). French bass, later tenor, star of the Opéra-Comique. Originally a medical student, E. made his début in *Le Déserteur* in 1790. Dalayrac wrote many operettes for his voice. After 1801, turned to *opera seria*, became legendary as

Étange, Baron d'. Character in *La Nouvelle Héloïse*. See Rousseau.

"Eterno Genitor" (hymn). See Metastasio.

Fabro parigino, Il (opera buffa). See Fioravanti.

Faniska (opera seria). See Cherubini.

Farinelli (=stage name of Carlo Broschi: b. Andria 1705; d. Bologna 1782). Italian male soprano of the "golden age", who enjoyed a European reputation between 1724 and 1737, after which he abandoned the stage for politics, becoming a sort of *éminence grise* at the court of Philip V of Spain. 77 note, 100

Farinelli, Giuseppe (b. Este 1769; d. Trieste 1836). Italian composer who worked mainly in Naples, Turin and Trieste. Student at the Turchini. Début, Naples 1792, with *Il Dottorato di Pulcinello*. Left some 50 operas, of which the best were *Teresa e Claudio* (1801) and *I Riti d'Efeso* (1803). Eclipsed by Rossini. 72, 249 note, 257

Faustina (=Faustina Bordoni, wife of the composer Hasse, known as: 1700–81). A soprano of noble birth. Début in 1716. Sang in Venice, Naples, Florence, Vienna (1724) and London. The remainder of her career was spent mainly in Dresden and Vienna. Her tantrums and mannerisms are satirised in Gay's *Beggars' Opera*. 60

Femme jalouse, La (moral comedy). See Desforges.

Fénelon, François de Salignac de la Mothe (b. Périgord 1651; d. Cambrai 1715). French divine, preacher, educationist and writer. In 1689 he was appointed tutor to the duc de Bourgogne, for whom he wrote his famous allegorical novel *Télémaque*. 152, 255 note

Fenice, la (Venice). See Theatres.

Ferdinand, Archduke of Austria, Duke of Massa and Carrara (1754–1806). Third son of Maria-Theresa, Viceroy of Lombardy and patron of Carpani. On 15 Oct. 1771, married Maria-Beatrice d'Este, and later became the father of that Francesco IV of Modena who served as model for Stendhal's abominable princeling, Ranuce-Ernest IV of Parma. 177

Festa-Maffei, Francesca (b. Naples 1778; d. St. Petersburg 1836). Italian soprano, pupil of Aprile and Pacchiarotti. Début Naples *c.* 1796. From 1809–11, she sang in Paris, where she was the most dangerous rival of Madame Barilli. Greatest triumphs at La Scala, 1815–17. Retired 1828. 242, 247

Feydeau (Paris). See Theatres.

Figure of a Woman (engraving). See Müller. Not identified for certain.

Possibly the *Portrait of a young Woman* (1506–07), in the Uffizi Gallery, Florence; possibly the madonna known as *La Belle Jardinière* (1507), in the Louvre, Paris.   129 note

Finta Giardiniera, La (opera buffa). See Mozart, W. A.

Finta Semplice, La (opera buffa). See Mozart, W. A.

Finti Rivali, I (opera buffa). See Mayr.

Fioravanti, Valentino (b. Rome 1764; d. Capua 1837). Italian composer who made his début in Rome in 1784 with *Le Avventure di Bertoldino*. Between 1789 and 1819, he was one of the most popular and prolific operatic composers of the period, but he was finally eclipsed by Rossini. Worked mainly in Naples, Lisbon and Paris: from 1816, *maestro di capella* at St. Peter's, Rome. Left some 75 operas.   72, 73 note*, 152, 202, 248 note

Works referred to:

    Cantatrici Villane, Le. Naples 1799. Given in German as *Die Dorfsängerinnen*. Revived Berlin 1930.   73, 152, 248 note

    Ciabattino, Il. Teatro Nuovo, Naples, date uncertain.   248

    Fabro Parigino, Il. Turin, 1797.   248 note

    Furbo (Il) contra il Furbo. Turin, 1795.   248 note

    Pazzie (Le) a vicenda = Con i Matti il Savio la perde, o vero la Pazzie a vicenda. Florence (Pergola) 1791.   248 note

Firmian, Graf Karl von (b. Trento 1718; d. Milan 1782). Austrian governor of Lombardy from 1759 until 1782. Under his rule the Lombard liberal renaissance was allowed to proceed almost unhindered.   172, 177

Fischer-Vernier, Josepha (Fischer-Bernier: b. Vienna 1782). Austrian soprano, who made her reputation in Vienna and appears never to have sung elsewhere. Eldest daughter of the famous bass Ludwig Fischer, sister of the tenor Joseph Fischer. Between 1806 and 1810 she appears to have sung mainly in Italian opera (*Sargino, Cantatrici Villane, Griselda*, etc.). She retired early, and ran a school for girls in Vienna.   146

Fleury (=Joseph-Abraham Bénard, known as: b. Chartres 1750; d. Orléans 1824). French actor, son of the director of the Théâtre de Nancy. Protégé of Stanislas Leszczynski. Sociétaire of the Comédie Française from 1778. Major interpretor of *comédie sérieuse* parts. Retired 1818.   241

Fourcroy, Antoine-François de (b. Paris 1755; d. Paris 1809). Celebrated chemist. Appointed to the Chair of Chemistry in Paris by Buffon in 1784. A notable teacher, whose reputation rests, not so much on his original discoveries, as on his methodical ordering of material already known. Together with Lavoisier, Bertholet and Guyton-Moreau, he produced the *Méthode de Nomenclature Chimique* (1787). Deputy to the Convention during the Revolution (succeeded to Marat's seat); an important influence on educational reform under Napoleon. 29 note

Francis (Franz) I. (b. Nancy 1708; d. Innsbruck 1765). Succeeded to title of Duke of Lorraine in 1729; married Archduchess Maria-Theresa, heiress-apparent to the Austrian Crown, in 1736; in the same year, relinquished his Duchy of Lorraine to Stanislas Leszczynski in order to end the War of the Polish Succession; in exchange, became Grand-Duke of Tuscany in 1737; co-regent of Austria–Hungary on accession of Maria-Theresa, 1740; Holy Roman Emperor, 1745. 167

Franck (Frank), Johann Michael (fl. 1720–40). Married to Rosina, half-sister of Matthias Haydn, father of Joseph Haydn. Schoolmaster and choirmaster at Hainburg, north-east of Vienna. 17, 18, 19

Frascatana, La (*opera buffa*). See Paisiello.

Frederick II ("The Great": b. Berlin 1712; King of Prussia, 1740; d. Potsdam 1786). Besides his military talents, F. was a flute-player of some distinction, and maintained an efficient opera-company at Potsdam. 51, 88, 103, 188–9

Frieberth (Friberth), Carl (b. Wullersdorf 1736; d. Vienna 1816). Austrian tenor, pupil of Bonno and Gassmann; member of choir of St. Stephen's. 1759, appointed *Hofstaat-Musikus* to Paul-Anton Esterházy, a post which was confirmed in 1762 by Nikolaus I. Sang tenor parts in Haydn's early operas; H. wrote *Il Ritorno di Tobia* for his voice. 1776, *Kapellmeister* to Am Hof and University churches, Vienna. *Kapellmeister* of Imperial Chapel. 11

Frieberth (Friberth), Joseph (d. 1805?). Singer in the Imperial Chapel c. 1770. Minor Austrian composer, friend of Gregor Werner, *Kapellmeister* to the Esterházy orchestra. Left some four operas, of which the best is *Die Kleine Ährenleserin*. 31

Frogs, The (comedy). See Aristophanes.

Furbo (*Il*) *contra il Furbo* (*opera buffa*). See Fioravanti.

Fux, Johann Joseph (b. Hirtenfeld 1660; d. Vienna 1741). Author of the most important treatise on musical composition in the eighteenth century: *Gradus ad Parnassum, sive Manuductio ad compositionem musicae regularem. Methodo novâ, ac certâ, nondum antè tam exacto ordine in lucem edita.* Vienna (Van Ghelen) 1725. Fux' personal pupils included Wagenseil; but all major composers, from Leopold Mozart to Schubert, owe something to his method.   24, 66

Gabrielli, Catterina (b. Rome 1730; d. Rome 1796). Italian soprano, pupil of Porpora. Daughter of a cook in the Gabrielli family, she was known as "La Cochetta di Gabrielli", hence as "la Gabrielli". Début, Lucca 1747, in Galuppi's *La Sofonisba*. Worked mainly in Vienna (1751–65), where she was pupil of Metastasio. A great coloratura, renowned also for her love-affairs and her avarice. One of the wealthiest singers ever on retirement.   15

Gafforini, Elisabetta. Italian soprano, fl. 1770–1815. Début Vienna, 1789. Sang mainly in Turin, Spain and Portugal. Last recorded performance at La Scala, 1815. Famous for comic parts, especially in operas by Fioravanti.   204, 248, 255

Galanti, Luigi. Neapolitan lawyer who, in 1803, published a guide: *Napoli e suo contorno con un appendice.* Stendhal copied out much of it into his diaries: see *Journal,* 11 Oct. 1811. His description of Galanti as "un grand abbé sec" is pure imagination.   81–5

Gallini, Giovanni Andrea Battista, known as "Sir John G." (b. Florence 1728; d. London 1805). Italian ballet-dancer, choreographer, teacher, theatre-manager and impresario, who settled in London *c.* 1753. After a successful performance given to the Pope, he was made a Knight of the Golden Spur, and thereafter styled himself "Sir John". Builder of the Hanover Square concert-rooms.   93

Galuppi, Baldassare, nicknamed *il Buranello* (b. Burano Island 1706; d. Venice 1785). Italian composer of note, who made his début at Chioggia in 1722 with *la Fede nell' Incostanza.* Worked mainly in Venice, London and St. Petersburg. His greatest operas were those written in collaboration with Goldoni.   49 note, 68, 85 note, 127, 142, 180, 243, 250, 251

Ganganelli, Giovanni Vincenzo Antonio (b. Rimini 1705; Cardinal, 1759; Pope Clement XIV 1769; d. Rome 1774). Responsible for the suppression of the Jesuits, 16 Aug. 1773.   177

Garat, Pierre-Jean (b. Ustaritz 1764; d. Paris 1823). One of the greatest singers in French musical history. Began his career as an amateur, turned professional only when the family fortune was lost in the Revolution. Début Hamburg 1794; Paris 1795; Professor of singing at the Conservatoire, 1797. After 1801, G. abandoned opera, and confined himself to the serious concert-platform. One of the greatest performers of arias by Gluck.   130, 246

Garrick, David (b. Hereford 1717; d. London 1779). English actor and dramatist; pupil, later friend, of Dr. Johnson. Début as Richard III in 1741; later director of Drury Lane, 1747-76. His play, *The Clandestine Marriage* (1766), forms the basis of Cimarosa's *Matrimonio segreto*.   76 note

Gasparini, Francesco (b. Lucca 1665; d. Rome 1737). Italian composer, pupil of Corelli. Teacher at the Conservatorio della Pietà, Venice; *maestro di capella* at San Giovanni Laterano, Rome; teacher of Benedetto Marcello. Left a variety of church and operatic music; also a book of theory: *Armonico prattico al cembalo* (1683).   16

Gassmann, Florian Leopold (b. Brüx 1729; d. Vienna 1774). Bohemian composer; 1771, appointed Imperial *Kapellmeister*, Vienna, in succession to Karl Reutter (*q.v.*). Killed by falling out of a coach. Teacher of Salieri. A major figure in the history of Viennese music; composed both church and operatic music.   16

Génie du Christianisme, Le (sentimental-religious treatise). See Chateaubriand.

Gentil-Bernard (=Pierre-Joseph Bernard, known as: b. Grenoble 1710; d. Paris 1775). French poet, librettist, humorist and satirist. Admired by Voltaire, who invented his nickname. Librettist of Rameau's *Castor et Pollux* (1737). At his best, a brilliant and witty versifier in the lighter vein of the eighteenth century.   73

George III. King of England.   94

George IV. Prince of Wales at the time of Haydn's visit to London. Later King of England.   94

Georgics (poem). See Virgil.

Gerardi (Gerhardi), Christine (b. 1777). Austrian soprano of Italian origin, who sang in the *première* of Haydn's *Creation*. She made her career almost entirely in the Schwarzenberg-Lobkowitz musical circle; achieved her greatest successes in Salieri's *Axur*, Gluck's *Alceste* and Handel's *Acis and Galatea*; praised by Wieland in the

Neue Teutsche Merkur, 3 May 1798. 1798, married Dr. Josef Frank, son of Beethoven's doctor. Last heard of in Wilna, 1804–09.   121

Gil Blas (picaresque novel). See Lesage.

Ginevra di Scozia (*opera seria*). See Mayr.

Giotto (Angiolotto di Bondone, known as: b. Colle 1266; d. Florence 1336). Greatest of the early Florentine painters, friend of Dante. 97

Giraùd, Count Giovanni (b. Rome 1776; d. Naples 1834). Roman playwright and satirical poet, friend of Buratti and Rossi. Stendhal admired his work, and refers to it frequently in *Rome, Naples and Florence*. The "social comedy", *l'Ajo nell' Imbarazzo* was written in 1807.   260*

Giulietta e Romeo (*opera seria*). See Zingarelli.

Giuseppe Riconosciuto (*azione sacra* in two parts). See Metastasio.

Gladiator, The. The famous sculpture, discovered near Anzio *c*, 1610, and known variously as the *Gladiatore morente*, or the *Gladiatore borghese* (from its original home in the Borghese Gallery, Rome), is now in the Louvre. It was one of the masterpieces "acquired" by Napoleon in 1800. It is in fact the marble statue of a warrior, erroneously interpreted as a gladiator.   210

Gluck, Christoph Willibald, Ritter von (b. Erasbach 1714; d. Vienna 1787). German composer, major figure in the history of French and Austrian music. Settled in Vienna in 1732, as protégé of Prince Lobkowitz; later received Italian training under Sammartini. Opera début, Milan 1741, with *Artaserse* (libr. Metastasio). Important influence on the *ballet d'action* with *Don Giovanni* (1761). Revolutionised the *opera seria* with *Orfeo ed Euridice* (1762). He anticipated Wagner by conceiving goera as a "total spectacle"; his ideal was sublimity through austere simplicity.   53, 60, 62, 75, 78, 87, 109, 112, 142

Works referred to:

    Alceste. Opera seria, libretto by Rainieri Calzabigi. Italian version, Vienna (Burgtheater) 26 Dec. 1767; French version (libr. F.-L. Lebland du Roullet), Paris (Opéra) 23 Apr. 1776.   62, 78*

    Iphigénie en Aulide. Opera seria, libretto by F.-L. Lebland du Roullet, based on Racine and Euripides. Paris (Opéra) 19 Apr. 1774.   87

13

tragedies, a basic *Origines juris civilis* (1713), and a treatise, *La Ragion Poetica* (1708).   31, 236

Graziano. Character in *The Merchant of Venice*.   40

Grétry, André Ernest Modeste (b. Liége 1741; d. Montmorency 1813). French composer of operas, best known for his *Richard Cœur-de-Lion*. Founder of the tradition of the *Opéra-Comique*. Stendhal knew his *Lisbeth* (*Grand Opéra*, 1797), and may have had it in mind when inventing his *Lisbeth folle par Amour* (*q.v.*).   47, 144, 251

Griesinger, Georg-August (fl. 1760–1820). Permanent *attaché* at the Saxon Legation in Vienna. He settled in the capital in 1799, in the suite of Graf von Schönfeld, and rapidly became a close friend of Haydn. His *Biographische Notizen über Joseph Haydn*, Leipzig (Breitkopf & Härtel) 1810, are a primary source of biographical information about the composer.   11

Guadagni, Gaetano (b. Lodi *c.* 1725; d. Padua 1792). Italian male contralto, later soprano. Début Parma, *c.* 1747. Pupil of Gizziello and later of David Garrick. Sang mainly in Italy, Vienna, Paris and London. Gluck wrote parts for him in *Telemacco* (1765) and *Orfeo* (1762). Retired 1776.   15 note

Guercino, Il (=Giovanni Francesco Barbieri, known as: b. Cento 1591. d. Bologna 1666). Major Italian painter of the Bolognese school, influenced by Caravaggio and Guido Reni.   36, 142

Guglielmi, Pietro Alessandro (b. Massa di Carara 1728; d. Naples 1817); Italian composer, pupil of Durante. Début with *Lo Solachianello 'mbroglione* (Naples 1757). This was followed by a list of over 100 operas. G.'s eldest son, Pietro Carlo G. (b. Naples 1763; d. Naples 1817) was also a prolific composer.   72, 85 and note, 180, 250

Guido d'Arezzo (Guido Aretinus, Fra Guittone: b. Arezzo *c.* 990; d. Pomposa). Early Italian musical theorist and teacher; Benedictine monk at Pomposa, later travelling to France and England. Is reputed to have invented the modern stave-system for musical notation; is known to have coined the names Ut-re-mi-fa-sol-la as names for the six notes of the natural hexachord, based on the Latin text of the hymn for St John Baptist's Day. His main work is the *Micrologus de Disciplina artis Musicae*.   96

Guido Reni (b. Calvenzano 1575; d. Bologna 1642). Major Italian painter of the Bolognese school, a pupil of Lodovico Carracci. 45, 97, 103, 124, 126, 127, 142, 151, 195, 204

Works referred to:

    Aurora (1614). Ceiling-fresco in the Palazzo Rospigliosi-Pallavicini, Rome. 127, 204

    Rape of Helen, The. Painting, in the Louvre, Paris. 126

    St. Michael = The Archangel Michael, now in the Church of Santa Maria della Concezione, Rome. 103

Habsburg Dynasty. Ruling family in Austria, later extending its influence by marriage over many other parts of Europe. Founded by Rudolf von Habsburg in 1278; ended with the abdication of the Emperor Karl I in 1918. 10*

Hamilton, Antoine (b. Ireland 1646; d. Saint-Germain-en-Laye 1720). Adventurer and writer of Scottish origins, educated in France. Returned to England in 1660 with Charles II; went back to France with James II in 1688. His most famous novel, the *Mémoires de Gramont* (1713) is based on the life of his brother-in-law, the Comte de Grammont. 240

Hamlet (tragedy). See Ducis.

Hamlet (tragedy). See Shakespeare.

Handel (Händel, Haendel), George Frideric (b. Halle 1685; d. London 1759). Naturalised English composer of German birth; major figure in English music of the eighteenth century. His oratorio, the *Messiah*, was first performed in Dublin, 13 Apr. 1742. 46, 85 note, 92, 94, 108, 109, 110, 112, 133–4, 137 note, 142, 171, 176, 181

Handel Commemoration Festivals. Originally planned to celebrate the centenary of Handel's birth in 1785; the first concert was actually given in Westminster Abbey on 26 May 1794. The great massed performance of the *Messiah* was so successful that it was repeated in 1785, 1786, 1787 and 1791, on which last occasion Haydn was in the audience. 108–9 and notes

Harrach, Counts of. Notable Austrian aristocratic family, whose property included the village of Rohrau, where Haydn was born. One Graf Harrach, Governor of Austrian Lombardy, had introduced the music of Sammartini to Vienna, thus paving the way for Haydn's symphonies. In Stendhal's time, Graf Carl Borromäus H.

13*

Mass No. 2 in E flat major: Missa in honorem Beatissimae Virginis Mariae (Grosse Orgelmesse), 1766.   104*
Mass No. 4 in G major ("Missa Sancti Nicolai"), 1772.   102
Mass No. 8 in B flat major ("Heiligmesse (?)"), 1796.   99
Mass No. 10 in B flat major ("Theresienmesse"), 1799 99(?), 104*
Orfeo. Opera seria, libretto by Badini. Originally entitled *L'Anima del Filosofo* (1791). Never completed, extracts published under title *Orfeo ed Euridice.*   93
Orlando Paladino. Dramma eroi-comico, libretto by Nunziato Porta. Esterház, 1782.   72
Quartet, No. 45 (Op. 50, No. 2, in C major).   35*, 62
Quartet, No. 83 (Op. 103, in B flat major—D minor, unfinished).   145
Ritorno di Tobia, Il. Oratorio, 1774-5.   108
Scottish Airs = *A Select Collection of Original Scottish Airs* (George Thomson). 1800-05.   145
Seasons, The. Oratorio. Libretto by Van Swieten, based on Thomson. Palais Schwarzenberg, 24 April 1801.   36, 62, 95, 112, 134-9, 144
Seven Words (The) of Our Saviour on the Cross. Commissioned by the Chapter of Cadiz Cathedral for the Three Hours' Devotion (*el Entierro*) on Good Friday:
    (a) Orchestral version (1785)
    (b) Version for String Quartet (1787)
    (c) Vocal version (1799).   38, 65
Speziale, Lo. Dramma giocoso, libretto by Goldoni, previously set by Pallavicini. Vienna (Palais von Sumerau) 1770.   72
Stabat Mater in G minor (1767-8).   38
Symphonies:
    (?) No. 1 in D major (1759).   31
    No. 6 in D major ("le Matin"), 1761.   31
    No. 7 in C major ("le Midi"), 1761.   31
    No. 8 in G major ("le Soir et la Tempête"), 1761.   31
    (?) No. 26 in D minor ("Lamentatione"), 1768.   66 note
    No. 45 in F sharp minor ("The Farewell"), 1772.   70

(?) No. 49 in F minor ("la Passione"), 1768.   66 note

No. 94 in G major ("The Surprise"), 1791.   71

"Toy Symphony" (probably either by Leopold Mozart or by Michael Haydn).   70, 71

Trios (6) for 2 violins and string bass with continuo (*c.* 1750).   29

Vera Costanza, La. Dramma giocoso, libretto by Puttini and Travaglia. Commissioned by Maria Theresa for the Court Theatre, Vienna, in 1776, but not performed until later.   72

Haydn, Maria Anna Aloysia Apollonia (wife). See Keller.

Haydn, Matthias (father): 1699–1763.   17, 19

Haymarket Theatre (London). See Theatres.

Helena and Paris (sculptural group). See Canova.

Helen of Troy.   61

Henri IV (b. Pau 1553). King of France, 1589; assassinated 1610. See Collé; Legouvé; Méhul.   198 note

Hercules. Greek mythical hero.   80

Histoire de la peinture en Italie (treatise). See Beyle.

Histoire des Républiques Italiennes (history). See Sismondi.

Homer. Greek epic poet.   23

Horace (tragedy). See Corneille.

Hymn on the death of Haydn. See Cherubini.

Idomeneo (*opera seria*). See Mozart, W. A.

Iffland, August Wilhelm (b. Hanover 1759; d. Berlin 1814). German actor and dramatist, one of the outstanding character-actors of the *drame bourgeois*. As a dramatist, he was chief rival to Kotzebue, but, outside Germany, the latter was all in all more popular.   260

Ifigenia in Tauride (*opera seria*). See Jommelli.

Institut de France. Centralised organisation, founded under the *Constitution de l'An III*, embracing the five major Academies of France.   95, 146, 149

Iphigénie en Aulide (*opera seria*). See Gluck.

Iphigénie en Aulide (tragedy). See Racine.

Iphigénie en Tauride (*opera seria*). See Gluck.

Italiana in Algeri, L' (*opera buffa*). See Rossini.

Jerusalem, Herr. A young man, son of a pious and learned theologian, and secretary to the Ambassador appointed to Wetzlar by the Court of Brunswick, who committed suicide as the result of an unhappy love-affair. Goethe was struck by the story, and used Jerusalem as model for his hero, Werther. Stendhal's *abbé* de Jérusalem arises from a misunderstanding of Goethe's text in *Dichtung und Wahrheit*. 136 note

Jesi, Giambattista. See Pergolesi.

Jessica. Character in Shakespeare, *The Merchant of Venice*. 73

Jeune Henri, Le (opera and overture). See Méhul.

Jommelli (Jomelli), Niccolò (b. Aversa 1714; d. Naples 1774). Italian composer, "le Gluck de l'Italie". Début Naples 1737, with *L'Errore Amoroso*. Worked in most Italian cities before moving to Vienna in 1749; close friend of Metastasio, whose *Achille in Sciro* he set in 1749. 1751, *maestro di capella* at St. Peter's, Rome: 1753–68, *Kapell-meister* at Stuttgart. 16, 56, 57, 66, 68, 72, 84, 85 note, 108, 142, 173

    Works referred to:

        Armida abbandonata, opera seria. Naples (San Carlo) 1770. Mozart is reputed to have attended rehearsals and the *première*. 84

        Benedictus. Not identified. Jommelli left several Masses, a *Te Deum*, and a *Requiem* in E flat major for the Duchess of Württemberg. 84

        Ifigenia in Tauride. Naples 1771. 84

        Miserere. Probably the *Miserere* for 2 sopranos and orchestra (libretto by Mattei), 1774; but possibly the *Miserere* for 5 voices in G minor. 84, 108

Joseph II. Emperor of Austria, 1780–90. A reforming ruler, strongly influenced by the *philosophes*. 172, 186–7, 188–9, 190

Journal des Débats Politiques et Littéraires. One of the great periodicals of the nineteenth century. Originally the *Journal des Débats et Décrets* (1789), it changed title in 1814. Its early editors included Fiévée, Geoffroy, Dussault, Hoffmann, Chateaubriand, Villemain, etc. 47

Julie. Character in *La Nouvelle Héloïse*. See Rousseau.

Juno. 36

Jupiter. 96

Kärnthnertor Theatre (Vienna). See Theatres.

Kaunitz, Wenzel Anton, Prince von (b. Vienna 1711; d. Vienna 1794). Austrian statesman of Moravian origins. Governor of the Low Countries (1745); Ambassador to the Congress of Aix-la-Chapelle (1747); Ambassador to France (1750–53). His policies were based on Franco-Austrian friendship, and prevailed almost exclusively under Maria Theresa; his influence declined under Joseph II. Between 1760 and 1775, he exercised a decisive influence on the Vienna Court Theatre, particularly in his enthusiasm for comedy in the French tradition.   150, 172, 177

Keller, Johann Peter. Hairdresser or wig-dresser in the Ungargasse, Vienna.   26–7, 32

Keller, Maria Anna Aloysia Apollonia. Elder daughter of the preceding. Married to Haydn on 26 Nov. 1760, in St. Stephen's cathedral. The marriage was an unmitigated disaster, and Haydn goes down to history as one of the most unhappily-married men of genius who has ever lived.   26*, 27*, 33

Keller, Theresia. Young sister of the preceding, with whom Haydn fell in love, and wanted to marry; but she decided to become a nun. Later, she left her convent, but by then Haydn was married.   26*, 27*

Kotzebue, August Friedrich Ferdinand von (b. Weimar 1761; assassinated Mannheim 1819). German dramatist who perfected the *Schicksalstragödie* (e.g. *Menschenhass und Reue*, 1790). He was also prolific in other genres: middle-class dramas, historical pageants, small-town comedies. His drama, *Die Kreuzfahrer*, with Babet Rothe in the cast, was seen by Stendhal in Vienna early in November 1809.   249*

Koželuck (Košeluch), Johann Anton (b. Welwarn 1738; d. Prague 1814). Czech composer, member of a large family of successful musicians. Settled in Vienna c. 1764, as teacher of composition; friend of Gassmann, Gluck, Hasse. After 1766, he worked mainly in Prague. His cousin and pupil, Leopold Koželuck (1754–1814), a virtuoso pianist, was also a well-known composer in a facile and graceful style; in 1792 he replaced Mozart as Chamber-Composer to the Court of Vienna.   69

Krumme Teufel, Der (opera buffa). See Haydn.

Kurz, Johann Joseph Felix (b. Vienna 1717; d. Munich? c. 1780).

Viennese comic actor, début in 1737. Although constantly in trouble with the censorship, K. revolutionised and revitalised the old *Hanswurst* tradition of Viennese farce, and paved the way for a more sophisticated type of local comedy, later exploited by Schikaneder. K's wife, Franziska, a light-opera soprano, some-time chambermaid, was renowned for her beauty. She died in 1755. 27, 28

Kurzböck (Kurzbeck), Magdalene von (fl. 1760–1820). Daughter of Joseph von K., writer and bookseller in Vienna. An accomplished pianist and amateur musician. Haydn admired her so much that he dedicated to her his piano-sonata, op. 92.   11, 146, 148

L***, duchessa, of Rome, of Naples.   16

La Bruyère, Jean de (b. Paris 1645; d. Versailles 1696). French writer and moralist. His major work, *Les Caractères*, appeared between 1688 and 1696.   240

La Fontaine, Jean de (b. Château-Thierry 1621; d. Paris 1695). French poet, universally known for his *Fables* (1668–96). *La Mort et le Bûcheron* is found in Bk. I, no. xvi.   64, 151, 213, 234

Laharpe, Jean-François de (b. Paris 1739; d. Paris 1803). French scholar and critic, a pillar of the classical tradition. His *Lycée, ou Cours de Littérature ancienne et moderne* was the standard text-book in French schools from about 1810 to 1840. In tragedy, he acquired some fame from an attempt to adapt Polish place-names to the French classical alexandrine; his *Coriolan* was given on 3 Mar. 1784. 10, 78, 97, 256

Lambertini, Prospero (b. Bologna 1675; Bishop of Ancona 1727; Cardinal 1728; Archbishop of Bologna 1731; Pope Benedict XIV 1740; d. Rome 1758). Greatest Pope of the eighteenth century. An eminent scholar and authority on canon law, with a sour mistrust of Jesuits and Freemasons, and a generous love of the arts. 224

Last Judgement (fresco). See Michelangelo.

Last Supper (fresco). See Leonardo da Vinci; Bossi.

Laura (=Laura de Noves, wife of Hugues de Sade: b. Avignon *c.* 1308; d. Avignon *c.* 1348). High-born Provençal lady, ancestress of the marquis de Sade. Seen by Petrarch in the Church of St. Claire, Avignon, on the morning of 6 April 1327. His ensuing love for her inspired sonnets and other poems which are the first examples of modern love-poetry.   236

Lavoisier, Antoine-Laurent (b. Paris 1743; guillotined 1794). Major French chemist, member of the Académie des Sciences at the age of 25; also a tax-farmer—a fact not forgiven him by Robespierre. Discoverer of oxygen.   29 note

Lebrun, Pierre-Antoine (b. Paris 1785; d. *c.* 1860) French poet and politician. Began life as infant prodigy and gross flatterer of Napoleon. His first tragedy was *Ulysse*, given at the Comédie Française, 28 April 1814, performed by Talma, Mlle Georges and Mlle Duchesnois. His best play was *Maria Stuart* (1820), which shows the influence of Schiller. Later a friend of Walter Scott, protector of Bérenger and Victor Hugo. 1831, Director of the Imprimerie Royale; Senator in 1853.   197* note

Lech★★★, Louis = Louis de Bellisle (*q.v.*). A typical complex riddle-pseudonym, of the type Stendhal loved. It suggests (i) the Lechi family in Brescia, whom Stendhal had met in 1811 and to whom he refers constantly; and (ii) the battle of Lechfeld, on the Lech in Bavaria, where Pépin le Bref defeated the Bavarians in 743 A.D. Louis de Bellisle's second name was Pépin.

Leda (painting). See Correggio.

Legend of St. Nilus (frescoes). See Domenichino.

Legouvé, Gabriel-Marie-Jean-Baptiste (b. Paris 1764; d. Montmartre 1812). French poet and dramatist of remarkable mediocrity. Début in 1792, with *La Mort d'Abel*; he exploited a vein of pseudo-pastoral simplicity which found favour with a public surfeited with Revolutionary and political propaganda. He also tried to imitate Shakespeare without disturbing the classical tradition. *La Mort de Henri IV, Roi de France* was given on 6 Jun. 1806 at the Comédie Française. 198 note

Lehoc, Louis-Grégoire (b. Paris 1743; d. Paris 1810). French civil servant and administrator, who had been a protégé of Necker and (among other things) Ambassador to Sweden. After his retirement, he took to writing tragedies as a hobby. *Pyrrhus ou les Æacides* was given at the Comédie Française on 27 Feb. 1807, and received the honour of being banned by Napoleon on account of its political allusions.   197 note

Leiden (Das) Jesu Christi (oratorio). See Weigl; Carpani.

Lemoyne, Jean-Baptiste (b. Eymet 1751; d. Paris 1796). French conductor and composer who worked in Berlin and Warsaw. Settled in Paris in 1778, where he quarrelled with Gluck. Left some 16 operas, of which the most popular was *Les Prétendus* (libretto by M. A. J. Rochon de Chabannes: one-act, Comédie-Lyrique, 1789). Rewritten by Mosca as *I Pretendenti delusi* (*q.v.*). 247*

Leo, Leonardo Ortensio Salvatore de (b. San Vito degli Schiavi 1694; d. Naples 1744). Italian composer and teacher, pupil at the Turchini. Début with *Pisistrato*, Naples 1714. 1741–4, First-Master at the Turchini. Wrote mainly church-music and operas, of which *Demofoonte* (libretto by Metastasio; Naples 1735) was the most successful. Piccinni considered Leo's setting of *Misero Pargoletto* as "a model of dramatic expression". 16, 72, 82, 82 note, 83 note, 85 note, 92, 180

Leonardo da Vinci (b. Vinci 1452; d. Amboise 1519). Major Italian painter of the Florentine school. His *Last Supper* was commissioned by Lodovico Sforza for the church of Santa Maria delle Grazie, Milan, and executed 1495–8. Owing to the disastrous degeneration of the original, copies such as those by Bossi (*q.v.*), Marco d'Oggione and Raphael Morghen are of great value. 257

Leopold I, Emperor of Austria and Holy Roman Emperor from 1658–1705. 175

Lesage, Alain-René (b. Sarzeau 1668; d. Boulogne-sur-mer, 1747). French dramatist, novelist and translator, best known for his satirical comedy, *Turcaret* (1709) and for his great picaresque novel, *Gil Blas de Santillane* (1715–35). 40, 115

Lespinasse, Julie-Jeanne-Eléonore de (b. Lyon 1732; d. Paris 1776). An illegitimate child, she lived for many years a humiliating existence, and from 1754–64 she was companion to Madame du Deffand. Visitors to the latter's *salon*, however, gradually discovered that the companion was as remarkable as the hostess, and soon her own *salon* was the glittering rival of that of her erstwhile mistress. Her *Lettres écrites depuis l'année 1773 jusqu'à l'année 1776* (Paris, 2 vols., 1809) were written to her lover, the Comte de Guibert. 221 note

Lettres de Mademoiselle de Lespinasse. See preceding.

Lettres d'Italie. . . . See Brosses, Président de.

Lettres d'une Religieuse portugaise. See Alcaforada.

Lettres écrites de Suisse, d'Italie, de Sicile et de Malte. . . . See Roland.

Lettres Persanes (novel). See Montesquieu.

Liechtenstein, Prince Johann-Joseph (b. Vienna 1760; d. Vienna 1836). Austrian statesman, general and patron of the arts. In 1805, he covered the retreat of the Austrians after the defeat of Austerlitz, and signed the treaty of Pressburg; in 1809, took part in the battle of Wagram, and became commander-in-chief of the Austrian forces after the resignation of the Archduke Charles.   150

Ligniville, Marquis de (fl. *c.* 1760). Member of a family which gave France two famous soldiers, the Marquis who befriended Mozart is described as a "musical courtier" who dabbled in composition "if writing church music in elaborate canons can be called dabbling". Apparently a disciple of Padre Martini in his love of *"canons énigmatiques".* 173

Linley (Lidley, Lydley), Thomas (b. Badminton 1733; d. London 1795). Probably the singing-master and concert-promoter, whose daughter Elizabeth Ann married the dramatist Sheridan. His adaptation of parts of Milton's *Paradise Lost* as the libretto of an oratorio was originally intended for Handel. Salomon acquired it and passed it on to Haydn, who had it translated by Van Swieten and used it in the *Creation.* 110

Linley, Thomas *jun.* (b. *c.* 1756; drowned *c.* 1778). English violinist who, at the age of 12, became the intimate friend of Mozart. Probably the son of the preceding, and brother of Mrs. Sheridan. Studied under Nardini; afterwards composed part of the music for Sheridan's *The Duenna.* 173

Lisbeth folle par Amour. Non-existent opera, compounded by Stendhal out of Paër's *Nina pazza* and Grétry's *Lisbeth*, in honour of his Viennese mistress, Babet (= Elisabeth) Rothe. Cf. also *Eliska.* 249

Lobkowitz, Franz Joseph Ferdinand Max, Prince (b. Prague 1772; d. Wittingau 1816). Leading dilettante in Vienna in Stendhal's time; member of the *Gesellschaft der Cavaliere* which ran all the Court Theatres from 1807 to 1813, during which time he was responsible for all matters relating to the Opera. Himself a violinist, 'cellist and first-class bass singer, he had written symphonies, and was the friend of Beethoven. Luigi Bassi and many other singers

Maddalena (painting). See Correggio.

Madonna al longo collo (painting). See Parmigiano.

Madonna alla scodella (painting). See Correggio.

Madonna alla seggiola (painting). See Raphael.

Malanotte, Adelaida (b. Verona 1785; d. Brescia 1832). Italian contralto of aristocratic birth, originally an amateur. Début, Verona 1806. Rossini made her reputation when he wrote *Tancredi* for her voice in 1813. Retired in 1821.   247

"Malbrouck s'en va-t-en guerre". French nursery song. Marie-Antoinette, hearing it sung by a nurse to her children, was caught by the tune and popularised it.   12 note

Malherbe, François de (b. Caen 1555; d. Paris 1628). French lyric poet and grammarian, who established the language of classical French poetry.   97

Malthus, Rev. Thomas Robert (b. Guildford 1766; d. Haileybury 1834). English economist, Professor of Modern History and Political Economy at Haileybury College. His *Essay on the Principle of Population as it affects the future Improvement of Society, with Remarks on the Speculations of Mr. Godwin, M Condorcet and other Writers*, first appeared in 1798, and was revised in 1803, again in 1826. Stendhal notes in his *Journal* (19 Mar. 1810) that he is reading it with extreme interest.   252–3

Mandragola, La (satirical comedy). See Machiavelli.

Manfredini, Elisabetta. Italian singer, member of the original casts of Rossini's *Tancredi* (1813), *Sigismondo* (1814) and *Adelaide di Borgogna* (1817). Nothing further is known of her career.   246

Mantegna, Andrea (b. near Padua 1431; d. Mantua 1506). Major Italian painter of the School of Padua.   97

Mara (Marra), Gertrud Elisabeth, *née* Schmeling (b. Cassel 1749; d. Reval 1833). German soprano, a pupil of Hiller in Leipzig. Début in Dresden, then moved to Potsdam until she quarrelled with Frederick II. Failed in Vienna, then changed her style and triumphed in London (1784–91). Thereafter sang mainly in oratorio.   15

Maratta (Maratti), Carlo (b. Camerano 1625; d. Rome 1713). Painter of the Roman school, pupil of Andrea Sacchi. Painted mainly madonnas, hence nickname *Carluccio delle Madonne*. Restored the Raphael frescoes in the *Loggie* of the Vatican.   142, 195

Marcello, Benedetto (b. Venice 1686; d. Brescia 1739). Venetian administrator, dramatist, pamphleteer, satirist and amateur composer, "one of the greatest musical intelligences of the eighteenth century". His play, *Il Teatro alla Moda*, is a major source of information concerning operatic conditions during the period. 68, 92, 109, 112

Works referred to:

Calisto in Orsa: pastoral cantata for 5 voices. Libretto (by Marcello) published in 1725; music now lost.   112

Capriccio, Il = Il Flagello dei Musici: set of 2 "burlesque madrigals" (i) for 2 tenors, 2 basses; (ii) for 2 sopranos, 2 altos. A farcical piece written to ridicule the castrati. 68

Marcellus II, Pope. See Servini.

Marchesi, Lodovico (b. Milan 1755; d. Milan 1829). Italian male soprano. Début, Rome 1774. Known as the last of the great castrati. Sang at the San Carlo, St. Petersburg, Vienna and London. One of the finest singers in Europe until his retirement in 1806.   15, 18, 123, 221

Maria Theresa (Theresia). Empress of Austria 1740–80.   177

Mariage de Figaro (comedy). See Beaumarchais; Mozart, W. A.

Marivaux, Pierre Carlet de Chamblain de (b. Paris 1688; d. Paris 1763). French dramatist, novelist and journalist, creator of the sentimental novel in France (*La Vie de Marianne*, 1731–41), and of numerous exquisite and witty comedies.   224

Marriage of St. Catherine, The (painting). See Correggio.

Mars, Mademoiselle (= Anne-Françoise-Hippolyte Boutet, known as: b. Paris 1779; d. Paris 1847). French actress, daughter of the actor Monvel. Début, Théâtre Feydeau, 1794; Sociétaire of the Comédie Française, 1799. For thirty-three years, the glory of the French Romantic stage; favourite actress of Napoleon.   143, 241

Martin y Soler, Vicente (b. Valencia 1754; d. St. Petersburg 1806). Spanish composer and organist. Début, Naples 1779, with *Ifigenia in Aulide*. Worked in Venice with Lorenzo da Ponte, and with him produced his masterpiece, *Una Cosa Rara, ossia Bellezza ed Onesta* (Vienna, 17 Nov. 1786), based on a story by Luis Veléz de Guevara. One of the most successful operas of eighteenth century.   181

Martinez, Antonia (1747–1812). Younger daughter of Niccolò M. 11, 30*, 31*

Martinez, Marianne (= Anna Katharina: b. Vienna 1744; d. Vienna 1812). Elder daughter of Niccolò M. Austrian composer of Italo-Spanish descent. Educated by Metastasio, received lessons from Porpora and Haydn. Friend of Mozart. 1773, elected member of the *Filarmonici* of Bologna. Left 12 piano-concertos, 3 oratorios, a mass, etc. It was she who introduced Haydn to Metastasio and Porpora.   11, 30, 31, 244

Martinez, Niccolò di (fl. 1710–80). Minor Roman diplomat, who settled in Vienna *c.* 1720, as Master of Ceremonies to the Papal Nuncio. Shared an apartment with Metastasio. By his wife Maria-Theresia, had two daughters, Marianne and Antonia, who were educated by Metastasio.   30, 31

Martini, Giovanni Battista, known as Padre Martini (b. Bologna 1706; d. Bologna 1784). Italian composer, musical theorist, violinist, harpsichordist, philosopher, theologian, and the greatest teacher of the eighteenth century. *Maestro di capella* to the Franciscan Order in Bologna. Remembered for his *Storia della Musica* (3 vols., Bologna, 1757–81), and his *Esemplare, o sia Saggio fondamentale pratico di Contrappunto* (2 vols., Bologna, 1774–5). As a teaching-method, he liked to use a form of contrapuntal riddle or *canone enigmatico*: the *Storia della Musica* includes a large number of these, including possibly those referred to:

"Decrepit Nun's Round" (*c. delle vecchie Monachelle*).
"Drunkards' Round" (*c. degli Ubbriachi* = possibly canon:
    Hilari merum bibentes Bromium patrem canamus canamus,
    Storia, II, 141).
"Round of Bells" (*c. delle Campane*).   56, 57, 69, 84, 104,
173

Martyrdom of St. Andrew (painting). See Domenichino.

Martyrdom of St. Peter (painting). See Titian, *St. Peter Martyr.*

Marzocchi (. . .). Italian tenor, who made his début in Paris at the Théâtre de l'Odéon in *Saulle* on 4 Sept. 1813, and thereafter disappears.   248

Mass (*Missa Papae Marcelli*). See Palestrina.

Masses (various). See Haydn.

Matrimonio segreto, Il opera buffa. See Cimarosa.

Maximilian, Archduke (b. Vienna 1756; d. Hetzeufeld 1801). Youngest son of Maria-Theresa; later Archbishop-Elector of Cologne. 178

Mayr (Mayer), Johann Simon (b. Mendorf 1763; d. Bergamo 1845). Italian composer of German origin. A prolific composer, whose influence on Rossini was considerable. Operatic début with *Saffo* (La Fenice, 1794), followed by 61 other operas. 1802, *maestro di capella* at Santa Maria Maggiore, Bergamo, which town he refused to leave for the rest of his life. Teacher of Donizetti; wrote one of the earliest on Haydn (1809). 62, 85 note, 124, 142, 248 note, 249 note, 247

Works referred to:

    Adelasio ed Aleramo. Libretto by Luigi Romanelli. Milan (Scala) 26 Dec. 1806. 249 note

    Finti Rivali, I. Milan (Scale) 1803. 249 note

    Ginevra di Scozia. Libretto by Gaetano Rossi, based on Ariosto. Trieste, 21 April 1801. 62

    Pazzo per la Musica, Il. 249 note

Medonte, Re d'Epiro (opera seria). See Sarti.

Méhul, Etienne Nicolas (b. Givet 1763; d. Paris 1817). French composer, especially of comic opera; profoundly influenced by Gluck. Début at Opéra Comique with *Euphrosine* (1790). Noted for his sustained melody, also for his development of the overture-form in the comic-opera tradition (e.g. *Horatius Coclès*, *Les Deux Aveugles*, etc.). His most famous overture, which imitates the yelping of hounds, is that to *Le Jeune Henri*, libr. by J.-N. Bouilly, Paris (Opéra-Comique), 1 May 1797. 137*

Melani, Jacopo (b. Pistoia 1623; d. Postoia 1676). Member of large family of Italian musicians, one of the pioneers of comic opera in Rome; noted for arias on a *basso ostinato*. His best work was *La Tancia, ovvero Il Podestà di Coloniola*, written for the opening of La Pergola, Florence, in Dec. 1656. *Il Girello* was revived in Rome, Jan. 1968. 112

Mélomanie, La (opéra comique). See Champein.

Melzi d'Eril, Francesco, Duke of Lodi (b. Milan 1753; d. Bellaggio 1816). Sometime vice-president of the Cisalpine Republic; Lord Chancellor of the Kingdom of Italy. Greatest Italian statesman of the Napoleonic period. His famous villa stands on the shore of Lake Como, a mile south of Bellaggio. 257

Mengs, Raphael (b. Bohemia 1728; d. 1779). German painter of great skill and little sensibility, very popular in the Napoleonic epoch. 103, 195

Merchant of Venice, The (play). See Shakespeare.

Merula, Tarquinio (b. ?Cremona; fl. 1600–60). *Maestro di capella* in Bergamo, 1623, later church organist in Warsaw, then Cremona. Composer of church music and madrigals; pioneer in the use of voices and instruments in combination.   67–8

Messiah, The (oratorio). See Handel.

Metastasio, Pietro (= Antonio Domenico Bonaventura Trapassi, known as: b. Rome, 3 Jan. 1698; d. Vienna, 17 April 1782).

Works referred to:

> *Achille in Sciro.* Dramatic poem in 3 acts, first setting by Caldara. Vienna, Hoftheater, 13 Feb. 1736, for the marriage of Maria Theresa with Francis of Lorraine. 221

> *Adriano in Siria.* Dramatic poem in 3 acts, first setting by Caldrara. Vienna, Hoftheater, 4 Nov. 1731, for the name's-day of the Emperor Charles VI.   245

> *Artaserse.* Dramatic poem in 3 acts, first setting by Vinci. Rome, Teatro delle Dame, 26 Dec. 1730.   21, 83

> *Attilio Regolo.* Dramatic poem in 3 acts. Originally intended for the name's-day of Charles VI, 4 Nov. 1740, but not given on account of his last, fatal illness; first setting by Hasse, Dresden Opera House, Carnival season, 1750. 233

> *Canzonetta a Nice = Canzonetta No. III: La Libertà—a Nice.* Written in Vienna, 1733.   228–33

> *Clemenza di Tito, La.* Dramatic poem in 3 acts, first setting by Caldara. Vienna, Hoftheater, 4 Nov. 1734, for the name's-day of Charles VI.   29, 181, 195, 204–5, 233

> *Demetrio Sotere, Re di Siria.* Dramatic poem in 3 acts, first setting by Caldara. Vienna, Hoftheater, 4 Nov. 1731, for the name's-day of Charles VI.   233

> *Demofoonte, Re della Chersoneso di Tracia.* Dramatic poem in 3 acts, first setting by Caldara. Vienna, Hoftheater, 4 Nov. 1733, for the name's-day of Charles VI. The lyric *Misero pargoletto* is in Act III, scene 5.   82, 82 note, 83 note

Didone abbandonata. Dramatic poem in 3 acts, first setting by Sarro. Naples, 26 Dec. 1724. M.'s first libretto.   236

"Eterno Genitor". Hymn. 237

Giuseppe Riconosciuto. Azione sacra in 2 parts, first setting by Porsile. Vienna, Imperial Chapel, Holy Week, 1733. 233

Olimpiade, L'. Dramatic poem in 3 acts, first setting by Caldara. Vienna, Hoftheater, 28 Aug. 1733, for the birthday of the Empress Elisabeth.   44, 84, 213–21

Re Pastore, Il. Dramatic poem in 3 acts, first setting by Bonno. Schönbrunn Court Theatre, Vienna, Spring 1751.   235

Sogno di Scipione, Il. Dramatic *"azione"* in 1 act, first setting by Predieri. Vienna, Favoriten-theater, 1 Oct. 1735, for the birthday of Charles VI.   178

Temistocle. Dramatic poem in 3 acts, first setting by Caldara. Vienna, Hoftheater, 4 Nov. 1736, for the name's-day of Charles VI.   233

Mia speranza! Io pur vorrei . . . (aria). See Sarti (*Achille in Sciro*); Marchesi.

Michelangelo (= Michelangelo di Lodovico Buonarroti Simone, known as: b. Caprese 1475; d. Rome 1564). Florentine School. His famous *Last Judgement*, forming the reredos of the Sistine Chapel, was commissioned by Pope Clement VII in 1534; finished under Pope Paul III in 1541.   74, 136, 141, 142, 174

Millico, Giuseppe (b. Terlizzi 1739; d. Naples 1802). Italian male soprano and composer. Gluck admired him unreservedly. Sang in London and Vienna as well as Italy. Left 3 operas, and a variety of cantatas, etc.   221 note

Milton, John (b. London 1608; d. London 1674). Major English poet, whose *Paradise Lost* is used as the basis of the text of Haydn's *Creation.*   110, 118, 121

Mingotti (Mingoti), Regina, *née* Valentini (b. Naples 1722; d. Neuburg a.d. Donau 1808). Wife of the famous operatic impresario Pietro Mingotti. Pupil of Porpora. Début, Dresden 1747. Implacable rival of la Faustina (*q.v.*). Sang in Italy and in London, but mainly in Dresden. Retired 1787.   60

Miserere (church music). See Allegri.

Miserere (church music). See Jommelli.

French composer, a protégé of the House of Orléans. Début with *Les Aveux indiscrets*, Paris 1759. Stopped composing suddenly in 1777, having written some 17 operas, of which the best-known are *Rose et Colas* (1764) and *Le Déserteur* (1777). 250

Montesquieu, Charles de Secondat, Baron de (1689–1755). French political philosopher, wit and historian, best known for his political treatise, *L'Esprit des Lois* (1748). His first work, *les Lettres Persanes* (1721), is a satirical novel in epistolary form, criticising every aspect of contemporary French society. 15, 57, 98 note, 151, 240*, 258

Monteverdi, Claudio (b. Cremona 1567; d. Venice 1643). One of the greatest Italian composers, who ranks beside Beethoven, Wagner and Debussy as a man who revolutionised the whole musical climate of an epoch. Like J. S. Bach, he was largely forgotten in the eighteenth century; Padre Martini (*q.v.*) alone recognised his true stature. 66

Monti, Vincenzo (b. Alfonsine 1754; d. Milan 1828). Italian poet, recognised leader of the neo-classic revival. During the troubled period in which he lived, Monti changed his allegiance repeatedly; but the quality of his verse remained intact. His *Bassvilliana* (*In Morte di Ugo Bassville*, 4 cantos, 1793) commemorates the death of Nicolas Hugon de Bassville (1753–93), who was murdered by the Roman populace in Jan. 1793, in the course of a riot protesting against the French seizure of Avignon from the Pope. 227–8

Morelli, Maria Maddalena, known as Corilla Olimpica (b. Pistoia 1727; d. Florence 1800). Florentine poetess, celebrated for her improvisations and for the conversation of her *salon*. Court-Poetess to the Grand-Duke of Tuscany from 1775. Little of her ephemeral art has survived. 173

Morgante maggiore (epic poem). See Pulci.

Mort de Henri IV, Roi de France (tragedy). See Legouvé.

Morzin, Graf. Bohemian aristocrat and dilettante, who kept an orchestra at Lukaveč, where Haydn was employed from 1759–62. Early in 1762, Morzin was forced to disband his orchestra for financial reasons, which left Haydn free to accept service with the Esterházy family. 31

Mosca, Giuseppe (b. Naples 1772; d. Messina 1839). Italian composer,

14

studied at Santa Maria di Loreto. Début with *Silvia e Nardone* (Rome 1798). Prolific, facile, but without real inspiration. His best-known work is *I Pretendenti delusi* (libretto by L. Prividali, based on Lemoyne's opera *Les Prétendus*), given in Milan in 1811; Mosca later claimed that this opera contained the first example of the "crescendo-technique" which was to become the hall-mark of Rossini, and which the latter had "stolen" from him.   85 note 247, 249 note, 251, 257

Mosca, Lodovico (b. Naples 1775; d. Naples 1824). Italian composer, brother of the preceding. Accompanist to the teatro San Carlo, Naples, later assistant *maestro di capella* to King Ferdinand IV of the Two Sicilies. Left about 10 operas, including a version of *L'Italiana in Algeri* (Milan 1808).   257*

Mozart, Anna Maria, *née* Pertl (mother).   164, 166, 170, 178, 179, 182

Mozart, Constanze, *née* Weber (wife).   179 note, 187, 193, 194, 199, 236

Mozart, Franz Xaver Wolfgang (b. Vienna 1791; d. Karlstad 1844) (son).   146

Mozart, Leopold (1719–87). His *Versuch einer gründlichen Violinschule* was published in Augsburg in 1756.   163, 164, 165, 166, 168, 169, 170, 171, 172, 173, 177, 178, 181, 182, 183

Mozart, Maria-Anna, known as Nannerl (sister).   164, 166, 167, 170, 171, 172

Mozart, Wolfgang Amadeus.

  Works referred to:

   Ascanio in Alba. Serenata Teatrale in 2 acts, libretto by Giuseppe Parini. Written for wedding of Archduke Ferdinand, third son of Maria-Theresa, with Princess Marie-Beatrix of Modena-d'Este, autumn 1771.   178

   Clemenza di Tito, La. Opera seria, libretto by Metastasio, with amendments by Caterino Mazzola. Written for the Coronation of Leopold II as King of Bohemia, Prague, 6 Sept. 1791.   29, 181, 195, 204–5, 249

   Così fan tutte, ossia la Scuola degli amanti. Opera buffa, libretto by Da Ponte. Commissioned by Joseph II. Vienna, 21 Jan. 1790.   143, 181, 200, 206

   Don Giovanni = *Il Dissoluto punito, ossia il Don Giovanni.*

Commissioned by Pasquale Bondini for Prague. Libretto by da Ponte, based on Gazzaniga. Prague, 29 Nov. 1787. 29, 60, 108, 116, 143, 181, 186–7, 200, 205–6, 245, 249

Entführung aus dem Serail, Die. Singspiel, libretto by Gottlieb Stephanie, based on comedy by Christoph Bretzner. Vienna, Burgtheater, 16 July 1782.   181, 183–4, 189

Finta Giardiniera, La. Opera buffa, librettist unknown. Commissioned by Maximilian Joseph III, Elector of Bavaria, for Munich Carnival, 1775. Munich, 13 Jan. 1775. 178, 181

Finta Semplice, La. Opera buffa, libretto by Marco Coltellini. Written for the Burgtheater, Vienna, in 1768, but not performed until later.   172, 181

Galimathias musicum (or *Quodlibet*). K. 32. The Hague, 1766. 168–9

Idomeneo, Re di Creta. (*Opera seria*). Commissioned by Karl Theodor, Elector of Bavaria, for the Munich Carnival. Libretto by Giambattista Varesco, based on Campra. Munich, 29 Jan. 1781.   179 note, 181, 186, 204

Lucio Silla. Opera seria, libretto by Giovanni da Gamerra, with improvements by Metastasio. Milan, 26 Dec. 1772. 178, 181

Mass in C major (K. 257). Munich 1776.   178*

Mass in C major (K. 262). Munich 1776.   178*

Mass, composed for Father Parhammer's Orphanage Chapel on the Rennweg. Vienna 1767. Music now lost.   172

Mitridate, Re di Ponto. Opera seria, libretto by Vittorio Amadeo Cigna-Santi, based on Racine. Milan (teatro Regio Ducale) 26 Dec. 1770.   177, 181

Motet: Veni sancte Spiritus (K. 47). Vienna 1767.   172

Nozze di Figaro, Le. Opera buffa, libretto by da Ponte, based on Beaumarchais. Vienna, Burgtheater, 1 May 1786. 48, 49, 59*, 74, 108, 111, 126, 136 note*, 142–3, 180, 200, 201–4, 245

Quartet in G minor, piano, violin, viola, 'cello (= K. 478?). 192*–193*

Re Pastore, Il. Festival opera, libretto by Metastasio. Commissioned by Prince-Archbishop of Salzburg to celebrate a

then the Persians. Capture of Baghdad, 1638. A competent ruler who died at the age of 29.   141

Murray, John (b. London 1778; d. London 1843). London publisher of Scottish origins (descendant of the Murrays of Athol), founder of a famous house. Set up the *Quarterly Review* in opposition to the *Edinburgh Review*; in spite of this, Stendhal consented that the English version of the *Lives* should come out with his imprint. Also publisher of Byron.   3

Mystères d'Isis, Les. A wholly unrecognisable distortion of Mozart's *Die Zauberflöte*, music by Lachnith (who included part of a Haydn symphony in the score), libretto by "le citoyen Morel, ci-devant Chedeville", given on 20 Aug. 1801 at the Théâtre de la République et des Arts. In 1805, it was transferred to the Académie Royale de Musique, where it was revived again in 1812, 1816, 1823 and 1826. Concerning this disreputable episode, see the translator's "The *Première* of Mozart's *Don Giovanni* in Paris", in *French Studies*, 1961, pp. 241–51.   195–7 notes

N***, Prince, of Rome. See under W***, Baron.   42

"Nach dem Todt bin ich dein". Viennese popular song, 1809.   44

Nardini, Pietro (b. Livorno 1722; d. Florence 1793). Italian violinist, composer and teacher; pupil of Tartini. 1753–67, solo violinist to the Ducal Court at Stuttgart; 1770, director of music to the Court of Tuscany. Leopold Mozart considered him the greatest violinist of his time.   173

Natal di Giove, Il (cantata). See Metastasio.

Naumann, Johann Gottlieb (b. Blasewitz 1741; d. Dresden 1801). German composer; pupil of Tartini, Hasse and Padre Martini. Worked in Italy and Copenhagen, but spent most of his life in Dresden. His one successful comic opera, *La Dama Soldato* (libretto by Mazzolà) was given in Dresden on 30 Mar. 1791.   248*

Nazolini (Nasolini), Sebastiano (b. Piacenza 1768; d. c. 1806). Minor Italian composer, début Trieste 1788, with *Nitteti* (libr. Metastasio)) Worked mainly in Italy, with one unsuccessful journey to London. Best work: *Semiramide* (Rome 1792).   72

Nelson, Horatio Lord (1758–1805). English admiral. Haydn admired his achievements, in particular the Battle of the Nile, and set some lines about it in cantata form. Nelson and Emma Hamilton visited

Orazi e Curiazi, Gli (*opera seria*). See Cimarosa.

Orestes. Greek mythological hero.   53

Orfeo (chamber cantata). See Pergolesi.

Orfeo ed Euridice (*opera seria*). See Gluck.

Orfeo ossia l'Anima del Filosofo (*opera seria*). See Haydn.

Orlandi, Ferdinando (b. Parma 1777; d. Munich *c.* 1840). Italian composer and teacher, pupil of Paër. Début, Parma 1801, with *La Pupilla Scozzese*. His greatest success was *Il Podesta di Chioggia* (Scala 1801). In 1806, became Professor of music at Milan; in 1828, professor in Munich. His *La Dama soldato* was given in Genoa, 20 Sept. 1808.   248*

Orlando Paladino (*opera seria*). See Haydn.

Orpheus. Mythological hero.   78

Ossian. Legendary ancient Scottish bard of third century A.D., whose poems were "discovered" and translated by the Scot James Macpherson (1736–96) in 1760. These poems, in spite of being the greatest literary fraud of all time, are the exquisite distillation of pre-romanticism, and took Europe by storm.   143

Othello (tragedy). See Shakespeare.

Pacchiarotti (Pacchierotti), Gasparo (b. Fabriano 1740; d. Padua 1821). Italian male soprano; pupil of Bertoni in Venice, where he was a member of the choir of St. Mark's. Début Venice 1756; made his reputation in Palermo, together with la De' Amicis. One of the finest singers in Europe 1771–92. Retired 1796. In his old age, Rossini paid him a visit of homage.   21, 123

Paër (Pär), Ferdinando (b. Parma 1771; d. Paris 1839). Italian composer who worked mainly in Venice, Vienna and Dresden until 1807, when he settled in Paris, as private *maestro di capella* to Napoleon. In 1812, succeeded Spontini as Director of the Opéra Italien; forced to take orders from Madame Catalani 1815–19; but then reinstated as director after the great *débâcle*. Co-operated with Rossini, 1824–6. One of the most popular composers of the period.   128, 246, 249 and note, 257

Works referred to:

   Camilla, ossia Il Sotterraneo (*opera semi-seria*). Libretto by Carpani, based on Marsollier des Vivetières; Vienna, 23 Feb. 1799.   246, 249 note

Italian composer, one of the greatest influences on the development of Western European music. Pope Marcellus II, who had complained about the "light and perfunctory music" performed in the Sistine, never lived to hear the *Missa Papæ Marcelli*, which was P.'s first masterpiece. Written in 1555, it was published in 1567, and is for 6 voices: soprano, alto, 2 tenors, 2 basses. The story of the "ban on music in church" is apocryphal.   66, 96, 97

Pálffy, Graf Ferdinand (b. Vienna 1774; d. Vienna 1840). Member of a famous Austro-Hungarian family, who devoted all his life and all his fortune to music. 1807-11, member of the *Gesellschaft der Cavaliere*; 1811, Director of Court Theatres; 1814, Lessee of the Hoftheater; from 1813, owner of Theater an der Wien. The supreme *mélomane* of all time. An earlier Graf Pálffy had been the patron of Sammartini, and the Pálffy library is reported to contain over 1,000 Sammartini MSS.   10, 54

Palladini (= ?Vincenzo Pallavicini, eighteenth-century Italian composer, b. Brescia, fl. *c*. 1720-60. A friend of Padre Martini; *maestro di capella* at the *Incurabili*, Venice, and from 1755, *mæstro di capella* at San Samuele.)   16

Pannard (Panard), Charles-François (b. Courville 1689; d. Paris 1765). French satirical poet and *chansonnier*, "le La Fontaine du vaudeville". Friend of Collé, Laharpe, Marmontel. Librettist for the Théâtre Italien.   240

Panurge. Character in Rabelais' *Pantagruel* (*q.v.*).   202

Paris. Trojan hero in the *Iliad*. See Virgil.   61

Parlamagni, Antonio. Minor Italian singer, member of the original casts of Rossini's *Pietra del Paragone* and *Matilde di Shabran*   247

Parmigiano (= Francesco Mazzola, known as: b. Parma 1504; d. Casal Maggiore 1540). Italian painter and engraver, strongly influenced by Correggio. His *Madonna del lungo collo* is in the Palazzo Pitti, Florence.   137 note

Parthenope: the French invasion of Italy in 1799 transformed the Kingdom of Naples into the Parthenopian Republic.   81

Paula, Hieronymus Joseph Franz von P., Count of Colloredo, Bishop of Gurk, Archbishop of Salzburg from 1772. Mozart wrote *Il Sogno di Scipione* for his installation-ceremony.   178*, 179*

Pavesi, Stefano (b. Vaprio 1779; d. Crema 1850). Italian composer;

14*

pupil at the Turchini (1795–9). Début with *Un Avvertimento ai Gelosi*, Venice 1803. A facile and prolific composer, whose only durable work was *Ser Marcantonio* (libretto by Angelo Anelli), La Scala, 26 Sept. 1810. An influence on Donizetti's *Don Pasquale* (1843).   60, 246, 248, 249 note

Pizzie a Vicenda, Le (*opera buffa*). See Fioravanti.

Pazzo per la Musica, Il (*opera buffa*). See Mayr.

Pèlerins de la Mecque (*opéra comique*). See Gluck.

Pellegrini, Felice (b. Turin 1774; d. Paris 1832). Italian bass, pupil of Ottani. Début, Leghorn 1795. Triumphs Rome 1805; La Scala, 1806; San Carlo, 1807–10. Paër originally wrote role of the Father in *Agnese* for his voice. Sang in Rome, Milan and Naples, later (1819–26) in Paris where he was associated with Rossini. After 1826, Professor at the Paris Conservatoire.   204, 247

Perez (Peres), Davide (b. Naples 1771; d. Lisbon 1779). Italo–Spanish composer, trained at Santa Maria di Loreto. Début with *Siroe*, San Carlo 1740. 1741, *maestro di capella* at Palermo, after which he settled in Lisbon. A sort of minor Handel. His greatest success was *Demofoonte* (Lisbon 1753). His *Credo* for two choirs was also composed in Lisbon, between 1752 and 1755.   16, 84

Pergolesi (Giovanni Battista Jesi, known as: b. Jesi 1710; d. Pozzuoli 1736). In spite of his brief existence, one of the most important Italian composers of the century.   16, 25 note, 43, 44, 49 note, 72, 83–4, 92, 107–8, 123, 124, 127, 128, 142, 152, 213–21, 222, 223, 224, 249 note, 250, 251, 258, 260

Works referred to:

Olimpiade, L'. *Opera seria*, libretto by Metastasio. Given Rome (teatro Tordinona), 8 or 9 Jan. 1737. An analysis of *Se cerca, se dice* will be found in *Grove*, VI, pp. 630–1.   44, 84, 213–21

Orfeo, L'. Chamber cantata: *Nel Chiuso Centro*, known as *L'Orfeo*.   219

Salve Regina. There are four settings of this text: Stendhal's reference is probably to that in C minor for one male soprano and strings (1735).   219

Serva Padrona, La. "Intermezzo", libretto by Gennarantonio Federico. Given Naples (San Bartolomeo), 28 Aug. 1733.

When revived in Paris in 1752, it sparked off the *Guerre des Bouffons*.   84, 108, 128, 224, 225*

    Stabat Mater, in F minor for male soprano, male contralto and small orchestra. Commissioned in 1736 by the Confraternità di San Luigi di Palazzo, for use on Good Friday. 84, 107, 123, 128, 219

Pertl, Anna-Maria. See Mozart, Anna Maria (*née* Pertl).

Petrarch, Francesco (b. Arezzo 1304; d. Padua 1374). The first modern Italian poet. His *Trionfi* are didactic poems in *terza rima*, and include the "Triumph of Love" and the "Triumph of Chastity" (*c.* 1342–3; re-worked 1367–74). See also under *Laura*.   51, 86, 227, 236*, 259

Phèdre (tragedy). See Racine.

Philidor (= François-André Danican, known as: b. Dreux 1726; d. London 1795). Composer and chess-player, best-known member of a large family of French musicians. Began his career as professional chess-player, but started writing operas as a hobby *c.* 1759; his works include an operatic version of *Tom Jones*. In spite of his eccentricity, a major figure in the history of the French comic opera tradition.   151

Picard, Louis-Benoît (b. Paris 1769; d. Paris 1828). French actor, dramatist and novelist, who for some time was director of the Théâtre de l'Odéon. His libretti include that for *Les Visitandines* (see *Deviène*). He also left some 25 volumes of novels, including *Les Aventures d'Eugène de Senneville et de Guillaume Delorme* (4 vols., 1813). 246*

Piccinni (Piccini), Niccolò (b. Bari 1728; d. Passy 1800). Italian composer, pupil of Leo and Durante at Sant' Onofrio. Début with *Le Donne Dispettose*, Naples 1754. In 1776 he settled in Paris as a protégé of Marmontel, where he was elevated (against his will) to the rank of champion of the anti-Gluckistes. Retired to Naples in 1789. Extended the duet as an operatic form, and increased the importance of the finale.   72, 84–5, 85 note, 108, 142, 248 note, 250

Works referred to:

    Ceccina (La), ossia la Buona Figliuola. Libretto by Goldoni, based on Richardson's *Pamela*. Rome (teatro delle Dame), 6 Feb. 1760.   108

Didone abbandonata (opera seria). Libretto by Metastasio. Rome (teatro Argentina), 8 Jan. 1770.   108

Pichl, Wenzel (b. Bechin 1743; d. Vienna 1805). Bohemian violinist, composer and teacher; pupil of Dittersdorf, later of Nardini. 1790, leader of the *opera buffa* orchestra in the service of Archduke Ferdinand at Monza, with Carpani as resident librettist. 1796, *Kapellmeister* to Archduke Ferdinand in Vienna. Composed largely for the violin.   11, 52

Pindar (521–441 2.C.). Greek lyric poet.   68, 74

Pirro (opera seria). See Paisiello.

Pirro, Re d'Epiro (opera seria). See Zingarelli.

Pitt, William, "the Younger" (b. Hayes 1759; d. Putney 1806). English statesman.   114

Plato (428–347 B.C.).   8

Pleyel, Ignaz Joseph (b. Ruppersthal 1757; d. Paris 1831). French composer of Austrian origin. Pupil of Haydn from 1774. 1783, *Kapellmeister* at Strasburg. 1799, settled in Paris as music-seller. On 24 Dec. 1800, it was P. who arranged the first performance of Haydn's *Creation* in Paris, on the way to which Napoleon was attacked with an "infernal machine" in the rue S. Nicaise. Publisher of Haydn's *Quartets*; also the link with Geo. Thomson of Edinburgh, leading to Haydn's arrangements of Scottish airs. 16, 150

Podestà di Coloniola (opera buffa). See Melani.

Polzelli, Luigia (b. *c.* 1760). Italian mezzo-soprano, married to a violinist, Antonio P., both employed by Nikolaus I Esterházy in 1779. Haydn's mistress until about 1790. Haydn had no luck with the women in his life, for after a few years she ceased to love him and became, if possible, even more avaricious than his wife.   33–4, 89

Porpora, Nicola (b. Naples 1686; d. Naples 1766). Italian composer; début Naples 1708, with *Agrippina.* 1715, *maestro di capella* at Sant' Onofrio. Visited Vienna in 1725, but received no commission, since Karl VI found his style too ornate. Worked in Venice, Naples, London and Dresden. 1752–7, second visit to Vienna; used Haydn as personal valet, and taught him the rudiments of composition. 15 note, 16, 24, 25, 66, 69–70, 82, 85 note, 123, 180

Porto, Matteo (fl. *c.* 1800–30). Italian *basso buffo*, début at Pavia, 1802. Milan (Carcano) 1805. *Primo buffo basso* at the Théâtre Louvois, Paris, 1810–14. Retired *c.* 1826. "A powerful voice, but slow and heavy articulation." 242, 246

Potier, Charles (1775–1838). French comic actor, whose glory was eventually eclipsed by that of his still more famous son, Charles-Joseph-Edouard (1806–70), hero of the *Porte-Saint-Martin* and the *Gymnase*. 247

Pretendenti Delusi, I (opera buffa). See Mosca.

Prétendus, Les (opéra comique). See Lemoyne.

Prometeo (ballet). See Viganò.

Psalms of David, The. 103

Pulci, Luigi (b. Florence 1432; d. Padua 1484). Italian poet, protégé of Lorenzo di Medici. His major work is the *Morgante maggiore*, a chivalrous epic in 23 (later 28) cantos, originally entitled *I Fatti di Carlo Magno* (1462–83). Partly a continuation, partly a parody of the *Chanson de Roland*, the *Morgante* is an extraordinary mixture of comic, burlesque and vernacular elements with profound philosophical and religious reflections. 212

Pyrrhus, ou les Aeacides (tragedy). See Lehoc.

Pradon, Nicolas (1632–98). French tragic dramatist, the unsuccessful rival of Racine and butt of Boileau's most vicious satire. 58 note

Quartets. See Haydn.

Queen of Prussia's Waltz, The. 23

Quinault, Philippe (1635–88). French dramatist and librettist, remembered mainly for his collaboration with Lully, for whom he provided a number of libretti, including *Alceste*, *Armide et Renaud*, etc. 197 note

Rabelais, François (b. La Devinière 1494; d. Paris 1553). French doctor, diplomat and writer, author of *Gargantua*, *Pantagruel*, etc. The episode of Panurge's Sheep occurs in the *Fourth Book*, ch. 8. 202*

Racine, Jean-Baptiste (b. La Ferté-Milon 1639; d. Paris 1699). French tragic dramatist. 37, 97, 130*, 134*, 135, 151, 197 note, 212, 213, 257, 258

Works referred to:

    Andromaque (tragedy), 17 Nov. 1667. 134

Madonna alla seggiola (= *Madonna della sedia*), 1516–17. Painting in Palazzo Pitti, Florence. 81, 124

St. Cecilia (painting, Bologna, 1513–16). Originally in San Giovanni in Monte; removed to Paris by Napoleon in 1800. 45, 113, 126, 239

Transfiguration, The (painting, Vatican gallery, 1519–20). R.'s last work; removed to Paris by Napoleon in 1800. 45, 82, 239

Re Pastore, Il (dramatic poem). See Metastasio.

Re Pastore, Il (dramatic festival cantata). See Mozart, W. A.

Regnard, Jean-François (b. Paris 1665; d. Dourdan 1709). French comic dramatist, one of the successors of Molière. He left a score of comedies of manners, of which the best is *Le Légataire universel* (1708). 243

Regnaut, Madame. Singer in Paris. Untraced. 254 note

Rembrandt (= Rembrandt Harmenszoon van Rijn: b. Leyden 1606; d. Leyden 1669). 36

Rencontre Imprévue (La), ou les Pèlerins de la Mecque (opéra comique). See Gluck.

Requiem. See Mozart, W. A.

Reutter (Reuter), Karl (b. c. 1707; d. Vienna 1770). Austrian organist, composer and teacher, son of Georg Reutter, organist at St. Stephen's Cathedral, Vienna. In 1731, Karl succeeded to the post of *Kaiserlicher Kammer-Organist und Kappellmeister an der Stefanskirche.* Collaborated with Metastasio and Caldara in producing Court operas. Composer of oratorios, including a *Ritorno di Tobia* (1733). 18–19, 23

Reynolds, Sir Joshua (b. Plympton 1723; d. London 1792). Major English painter who, however, did *not* paint Haydn's portrait: this was done by Hoppner. The portrait is in Buckingham Palace. 93–4

Ritorno di Tobia (oratorio). See Haydn.

Roland de la Platière, Jean-Marie (b. Thizy 1734; d. Paris 1793). French writer and statesman, Minister of the Interior in 1792. Friend of the Girondins; committed suicide on hearing of his wife's execution. His works include the *Lettres écrites de Suisse, de Sicile, d'Italie et de Malte, par M *** à Mlle *** à Paris en 1776, 1777 et 1778* (Amsterdam, 1780, 6 vols.). 250 note, 252

Romanina, La (= Marianna Bulgarelli, *née* Benfí, known as: fl. 1700–
40). Roman soprano; sang in *première* of Vinci's *Silla Dittatore* in
Naples (San Bartolomeo) 1723; otherwise little is known of her
career, except for her relationship with Metastasio, whom she
befriended after the death of Gravina.   236, 244

Rospigliosi. Famous Roman family, powerful since about 1295, but
acquiring its immense wealth at the end of the seventeenth century,
when Giovanni Battista R., General of the Papal Militia, married
Maria Camilla Pallavicino, a Genoese millionairess. The Palazzo
Rospigliosi-Pallavicino, on the Quirinale, dates from 1704.
127, 204

Rossini, Gioacchino (b. Pesaro 1792; d. Paris 1868). Italian composer,
as yet (1814) unknown outside Italy.   73*, 249 note, 255*,
257–8
Works referred to:
    Demetrio e Polibio. Opera seria, Rome (Valle), 18 May 1812.
    249 note*
    Italiana in Algeri, L'. Opera buffa, Venice (San Benedetto),
    22 May 1813.   249 note
    Tancredi. Opera seria, Venice (Fenice), 6 Feb. 1813.   257–8
    Turco in Italia, Il. Opera buffa, Milan (Scala), 14 Aug.   249
    note

Rothe, Babet (b. Vienna 1783?). Viennese actress and singer, specialising in ingénue and soubrette parts at the Theater an der Wien.
Stendhal's mistress in Vienna in 1809, and the mysterious "Eliska"
or "Lisbeth" referred to in various enigmatical passages in the
Lives.   249*

"Rotunda", The. Architectural monument on the Isle of Capri.   124

"Round of Bells, The" ("canon énigmatique"). See Martini.

Rousseau, Jean-Jacques (b. Geneva 1712; d. Ermenonville 1778).
French philosopher, novelist and musicologist.   12 note, 24,
29 note, 114*, 151, 194, 205, 210*, 221*
Works referred to:
    Devin du Village, Le. "Intermède" in 1 act, libretto and music
    by R., produced at Fontainebleau, 18 Oct. 1752. In 1753,
    Favart and de Guerville produced a parody of this work,
    Les Amours de Bastien et de Bastienne, which was later
    adapted by Mozart's librettist, Weiskern.   205

Dictionnaire de Musique (1767).   12 note, 29 note

Nouvelle Héloïse, La (novel, 1761).   114, 210*, 221*

Rubens, Peter Paul (b. Siegen 1577; d. Antwerp 1640). Major Flemish painter.   129, 142

S***, Contessa, of Rome. An illusion to the "Countess Simonetta", Stendhal's private name for his mistress Angela Pietragrua, of Milan. 42

Sacchini, Antonio Maria Gasparo Gioacchino (b. Florence 1734; d. Paris 1786). Italian composer: pupil of Santa Maria di Loreto, under Durante. Début, Venice 1756, with *Fra Donato*. Worked in Rome (1764–70) and London (1771–82), and left a large number of operas, of which the best was the posthumous *Oedipe a Colone* (1787).   49 note, 72, 78, 85, 85 note, 87, 118, 123, 131, 142, 152, 250

St. Cecilia (painting). See Raphael.

St. George (painting). See Correggio, *Madonna detta di San Giorgio.*

St. Jerome (painting). See Correggio, *Madonna detta di San Girolamo.*

St. Michael (painting). See Guido Reni, *Archangel Michael.*

Saint-Preux. Character in *La Nouvelle Héloïse*. See Rousseau.

Salieri, Antonio (b. Legnano 1750; d. Vienna 1825). Italian composer; pupil of Gassmann, who took him to Vienna in 1766. Friend of Metastasio. Début, Vienna, with *Le Donne Letterate*, 1770. 1774, resident composer to the Court of Vienna; 1788, Court *Kapellmeister*. Over-all director of the Viennese Opera for twenty years, until succeeded by his pupil Weigl. A friend of Haydn, Beethoven and Schubert.   147

Sallust (= Gaius Sallustius Crispus: *c.* 86–34 B.C.). Roman historian and stylist. His *Catalinæ Coniuratio* was written in 44 B.C.   151 note

Salomon, Johann Peter (b. Bonn 1745; d. London 1815). German violinist, composer and impresario; already an enthusiastic Haydinist by 1765. Settled in London as concert violinist, 1781; began his career as concert-organiser the hard way, by organising la Mara (*q.v.*). Brought Haydn to London in 1790–91 and again in 1794; suggested that he should write the *Creation*. 1813, founded the London Philharmonic Society. Many of Haydn's last Quartets are written to suit S.'s style as a violinist.   89, 110

Salve Regina (church anthem). See Pergolesi.

Scala, La (Milan). See Theatres.

Scarlatti, Pietro Alessandro (b. Palermo 1660; d. Naples 1725). Major Italian composer, pupil of Carissimi and of Stradella. Founder of the eighteenth-century Italian operatic tradition; also of the cantata and of other forms of vocal church music. Father of the keyboard composer Domenico S. Founder of the Neapolitan school of composition. 16, 72, 82, 83, 84, 92, 97, 98 note, 180

Schachtner, Andreas (fl. 1750–80). Austrian poet, composer and instrumentalist; Court-Trumpeter to the Prince-Archbishop of Salzburg. A contemporary of W. A. Mozart, concerning whom he left some memoirs. 168–9

Schauspieldirektor, Der (comic opera). See Mozart, W. A.

Schlichtegroll, Adolf Heinrich Friedrich von (b. Walthershausen 1764; d. Munich 1822). Studied at Gotha, Jena and Göttingen; from 1791, Headmaster of the Landesschule in Gotha; assistant librarian to the Duke of Gotha. From 1790, began to publish annual series of volumes of obituary notices of notable Germans who had died during the previous twelve months. Thus Mozart appears in 1791; J. C. Bach in 1795, etc. The series ran to 34 vols., and continued until 1806. 163

Schneider (. . .). Owner of the Hôtel d'Angleterre, Florence, where Stendhal had stayed on 27 Sept. 1811. 241

Schwarzenberg, Prince Josef Johann Nepomuk von (b. Vienna 1769; d. Frauenberg 1833). Member of a famous and powerful Viennese family, who threw open the gardens of the Palais Schwarzenberg to the public. President of the "Theaterunternehmungsgesellschaft", or *Gesellschaft der Cavaliere*, 1807–13. 108, 110, 138

Scottish Airs. See Haydn.

Seasons, The (oratorio). See Haydn.

Seneca. 152, 153*

Senesino (= Francesco Bernardi, known as: b. Siena 1680; d. Siena 1750). Italian male mezzo-soprano or contralto; pupil of Bernacchi. Little is known of his early career; sang in Dresden 1719. Mainly remembered for his long association with Handel in London (1720–33); created many parts in Handel's operas and oratorios. 100–1

Senneville, César de. Character in the novel: *Aventures d'Eugène de Senneville*. . . . See Picard.

date, the Persians being the major *theorists* in oriental music. Stendhal's touching fable is borrowed from Haller.   141

Sofonisbe, La (opera seria). See Traetta.

Sogno di Scipione, Il (dramatic poem). See Metastasio.

Sogno di Scipione, Il (azione teatrale). See Mozart, W. A.

"Song of the Man-at-Arms" = "Chanson de l'Homme armé" (*de Lome armé*, etc.). Title of old French *chanson*, the melody of which was used by the great masters of the fifteenth and sixteenth centuries (Carissimi, Palestrina, Josquin des Prés, etc.) as the *canto fermo* for a certain type of Mass: the *Missa Lomme Armé.* For words, tune, etc., see *Grove,* IV, 342–3.   96

Spectateur (Le), ou le Socrate Moderne, où l'on voit un Portrait naïf des Mœurs de ce Siècle. Translated and considerably adapted from Addison, Steele, etc., *The Spectator.* Innumerable editions in the eighteenth century; the *Nouvelle édition, corrigée et augmentée d'un nouveau volume*: Paris (Brocas) 1754, in 9 vols., corresponds to the pagination given by Stendhal.   128

Speranza, Padre Alessandro (b. Nola 1728; d. Naples 1797). Italian musical theorist, teacher of singing and counterpoint. A pupil of Durante at Sant' Onofrio, he was successively *maestro di capella* to several religious foundations in Naples. His pupils included Zingarelli and Selvaggi. His compositions include a *St. John* and a *St. Matthew Passion.*   57

Speziale Lo (opera buffa). See Haydn.

Stabat Mater (anthem). See Haydn.

Stabat Mater (anthem). See Pergolesi.

Sterkel, Johann Franz Xaver, known as the abbé Sterkel (b. Würzburg 1750; d. Würzburg 1817). German priest and brilliant amateur musician. 1770, priest and organist at Neumünster; 1778, Chaplain and pianist to the Elector of Mainz at Aschaffenburg. Opera début, San Carlo 1782, with *Farnace.* A sort of eighteenth-century Liszt, he impressed Beethoven as the first really world-class pianist he had ever heard. Left some 10 symphonies, numerous quintets, quartets, etc.   69

Stradella, Alessandro (b. Montefestino 1642; murdered Genoa 1682). Italian singer, violinist and composer. In opera and church music, his style was similar to Corelli. Important in the evolution of the oratorio from Carissimi to Handel; exerted some influence on

Purcell. According to legend, his "magical singing" which saved his life was in his own oratorio, *San Giovanni Battista*; Ortensia was betrothed to Senator Alvise Contarini.   139–41

Strinasacchi (Strina-Sacchi), Teresa (b. Rome 1768; d. London *c.* 1830). Italian soprano; début Mantua, 1787, in Paisiello's *Le due Contesse*. Member of the first post-Revolutionary Italian opera company in Paris, 1801–03; sang again in 1804–05, with particular success as Carolina (*Matrimonio segreto*). Returned in 1816, but the experiment was disastrous. Died in extreme poverty.   143, 247

Studies in Literature = Istoria della volgar poesia, etc. See Crescimbeni.

Swieten, Baron Gottfried van (b. Leyden 1734; d. Vienna 1803). Dutch musical amateur and patron. His father, Gerhard van S., had settled in Vienna in 1745, and became Maria-Theresa's favourite physician. Gottfried received a diplomatic training; in 1771, was appointed Ambassador to the Court of Prussia, where he imbibed a taste for Handel, Haydn and C. P. E. Bach. 1778, Curator of the Imperial Library in Vienna; 1781, President of the Education Commission. Founder of the *Musikalische Gesellschaft*. Patron of C. P. E. Bach.   11, 109–10, 112*, 116, 122, 134, 144, 180

Symphonies. See Haydn.

Tableau des Etats-Unis (treatise). See Volney.

Tacchinardi, Niccolò (b. Livorno 1772; d. Florence 1859). Italian tenor, originally a painter, then first-violin at la Pergola. Début as singer, Livorno 1804. Sang in Milan, then in Rome, where he became friend of Canova. Triumph in Paris, 1811–14, especially in the part of *Don Giovanni* (in spite of his hunchback and extreme ugliness!). Retired 1831.   122, 242, 243, 247

Tacitus (A.D. 55–120).   210

Talma, François-Joseph (b. Paris 1763; d. Paris 1826). French actor, originally trained as a dentist in London. Début at the Comédie Française in 1787. One of the great reformers of the French stage, Talma completed the break with the classical tradition, and inaugurated a new phase of romantic realism.   134

Tancredi (*opera seria*). See Rossini.

Tarchi, Angelo (b. Naples 1760; d. Paris 1814). Italian composer and teacher. Student at the Turchini; début Naples, 1781, with *l'Architetto*. From 1781–97, he worked in the Italian tradition; his most successful works were *Le due Rivali* (Rome 1788) and *Lo Spazza-Camino* (Monza 1789: see Carpani). In 1797, settled in Paris, and changed over to the French tradition: achieved one success with *D'Auberge en Auberge* (Feydeau 1800), but the rest failed. 72

Tartini, Giuseppe (b. Pirano 1692; d. Padua 1770). Italian violinist, teacher and composer. In 1728, founded the school of violin-playing at Padua which formed the skill and style of the whole century. 16, 46, 51

Tartuffe (comedy). See Molière.

Tasso, Torquato (b. Sorrento 1554; d. Rome 1595). Italian epic poet, a favourite source of eighteenth-century libretti. His works include *Rinaldo* (1562), and the great *Gerusalemme liberata* (1575). 8, 11, 194, 227, 228

Temistocle (dramatic poem). See Metastasio.

Tempest, The (episode from *Orlando furioso*). See Ariosto.

Tenducci, Giusto Ferdinando (b. Siena *c.* 1736; d. after 1800). Italian castrato and composer, also known as "Senesino" (cf. Antonio Bernacchi, under this entry). Main successes in London and Dublin. An extravagant, vain but brilliant soprano; also arranger, impresario and composer. His writings include a treatise on singing, and the score of an English comic opera, *The Campaign* (1784). 123

Teniers, David the Younger (b. Antwerp 1610; d. Brussels 1694). Major Flemish genre, landscape and portrait painter, specialising in scenes of village life. 61

Terrasson, abbé Jean (b. Lyon 1670; d. Paris 1750). French writer, historian, philosopher, a member of the Oratorian community. Important predecessor of the great generation of the *philosophes*. His novel-encyclopedia, *Séthos: Histoire ou Vie tirée des Monuments —Anecdotes de l'Ancienne Egypte* (3 vols., 1731) furnished part of the material for Schikaneder's libretto of Mozart's *Zauberflöte*. 196 note

Tessé, Comtesse de (fl. 1740–80). Lady-in-waiting to the Dauphine in 1764. 170

Theatres:

Bergère, théâtre de la rue B., Paris. See Conservatoire. 122, 149

Fenice, teatro della (Venice). 126

Feydeau (Paris 1788; originally Théâtre de Monsieur).   47, 251, 255

Haymarket Theatre, London (1705; rebuilt 1789; also known as the King's Theatre and the Italian Opera).   93

Kärnthnertor (Carinthian Gate) (Vienna).   27

Louvois (Paris: one of the many homes of the Opéra Bouffe).   243

Odéon, Théâtre de l' (Paris, 1797).   13–14, 200, 242, 243

Opéra (Paris: also known as the Opéra-Français, the Grand Opéra, the Théâtre de la rue Lepeletier).   60, 75, 122, 196–8 notes, 253

Polichinello, teatro di (Venice).   260

Scala, teatro alla (Milan; originally the teatro Ducale; rebuilt 1778).   240, 253

Théâtre-Français (Paris: founded 1680; also called the Comédie Française).   240, 250, 260

Wieden, Theater auf der (Vienna).   146

Thénard, Etienne-Antoine, known as Thénard l'aîné (b. Paris 1779; d. Paris 1825). French comic actor, specialising in the roles of valets Début, Paris 1807, in *Le Dissipateur*. Sociétaire of the Comédie Française from 1810. Reached his mature style only in 1812. Famous as Figaro; also in parts by Molère.   247

Thomas, Antoine-Léonard (b. Clermont-Ferrand 1732; d. 1796). French poet and belle-lettriste, who specialised in the *Éloge* as a literary genre. Pious, and therefore an enemy of Voltaire, who treated him mercilessly: the perfect illustration of Gide's phrase: "C'est avec de bons sentiments qu'on fait de la mauvaise littérature."   194–5

Thomson, James (b. Ednam 1700; d. Richmond 1748). Scottish poet, best known for his long descriptive poem, *The Seasons* (1725–30), on which the text of Haydn's oratorio of this title is based.   134

Timoleone (political tragedy). See Alfieri.

Tintoretto (Jacopo Robusti, known as: b. Venice 1518; d. Venice 1594). Major Venetian painter, a pupil of Titian.   13, 141

Titian (Tiziano Vecelli, known as: b. Pieve di Cadore 1477; d. Venice 1576). Major Italian painter of the Venetian school.   13, 53, 142, 209, 239

Works referred to:

Crown of Thorns, The. Painted in 1542 for the Church of Santa Maria delle Grazie, Milan; stolen by Napoleon in 1799, and now in the Louvre.   239

Martyrdom of St. Peter (*St. Peter Martyr*). Climax of T.'s second period: *c.* 1528–30, painted for the Church of SS. Giovanni e Paolo, Venice. The original was destroyed by fire in 1867, and replaced by a copy by Cigoli.   209

Traetta, Tommaso Michele Francesco Saverio (b. Bitonto 1727; d. Venice 1779). Italian composer, pupil at Santa Maria di Loreto under Durante. Début, San Carlo 1751, with *Farnace*. Worked in Parma, Venice, St Petersburg and London. Left some 40 operas, whose dramatic power foreshadows that of Gluck. His *Sofonisbe* (*opera seria*, libretto by Verazi, based on Zeno, *Scipione nelle Spagne*) was given in Mannheim in Nov. 1762.   84, 85 note, 250

Transfiguration, The (painting). See Raphael.

Trapassi, Antonio. See Metastasio.

Trauttmansdorf (Trautmannsdorf). Notable Viennese aristocratic family.   10

Trionfi, I (poems). See Petrarch.

Trios. See Haydn.

Turcaret (satirical comedy). See Lesage.

Turco in Italia (*opera buffa*). See Rossini.

Twelfth Night. See Shakespeare.

Two Shy and Innocent Girls (painting). See Domenichino.

Ugolino, Count. Character in Dante's *Inferno.*

Ulysse (tragedy). See Lebrun.

Una Cosa Rara (*opera buffa*). See Martin y Soler.

V***, Vicomte de.   39

Van Ostade, Adriaen (b. Haarlem 1610; d. Haarlem 1684). Flemish painter, pupil of Franz Hals. Specialised in scenes of low peasant life with drunken labourers and hags, and "dimly lit interiors with a single source of illumination".   61

"Variations on the G String". See Paganini.

Vasari, Giorgio (b. Arezzo 1511; d. Florence 1574). Florentine painter, pupil of A. del Sarto and Pontormo. Best known for his book, *Le Vite de' più eccelenti Architetti, Pittori e Scultori italiani* (1550, revised 1568), "perhaps the most important book on the history of art ever written").   14

Velluti (Vellutti), Giovanni Battista (b. Montolmo 1780; d. Bruson 1861). Italian male soprano, last of the famous castrati. Début, Forlì 1800; major reputation made in Rome, 1807, in Niccolini's *Traiano*. Sang in Naples, Milan, Turin, Vienna (1810 and 1812) and London. Retired 1828.   244, 245–6

Vendanges, Les (ballet). See Angiolini, *Die Weinlese*.

Venus.   36

Vera Costanza, La (opera buffa). See Haydn.

Vérité dans le Vin, La (comedy). See Collé.

Veronese, Paolo (= Paolo Cagliari, known as: b. Verona *c.* 1528; d. Venice 1588). Major Italian painter of the Venetian school. His *Wedding-Feast of Cana*, an immense canvas some 20 ft. high by 32ft. broad, was originally painted in 1563 for the Refectory of the Convent of San Giorgio Maggiore, Venice. Stolen by Napoleon in 1799, it is now in the Louvre. The central group, taken alone, *could* be mistaken (as Stendhal mistakes it) for a "Last Supper". 13, 64, 75, 238,

Versuch einer gründlichen Violinschule (musical treatise). See Mozart, Leopold.

Viadana (Lodovico Grossi, known as: b. Viadana *c.* 1564; d. Gualtieri 1645). Italian composer, pupil of Costanzo Porta. Franciscan monk who was *maestro di capella* at Mantua, later at Fano. Reputed inventor of method of building up a composition from the bass instead of from a *canto fermo*, thus giving independence to melody as a specific element in music. Author of *Cento Concerti ecclesiastici ... con basso continuo per sonar nell' organo* (Venice 1602).   13

Victoire, Madame (= Louise-Thérèse-Victoire, known as: b. Versailles 1733; d. Trieste 1799). Second daughter of Louis XV; quiet and pious aunt of Louis XVI, who lived all her life at Court until driven out by the Revolution.   170

Viganò, Salvatore (b. Naples 1769; d. Milan 1821). Italian composer and choreographer, pupil of his father, nephew of Boccherini. Début as choreographer with *La Fille mal gardée* (Venice 1790). Worked mainly in Vienna and Milan; major figure in the development of the "ballet d'action" in the Italian tradition. His ballet, *Gli Uomini di Prometeo, o sia la Forza della Musica e della Danza* was written for the Imperial Ballet of Vienna. 61, 117,

Villars, Marquis de. French ambassador to the Court of Savoy. 140,

Vinci, Leonardo (b. Strongoli 1690; d. Naples 1730). Italian composer, pupil of Greco. Début with *Lo Cecato fauzo*, Naples 1719. One of the more vigorous successors of A. Scarlatti, he worked with the singer Farinelli and contributed to the development of the dramatic aria as a musical form. His *Artaserse* (*opera seria*, libretto by Metastasio) was given in Rome (teatro delle Dame) in 1730, with Farinelli, in the cast. 16, 60, 83, 85 note, 142

Virgil (Publius Virgilius Maro, 70–19 –.c.). 80, 81, 101, 129, 152, 213, 226, 240

Works referred to:

    Aeneid. 80, 129

    Eclogues. 129

    Georgics. 226

Visconti, Ermes, Marchese di San Vito (b. Milan 1784; d. Crema 1841). Italian writer and political figure; contributor to *Il Conciliatore*. The main advocate of "Romanticism" in Italian literature: *Idee elementari sulla Poesia romantica* (1818), and an important influence on Stendhal's own literary theories. 55 note

Visitandines, Les (opera). See Deviene; Picard.

Volney, Constantin-François de Chasseboeuf, Comte de: b. Craon 1757; d. Paris 1820). French scholar and philosopher of noted liberal opinions, popular in his own time for a characteristically pre-romantic poem, *Les Ruines, ou Méditations sur les Révolutions des Empires* (1791). His *Tableau du Climat et du Sol des Etats-Unis d'Amérique* was published in 2 vols. in 1803. 42 and note

Voltaire (François-Marie Arouet, known as: b. Paris 1694; d. Paris 1778). French poet, dramatist, historian, philosopher, etc. His tragedy *Zaïre* (1732) was inspired by Shakespeare's *Othello*; his satirical fable, *Les deux Siècles*, appeared in 1771. 64, 111, 151, 252, 260

Volterra, Daniele da (= Daniele Ricciarelli, known as: b. Volterra 1509; d. Rome 1566). Tuscan painter, pupil of Sodoma and Peruzzi, later of Michelangelo. His major work is a series of frescoes in the Orsini Chapel, Trinità dei Monti, Rome, entitled the

History of the Cross (1540–47). The principal composition of this series, the *Descent from the Cross*, may in part be by Michelangelo. 239

Voyage de Roland (travel-book). See Roland de la Platière.

Voyage en Italie (travel-book). See Duclos.

W***, Baron. (Also Prince N***. A reminiscence of Count Lodovico Maria Widmann Rezzonico, a Venetian aristocrat who was a Colonel in the Guard of Honour attached to Prince Eugène, and who vanished during the Retreat from Moscow. Earlier, he had been the *amant en titre* of Angela Pietragrua.)   40*, 42*

Wagenseil, Georg Christoph (b. Vienna 1715; d. Vienna 1777). Austrian keyboard-player and composer, pupil of Fux and Palotta; Imperial Court Composer, 1739–77. Music-master to Maria-Theresa and her children, including Marie-Antoinette. A popular composer of *opere serie* and church music.   167

Wahlverwandschaften, Die (novel). See Goethe.

Weber, Constanze. See Mozart, Constanze.

Wedding-Feast of Cana, The (painting). See Veronese.

Weigl, Joseph Franz (b, Bavaria 1740; d. Vienna 1820). German 'cellist and composer who made his career in Austria. First 'cellist to the Esterházy orchestra, 1761–9; one of closest friends of Haydn, who stood godfather to his son Joseph.   11, 55

Weigl, Joseph (b. Eisenstadt 1766; d. Vienna 1846). Son of the preceding and godson of Haydn. Austrian composer, pupil of his father, Haydn, Gassmann, Albrechtsberger and Salieri. Début with *Die unnützige Vorsicht* (Vienna) 1792. Resident composer, later Kapellmeister, to the Court Opera. His main successes include *Die Schweizerfamilie* (1809); *Das Waisenhaus*; *L'Amor Marinaro*, etc. *Die Uniform* (1798) is a setting of a libretto by Carpani.   11, 109, 150

Work referred to:

> *Leiden Jesu Christi, Das* (oratorio). Setting of a German translation of Carpani's *La Passione di Nostro Signore Gesù Cristo*; performed at the Court of Vienna, 1804. The same text was later set by Pavesi.   109

Weinlese, Die (ballet). See Angiolini.

Weinmüller, Karl Friedrich Klemens (b. Dillingen 1764; d. Oberdöbling 1828). Austrian bass singer. An orphan who was adopted by the Prince-Bishop of Treves. Early career in Wiener-Neustadt, St. Pœlten and Hainburg; appointed to choir of Imperial Chapel 1797. Famous for his renderings in Haydn's *Creation* and Mozart's *Requiem*; but also outstanding as Leporello, Sarastro and Figaro. Retired 1825.   146

Wellington, Arthur Wellesley, Duke of (b. Dublin 1769; d. Walmer 1852). English general and conservative statesman. Created Marquis in Oct. 1812.   239

"Wenn ich war in mein" . . . (Tyrolean folksong = ?*Als ich in meinem Dorfe war*).   50

Wenzl (= ?Johann Karl: b. Ruppau *c.* 1759; d. Prague *c.* 1820). Austrian composer and violinist.   168

Werther (novel). See Goethe, *Die Leiden des jungen Werther*.

Wieden, Theater auf der. Built in 1787 by Christian Rossbach; taken over by Schikaneder, who used it for the *première* of *The Magic Flute* in 1791. By 1801, proved too small as a theatre; was replaced by the new Theater an der Wien, and thereafter used mainly for concerts.   146

Wilhelmina ★★★. See under M★★★, Wilhelmina von.

Wilhelmina ★★★. See under Correr, Pietro.

Winckelmann, Johann Joachim (b. Stendhal 1717; murdered 1768). German archeologist and historian; the first scholar to apply modern scientific methods of research and classification to the monuments of classical antiquity. Inspirer of the neo-classic revival of the late eighteenth century, and a powerful influence on creative artists such as Gluck, Mengs, Canova, Goethe, etc.   55 note

Young woman led before the Tribunal of Alexander (painting). See Domenichino: *Timoclea led before Alexander*.

Zaïre (tragedy). See Voltaire.

Zamboni, Lodovico (b. Bologna 1767; d. Florence 1837). Italian *basso buffo*. Début Ravenna, 1797, in Cimarosa's *Fanatico in Berlina*. Worked in Modena, Parma, Florence, Rome and Venice; 1810, La Scala. Rossini wrote the *Barbiere di Siviglia* for his voice. Retired 1825.   247

Zauberflöte, Die (opera in the Viennese tradition). See Mozart, W. A.

Zingarelli, Niccolò Antonio (b. Naples 1752; d. Torre del Greco 1837).

Italian composer, pupil of Santa Maria di Loreto, trained under Fenaroli as a violinist. The best composer of *opera buffa* between Cimarosa and Rossini; some of his works held the stage for nearly a century, e.g., *Il Mercato di Monfregoso* (1792). 1804, *maestro di capella* to the Sistine Chapel.   57, 72, 85 note, 88, 109, 123, 142, 226*, 243*, 248 note

Works referred to:

   Alsinda. Z.'s third opera, his first at La Scala (22 Feb. 1785). 57

   Distruzione di Gerusalemme, La. Originally an oratorio, later rewritten as an opera: Florence (teatro de' Infocuati), 27 Nov. 1803; Rome (Valle) 1805.   109, 243

   Giulietta e Romeo. Opera seria, libretto by Giuseppe Maria Foppa, based on Shakespeare. Milan (Scala) 1786.   57, 88

   Pirro. Re d'Epiro. Milan (Scala), 26 Dec. 1791.   88, 226